Meth Monster

Crankin' thru life
A look into the abyss of an
American drug pandemic

by

D.C. Fuller

authorHOUSE®

AuthorHouse™
1663 Liberty Drive, Suite 200
Bloomington, IN 47403
www.authorhouse.com
Phone: 1-800-839-8640

First published by AuthorHouse   5/10/2008

ISBN: 978-1-4343-3834-1 (sc)

Library of Congress Control Number: 2007907937

Printed in the United States of America
Bloomington, Indiana

This book is printed on acid-free paper.

7/14/06

"KNOW YE, THIS WAS THE KINGDOM OF KICKS
SPEED, BIKES, WEED AND CHICKS. ALL HOPE
WAS LOST, ALL YE WHO ENTERED HERE."

Dedicated to:
THE LORD above for keeping my brain cells in my head.
Kona, the first thing I ever loved besides my motorcycle and crank.
Ralph, my first citizen friend who gave me a
place to go when I decided to quit.
Debbie, who provided a soft place to land and
the time and place to detox and recover.
My mother, who loved me no matter what.
Matt, for the covers.
My daughter Jessie, without her this would've never been.
Orin for the closing poem.
If somewhere in this book you think you recognize yourself,
you're probably right, it's me and I'm talking about you or us
and the things we did. I know some of you took an even rougher
road than mine, I hope you're alright. I made it out the back
door of the "too much fun in a no fun zone" in one piece, more
or less, hope you did too. This is especially dedicated to you.

Information Is Power

HOPEFULLY the information about meth and the destructive power of this drug contained in this narrative will help you make the decision to get off it if you're on it, help you help someone you know get off it if you're not or prevent someone from even thinking about using it if the temptation ever arises.

Though some of the things you'll read in here are funny, addiction to any drug certainly isn't, especially meth. By becoming an addict you give away your personal power, a very dangerous thing in this day and age because you become a victim of your own ignorance. Which might not sound so bad until you think of this, without you we can't change this fucked up world that has us so miserable. It will take everyone getting involved to bring this world back to where it should be. If you're addicted to drugs you don't care and if you're an inmate or a convicted felon you don't matter. Think about it and we'll talk more about it at the other end.

When I used this drug only about one percent of the population even knew what it was, it was relegated for the most part to outlaw bike clubs and their direct associates. When members of that radical counterculture died from it directly or indirectly, society as a whole was relieved. That passing was a relief to "normal" members of society because that meant there was one less scary monster prowling the streets.

THAT WAS THEN, THIS IS NOW, this form of chemical suicide is no longer just the property of that one percent, it's invading every home in America making victims of fathers and mothers, sisters and brothers one at a time. It is now more frequently used by "soccer moms"

1

than it is by the outlaw bikers that claimed it as their drug of choice for decades before this pandemic began.

There really isn't one good reason to let yourself be talked into using meth. On the contrary you should do your best to convince the would-be convincer to quit right then. There are a million reasons to run from this chemical atrocity and never look back. Read this story, be entertained by it, informed by it, but most of all learn something from it. At the other end of this narrative we're gonna find out some of the reasons why this is as close as anyone should ever get to methamphetamine or any other mind altering addictive drug for that matter and they're all addictive, except pot.

Disclaimer

THIS BOOK IS NOT POLITICALLY CORRECT!

THE STUNTS OUTLINED IN THIS BOOK WERE PERFORMED BY A DRUG-INDUCED LUNATIC AND SHOULD NOT BE TRIED AT HOME OR ANYWHERE ELSE!

THIS BOOK WASN'T WRITTEN BY A DOCTOR OR A WRITER; IT WAS WRITTEN BY A PERSON OF THE STREET, AN EX-JUNKIE AND IS VERY GRAPHIC IN PLACES. CRANKSTERS DON'T SNORT, SLAM OR SMOKE THEIR DOPE WITH THEIR PINKIES EXTENDED DAINTILY, THEREFORE THE LANGUAGE IS PRETTY COARSE AT TIMES AS WELL. IF THIS OFFENDS YOU IN ANY WAY, COVER YOUR EYES OR WEAR A HELMET WHILE YOU READ IT, BUT READ IT! IT MAY SAVE YOUR LIFE OR THE LIFE OF SOMEONE YOU KNOW. NEVER FORGET THERE'S MORE THAN ONE WAY TO DIE, AT THE SCENE IS THE EASIEST WAY OUT. STAYING ALIVE ISN'T ALWAYS LIVING AND IT ISN'T ALWAYS EASY.

IF YOU CHOOSE TO BECOME INVOLVED WITH METH, BELIEVE ME BEFORE YOU'RE SCRAPED OUT OF A GUTTER SOMEWHERE OR RELEASED FROM THE JAIL OR PRISON YOU END UP IN, YOU'LL HEAR LANGUAGE AND DO THINGS THAT'LL AMAZE YOU AT HOW LOW YOU TOO CAN GO. YOU'RE BETTER OFF READING IT NOW, BEFORE YOUR VERY OWN DOWNWARD SPIRAL BEGINS. HOPEFULLY READING THIS WILL STOP IT BEFORE IT STARTS.

This book is the truth and the whisperings of a million meth monsters in the middle of a million nights. If you recognize yourself in here and you don't like what you read, tough shit!

Until we become a communist country {which isn't too far off, fascist actually} the First Amendment still exists and I'm entitled to and will express how I feel about that life, the fact is it's my story and I'll tell it any way I want to.

If I portray you for what you were to me and you don't like it, too bad! I don't care about your feelings any more than you cared about mine. If my opinion of you sucked then, you can bet it hasn't gotten any better; I'm recounting things like they happened like it or not.

The origins of **METHAMPHETAMINE** are fact and well documented throughout the history of the Third Reich. An ultra-white race of overzealous, psychotic fuckheads with the idea that they were the one pure race founded by a self-loathing, antisocial, idiotic, meth-addicted mongrel who should've been the first one killed if the ideology that he preached was to be followed to the exact letter.

This bunch of lunatics brought you the Second World War and a plethora of mechanical and chemical devices used in the torture and annihilation of millions of Europeans and Jews and were the creators of *this* particular chemical atrocity.

I've also heard that the Japanese invented it around the turn of the century, but couldn't find a use for it till the Second World War with the help of the Germans. Whichever the case, WWII was the first time **METH** was used in the world.

I lived outside the law until 1995; at one time in this world the truth was an absolute thing with no gray areas which is still true in reality. In the world outside the law, truth is relative to circumstance and manipulated to attain a desired outcome, the same way the government uses it today.

Unfortunately that has become the norm in all aspects of life, your religious leaders lie to you, your government lies to you, your employer lies to you, your spouse lies to you, law enforcement lies to you, the media lies to you in every newscast, there is no truth in our society, lying has become an accepted form of business and life. In essence our whole society lives outside the law now, from The President {who's the biggest liar on record to date} on down.

Deceit is taught in classrooms across this land daily, it was when I was a kid. All the things we were taught were bullshit {Columbus never discovered America, in fact he never even came closer to it than the Bahamas}. You'll find this out when you get out in the world or look beyond your own front door.

In school anyone can major in Political Science; the science of spinning the truth to suit your own end. The science of creating the truth, spun from a lie fabricated outta thin air, told to so many people and said so often that the truth is lost and the lie replaces it. This was foretold in the bible **"WHEN GOOD BECOMES EVIL AND EVIL BECOMES GOOD."** I don't remember the book {Revelations I believe}, that really doesn't matter, that's what's happened, for your sake look around you, read the bible {Old and New Testament} if you wanna know exactly where that's written, heaven knows you probably need to, just as much as I do.

A historical fact is that white people have been the scourge of the earth destroying entire civilizations down through history in the name of their God **{WEALTH}** and civilization. I never read anywhere in the bible where God or Jesus said to crush the sculls of the unenlightened and pound Christianity into their corpses to scare the living into submission, I was always taught that God was just and loving.

I'm not proud to say I'm white or Christian {I believe deeply in God but I'm not a Christian in today's sense of the word because Christianity in this day and age is a farce, pushed on society for the financial gain of its leaders and nothing more. The business of Christianity worships the dollar in the name of God}. White man since before the days of Christ has destroyed, deceived, raped and subjugated every people {especially their own} they've encountered to further their own financial ends and are doing so as we speak. Dick Cheney and George W. Bush are prime examples.

I believe white man to be the spawn of the devil on earth and I know I'm of that ilk because of the life I've led as evidenced in the following narrative and the part we've played in the destruction of all things earthly right down to the planet itself. Every other civilization down through the millenniums have felt the lash of the white devil and everything we call progress has taken us further away from the truth and closer to a living hell of our own making right here in our own back yards as evidenced by our deviant society spiraling further and further outta control.

Whites are the only civilization that conceived of the ownership of the earth and placed a monetary value on it. Today without money you are simply cast aside to starve because you're unable to contribute to the coffers of the powers that be. **Money is the basis of our so-called Christian societies.** What is the one thing that is reported on during every broadcast of the nightly news and I mean every night? **THE STOCK MARKET!** In essence; how much money the liars and cheats of this world fleeced the public out of today, the root of all evil is reported on during the nightly news, **EVERY NIGHT!**

The so-called religious leaders of today, every last one of them use religion to fleece the public and pillage the unknowing to foster their own greed. **"THE LUST FOR MONEY IS THE ROOT OF ALL EVIL!"**

If people would only stop following blindly, read the bible or whatever book their religion adheres to; stop interpreting with their minds and start adhering with their hearts, the politicians and religious liars of the world would be seen for the thieves and trash that they are and would be cast down to the gutter were they belong. Especially the pope, the figurehead of a pagan based, Satan worshipping cult that makes up their religion as they go along and were the leaders in the persecution of the followers of Christ until the Emperor Constantine "converted."

"THOU SHALT PLACE NO OTHER GODS BEFORE ME." The statue of Mary is worshiped and prayed to by the Catholics instead of the God who created her, Paganism at its finest!

Bartering {the exchange of goods for goods or services or both} is against the law, why? It can't be taxed! No money to be stolen from a bartered transaction.

So much for truth; everyone wants the truth, but no one wants to tell it or hear it. It's against the law to say what you think about the politician that extorts billions of dollars in taxes from the working class of this country every year and allows pork barrel spending because he's getting kickbacks from the people who help him waste your tax dollars with frivolous spending and over inflated budgets. Our school systems are almost the worst in the world, why? Because an educated and informed public is harder to oppress, the well educated can't be easily controlled.

Our country is producing less educated people every year because the opportunities aren't there for people with average or less than average finances or credit. The public schools lay a horrible foundation to build on academically because they're underfunded, the teachers underpaid and everything they teach is bullshit. This will continue to worsen over time because this falls in with the grand design of the elitist and separatist {soon to be fascist} ruling class bent on destroying and enslaving this country from within.

If the government can keep the people ignorant of what's going on around 'em and wasted on drugs so they fight amongst themselves and spend more time trying to kill {there are many ways to kill and drugs is one of them} each other than they do getting an education it's easier for them to run their own agendas, spend your hard earned money on themselves and insulate themselves even further from the people they profess to serve.

Our politicians and religious leaders are only here to rob us blind until we are no longer economically viable {a fancy term for broke} then we're left to rot or freeze on the streets of some city without a second thought. Once we have nothing more to take we're just dead weight to the elitist pigs that control our government, the easiest way to get rid of us is to simply let us die in the gutter.

Drugs are just one of many ways the shadow government that controls our government oppresses the population. Granted we all choose whether or not we use drugs, but when that's all we know because it's impossible to get a job that will support ourselves let alone a family, but manufacturing and selling illicit drugs can make you comfortable overnight. The uneducated {even the educated} turn to drugs every time, myself and millions of others have, just look at the population behind bars in this country for drug violations. It's pretty simple, hungry and needy or drugged out and oblivious, not everyone in this country has the same advantages; if we did the world would be a better and far more peaceful place.

Crank, Ice, Cat, Crack and pretty much every synthesized drug on the street today, where do you think they came from, a kid playing with a chemistry set in his father's garage? They originally came from government labs {not necessarily our government, but a government none the less}; developed by government scientists to be added to **THE WAR ON DRUGS,** another farce perpetrated by the government to hit us for more tax dollars. Our government is funding both sides of this so-called war in order to keep the albatross flying and give us something else to think about, hiding the real issues that are the foundation of our misery and generating thousands of useless jobs for the peons that the politicians use to insulate themselves from us.

The truth is every drug is an escape. **METH** is the ultimate escape, on meth you're **ten feet tall-n-bulletproof**, everything bounces off you like you're made of steel, no pain is felt, no idea's too wild, nothing's impossible and anything and everything is doable. What better a drug could you ask for to hide from reality in? A drug that envelopes your entire life till you're completely engulfed by it, altering your immediate reality enough to be considered delusional and getting you into trouble around straight people.

How's this for truth? Sucks doesn't it and you ain't seen nothin' yet. Now let's get to the story of probably one of the most heinous of drugs ever conceived, **METH.**

Definition Of Terms

I guess the first thing we should have is a definition of terms so we'll know what I'm talking about.

CRYSTAL CREATURES and **METH MONSTERS** aren't people who use meth. They're the hallucinations created by the compounding fatigue and the frying of millions of brain cells by being awake for days on end and ingesting the poison that is Meth.

CRYSTAL CREATURES are the flashes of dark movement seen in your periphery from the first to the third day of use, usually seen near the floor or ceiling.

As your time awake increases the hallucinations get closer and more frequent, till it seems they're standing right over your shoulder, whispering curses, threats, or whatever your brain can dig out of its depths to scare the shit outta you, in your ear.

They're also noises like things banging, phones ringing, taps on window panes, knocks on doors, conversations overheard from other empty rooms, voices in your head, people seen in your house or shop, things misplaced or thought to be missing completely.

The amazing thing is there's nobody there and you know it, but one part of your brain is playing a game with another part and you're not invited. These are **METH MONSTERS.** We used to say that **you chased CRYSTAL CREATURES** and **METH MONSTERS chased you.** At this point if you haven't got a grip, the paranoia that leads to methamphetamine psychosis takes over, usually with some unwanted results. Basically your mind is playing tricks on itself and you're loosing the game.

- **ANHEDONIA** - the inability to experience pleasure because dope has burnt the pleasure part of your brain to a cinder.
- **CRYSTAL** - The purest form of meth.
- **GLASS** - Another name for crystal.
- **PEANUT BUTTER** - Impure not gassed and washed enough, a lot of red phosphorous residue. This stuff has caused liver failure after one weekend of partying.
- **CRANK** - Anything that isn't glass or crystal, a generalized name for everything meth.
- **GAAK** - Just a nickname because the drip makes you make that noise when it starts dripping down the back of your throat.
- **DRIP** - The residue that runs down the back of your throat after you snort a line.
- **SHMEGMA** - Residue on anything you use to use speed.
- **FISHING** - Flopping on the floor in convulsions and muscle spasms after slamming a massive amount of dope, like a fish outta water.
- **GEEZER** - `70s drug term for a needle user.
- **JUNKIE** - Originally used to denote a heroin addict, used here to describe any chronic drug user.
- **BINDLE** - A paper fold used for coke, doesn't work with crank, it'll eat right through it.
- **RIG** - a syringe.
- **TRACKS** - The marks left in the skin from needles.
- **REGISTER** - The first sensation of drugs in your system when you slam, created by the drugs on the outside of the needle from getting the air outta the rig before you slam.
- **GO FAST** - Biker/Trucker term for speed.
- **HIGH SPEED CHICKEN FEED** - Truckers term.
- **RIPPER** - A gigantic line guaranteed to get you high.
- **LEGS** - The length of time the dope keeps you high, this varies from recipe to recipe.

- **SPRUNG** - You've been up for days but you're still getting high on each line you do. You've got a firm grip on something you're just not sure what, but you've definitely got the energy to hunt it down and kill it.
- **"YOU'RE OUTTA MY MIND"**- A funny way of telling you I'm done with whatever it is and/or you.
- **"GOING BOWLING"**- Getting stoned, ya know smoking a bowl.
- **"ON YOUR LIPS"**- Obliterated drunk, totally incoherent, talking out your ass.
- **AMP'D** - Too high to pick a thought and run with it, millions of thoughts are screaming through your brain at warp ten, like having a traffic jam for a brain. Sometimes outta this'd come the answers to all the questions of the universe in a flood, a revelation, then the traffic jam would return and I'd just be too high, but I'd know why.
- **AMPING** - An oily sweat exuded from your skin when you're too high but not completely overdosed, this usually smells like the dope you're doing. This is the first sign of "too much fun in a limited fun zone," it only gets worse from here. Best thing to do is focus on something to keep you busy for the next eight or ten hours, something that doesn't involve chewing your fingers to a nub or picking a huge hole in your face and remember it's only the drugs, you'll come down eventually if you just hang on no matter how bumpy it gets. The sweat is your body doing everything it can to get rid of this poison as fast as it can. I went thru this many times because of my "just say yes" policy
- **METHROADS** - These were little pills with crossed tops made with meth. Someone had gotten ahold of a pill press and started turning them out by the thousands making 'em outta crank. In their day these little beauties hospitalized more than a few people.
- **CROSSROADS** - The tame pharmaceutical version of methroads.

- **WALLSHOT** - Using two needles {one in each arm} to shoot a massive amount of dope.
- **BLACK BEAUTIES** - These little babies were the cats meow of pharmaceuticals, one'd keep you going from L.A. to N.Y. hence the nickname {west coast turn around}. They were the very best dope Uncle Sam ever kicked out to the masses. They weren't around long because people were having "too much fun in too many no fun zones." Especially the truckers, who if they didn't time the trip right would run outta buzz before they ran outta trip. The crash from Black Beauties was unreal; it came on quick and hard resulting in some ungodly traffic crashes. Exactly the reason for the 20/20 exposé called Killer Trucks back in the early ` 80s which prompted the C.D.L & the drug testing that is in place today.
- **POCKET ROCKETS** - Black Beauties.
- **SHOOTING GALLERY** - A place where slammers go to shoot dope, generally an abandoned building or any outta the way place where they can't be seen or heard.
- **COOKS** - Manufacture crank, the process is called cooking.
- **WHACKED/STEPPED ON** - Cut, anositol is the best for crank, but idiots cut it with everything from sugar to Drano.
- **ANOSITOL** - Vitamin B-12, an enzyme that aids in digestion, it also aids in the absorption of crank. I've cooked dope that was textbook perfect, but gave very little buzz and had no legs. Whacked with a little anositol, this stuff turned into the killer it should've been to begin with.
- **HYPER-BABBLE** - Nonstop diarrhea of the mouth.
- **WARP-MUMBLE** - Unintelligible diarrhea of the mouth.
- **CRANKSTERS** - Race through their lives of busy nothingness in a casually frantic search for the eternal buzz.

- **TWEAKERS** - Sit-n-spin, spend three days and nights playing Tetris nonstop or dig in dumpsters all night for what they think is buried treasure. Sometimes spending hours dismantling a car stereo, attaching all the scattered components with jumper wires, then attaching it to a home stereo and making it sound like a live band playing right in front 'a ya. All for GOD knows what reason. Been there, done that!
- **TWEAKING** - What tweakers do.
- **SPEED FREAKS** - People that use speed as a means to an end to the exclusion of any other upper, a tool to prolong the work day and increase productivity. I'd consider myself one of these, our M.O. was to snort a line, smoke a joint, and build something.
- **METHER** - A term used on me by a Missouri Highway Patrolman who'd searched a vehicle from stem to stern three times and found nothing though convinced he had something. "Little did he know," the full story of this adventure will be told in another book at a later time.
- **JONESING** - Consumed with a near uncontrollable need to get high. You might even be high as a kite already, but still want more. Been there, done that. I jonesed for about eight years after I quit. It got easier as time went on, but I know I wouldn't've made it eight minutes in California my jones was so strong. The longer the use time, the longer the recovery time, the deeper the depression, so deep the real you gets lost for a while. The consumption of your life isn't completely clear until you try to climb outta that pit. It's easy to see the material things lost, you haven't got shit! It's a hard fact to face; you *think* you can't live without dope
- **LINES** - Crank chopped into a fine powder & plowed into long thin piles to be snorted.
- **BUMP** - Not quite the process of laying out a line, a pile on a piece of whatever.
- **BLAST** - Same as a bump, it's all getting high.

- **TUNE UP** - Getting high, doin' a line.
- **EIGHT-BALL** - 1/8th of an ounce.
- **OD** - Overdose.
- **BUNK** - Shitty worthless fake dope.
- **REUP** - Getting a new supply.
- **TEENTH/ TEENER** - 1/16th of an ounce.
- **PIN JOINT** - A tiny joint, far smaller than a cigarette sized normal joint.
- **"JOINT SESSION"** - Smoking a joint with friends.
- **DUMPSTER DIVING** - Rooting through dumpsters in the middle of the night looking for whatever neat shit you can find. I'm no stranger to this either, you'd be amazed what's thrown away, especially by businesses.
- **TOOTER** or **TOOTER TUBE** - A pen barrel, rolled up dollar bill, super sized stainless steal barrel with custom nasal adapters {speed freaks are very industrious and develop talents quickly}, anything used to snort dope.
- **ROLLING OVER** - Snitching on friends and associates to save your own ass.
- **DAVE LANE** - California numbers their lanes from the center divider out, number one being the closest and fastest. The Dave Lane is the dotted white line between the number one and two lanes.
- **BRO** - Bend Right Over.
- **SUSPECT / HANGAROUND** - First stage of entry into a motorcycle club.
- **PROSPECT** - Second phase of potential membership in a club. In this phase if you're serious about being in the club you lose your wife, your home, your freedom several times. You go through various mudchecks, you loose all the vestiges of your old life so all you have to live for is the club. The degree of this varies with the intensity of the club, outlaw clubs have the most intense program because they have the most to lose. The goal of all of this is to become a patchholder or brother.

- **PATCH** - The insignia of a motorcycle club, usually worn on a vest over the rest of your clothes so that all the public can see.
- **PATCH FEVER** - When prospects finally earn a patch in a motorcycle club it's a big event in their lives and they often go off the deep end, throwing their weight around, acting tough, scaring citizens and generally being a pain in the ass.
- **PATCHHOLDER** - The person your mothers warned you about.
- **MUDCHECK** - Measuring your toughness.
- **DUMP TRUCK** - A court appointed lawyer {public defender}.
- **CCW** - Carrying a Concealed Weapon.
- **SCOOTER** - A motorcycle {preferably a Harley}.
- **DRESSER** - A Harley with saddlebags and windshield.
- **STROKER** - A Harley or any engine where the distance between the crank pin and the sprocket shaft is lengthened to achieve more piston travel enabling the engine to inhale more mixture and compress it tighter before firing it.
- **CAGE** - Old time biker name for a car.
- **CHURCH** - The weekly meeting of a bike club.
- **CRIMEY** - Partner in crime.
- **PCH** - Pacific Coast Highway.
- **PALAVER** - Useless talk.
- **TANK SLAPPER** - The front end of your scooter starts wobbling so violently that the handlebars slap the gas tank.
- **GLADIATOR SCHOOL** - A term denoting the toughest of prisons.

Different Forms Of Use

- **SNORTING** - Is inhaling through your nose using a tube, usually a straw, barrel of a pen, or rolled up currency. This is the middle of the road as far as blast off time. The only real disadvantage to this method is the nasty drip down the back of your throat. Clearly Canadian peach water or Calistoga Black Current water cut the drip the best for me.
- **EATING OR DRINKING** - This method takes the longest to get off; the high is more mellow and lasts much longer.
- **SLAMMING** - Or Intravenous use is the quickest and the highest, on occasion people's hearts have ripped holes in themselves due to the mixed signals sent to the muscles by the traffic jam called your brain.
- **CHASING THE DRAGON** - Is a form of smoking where you put a small amount of product at the top of a six or eight inch long, two or three inch wide piece of tinfoil, you inhale through a tube placed in your mouth. With a lighter or constant flame you tickle the bottom of the foil never exposing the product to direct flame or high heat. The goal here is to melt the product to vaporization without burning it while inhaling the vapors. This results in a very different high, many people who snorted for years and maintained well lost it completely after a very short run of smoking. Not a good thing. This method is also used to eyeball the PH

balance of a batch of dope by noting the niacin scaling pattern on the foil when light heat is applied.

- **SMOKING** - This is done using a carefully broken light bulb. At most head shops you can now get pipes made in this same design. The globe allows the smoker to roll the pipe to keep it from getting too hot and burning the dope before it vaporizes correctly. This type of use does a great amount of damage to the respiratory system in a very short period of time and completely changes your personality instantly. Something about this type of delivery is hard on the brain and can cause psychosis in a very short period of time. Chasing the dragon is the same thing, just a different method.

List Of Indicators

Since the average age of the first time meth user is twelve {I was thirteen the first time I used amphetamines, but that was only because they were very widely prescribed and as available then as meth is now} I'm directing this particular segment to the parents of pre and early teens.

Law enforcement has a thing they call a list of indicators. Meaning when they make a traffic stop or enter a home or any type of property there are certain things they look for that indicate a crime of some type {in this case meth production} has been, will be or could be going on.

The following list is the toxic and caustic household items and a few other things that have replaced the original ingredients used to make meth. These adulterated ingredients are a major contributor to the disastrous effects that meth has on the mind and body of the user in a very short period of time.

From the first use meth changes your physical chemistry altering and short circuiting a multitude of thought processes that are easy to spot. Normal speech patterns are altered, restlessness, twitching, constant scratching, rubbing, picking at the skin {I had one friend that picked a hole in his forehead so huge and deep that it made me sick to look at him and I had to just stay away from him in order to keep from puking in his face}. This is far from a complete list of symptoms, they vary from person to person and recipe to recipe, all but a very few users are altered in some immediately noticeable way. These are only the most common and least dangerous behaviors. Behavioral changes can escalate all the way up to murderously delusional states and totally irrational rages brought on by the meth monsters whispering all kinds of deludedly insane things inside your head. The trouble starts when you begin listening.

The following things can be found in most homes across the country, rarely all at one time or in the amounts needed to cook a significant quantity.

ISOPROPYL ALCOHOL, **BRAKE OR CARBURETOR CLEANER**, **ETHER** starting fluid, **DRANO** or **BATTERY ACID**, **RED PHOSPHOROUS** kitchen matches or road flares, **IODINE**, **LITHIUM BATTERIES**, **TRICHLOROETHANE** cleaning solvent, **MSM** or **ANOSITOL** both aid in absorption, the best cuts for crank, **HEET** diesel fuel treatment, **MURIATIC ACID**, **LYE** and **ACETONE**.

If you find these things in any quantity or hidden anywhere around your property or simply laying around the garage and you didn't put 'em there you should be talking with your kid especially if you've noticed any weirder than normal behavior lately. Most of these things are toxic and caustic, some to the point of death and others can cause serious chemical burns when contacting the skin.

If you suspect someone you know of using crank the least you could do is show 'em the crap this shit's made out of and let 'em know exactly what they're sticking in their bodies {no wonder they look so hammered so fast}.

The last and most deadly ingredient is **ANHYDROUS AMMONIA**; one whiff of this can instantly freeze your lungs and kill ya. Several years ago I was listening to the local news in a small farming community in Illinois one morning. Earlier that year a law had been passed requiring farmers to padlock the spigots on their anhydrous ammonia tanks that they kept in their fields for fertilizer and varmint control {when shot into a gopher or woodchuck hole it freezes 'em instantly} to keep cranksters from stealing it to cook their dope with.

This particular news item was about five teens found partially frozen in front of an anhydrous ammonia tank by a farmer. Apparently when they found the padlocked spigot they simply knocked it off. The fluid drained out on the ground, they breathed the fumes, froze their lungs, collapsed into the growing pool and froze every part of their bodies that contacted the ammonia. The oldest was seventeen, the youngest fifteen; all shining examples of crankster mentality.

If you find this anywhere around do not under any circumstance breath the fumes. Remove it to a well ventilated area and call the proper authorities or a local farmer, they use it all the time safely, hell it was probably his to begin with.

I don't really recommend having your child locked up except as a last resort, for the simple fact that surrounding an impressionable teen with criminals will only end up making him or her a better criminal. I do recommend swift and immediate intervention of a severe nature.

The only way to break the grip of meth is to catch it before it has a chance to suck the new user down into an abyss that few return from. With forty million meth addicts and ten thousand new users daily, most around the age of twelve, we'll have our work cut out for us stemming the tide of the meth pandemic in this country, but unless we all turn to meth {I've done my time in hell, thanks} it'll never be too late!

Degrees Of Highness

Before I explain the degrees of highness it should be known that these vary by recipe, personal reaction to same, state of mind, and length of time up.

- **SPUN** - Aggressively in search of the eternal buzz at warp speed and at all cost, the movie by the same title is an accurate portrayal of the busy nothingness of crankster's lives.
- **SPRUNG** - Tightly unwound.
- **SIT-N-SPIN** - Certain types of dope create this effect in even the most experienced speed freak, sitting-n-spinning consists of idle nothingness at warp speed for hours obsessively chewing nails, picking at the face or whatever, *PLAYING TETRIS FOR THREE DAYS*, obsessive behavior of all sorts generally directed at ones self. Depending on circumstance and personality some recipes make you get up and go to work while others scatter your thoughts and cause you to momentarily obsess for hours into days about everything, nothing, the stupidest things.
- **WIRED** - Ready to **GO** do something **NOW** even if it's wrong, all dressed up with everywhere and nowhere to go.
- **FLIPPIN' IN** - Too fucked up to even speak, thoughts are a blur, all you can do is sit there and look like you shit your pants.

- **FLIPPIN' OUT** - So fucked up you can't shut the fuck
up to save your life.

Normal behavior is also the norm for normal people. My friends and I used to say that if you flipped in or out on the shit, the gun was fired before you ever snorted the first line. Normal {always remember normal is relative} people being people like myself that stayed up for weeks on end and developed, followed through, and finished numerous projects, owned businesses, paid taxes, made money, worked our asses off in the name of fun because to us this is what it was and crank was just a tool to extend our playtime. We never lost our minds, we never lost our morals{these varied on a minute by minute basis depending on circumstance and desired outcome, but we never lost sight of 'em}. Basically we lived by a kind of code {honor among thieves} like the outlaw bike clubs adhered to, that had nothing to do with society's laws.

We bent the rules far beyond the breaking point on a daily basis, through all of it {life was the filter we used to find our own level of party and participants, once found the loose collective becomes we and a circle is formed} we all realized we were just getting high. High seemed like it would last forever, as long as you didn't run outta dope. The resulting crash was deafening when you did, but only you could hear it. Those around you hear nothing or see nothing, you've disappeared off the face of the earth, usually for days, at least until you get more dope, that's the only thing that works, that or a long, long sleep.

At times when reading this book I may sound pro speed. I'm not, but I did have one hell of an adventure using this drug for years and years. Understand I'm the exception, not the rule. While many people around me succumbed to the effects of crank, I maintained as always. In fact I made a game out of using prodigious amounts of dope and staying a step ahead of the cops and often said "It was my job to break all the laws I could and not get caught. It was their job to catch me." That is not the norm, most spun cookies don't even think about it till it's too late.

"When you live outside the law you have to be honest," with yourself at the very least, I've seen people mentally debilitated at their first use. Already disadvantaged they should leave the game; instead they ended up in jails and other institutions or another statistic because they didn't.

Meth is an insidious vacuum that eventually sucks everything outta your life. I mean everything, health, finance, common sense, morals, and self-respect. You can't stay one step ahead of meth, with the ups and downs, each down going lower and each up never getting quite as high as the last, a one step up three steps back kinda' thing. Then always on the horizon, the inevitable bust. The list goes on-n-on, till you get to your personal bottom.

This shit will kill you by degrees until you're in a box at a very early age, but on the way down {especially if slammed} you'll hurtle over new low after new low like an Olympic Athlete until you end up in a shooting gallery sitting in your own shit, piss, puke, and blood living for the rush of the needle; one bodily function after another shutting down till you're just a hollow stick figure that your family can't recognize in the morgue when they come to claim your body, if they even know where you are.

I've seen a few people take this road; I've looked down that road all the way to the end, nothing for me down there. I could've easily gone, but after seeing the results first hand, no thanks. I still think of the friends lost way down there. Saddest of all, nothing could've been done anyway. **<u>METH IS ALL CONSUMMING!!!!</u>**

The Wonders Of Meth

The first wonder of speed is that it doubles your work time. I used to start ten projects a week, three major ones, seven minor ones, and could schedule my dope so that I managed to stay up all week, from Sunday night to Sunday morning on very little dope if need be. You can get a lot accomplished and a lot of playing done when you utilize every minute of almost every day.

Fun for me was to snort a line, smoke a joint, and build something, continually. Part of the game was chasing the crystal creatures around all week until they became meth monsters and started chasing me, then the real fun began. My shop was in the middle of nowhere, after eight o'clock at night I had no neighbors. Meth monsters and other things that thrived in that environment added up to an adventure every line.

In the beginning of use the wonders of your increased abilities never cease to amaze you. You feel invincible and more alive than you've ever felt in your life. It's like for the first time your eyes are truly open and you can feel to the depths of your hell. No mission is impossible, everything is probable, you commonly find yourself saying "we're not done yet?"

As use continues things start to slip away like your health, because you don't take care of yourself. Your money, it all goes on drugs. Your possessions, you turn 'em into money or meth, no matter how little you get and the worst of all your time {you'll never get that back}. Eventually the only positive feeling in your life is when you're high. Any other time the depression is overwhelming. This is one of the most important factors in your continued addiction, now all you have is the drugs.

A time comes when, like heroin speed becomes a maintenance drug. Without it you simply can't function, you can't think or move and all you can do is sleep for days. When you're awake you're so depressed that death is a better alternative to life without crank {with any luck you're too tired to act on the thought} and you wish it'd come quickly, but get a line in you and you're on top of the world again even though nothing has changed but your altitude.

The final wonder of methamphetamine addiction is where the hell your life went. That means possessions, money, property, self-respect; all of these things were flushed long before you even got a glimpse of the bottom. If you haven't given up dope yet, you can't even see the bottom, but its coming. Everyone gets there, and it's always different, yet horribly the same. Nobody gets out alive; it's just a matter of time and for some a very short time at that.

The Origins Of Meth

The very first speed sold was Benzedrine inhalers {bennies}, these were marketed in Germany in the early thirties, people broke these open and swallowed or soaked the amphetamine filled cotton and drank the fluid to get high, this was called "poppin' bennies." All amphetamine is a synthetic with effects from mild to wild depending on the amount used, bennies were for all intents and purposes pretty mild.

Seeking a more intense high the Third Reich created methamphetamine {petroleum amplified} using Benzedrine for its base. This drug fueled the Axis Powers throughout the Second World War. Germans from The Fuehrer {who was shot up five times a day} to the lowliest foot soldier had an ample supply of crank to keep 'em going. Being allied to the Germans, the Japanese took full advantage of this better war through chemistry philosophy; crank fueled the Japs right down to the last kamikaze. If you had a never-ending supply of this shit you didn't have to worry about feeding your troops, just keeping 'em high and armed.

The paranoia and psychosis that would inevitably set in would feed the flames of combat if they could only be directed at the enemy and not within. Unfortunately you become paranoid of the things you see every day, not what someone tells you to fear. The distrust and violence are inevitably aimed at your own subordinates almost as intensely as your supposed enemy.

Hitler in the first year of the war had most of his staff executed for imagined treasons and distrusted all but a handful of the ones he let live. He had all of them under constant surveillance. That was what the Gestapo did, spy on the government and the people and kill anyone that had even a questioning thought. The Gestapo was a government agency founded on paranoia and the knowing that what they were doing was the most absolute wrong ever committed against their fellow man.

This is why the Blitzkrieg {crank was the blitzkrieg that fueled the blitzkrieg} was so intense and the Japanese and Germans moved so rapidly and ruthlessly towards their objectives.

After the war was over methamphetamine was introduced worldwide. The response was overwhelming; everyone loved this new wonder drug. It could be purchased legally over the counter in any store, and if you didn't live near a store it could be purchased mail order through all of the different mail order catalogs of the time, including Sears and Montgomery Wards. "The kit" as it was called contained a syringe {to shoot up with, best form of ingestion}, a spoon {to cook it down for the syringe with} and an ampoule of crank, all for five dollars.

In post war America the speed epidemic started and gained startling momentum, soon everyone was on speed, by the late `40s seventy percent of the population was addicted to meth. It was a definite favorite among artists and writers, in 1950 Jack Kerouac wrote "On the Road" in twenty days while under the influence of meth.

As society spun outta control the government had to get a grip on speed use and finally banned over the counter and mail order sales. You now had to have a prescription from a doctor, but you could get a prescription by simply visiting your local doctor and complaining of any one of over thirty maladies and be prescribed speed. Speed was the most prescribed drug of all time in America.

Eventually (early seventies) the drug was removed from the market completely. People were destroying themselves with it, daily. The bootlegged form of the drug then moved underground and for several decades was found almost exclusively in outlaw motorcycle clubs and truck driver's pockets or pill bottles.

These two subcultures operated on the fringes of society without very much interaction. Back then to get speed you had to know someone. Other drugs more readily available caught the attention of the using public; meth kinda' took a back seat, except in California and areas where outlaw motorcycle clubs kept the drug flowing in their circles, occasionally small quantities escaped to a few citizens here and there, but as a whole the unknowing public was far more in love with cocaine and crap like that.

This continued until the mid-eighties, when with the help of the internet anyone could find a recipe online. In the late-eighties/early-nineties the "Mexican Mafia" got ahold of the recipe, and began flooding the southwestern United States with cheap, unstable, high grade product. At one time everyone I knew in Southern California was using. This included cops, lawyers, doctors, citizens in all walks of life. Now the most frequent users are stay at home moms and the shit's cooked in garbage can labs in your neighbor's garage.

For years crank wasn't identifiable by law enforcement. If you got stopped and had crank in your possession they tested it with bleach (the test for cocaine). If it didn't turn blue they didn't know what it was. I used to tell 'em it was a special soap powder that you mixed with water to acid wash aluminum. Being in the motorcycle business I could point to my beadblasted heads on my bike and tell 'em this is what this wash did. They'd look at me in disbelief for a moment and then as if realizing they didn't have a clue they'd agree and let me go, most of the time giving back the bag of dope. Occasionally I'd have to dump it out but that's still better than going to jail.

When I left SoCal in 1995 every cop in Ventura County was convinced everyone was on crank. They were probably eighty percent right, some of them were even on it. I know I sold it to 'em. Now they had the knowledge to identify crank, and cranksters alike. The sweep was on. At that time the economy in the area was so bad that everyone had a pocketful of crank, but very few had two nickels to rub together.

How It Works

Meth is a central nervous system stimulant, meaning heightened senses, a higher threshold of pain, euphoria, increased thought processes, creativity and problem solving skills are enhanced. In short the **"ten feet tall-n-bulletproof"** syndrome comes into play and depending on the dope lasts up to thirty-six hours or more.

Unlike cocaine the other popular stimulant where you're high for twenty minutes and jonesing for more for the rest of your life; a waste of time and money if you ask me and that's all I can tell you about coke. I tried it several times in my early drug years and wasn't impressed.

I loved crank the very first time I used it and do to this day, I just know better now. I've been close enough to the end of road to see it from where I stood and know I didn't wanna go there. I chose to live, but not before I stared death in the face a few times.

Four Baser Instincts

Every creature on earth has four baser instincts that control our unconscious thought. These are Hunger, Survival, Proliferation of the Species {sex}, and to **Alter our State of Consciousness**. This is the one we're concerned with; it is also by far the most powerful and deadly.

At a certain time of year in Africa the fruit of a particular tree {I can't remember the name of} ripens, falls to the ground and ferments. Every form of creature from far and wide comes to partake of the bounty. Predator and prey alike converge at one time and party till everything is gone then they go their separate ways, momentarily all other instincts are overridden for the sake of a party.

A monkey, when given the choice of food, sex or cocaine, will kill itself with dope and never think of anything else. People will lie, cheat, steal, flush their entire lives and kill {even family members} to kill themselves with dope. So much for civilization. Every twenty-two seconds our brain seeks to alter its state of consciousness. Crank fills that particular desire in a way no other drug does. For me and all my friends it was a way of life that overshadowed everything we did. I couldn't go to court without getting high, shit I couldn't even go do my community service without being high. With this going on in our heads it's very hard to stay on the farm when we've seen the lights of L.A., even if it was just in our minds.

Methamphetamine Psychosis

Methamphetamine Psychosis is what the mental mess created by crank is called. The common and only treatment I've ever heard of is Lithium and Haldall. This somewhat rights the imbalance of chemicals in the brain that cause this as long as it's being used. Stop taking it and you're right back in your own little world and it doesn't even work for everybody.

The onset of this varies from person to person. Sometimes this happens with the very first line. My theory on that is that the gun was already fired and that person was already an accident looking for a place to happen and anything could've tipped 'em over the edge, it just happened to be crank that did it for 'em.

The following is almost a drug addict's boot camp. It seems that everything in the next part of this narrative was simply readying me for my arrival in L.A., the big candy store. These are only the high points to get us to the real story of the fifteen year crank binge that is the basis of this story.

I'm The Person Your Parents Warned You About!

I was born an outlaw. This doesn't mean I was born in a hideout to hoodlums or gangsters. My parents were upright, hardworking middle class people. I mean I had the **"rules were made to be broken, especially by me"** gene in my DNA. They broke the mold, then they made me. From birth I was compelled to break every rule I encountered at a casually reckless pace, with consequences rolling of me like water off a duck's back.

An asswhippin' of phenomenal proportions only lasted as long as the crying time it took to recover. Then if I wasn't somehow prevented from returning to the activity in question I was right back at it like nothing happened. I was not intentionally bad just busy beyond distraction and rules were a definite distraction.

Before I even learned to walk I was trouble with a capitol T. My first word was **NO** and that was the answer to everything. At eight months I toddled, at nine months I was almost unstoppable, everywhere at a dead run, sounds pretty normal to me. Our family doctor said I was vaccinated with a phonograph needle cause I couldn't be quiet.

At around three years old I remember my mother interceding in an escalating beating being meted out by my dad. He was so furious he held me up to face level, his cigarette and coffee breath blasting me in the face, his eyes locked with mine as he shook me screaming "this kid's either gonna be dead or in prison by the time he's sixteen and if he's dead I hope I'm the one that kills him!" With that he slammed me to the floor and stormed off into the living room.

I tormented my dad to no end. One of my favorite things to do while he was driving was to sneak up behind him from the back seat, get right next to his right ear and yell **"FLOOR IT DADDY-O!"** Before he could get to me I'd dive for the other side of the car shrieking with laughter while my mom told him to keep his eyes on the road.

One day I did this when we were pulling into Langelle's Mobil Station to get gas. He floored it all right, all of about fifty feet. Then he slammed on the brakes and threw the car in park, jumped out his door before the car even stopped, jerked open the back door, hauled me outta the car by one leg screaming, stood me up, hauled my pants down and blistered my ass with his work hardened calloused hand till I was begging him to stop between shrieks of pain from each whack. It was probably two weeks before I did that again.

My mom never understood why, she just accepted me. Maybe she could tell why by looking at me; when I was a little kid I had three unbelievable cowlicks, one on each corner in the front that resembled horns, the third was in the middle of the back of my head like a middle finger in a perpetual "fuck you." It didn't matter what kind of glue you used you couldn't keep 'em down. The only way to tame 'em was to shave 'em, which was a frequent punishment of my dad's. The horns are gone, hair doesn't even grow there anymore, does that mean I'm finally purged of my evil I wonder?

Sometimes my mom'd ask me why I couldn't just behave, but I couldn't give her an answer I didn't have, hell I didn't know. When I was younger I thought that my dad was the meanest bastard a kid could have for a dad. Now that I'm his age {he was fifty when I was five} I realize he had a big helping of patience, because if I had a kid like me he wouldn't've made it to age two, I'd have killed him long before.

By the time I was in kindergarten I'd been banned from all the neighbor's yards and forbidden to play with all the neighbor kids, just more rules to break. I should probably add before I get much further that my ancestors where Vikings {the scourge of the known world at one time}. I'm a Taurus {bull in a china shop syndrome}. As a child I was frenetic, ultra-hyperactivity caused by food colorings, flavorings and preservatives {bull in a china shop syndrome at warp ten with a taste for whatever I could make happen next}.

At the end of the day the only one around me that wasn't exhausted was me. Everyone else'd been run through a continual ringer of behavioral issues that started when my eyes opened and sometimes continued after I was asleep. Usually these took the form of calls from other parents who were just discovering things washed up in the wake of a busy day of pillaging the neighborhood.

I could tell by the tone of the ring on the phone that I was in trouble. My dad's voice confirmed it, but my mom'd make it wait till tomorrow once I was in bed. Tomorrow was another day and I'd probably had enough beatings for one day as it was. The tone of my life had been set in my formative years, somehow that tone had already become immutable, I was already the person your mother warned you about.

My kindergarten teacher was also our neighbor three doors down; she had a pretty good idea what she was in for when my mother and I walked through the door the first day of school. The highlight of that year's behavioral issues came after a Tarzan movie marathon the previous Saturday. My teacher'd left us to recess unattended for a few moments; things started as a simple Tarzan yell competition and quickly escalated into me stripped to my underwear, barefoot, swinging from the roof of the girl's playhouse to the stage by the gold braided curtain cord for the purple velvet curtain that graced our stage, all the while doing my very best Tarzan yell at the top of my lungs.

I had this competition in the bag till the teacher walked in midswing. I spent a good portion of kindergarten with my head down on my desk. I was also introduced to the wooden ruler, the yard stick, the blackboard pointer and every corner of the room. I developed an intimate relationship with all of 'em with the blessing of my parents who'd given up years earlier and was resigned to the fact that a beating was the only thing that got my attention.

Things got much better in the first grade. My desk and all was put out in the hall for the entire second semester of the year. The notes sent home thrown in the trashcan in front of Hillson's store. Thought I had it whipped I did, didn't know about the mail, parent/teacher conferences that kinda' stuff.

During my stay in the hall one of my partners in crime and I broke a water fountain off the floor, flooding and ruining the finish on the lobby floor. My partner'd been sent to the cloakroom for acting up in class. This means he was standing face in the corner about twenty feet away from me. My desk'd been placed very close to the water fountain next to our classroom. During the shear boredom of hall life I'd taught myself to squirt water over thirty feet by placing my finger on the nozzle of the fountain just right and developed deadly accuracy doing it.

While my crimey stood face in the corner I started squirting him in the back of the head from the water fountain. He kept motioning me to quit which egged me on even more. About the forth squirt he came flying at me from outta the cloakroom. I ran around the banister post and up the stairs to a landing where the stairs split, both sides going up to the second floor balcony which went all the way around the atrium, the landing midway up the stairs had another water fountain on it.

As I ran up the stairs and around the balcony shrieking with laughter my partner stopped momentarily on the landing to squirt me from that fountain, then ran up the other side to head me off at the pass. While we were in the midst of this the teachers and all the students both upstairs and down that could get out the doors behind 'em were boiling out into the lobby and onto the balcony to see what was going on. I wheeled at the top of the stairs and ran in the other direction with my buddy hot on my heals.

He caught me all the way around on the other side of the balcony at the top of the stairs. We both tumbled down the stairs in a twisting heap and crashed into the water fountain on the landing sending it end over end down the bottom half of the stairs with the tin sides flying in all directions and a horribly loud crash, crash, crash all the way to the middle of the lobby floor, where it landed in pieces. Water from the broken copper tube that fed the water fountain sprayed twenty feet in the air soaking the entire lobby floor and fucking the finish up royally.

The beating we got with those inch square yardsticks was phenomenal. Neither of us could sit the rest of the day and after school we had to clean every eraser in the place before we went home. No big deal for me, I walked to school, but my buddy took the bus. His parents had to be called to pick him up, so he was in trouble immediately. My mom simply thought I'd been dilly-dallying around coming home so I didn't get into any more trouble then and the note that came home with me never made it any further than the trash can in front of the store like all the others. The next day my buddy came to school with a note from his parents instructing our teacher to keep us as far apart as possible in the future.

After that I accidentally hit my teacher right between the eyes with an iceball during a snowball fight we weren't allowed to be having in the first place, with the same kid who helped me break the water fountain that I was forbidden to even be around, breaking her horned-rimmed glasses in two and knocking her unconscious.

By the end of the semester the principal {Miss Murray} had broken two and a half cases of inch square yardsticks over my ass for those and a myriad of lesser infractions that kept pretty much the whole four room schoolhouse in a constant uproar the whole quarter.

All of this caught up with me at the quarterly parent/teacher conference, when a letter was *mailed* home to my parents. My dad had to leave work an hour early because his attendance was required at this conference as well as my mothers; nothing interrupted my dad's work and lived. I stood in the corner waiting for I didn't know what yet as ordered by my mother the instant I set foot in the house after school on the afternoon of the conference.

As I stood in the corner wondering what I was being punished for {I still had no idea that I'd been busted} my dad's car pulled in the driveway more than an hour before he was due to get off work. I swallowed so hard I had to puke my tongue back up to keep from choking on it; if I was the reason my dad was home this early I was dead.

I could tell my dad was fit to be tied by the way he made the whole house shake as he stormed up the stairs. The back door opened, that same instant his huge rough hand was squeezing the back of my neck as he pulled me backwards outta the corner by it far enough to give me two whacks on the ass that lifted my feet off the floor with each one. He stuffed me back in the corner, with his mouth right next to my ear he growled "you stand right there and don't even think about moving till we get back." I heard the back door again, then the car left the driveway. I didn't dare to look or even make a sound, especially cry; my dad was really good at giving me something to cry about.

I stood in silence for I don't know how long; finally noticing there were no other sounds in the house, had my mom gone with him? I softly called "mom" and got no answer. I hadn't figured out why for sure, but I had a good idea it had something to do with school, if that was true I was fuuuuuuuucked!

I heard the car in the driveway, then the back door. I was jerked backwards by my neck *over* the kitchen table this time. I remember very little of the beating or the rest of the evening for that matter. The next morning and every meal after that for about four or five weeks I stood to eat. Sitting was impossible, the welted, blistered flesh of my backside couldn't handle the pain. Even worse than the beating was the grounding, the rest of the school year, during the week and on the weekend until all my homework was done and there wasn't any such thing as no homework whether there was or not, so it never got done, meaning I never left my yard.

The next morning a note was sent to school with me that I made sure the teacher got straightaway. My desk was back in the classroom, but set off to one side of the room and I was excused from sitting due to its impossibility until further notice. Seems as though it took about a month before my ass gave me that notice too.

I graduated the first grade with four Fs, a D- and a note from the teacher explaining that I was passed to second grade because no first grade teacher would have me in their class. I could do the work, I simply refused to because I was too busy being a constant disruption. The real kicker was the bill for five cases of yardsticks that the principle broke over me in the course of that year. I was grounded until the day before the next school year.

Another tone was being set. A loner was evolving, I was learning to trust no one, do things solo and keep my mouth shut about it.

When I was a kid there used to be a television show on called Art Linkletter's House Party. One of the segments on that show was called Kids Say the Darndest Things. Each day a new question was asked to a panel of five to seven year olds. On one particular day the question was, why do you think Abraham Lincoln was assassinated? One little boy immediately answered "because he was in John Wilkes booth." This show aired just a few days before President Kennedy was assassinated.

The day he was assassinated I'd been in rare form all day, driving my teacher {Mrs. Conley} crazy with one disruption after another. She was called outta the room momentarily by the principal {Mrs. Downy} and given the news about the killing. When she came back into the room she was very somber as she asked us to quiet down. We could all tell that something was wrong and did so immediately.

You could've heard a pin drop after she made the announcement to the class. Instead the whole class heard me say half under my breath "he must've been in John Wilkes booth too" and exploded with laughter. Which was immediately silenced, I was jerked outta my seat by my right ear, paddled all the way out into the hall and left standing in a corner.

After being discovered by Mrs. Downy I was paddled again. When she found out what I'd said to end up out in the hall I was taken downstairs, my mouth washed out with soap and kept after school to write sentences on the blackboard till my arm fell off. Once I'd completely filled the blackboard I had to erase it and clean all the erasers in the school before I went home for Thanksgiving vacation.

My meteoric rise through the ranks of Scarborough's worst students was nothing short of underwhelming. By the third grade teachers drew lots to see who'd be stuck with me the next year and groaned when they drew the wrong one. In later years this affected my sister by having to prove to every teacher she had she wasn't like me. That was the indentation left by me in our school system.

I scraped by with record low grades and a lot of detentions {I learned to write with six pens at a time to finish my sentence writing assignment in twenty minutes and have twenty-five minutes to get more detention in} suspensions, and notes explaining why though with failing grades I was passed to the next grade, till the eighth grade. By then I'd experimented with every drug that came my way and was trying to be a regular pot smoker. I hadn't experimented with needles yet, but that wasn't far in the future.

Poppin' Dexies

Early in the year of the eighth grade my friend's dad suffered a heart attack. One of the prescriptions he brought home was Dexedrine. My friend and I didn't know what they were, but finding out went right to the top of our to do list.

Dexedrine is a synthetic speed with a much milder ride than crank. Taken in the prescribed dosage only a slight pick me up is noticed. At that period in our lives {too much was never enough} the object was to do as much of something as absolutely possible and try to maintain in everyday situations. We were turning drug use into an extreme sport with death or a trip to the hospital to have your stomach pumped as the gold medal. To this day I'm still an extremist, all or nothing, no middle ground.

That year thanks to the focus that the dexies gave me I completed the year with mostly As and Bs the lowest grade was a C+ all year. The dexies'd worked on me much the way Ritilin works on hyper kids today. Unfortunately this wouldn't last; the prescription was changed after another heart attack the following summer.

I'd become confident in my new found ability, enough so that I elected to take college courses in the ninth grade; including algebra {I'm numerically dyslexic and have a terrible time with numbers of any kind, let alone numbers and letters}. Needless to say without the speed to settle the natural chaos in my brain I didn't stand a chance. Failing everything miserably I went back to being the disruption I always was, I was good at being bad, I had a lot of practice.

This last paragraph might sound like I had a clue what caused the focus, not so. It was decades later when I understood the drug Ritilin {very pure pharmaceutical speed used to control hyperactivity} that I connected the dexies with the good grades of the eight grade.

I flunked my way thru school till I was old enough to quit without parental consent. For years school'd been a party place, a place to buy, sell, trade and use drugs. There's no way you can spend the day in school tripping on acid or mescaline or sometimes both and retain even your name let alone anything else.

I left school with no hopes, actively in search of the eternal buzz, not knowing what it was yet. That summer was an explosion of partying, the drinking age was lowered to eighteen, I finally had my own car to drive, drugs of all kinds were everywhere. The Casco Bay area was one of the hottest drop-off points for pot smugglers, a pound of pot was one hundred and twenty-five dollars and it was everywhere, the year was 1974.

My First Tweakend

In a bar I can't remember the name of on East Grand Avenue in Old Orchard Beach early one Friday evening a friend and I were shooting pool when challenged to play teams by two Canadians {at that time coastal Maine was the vacationland of the Canadians}, thru the course of the next few games we became acquainted.

We finally took a break and went outside to smoke a joint inviting the Canadians along as well. In the course of our conversation they explained that pot was very hard to get in Canada and very expensive if found. After hearing about our pot situation they showed us something they had with a similar situation to it in their country, they called it "Pink Crystal." It came in rock form. The rock glowed iridescent white with little flashes of color like a diamond, but when you held it up to the light and looked through it, it had a light pink tint not noticed before and it flowed freely and cheaply in Canada like pot did here.

When we expressed an interest in trying it, we walked around the corner to their motel room, with them all the while explaining how this drug was snorted, something we hadn't yet done. Once in the room a mirror, razor blade and tooter tube was brought out. One of the guys shaved a small pile off the rock onto the mirror. This he chopped even finer. He separated the pile into four smaller piles, made each pile into two minuscule lines. He picked up the tooter, stuck it up his nose and inhaled a line up each nostril, passing the mirror around the circle we all followed suit.

I sat on the end of the motel bed after I snorted my lines. My ears started to ring, I felt like every hair on my body was standing on end. A warm rush started at the base of my spine and like a wave rose and spread up my back till it washed up my neck from behind, over my skull, down my face to my chest and then **I WAS FUCKIN' HIGH!** High like I'd never been before, but at that moment knew I always wanted to be.

My drug of choice was found, it was love at first drip. Those first lines the size of two matchheads propelled us through an endless party that entire weekend. In the course of that weekend a deal was struck with the Canadians to trade weed for speed even up, The French Connection'd been made. Unfortunately due to international logistics problems we only made a couple of trades then everything went sour. This was just a minor problem because now that I knew what I wanted, I just had to figure out where to get it.

My search uncovered all kinds of speed mostly the less intense forms of dexies and bennies. Occasionally methroads would come around, but never regularly or in a great quantity. In the course of my never-ending search I came across the best thing the government ever provided a budding speed freak, Black Beauties. These timed release babies when eaten'd keep you going thirty-six to fifty hours depending on your tolerance and body weight.

We eventually got around to breaking open the capsules, crushing the white and brown beads and snorting the powder. The rush from this'd make ya shit yer pants the first time ya did it, the drip was like gasoline-n-lye, your hair stood on end {at least it felt that way, even if it was two feet long}. Your face got hot flaming crimson, breath was short, thoughts a blur, it took a few minutes for this to level off, but when it did you'd better have something to do, cause you suddenly had a lotta time on your hands.

This was around the time that needles came to add a new dimension to getting high and a source for crank was found at the local bike club's clubhouse. At the same time as needles came Percodan, Seconal, Valium, Quaaludes, LSD 25, cocaine, heroin, and the junkie 101 chemistry classes required to learn how to cook these things down to be used in a needle, all except the LSD it was already in liquid form.

At this same time a skylight was found to be ajar in the roof of a local pharmacy. Obtaining these pharmaceuticals was a simple midnight recon down the street. We always returned with huge apothecary jars of drugs, syringes and all kinds of things of extreme interest to a novice up and coming geezer.

On one of these forays I found a matched set of stainless steel dental syringes with finger loops, interchangeable glass barrels, and needles from numbers one thru five in a beautiful teakwood box. These became a prized possession of mine. I polished the increments off the barrels so you had no idea the dosage you were taking and these became the suicide rigs used in our fishing contests.

Gone Fishin'

This next bit'll give a whole new meaning to the word fishing. You can bet your bass you ain't never done this kind of fishing or maybe you have. During the course of experimenting with combinations of all the drugs named earlier I discovered that my favorite combination was Percodan and crank in a near 50/50 mix. I'd grind the percs up in a mortar and pestle and mix the powders. Cook 'em down to an opaque fluid, load each rig, then do a wallshot. Working in the first rig gradually till I got a register, then slamming both rigs at the same time.

This is where the term extreme sport drug use came from. There were three challenges to this type of insanity. The first was getting the rigs outta each arm before you went into convulsions and snapped the needles off. The second was not busting your head open when the convulsions hit and you hit the floor fishing like a mackerel outta water.

At this point we'd get out the yardstick and measure the height of the bouncing off the floor {fishing}. The highest bounce being the winner. The last, but far from the least challenge is to stay alive during the next forty-five minutes that you had a traffic jam for a brain and no control over yourself. Unfortunately the winners of this contest have on occasion died before receiving their trophy and quite a few others had to wait till they got released from the hospital to get theirs. If a trip to the hospital was called for, he or she was loaded into the back seat of someone's car and dumped on the sidewalk in front of the emergency room door when no one was looking.

One particular birthday party {I think it was mine} really got outta control. A friend worked as a medical supply delivery driver which gave us access to a world of professional drug paraphernalia, which to us was the equivalent of L.L.Bean for junkies.

Taking advantage of this connection we helped ourselves to five large cylinders of nitrous oxide and several hundred feet of rubber tubing and the necessary valves and fittings needed to create about a dozen nitrous stations around the living room of my girlfriend's apartment.

All you had to do was stick the mouthpiece in your mouth, open the valve and inhale till you keeled over laughing {don't forget to close the valve asshole, party responsibly at all times}. Part of the reason for this contraption was inhaling nitrous directly outta the cylinder could freeze your lungs and kill ya, a real buzz kill. To avoid that, the nitrous had to be warmed in a balloon or in all the hundreds of feet of tubing strung about the room to the various inhalation stations.

The nitrous was just the beginning of the party favors to appear at this rights of spring and birthday extravaganza. There was coke, pot, six types of speed, LSD 25, peyote buttons, mescaline and all types of pharmaceutical drugs both ups and downs. Of course everything was drowned in mass quantities of alcohol of all kinds.

This party was so well known throughout the community that even the cops showed up several times and helped people to jail and the hospital, which I thought was pretty nice of 'em considering the number of times their cars got pelted with rocks and beer bottles. One guy even stood on the roof of the front porch and pissed on 'em as they walked up the stairs.

They remained very cheerful as they threw Doug off the roof and beat him damn near to death with their nightsticks, hogtied him and chucked him unceremoniously into the back of the paddy wagon. Believe it or not this kind of fun was had by all but a very few who chickened out and left the first time the cops came to break up the party. For those who stayed that meant more drugs and alcohol per person and a guaranteed good time for the hardcore users and abusers.

Once the lightweights were outta the way the party really took off with gangbangs in the bedrooms, puke paved floors and walls and people slamming everything they could get into the barrel of a rig. What they couldn't slam got snorted or smoked and when everybody was fucked up outta their minds the cops showed up with their portable light shows and gave everybody that could fit a ride in their police cars.

After five days of this and three trips to jail for me, the party was definitely winding down. Most everyone was in jail, the hospital or their parents'd found 'em and dragged 'em home.

The Indian In The Cupboard

Myself and another diehard were sitting on the couch watching a western on an old black and white TV. A pack of whooping Indians on horseback was riding at the screen guns blazing. The lead Indian's horse was shot out from under him and he fell to the ground rolling. He rolled right outta the TV onto the floor in front of it changing from black and white to natural colors as he did so. Simultaneously my friend's and my head snapped toward each other and we screamed **"DID YOU FUCKIN' SEE THAT?"**

When we screamed the two inch tall Indian looked in our direction, quickly scanned the area for cover and ran under the couch we were sitting on. We jumped up, dove to the floor and looked under the couch. The little bastard shot two arrows at us while running for the other end of the couch and the chase was on.

We chased that two inch tall Indian all over the room breaking furniture and everything in our path to get to this guy. He finally ran around the corner into the kitchen and jumped up into the kitchen cabinets. In a blast of hallucination chasing genius we piled all the destroyed stuff in the middle of the room, pulled up and wrapped the new wall to wall carpet around the debris and tied it like that so the Indian couldn't sneak back into the living room {we were both amazed at how fast and smart he was for his size} and hide in it. Once we had that done we started on the kitchen, he wasn't gonna get away from us.

By the time my girlfriend got home we had the kitchen cabinets ripped away from the wall the entire length of the room. A huge hole was ripped in the wall where he'd jumped into a small hole earlier.

The plumbing was leaking {spraying} all over the room. We were both soaked and filthy and water was running all over the floor, where it hadn't run we'd tracked it.

She walked in on us while we were shoulder deep in the hole in the wall, convinced we almost had him. I heard this noise {I can't describe it}, turned around and she was standing there shaking all over, her face was purplish red. She kinda' spit a few unintelligible sounds at us and flew outta the apartment never to be seen again. What the fuck was her problem? If we caught that Indian could you imagine how rich we'd get? Her interruption gave him the chance he needed to get away without a trace. That fuckin' bitch'd ruined everything.

Noticing the time, we went to the bar soaking wet and absolutely filthy for happy hour. When we got back water was running down the stairs and the plaster ceiling in the apartment below had fallen in pissing the neighbors off immensely. Leaving the fucked up mess like we found it, we turned the water off to the whole building and passed out.

When I awoke out of my drug-induced coma three days later there was no sign of that Indian anywhere. Even the arrows he'd shot at us were gone {I'd saved 'em in a shot glass}.

Decades later a movie named "The Indian in the Cupboard" came out. The first time I heard that I fell out laughing and I'm sure my partner in crime that day did too if he was still alive and remembered the event.

During this time I was working for a sandblast outfit, sandblasting the inside of huge oil storage tanks. On this particular day I'd taken a break and gone to the truck to get high. I kept two ampoules of dope in the bottom of my thermos, one contained pure crank to keep me going for work, the other was my 50/50 mix of percocrank.

I accidentally got the wrong dope in the rig and slammed a dose of percocrank. I went into convulsions and upon coming to found one of the owners staring at me through the passenger side window of the truck, his eyes as big as pizzas. In my convulsions my head'd broken the back window outta the cab and I'd torn two huge pieces outta the padding on the dashboard with my clinching fingers trying to hold on during the unexpected ride. Needless to say I was fired on the spot, which suited me fine; working was seriously cutting into my party time anyway.

For quite a while I staggered from job to job, partying always being the only goal. Never working anywhere long, gone with the first good paycheck or the first hassle whichever came first. In that period of time I lost my driver's license, was incarcerated numerous times {I actually got my GED in jail, on the form it states for place of graduation, Cumberland County Jail} for all types of crimes, mostly fighting, drugs, traffic violations and other stupid shit that idiots on drugs and alcohol do. Luckily for me everything was considered minor back then, if those same things where done today I'd've been under the jail somewhere for a long time.

On a freezing cold, snowy morning {about 3:00AM} while hitchhiking and freezing simultaneously, I had an unusual fit of lucidity and realized that I was fast becoming the person my mother'd warned me about. I was doing life on the installment plan, the only real home I had was the county jail. I was making far more backward progress than forward, through my casual recklessness I'd trashed every aspect of my life. Still in my teens I'd already bought my ticket, taken my seat and had my ticket punched on the downbound train of addiction.

My first conscious effort at slowing the momentum of this beast was to swear off needles. Early one snowy morning, I walked to the middle of the Million Dollar Bridge, said goodbye to the beautiful teakwood box and its contents that'd so quickly helped me through the train station to my elected seat on this accursed rail line and pitched it into the blackness of Casco Bay.

You're probably thinking that this would've been a good time for an intervention and a trip to rehab. They didn't even have that shit back then. I call it shit because that stuff only works on dedicated quitters, if people don't wanna quit they won't. Everything in their being screams **NO** silently in their heads until it drowns out any rational thought other than how to get out or play the system. **They only go through the motions to get free and get back to the dope.** They'll lay low until the coast is clear *in their minds*, then they're right back where they left off without so much as a hitch in their giddy up. In fact usually harder at it than ever, like making up for lost time.

I did although avail myself of the rehab of the day, which was to quit chemicals and hard liquor, only smoking weed and drinking beer. At first this reduction in stupidity was met by jeers of pussy, lightweight and lagger from the crowd I hung with. Over time that crowd slowly almost imperceptibly slipped away to prison, jail and overdoses causing death or worse, several ending up in mental institutions never to return. Some became full blown {living in a box or ditch} alcoholics and junkies that didn't even know their names, suicides {hung himself in jail on Christmas Eve at eighteen years old} or found naked frozen to death in a snow bank {never figured that one out}.

Eventually I found myself alone again, friends gone, girlfriend gone, the advantage to this wasn't immediately clear, but it eventually donned on me that this would be the best time to make a major change. This change became easier to make as time went by because drug connections were lost. Eventually getting a bag of weed became a two day ordeal and I wasn't really much of a drinker by myself. Near sobriety was becoming a way of life interspersed with the occasional tweakend or week long party when the godless were in alignment.

I walked into a pretty good job where I learned the hardest part of driving a tractor-trailer {backing up and adjusting turns for length}. That way the drivers could spend a little more time in the break room in the morning while I taught myself how to drive a tractor-trailer on our yard and load their trucks for 'em.

Driving was something I enjoyed and was good at except when I ate waaay to much windowpane acid and couldn't see through the fog between me and the windshield. I was freakin' out about it and laughing hysterically at the same time, no one else thought this was very funny and I was relieved of duty voluntarily in my own car by someone that didn't even have a license.

Things went forward for a while; I got my license back, got off probation, stuff like that, positive stuff. Well, we just couldn't have that now could we? Working regularly provided regular money which caused me to find a regular connection for weed at first, then speed again. Pretty soon I was back to being high all day at work, drinking lunch at the bar down the street and acting stupid the rest of the time. A fained slow period was the best reason for a lay off they could come up with. I know it couldn't've had anything to do with the numerous times I'd been warned about my reckless attitude and actions, no way. What an IDIOT!

It was now officially time to get the fuck outta town. It'd been set up by my father years earlier, that when I became too much to handle I'd be shipped off to live with my extremely religious aunt. She seemed to think she could straighten me out. I was gravitating to truck driving because of its lack of immediate supervision and an aptitude for all things mechanical.

The area I moved to was ripe with driving jobs, it wasn't long before I had a chauffeur's license and a job I'd bullshitted my way into and was not in the least bit capable of doing. I didn't last there very long, after tearing down a hundred feet of cyclone fence and dragging it down Crosstimbers Road, my services were no longer needed.

I eventually became a proficient driver, but not till I grew up a lot. It'd been a long time since I'd used chemicals of any kind. I still smoked weed, only because that was all that was readily available. Speed wasn't on every street corner like it is now and I'd've never gotten away with those kinds of actions around my aunt and uncle so it didn't even enter my mind all that often.

After the next succession of careless failures, I was blinded and choking by the smoke from all the bridges I had flaming around me. Time again for a change, this time a little discipline was in order and The Marines were called out.

My service to my country was nothing short of underwhelming. It was absolutely unbelievable that anyone could get in that much trouble in such a short time and live to tell about it. I bent or broke almost every rule I encountered from the very beginning. A lieutenant in boot camp told me The Marines would break me of my bullshit.

By the time I graduated he'd stomped three starched covers and one Smokey Bear hat into mud puddles and lawns because of something I'd done. Two years after induction with six months in the brig for selling drugs came my expulsion. I was given a general under other than honorable conditions discharge and the door forcefully slammed on my ass on the way out.

All the better, I didn't do well in that environment at all. Too many rules to break. I was absolutely exhausted when I was finally released. That rule breakin' is hard work and calls for an extended play period for the required amount of rest.

While in The Marines I'd been broadsided on my motorcycle, a contributing factor in my early discharge, I simply wasn't worth having around. The settlement from this provided me with a small nest egg, a car and a motorcycle. Why leave now, the party was just starting right?

When I was in the wreck I already lived off base, so nothing changed very much in that respect except that I *never* went to work anymore. Finally I was called into the company gunny's office and told that I was nothing but trouble and they wanted me out. What took 'em so long?

Finally I was free to pursue the life I was meant for {drug-induced scooter tramp}. I proceeded to become immersed in the local drug and motorcycle scene. Knowing that work would severely inhibit my drug doing I avoided it at all costs. I still had to have money to live and I was pissing my nest egg away pretty fast. I heard about a security job that was right up my ally, guarding a Quaalude airport in the middle of the night. What better job for a speed freak?

This airport was a predetermined dirt road in the middle of the North Carolina nowhere big enough to land a Cessna on for ten minutes. Several of us stood around with automatic weapons watching the perimeter while the rest unloaded fifty-five gallon drums of Mexican 714s into a pickup truck, then we all split.

The whole thing took less than half an hour. Payment was a bag of ten thousand ludes or ten thousand dollars, your choice. This only lasted a couple 'a more times though, the plane tagged a tree in the dark and crashed in a ball of flames. I narrowly escaped the scene before the entire area was aflame, that was the end of that job and it was time for a drink.

I hung around for a little while doing whatever dope came my way, but never got a regular line on my drug of choice. It seemed that the right coast was more interested in going down instead of up. Pot, downs of all kinds, PCP, cocaine and all kinds of hallucinogens were available, not much speed with any regularity though. Most of what I could get was from other jarheads and that was milder forms of the pharmaceutical varieties only, like the dexies I'd first used in the eighth grade occasionally some bootleg Black Beauties, never any crank though.

The end to this came as the result of a Friday night of drunken gunfire, arrest, hospitalization, and escape. After this I hid out long enough to get my shit together, then I was gone from that part of the country for good. I headed for my family's home, spent eight months runnin' scams, ridin', met a gal and together we went down to Florida. There we had a series of unfortunate mishaps that caused us to pack up and head for the left coast.

We left on New Years Eve and arrived in L.A. four days later after an uneventful trip from coast to coast. When we crossed into California I got a rush like I'd never felt before, there was a kinda' glow to the air itself. I felt energized, plugged in, the atmosphere, the ambiance, was like a huge power source that surged through me from head to toe.

I'd wanted to be in Caly since I was old enough to know that Maine sucked. Everything that I held sacred, hotrods and Harley-Davidsons roared through the streets of California year-round unencumbered by the snow and deep cold of the northeast, the truest form of paradise to me. I still to this day get that very same feeling every time I go out there. I can't remember where my girlfriend was born {Gardena I think}, she was raised in California and we were going back to her home town as much as she hated the thought of it. As we dropped down Chiriaco Pass into the Indio valley I had my first glimpse of what I thought'd be my personal paradise {little did I know}.

I thought this was the end of my "boot camp." By this time I'd developed most of the code that I spoke of earlier, but other incidents created future revisions. It lists as follows;

TRUST NO ONE, especially women!

Friends will fuck you over faster than enemies, they know more about you.

Don't fuck with citizens {you're a citizen}.

If you live outside the law, you have to be honest.

Honesty is relative to the situation.

Change women like socks, never let 'em get too close.

Dickhead doesn't mean you're the head dick.

Peckerhead doesn't mean you're the head pecker.

You're only free when you're goin'.

People are expendable {better them than me}.

If you can't do the time, don't do the crime.

Your word is worth your life.

Your life is worth nothing to anyone but you.

Plan your play and play your plan.

Ride hard, die fast, and leave a good looking corpse.

You don't piss off the drug man or the motorcycle shop.

Don't own anything that you're not willing to leave on a moments notice.

Always be ready to go.

Too much is never enough.

Just saying yes is the easiest way to avoid conflict, internal or otherwise.

Family are people you just happen to know and don't necessarily like.

Do your crimes by yourself and keep your mouth shut.

Never take pictures, never leave fingerprints, if caught deny, deny, deny.

If you don't deserve it, you won't keep it no matter how much you paid for it.

People = shit, the more people, the more shit.

Never shit in your own back yard and never eat where you shit.

Laws were made to be broken {especially by me}.

It's only illegal when you get caught.

One cop can ruin your whole fuckin' day.

It's all a game; it's my job to break as many rules as I can and not get caught and it's their job to try to catch me.

Play to win cause prison or worse sucks.

Payback's a bitch, give back ten times what you get.

Know your enemies, especially the cops, never underestimate stupidity.

Expect no mercy, especially from the law.

Never bring a knife to a gun fight.

Never do business with women, emotions have no place in illegal activities.

Never talk about anything on the phone, never use names.

The worst day on the street, is better than the best day locked up.

Three can keep a secret if two are dead.

Sometimes being 86d is the best compliment you can get.

These rules of survival go together to form a loose code of conduct followed when navigating through the so called "dark underworld" of outlaw bikers, cranksters, and the illegal activities they engage in on a minute by minute basis, where your word and deed is worth more than money especially when things go wrong as they often do in the drug world.

In this world that's always operating on the fringe of mainstream society there are no credit checks, only mudchecks. Law enforcement is the enemy and people are an asset or a liability depending on the moment. A simple traffic stop can turn a close friend or business partner into the downfall of an entire circle of users and suppliers. Turning this network into inmates or corpses, inmates if they don't snitch, corpses if they do. Hell you can become a corpse just by calling to much attention to yourself. By calling attention to yourself you become a liability to your circle by inadvertently calling attention to them as well, one way or the other you're gonna be gone.

If you're busted and released too soon everyone knows you rolled over {typically the cops always want three names} and you're not worth shit anywhere. Sometimes they cut you loose quickly {kind of a shaking the bushes thing, to see who falls out} to see how long you live on the street and who starts shootin' at ya because they think you rolled over on 'em.

A smart junkie would simply go away and not provide a rat to be chased, but junkies aren't smart and the domino effect starts, eventually bringing everyone down. I don't think this world is so dark, just different and to the average citizen fast, loud and scary. The part of this world that is the most attractive is the fact that there's only one thing to worry about, the cops. Everything else, money, dope, women is all covered by the one thing, **crank**, as long as there's a steady supply of that flowing life is good, very good, when it stops though shit gets bad real fast.

You can tell people are scared by fast and loud by the way they slam their car door locks down at a traffic light as you whiteline down between the cars on a sparkling San Fernando Valley afternoon. This is good; it keeps the public at arms length and outta your business. Most don't even dare to look in your direction. That too is good because it's easier to be obvious with what you're doing if people make a point of not looking at you, especially if they're afraid of what they'll see.

With all this outta the way let's get down to the story of a fifteen year love affair with one of the most deadly drugs to ever be turned loose on the citizens of this world. I say deadly because in this drug world there's more than one way to die, some permanent, some not so permanent, all end in the same place eventually, the only difference is the road taken and the scenery along the way. Some flip out or in and never come back, some rot in prison, some rot on the street, some die in a shooting gallery with a needle in their arm. Most of the people that are smart enough to quit develop what I call eventual death diseases {Hepatitis C, Liver Cancer, Respitory Ailments, different types of brain, heart, and kidney problems}, dying at very early ages, Mid to late fifties and so on. I myself am dying slowly from Silicosis, a degenerative lung disease caused by the inhalation of silica sand dust and painfully from extreme arthritis, a side affect caused by the silica dissolving into my body. The prices we pay for the lives we lead.

Eventually I'll just suffocate to death because the scar tissue in my lungs won't oxygenate my blood. This has nothing to do with my drug use and everything to do with the lack of required safety equipment when I sandblasted as a teenager and years of exposure working around beadblast booths in motorcycle shops.

The City Of Angels

We arrived in L.A. right after Natalie Wood drowned off Catalina Island and the Signal Hill Police Department beat to death and then hung in a cell to fake suicide a young black college student who also happened to be a first round NFL draught pick home for Christmas Vacation.

I remember how crushed I felt inside at hearing the news about Natalie Wood; I'd always had this place in me for her, kind of a crush I guess, ever since I was young. The student was a sample of the brutality of everyday life in L.A., something that I quickly became accustomed to and began gradually to thrive on. Living closer and closer to the proverbial edge as the last of my naiveté melted away with every new acquaintance and situation I encountered .

This place'll eat you alive and you won't even see it happening till it's done. One minute you're just beginning to get a grip on some of the happenings in a city like L.A. and then you're slammed halfway through a cyclone fence by a lowrider one block from home, only two weeks after arriving in this meat grinder called a city. Ever happen to you? Happened to me, actually us, my ex and I at the same time on the same bike. Who'd 'a thunk? She'd just started a waitress job at a local restaurant and I hadn't found a job yet.

We'd been out riding that afternoon and were on our way home on Eastern Avenue in Billy Goat Acres. A lowrider in the left turn lane flashed his headlights for me to go ahead. As I entered the intersection he floored it and broadsided us shattering my ex's left leg from knee to ankle, crushing the bike and sending me headfirst under the fence on the corner to have the top of my head bitten by the guard dog inside.

My ex spent three months in U.C.L.A. Medical Center in traction, I got a broken leg, a punctured leg, treated and released. Seems like the bad luck'd followed us from Florida like the plague. If we'd only had verifiable jobs we'd've been in so much better shape because we'd've been eligible for assistance under the Victims of Violent Crimes Act. Instead we were shit outta luck in a city where it's only too clear where you'll end up if you don't do something quickly when you're shit outta luck.

I found out very quickly that I was on my own to deal with all of this crap. I went to the hospital every day and stayed with my ex till visiting ended for the day, then I'd go home and wonder what the hell I was gonna do.

A couple 'a weeks into this program someone stole our puppy. He'd been my only company in this whole mess and now he was gone hopefully to a better home, by then the pickins were getting mighty slim around our house.

When we got to town we bought a `64 Impala with a six cylinder, three on the tree. That old car was as dependable as the sun. One evening my ex's mom came to the hospital to visit with me. It was this night that the Chevy decided it needed a new clutch. While waiting for the tow truck a bunch of drunks pulled into the liquor store parking lot where we were waiting and began to party in the parking lot.

We were on Soto Street which is the heart of one of the barrios in downtown L.A., so cops steer clear of only the most heinous of crimes. They stay away from simple things like drinking in a parking lot unless there's a lot of 'em with nothing to do. In L.A. a small thing like this can turn into a shooting or worse and I've been told many times by several different cops out there that they don't get paid enough to die for you. To avoid the problems they look the other way and concentrate on less confrontational law enforcement {traffic tickets and the like}.

I was afraid this'd happen before we could get outta there. My ex's mom was a raging alcoholic that needed no excuse for a bender. Watching the alcoholic waltz going on in the parking lot was more than she could bear. She'd kept her promise and been sober in the hospital, but she was outta the car and drinking before I could say shit.

By the time the tow truck got there she was completely incoherent and insisted on being left with her new friends. She paid for the tow truck and dismissed us both refusing to listen to anything I said. I called my sister-in-law, told her what and where was going on and left in the tow truck to try to figure out this new problem.

I found out then that family wasn't worth shit, going to the bar, or doing anything else was far more important than helping me. Stranded without transportation I had to do something fast. Hobbling around on crutches I got the car on blocks, removed the transmission, clutch and flywheel for resurfacing.

All I needed was a ride to the auto parts store to get the flywheel resurfaced and the new clutch, even that was too much to ask. I ended up walking the six mile round trip on crutches with a thirty pound flywheel in one hand on the way up and the flywheel and a forty pound clutch assembly in my hands on the way back. After this ordeal putting the car back together was a breeze.

That afternoon with the help of a couple 'a kids from the neighborhood the Chevy was on the road again and a new life law was written {there comes a time in your life when family are people you just happen to know, you don't necessarily like 'em and you can't trust 'em or depend on 'em} and some new friends were made that proved very useful in the coming weeks.

Things got back to normal. I got off the crutches and actually got a job in a bike shop in Bellflower wrenchin' on Harleys. The first day I was introduced to the head mechanic called Wrench. He was good at what he did, but was difficult to deal with because he was prospecting for a local motorcycle club and though he didn't have his patch yet, he had a head fulla patch fever like I'd never seen before.

Wrench came and went as he pleased, did what he wanted, when he wanted, all of it at warp speed. I wondered where I could get that kind of energy, but he wasn't saying. The next person I met was Bo. He worked around at several different shops getting paid by the job and on to the next. Bo had no affiliation and he was far more open about everything {misery loves company}.

When I asked him about the local dope scene we went out back and he showed me first hand. That afternoon we went to his place for lunch. He told me how uncool the people I worked for were, all the different kinds of dope available and who to get ahold of in case I couldn't find him.

Word gets around fast because the next day Wrench was a totally different person, he opened up about where we worked. The owner was a reformed partier turned narc, his kids {who worked there too} partied but'd snitch anyone out to save their own asses, so I'd better watch mine.

After that I was plugged into a river of crank that flowed like water, the only restriction was the money it took to get high. Living no matter how spartanly costs money and I didn't make that much. A quarter gram a week was all I could afford and not even every week at that {crank wasn't in control yet, it was just a bad influence}. My priorities were still geared to taking care of the business of getting our lives back together and back on track.

I got in the groove of working all day and at the end of every day I'd stop at some drive thru, pick up some food and make the drive downtown to spend the rest of the evening at the hospital. This went on for weeks into months until finally the day came when after almost three months of traction my ex was released.

I left work at noon that day, got to the hospital at about one-thirty and we were headed home about an hour later. It was quite an ordeal for my ex to simply get to the car let alone get in it. It took everything she had to make that little trip to the car, the ride home wasn't any lark either.

I remember how I felt pulling into our driveway with my shattered ole'lady, my eyes falling on the crushed, twisted remains of the scooter that was to become my only love besides dope eventually.

When she was finally seated and comfortable in her own house we smoked our first joint together in months. It was good to have her home, for the first time in months this place felt like a home.

During the first few weeks after the accident {for lack of a better word} a few of the neighborhood kids'd see the front door open and stop in to chat during the day. They told me about the vato that hit me, were he lived and that he'd gone back to Mexico the same night he hit me fearing arrest or retaliation. Same shit the cops told me the day I went to see 'em after it happened. They told me he belonged to the baddest gang to come out of East L.A. and that he was in Mexico a couple 'a hours after it happened so there was nothing they could do. I went away mad, but I went away.

During the next few weeks the kids stopped by often, they helped me with the car when I had to do the clutch. They brought me news of The Hood. I laughed when they told me that the vatos that lived in the apartments with the one that hit me thought I was in a gang and were waiting for a war to break out {I knew virtually no one}. I certainly wished I could make that happen, but I strongly doubted it.

One afternoon I was sitting on the couch and could see the kids boiling up the street on their bikes like they were on fire. They came screaming up into the yard and into the house all shouting at once.

When they finally shouted themselves out I gathered that the vato that hit me was back and living in the same place he had been when he hit me. They wanted to know if there was gonna be a war now and all kinds of silly shit like that. We shot the breeze until it was time for me to go to the hospital that day and then they left.

That evening my ex and I discussed it and the next day I went to see the detective I'd talked to the first time. He didn't seem to care that this guy was back, in fact he seemed annoyed that I was even bothering him with this, which gave me an instant attitude. He pulled me into an office, motioned me to a chair and once seated informed me that this vato belonged to the King Cobras, the baddest street gang to ever come out of East L.A. The police department was outmanned 10/1 and outgunned 100/1 and there was no way they'd be going to bat for some scooter trash and his woman, they didn't get paid enough to commit that kind of suicide.

I thought it was pretty funny that when I said I'd take care of it myself he jumped all over me with threats of arrest and prosecution, saying that no one is gonna get away with vigilantism in his town. I left there with an extreme hatred for the cops that isn't any better today. Of course I'd just been shooting off my mouth 'cause I was pissed, I had no idea of doing anything.

Before we got hit we'd found a few local watering holes. On the evenings when I just couldn't take being home alone anymore I'd go down and have a few beers and hobnob with the uppercrust of the local riffraff. Not that I was any better, they were all far more practiced than me is all.

The next time I visited the bar the conversation eventually turned to the conversation with the detective and its bullshit outcome. One of the regulars made the statement that I'd have to take care of it myself, then the point was made that the cops'd assume it was me if anything happened so I'd have to stay out of it.

Plans were made by cranked-up drunks {it's amazing how much you can drink when you're wired}, until that horse was beaten to death many times over. Bars are open till 4:00AM in L.A. which gives cranksters lots of time to drink and snort and smoke. On the nights that I'd go to the bar I'd close it out, go have breakfast and get high in the car in front of the shop till someone showed up and unlocked the door so I could go to work.

The problem with this comes around three in the afternoon when you're outta dope both inside and out and you've run outta steam and money, that's the only time that doin' crank sucks. Well the next day after we made all the drunken plans was a day like that and that put a damper on the idea of doing that again. I didn't go back again until long after Ma {my ex} got outta the hospital.

One Saturday afternoon fairly soon after Ma got out we were sitting around watching The Three Stooges and getting stoned when the neighborhood kids showed up saying that the vato that hit me and his whole family, brothers, sisters, kids and all just disappeared in the middle of the night. They figured that they'd skipped back to Mexico after committing some crime or other. That was how they operated, but usually the only ones that split were the ones that did the deed. They'd show up a few months later with a fake ID like nothing ever happened and go on about their business.

We discussed all this out on the stoop in the sun that afternoon and had a laugh at some of the things our imaginations conjured up for an outcome. We finally settled on an INS roundup {those happened all the time in L.A.}. The kids went on their way and we finished our day and eventually our weekend.

It'd been awhile since I'd done any speed regularly because we couldn't really afford it. I'd started rebuilding my scooter and that was taking all the spare money I could make. Crank isn't really good for people recovering from any kind of serious injury for many reasons, so for quite a while I didn't even think about it.

I was in love with the buzz from speed and weed, but I could do without the speed. There were some problems like cost and constant availability that weren't there with weed so we stuck to that for a while, till the neighbors moved into the back part of the duplex.

Mark and Debbie were related to the managers of the property. Mark had a little girl from a previous marriage and he and Debbie were newlyweds. We hit it off right away and the five of us became friends quickly. I can't remember if he had it when they moved in or if he got it shortly afterward, but he had a raggedy-assed `69 Sportster that fouled plugs on a daily basis and broke down weekly, almost always far from home.

Working in a bike shop I helped Mark with his rolling wreck constantly, it gave us both something to do after work and on weekends. We'd get a twelve pack and bag of weed and sit out on the patio, work on the bike and get a buzz. One weekend Mark brought home a bag of crank, we added that to our pallet of party favors and had an even better time that weekend.

The dope that Mark bought home was from the street and had been whacked several times before it got to Mark's hands. I told Mark I'd get the dope for the next tweakend. We had our usual uneventfully fun tweakend and spent Monday and Tuesday dragging through life as we recovered, comparing notes on how raggedy we felt over a few joints and beers after dinner, fat and happy getting ready for next tweakend.

Peanut Butter Like No Other

I'd hate to see what this shit'd do to a piece of bread; I know it sure could fuck a liver up. I kept my word that tweakend and brought home the dope. Little did I know that I was buying almost directly from the cook and the dope wasn't whacked at all. When I got it my buddy told me that this same dope'd killed several people down in Dago, to be careful with it and don't do as much as we were used to doing.

This incident right here is the one that prompted my method of using. I'd do little bumps and wait to see how high I got before doing any more. This method helped conserve dope and brain cells, besides that the first sign of an overdose is falling asleep and that kind of defeats the purpose of getting high doesn't it? I wonder if that's called partying responsibly? I had a tattooist friend that always used to say "everything in moderation." I know someone far greater than he said this first {I think it was Ben Franklin}. I guess the novelty is that you wouldn't picture this coming outta Sully's face, looks are almost always deceiving.

Well anyway when I got home that Friday evening the girls already had the grill going and the weekend kicked off with a good dinner under the balmy California sky. Even in the city at certain times of the day the air itself seems to glow and there's nothing like a Southern California evening with good friends and a good buzz. That evening was one of those nights. After dinner with the little one off in her bath and getting ready for bed we gathered around the mirror-n-blade.

I warned everyone about the dope we were about to do. We each did a little line and started into the evening. By the time I got out to the patio I knew something was up and it was me. I got that familiar heat rush up my back, over my head and down my face to my chest. Only it was ten times hotter than I'd ever felt before. I started amping and when I looked everybody else was to.

I remember laughing when I saw the "holyfuckinshit" look on Mark's face. It wasn't long before we all headed for the toilets, Ma and I to ours and Mark and Debbie to theirs.

In a few minutes we gathered back on the patio and had a laugh about what'd just happened. Debbie declared then that she didn't want any more and Ma agreed, not any time soon anyway. Mark was a little braver, he didn't say never. That weekend our little party got so outta hand that the cops showed up at about 5:00AM because of a noise complaint. All they found was the four of us listening to the radio and talking, a real wild time.

After we got over the initial rush of the dope it was an excellent buzz, so good in fact that there was a lotta dope leftover come Monday morning. We'd all done a little more and stayed up almost the entire weekend. I figured we could all use a bump to get our day started.

When I turned the corner an ambulance was in the driveway at Mark's house. He was already inside and they were starting out the drive. Debbie said they thought his liver'd shut down. Later that was confirmed when she came back from the hospital. He'd nearly died before they'd gotten him stabilized.

He was in the hospital for three days and didn't look so hot when he got home. I was the only one that did a blast that morning and many mornings after that. The following weekend was real quiet because I didn't tell anybody that I got some more peanut butter and nobody asked. Everybody else was scared of the shit except me, I loved it. It was so good that I could stay high all week on just a half gram, about forty dollars worth. As addictions go it seemed like a pretty economically sound decision, I was sold.

All good things come to an end though. Thank God, that dope ran out and the dope that was always around now took three times as much to get me buzzed. It's a good thing the money that it'd take to stay high was outta the question and I had to just stop and take a break for a while. I hadn't learned to eat while I was high yet, so each run took a lot outta me and I'd loose and regain weight quickly.

Crank gets you high by burning all your stored energy at one time. This energy comes from the food you eat and is stored in your body for the times when you need it. A chemical reaction in your body releases the amounts of energy you need in a measured dose according to the task you're performing. Crank opens the flood gates wide open and you get high. When your body has burned all its stores, it starts burning itself and you start to get that scabbed-up cadaver look.

When you look like that on the outside, imagine what's going on inside. Each cell is eating itself from the inside out, you're not gonna last long like that. I've seen it take less than a year from the first line to the grave especially in women and girls.

I know one girl that lost it the very first line she did and couldn't make a coherent sentence for two years after that. Everybody was doing the same dope and this didn't happened to anybody else. This just goes to show ya that "sobriety is for people who can't handle dope."

Once I learned this little secret and started practicing it, forcing myself to eat no matter how high I was. I found that not only did I feel better, my buzz lasted longer and the crash at the end wasn't quite as bad as they'd been before I discovered this information. I was actually turning addiction into a science and eventually I made a game out of getting high and staying high, awake and functioning. I thrived on that game for years.

After the peanut butter tweakend our parties were much tamer and we didn't do a lotta dope. Just weed and beer, occasionally some Jack. As usual another good thing was coming to an end.

We'd come to be the parents of a bouncing pitbull puppy named Dawg {the first I ever saved from parvo}, he had pretty much the whole front yard in his chain reach.

When we moved into the place it had a lush sod based yard with a big palm tree at each end. The driveway was a half moon that passed right in front of the door and exited to the street at each end. Between the front door and the driveway was a porch that ran the length of the house. The front of the porch was planted in rose bushes from end to end.

The owner of the house drove by one Sunday and saw the rose bushes gone {eaten right down to the ground}. His sod lawn was a dust bowl {scraped clean by Dawg's chain} and ordered the managers to evict us immediately. They hated to do it and tried to talk 'em out of it, but we had to go.

We had a hard time finding a place we could afford. We found one, one block from Watts, a quiet little converted garage on a back lot. It was fully fenced and secluded on a dead-end street in Lynwood one block from Alameda Avenue the dividing line for Watts. Our street was rather unique because it was in the middle of a predominantly black neighborhood and was populated mostly by middle class first and second generation Latino families. It was very quiet, at night with helicopters and searchlights flying all over the city around us, we were very seldom bothered by direct flyovers.

The old streetlights on our street weren't as bright as the high pressure sodium's that kept the nightly fog burned off the newer neighborhoods and large boulevards that sprawl all across the Los Angeles basin from ocean to mountains. These lights are so bright that you can wear your shades all night long when riding in L.A. instead of having to switch to clear glasses after dark.

We'd found a very cool place, except we were miles away from our walk to friends. That put an end to most of our weekend parties and a damper on our friendship. We saw each other as much as possible, but it just wasn't the same.

I still wasn't so dependent on crank that I couldn't walk away from it and I did for two reasons. **1**. Ma's leg'd never heal if she used and it was no fun being high by yourself {at least it wasn't back then, but that would change}.**2**. The weed we began getting from a neighbor was so stoney that you couldn't make it out the door to go get the crank.

As we got to know our new surroundings we found out that our house was an illegal conversion. Our story if asked was that we were related to our neighbor up front. Upon hearing this, a scam loomed on the horizon that'd give me the money to finish the rebuild of my destroyed scooter. Part of the story was that we lived there for free {that made the conversion legal because the property was zoned single family, we were family according to the story}, so I stopped paying rent.

Landlords can't file eviction papers on an illegally rented building, what was he gonna do? He did the only thing he could do, he harassed us on the phone. I changed the number. He started coming around during the day and hollering at the gate to be let in. Ma had a hard time getting to the gate on a good day, so she simply ignored him and he went away eventually.

I was always at work when he came by, so Dawg stayed near Ma instead of going out and barking at him. I figured I was doing him a favor because at the time in L.A. there was a big thing on TV and radio to report slumlords and he certainly was a slumlord of the first degree. The place looked good on the outside, but things like the furnace being improperly vented and almost killing us when we tried to use it and the house being overrun by fire ants on a regular basis added up to a big "fuck you" from me. When he told us it'd cost him more to fix the furnace than we were worth, payback became my only intention. I think I got my monies worth and he got the shaft.

Blackballed

One day Bo and I were out back doin' a blast. I looked up and there was the boss looking at us. Bo was already a long way down on his trip to the bottom. I could tell by the long sleeve shirt {hiding the tracks} in the middle of the summer, the weight loss, the sores from picking at himself and his filthy, smelly appearance {when your only intake is crank you begin to smell like it} that the word on the street that he was slammin' was true.

He tried to deny it because that's the end of life as you know it. Once you're labeled as a geezer you'll never be trusted in any of your old circles of friends. The only friends you'll have now are in the same cement canoe with chicken wire paddles you are and they're not your friends. The only friend a junkie has is their next hit. Though they hang in packs that's more to scavenge what they can from the group and keep their buzz going at whatever price they have to pay to do so. Nothing is more important than that next hit, not even self-respect. One junkie'll suck another's dick and let him piss in his face in front of God and everybody if he even thinks it means he'll get a hit.

The next time I heard anything about Bo, he and his girlfriend were found dead on a pile of garbage in an alley, needles in their arms. The rumor was that they'd ripped off the wrong dude n-been tripped with some bad dope in order to get rid of 'em in a way no one'd question. In L.A. bodies are found every day all over the place, so frequently that it doesn't even make a space filler in the paper.

Most of the time they're simply scraped up like so much refuse and if there's no ID on 'em they're simply incinerated, no questions asked. I'm sure somewhere a mother or some family member wonders occasionally what happened to 'em, but they'll probably never know.

I know it always worried my mom, but if she knew what I was doing it'd've worried her as much if not more. Every time I talked to her I'd remind her that no news was good news. That was the only band-aid I could put on that wound.

Anyway that was my last day at Chicken Delight as the shop was called on the street. I figured this wouldn't be any big deal there were plenty of shops in the area that built Harleys. I'd have another job tomorrow, no sweat.

Bad news traveled faster than I could ever imagine though. Once it got around it was Bo I was with, I was labeled too. As soon as I said my name I was done, I was told I wasn't needed. Since I was new to the area and not savvy to the politics of the bike shops {everybody knew everybody else and I was the outsider} the owner made sure the word got around overnight.

I told you that to tell you this. Remember I told you about the landlord coming by? Well one day I was home and several of us were sitting around getting stoned. I heard something outside the gate, it was the landlord. Dawg didn't allow anyone in his yard he didn't know and since I was home he didn't feel the need to stay near Ma. The landlord seeing the car in the driveway pushed the gate open and started inside.

Dawg was off the stoop like a missile. He hit the gate so hard it slammed the guy ass-over-teakettle into the front yard of the house next door. The gate slammed shut and two of the boards that made up the gate got knocked loose from the bottom. Before I could get to the scene he was in his car and gone.

In the afternoon our little dead-end street was always packed with our neighbors. Everyone was out visiting, kids filled the street on all kinds of bikes and skateboards and every kind of contrivance. Parents were on stoops and in their yards, so there was a big audience for this event. I didn't know my neighbors very well except the people in the front house.

This incident made Dawg a hero to the neighborhood. After that the kids'd come and ask if Dawg could come out and play with 'em. It was nothing to see Dawg tied to a bicycle with five kids piled on it.

He'd be pulling 'em up and down the street at a dead run, tongue lolling out, eyes glowing cause he was having so much fun. He loved kids and lived to play with 'em.

Seems that our landlord owned a good number of the houses on that street and was your typical slumlord. He owned many illegal places like ours housing several generations of a family on the same property. Many Mexican families live that way anyway. Partially because they value their families and all their familial ties far more than their white counterparts and they simply can't afford to live any differently.

Most of these people have no idea about codes, they pay their rent, they don't make waves and slumlords love 'em. After that afternoon we got a letter from the landlord asking us to please let him know when we were leaving and that was the last we ever heard from him.

With that problem outta the way, all I had to do was find a job which was easier said than done. It'd been sent around by a certain party that I was a slammer and that was almost as good as a death sentence. Soon as I said my name the initial interest in their possibly new wrench died a quick death and I was cold shouldered outta the shop.

I couldn't afford not to work for long and the only other thing I could do was drive a truck. I'd let my class one license go a couple of years earlier and in California you had to take a driving test, which means you've gotta' come up with a truck. The easiest way for me to do that was to go to a three week session of driving school to get me through the California driving test.

I borrowed the eleven hundred dollars from my ex's mom, got my class one and went back to working a real job hauling gas around L.A... That was regular for a little while, long enough for us to start getting caught up and actually thinking we might begin to get the bike back together soon, but.....

My boss was an owner/operator that was contracted to Union 76 to deliver gas to their stations all over Southern California. His contract came due for renewal and due to some service issues, conditions were made that he wouldn't agree to and we were locked out. So much for so little, work got pretty sketchy after that.

It's around that time Ma decided to visit her kids, while she was gone I fucked around on her with one of the girls in the neighborhood. I was honest about it when she returned, but things were never the same after that. She had someplace else that she needed to be. Everything we'd done since the time we'd left her house in Maine had been one disaster or another false start after another.

I got a job driving over-the-road, they were much easier to get than a local job. I stored my things where I could with friends and such, lent the old Chevy to one of her mother's friends with some of my motorcycle parts in the trunk. We gave away what we could and left the rest, climbed into that Freightliner and after a round about way Ma and Dawg ended up in Maine and I was alone again.

I ran for a few more months. It wasn't the same without Ma and Dawg. In that time I saw Ma a couple 'a times for a day or two each time and that was pretty much the end of it. She'd moved on, so I did too.

Without Ma and Dawg trucking wasn't the same and I decided to get out, but the company I worked for wouldn't get me home. After weeks of begging for a load home, I finally just shut up and took what they gave me. Finally they gave me a load to Southern California, I was so pissed by then that I left everything in a Zody's parking lot in Watts and ended my career with TSMT.

Hemet

With the bullshit of trucking set aside for a while I could concentrate on getting deep into the cranked-up subculture of the Southern California scooter tramp. I traded the often drugless, homelessness of trucking for the drug-induced, party till ya puke, sleep where ya drop, home is where your scooter's parked homelessness of Southern California trampdom.

When I set about retrieving all the things that we'd stored with friends and wherever we could in the low budget rush to get outta town. I was pretty fuckin bummed to find out that the most important thing the car, had been towed. The car wasn't all that important, it was the parts for Christine in the trunk {including a great pair of custom made leather saddlebags} that I had a fuckin' stroke over. FUCK! I could 'a sat down after getting everything together and had a running scooter before I had to look for a job or any of the other shit it takes to live this fuckin' life.

Instead I had to find a job with limited transportation and at the same time inventory all my parts, figure out what's missing and find a way to get it in my hands with no money. At the same time I was cultivating a blossoming crank habit {keeping all this going took a lotta dope}. The biggest part of being a scooter tramp is **HAVING A SCOOTER**, not having a scooter makes ya just another bum wearing a Harley T-shirt and a chain-drive wallet.

One afternoon while at my favorite scooter shop I was reintroduced to a dude, I'll call him Hemet, not his name, he lived there. I'd met him at Chicken Delight almost two years earlier and we'd talked for a few minutes at lunch time, but I hadn't seen him since.

This time we both had plenty of time, we ended up going out to his car and doing a couple 'a rippers, smokin' a bowl {a man after my own heart} and sitting on the wall out front of the shop watching traffic go by just shooting the shit for a good part of the afternoon. Hell I'd hitched down to the shop because my buddy's wife had his car and I wasn't really looking forward to hitching back.

During the drive home we stopped by Hemet's mother's house in Paramount, he introduced me to his mom and gave me her phone number saying if I couldn't get ahold of him at his number to call there, she'd probably know where he was. We stayed a little while sitting out by the pool in the sun talking. I remember how like a TV show it felt, being from Maine I'd only seen a few swimming pools in my life.

I never had one to relax around {we used to "pool hop", hopping people's fences and jumping in their pools for a swim in the middle of a hot summer night until the lights went on. Occasionally getting rocksalted by a shotgun blast if you're too slow getting over the fence, like I was once, not very relaxing}. To me this was kinda' like bein' on a movie set the scene was so idyllic. I actually felt weird and outta place, my engineer boots and greasy Levies had no place by this pool. I couldn't believe this typically upper middle class Southern California mom wasn't appalled with her son's judgment for one thing and for bringing his lack of judgment to her house for the second.

I was relieved when we finally left. I hate trying to answer the "how did" and "where did" questions that moms always ask when ya first meet 'em. I never make a good first impression and all the ones that follow are rarely any better. I've found it much easier to keep pretty much to myself most of my life. I just don't do well with many people. You can't trust many of 'em {everyone has their price and its usually pretty fuckin' cheap} so I'm close to no one, this comes in handy, living outside the law.

On the way up Eastern Avenue we stopped in a parking lot to do another ripper, that was when I asked if he could get me any. After he laid out the lines he closed the bag and gave it to me {probably a quarter ounce or more, biggest bag I'd ever seen}. While we were cruising to Mark's place he enlightened me on the joys of cooking and made an offer I wouldn't refuse.

When I first landed back in L.A. I stayed with Mark and Debbie, crashing on their couch at first. I moved out to the front porch quickly though because they kept it so damn hot in their place and a severe lack of housekeeping skills left the place absolutely fuckin' filthy. The place was a shithole and cockroaches crawled everywhere, it was nothing like when Ma and I lived there.

That evening I began my career as a dope dealer in earnest. I sold a quarter ounce outta the bag Hemet gave me and still had plenty of stash left for myself. That sale got me all the parts I needed to finish Christine just in time for Christmas. In fact it was Christmas Eve when I did ninety percent of the assembly on the old bitch.

When Mark and Debbie and the kids {they'd had a baby while I was out on the road} left to go to his in-law's house she was a bare frame on a milk crate. When they got back around midnight I was just beginning to finish wire the bike. The wiring is begun in the early stages of assembly. The rear fender and any other wires you want to hide are run first, then the hard parts are assembled. When the bike is on its wheels the finish wiring is done. I was almost ready to ride the damn thing. It was Christmas Eve though and they had kids so everything stopped for the Santa Claus thing and didn't get finished till the next day.

Early the next afternoon we were out in the driveway makin' smoke n-loud noises till the carburetor was dialed in. I was finally back in the saddle again on a two year expired Maine license plate, no motorcycle endorsement and no insurance. **"WHAT THE FUCK, RUN AMUCK"** and so I shall. Our first ride was gonna be to Mark's father-in-law's house to return his soldering gun {the key word here being gun}.

We made it to the first corner, but not all the way around it before Billy Goat Acres finest was on us like stink-on-shit. Mark rode his bike pretty much everyday without a problem, so I quickly figured out it was me as usual. I just didn't know how much yet.

I had the soldering gun {there's that word again} inside my leather jacket, which wasn't too bad when I was sitting on the bike and if we hadn't been stopped would 'a already been outta there. Standing there with my hands in the air, the tip of the soldering gun poking me in the ribs wasn't funny for very long at all, help was on the way though.

As soon as the first cop read the name on my driver's license he called for backup. Seems I was a suspect in a multiple murder {wonderful}.

As we stood around waiting for the grass to grow a bunch more cops showed up. Still nothing happened, finally a lieutenant showed up and the real circus began.

Until the lieutenant showed up nothing happened but a lotta whispering behind the backs of their hands, stern or puzzled looks and a reiteration to shut-up if we spoke, but they didn't come near us to cuff us or anything. A couple had their guns drawn and kept a close eye on every move I made, that was it.

The lieutenant was having a conversation on his radio as he pulled up. You could tell he was the one that everything was waiting for because as soon as he showed up the peons jumped into activity trying to look both busy and important.

He got outta the car when he was done on the radio and asked for my ID. The cop holding it passed it over, he looked at it a minute, then looked at me. When he did I saw that he was the same cop that pretty much told me to fuck off over the accident that Ma and I were in, except this time he was in uniform.

He motioned for a cop to bring me to him and had a fuckin' full blown conniption fit when he realized that I wasn't handcuffed. The cop started to cuff me and he screamed something about if I was gonna kill anybody they'd be dead by now. With that I couldn't help but make the comment "if this is how badly you guys can fuck up a traffic stop its no wonder you won't go after that fuckin' gangbanger. You'd all be dead before you got to his house. What do you put in your want adds? Looking for Barney Fife, only idiots need apply!"

When I said this Mark's face turned ashen like he'd just been kicked in the nuts. The lieutenant snapped and pulled me aside mumbling about idiots under his breath. When he pulled my jacket sleeve it shoved the tip of the soldering iron into my ribs and made me flinch. Seeing this he asked what was wrong. I told him I had a soldering gun in my coat and all hell broke loose. Two cops hit the deck, three pulled their guns and were pointing 'em at the lieutenant and I. Fuck, I thought they were gonna shoot both of us. One idiot was screaming to get down, another was screaming don't move.

The lieutenant got his lunatics under control and disarmed me. We then walked around to the other side of his car and he questioned me about the vato that ran my ex and I over almost two years earlier. I told him I'd been driving over the road for the past eighteen months and had only been to L.A. three times in that period of time.

I wanted to know why they gave a shit about this gangbanger and not the people he hurt. He looked at me for a couple 'a long seconds and the freaked out cop look {you know, that "deer in the headlights," kinda' shaky, on the ragged edge of a meltdown because of incomprehension and the lack of control of the situation, can't hold their iron still once they've jerked it out, look} melted off his face and real control came back to him.

Cops have it drilled into their heads that they must control even the most uncontrollable people or situations. I've always unnerved most law enforcement officers when our paths've crossed and our paths've crossed frequently. I'd say I'm much more used to them and could read 'em within seconds of initial contact, than they are the casual intensity of the barely contained mayhem lurking just behind my eyes.

Just recently I had a receiver at a place I was delivering to tell me I looked like a natural born killer and that outside of this environment he'd've avoided any type of contact at all. I just laughed and told him a few things about my life.

The lieutenant realizing I wasn't the culprit explained that the vato, his brothers and their entire families'd been rounded up and taken somewhere in the desert and beaten to death. Polaroid's had been taken in various stages of the multiple murders, these were thrown all over the floors of the apartments they lived in for whomever to find.

I asked the lieutenant if I looked like someone who'd do that.

He replied that I was the first person he thought of. See what I mean about first impressions. I chuckled and asked him why he wasn't glad they were gone. He relaxed a little more and said he actually was because since the incident the gang they belonged to had kept a very low profile. They were almost nonexistent and that took a big load off his department.

When I asked what they were gonna do if it'd been me, give me a medal? he looked at me sideways, grinned and said "maybe." All residual tension melted away and both of us had a little laugh at the joke we'd inadvertently collaborated on.

My license was returned and we were sent on our way without mention of the only crimes committed, no motorcycle endorsement, expired tags and no insurance. After returning the soldering gun we went right back to Mark's house instead of taking the ride we'd planned. I'd pushed my luck as far as I dared that day. I didn't want my bike towed off before I could even get it registered. I'd probably never get it back since I didn't have a California title yet.

The next business day I got me and Christine legal and was back in the saddle for real. First place I needed to go was Hemet. I made a call, got some directions and hauled ass. Whitelining east on the Riverside Freeway, rocketing between the cars just inches away on each side {one wrong move n-you're fucked}, loud pipes saving lives at 140 + decibels, we were passing traffic like it was standing still. The sun was blazin', the girls were gorgeous, with a killer buzz between my ears life was fanfuckintastic!

Too soon I was flippin' down my kickstand in front of Hemet's house. As I walked up to the house, the door opened and a huge gold-n-white pitbull came charging at me {I've always loved pits, in my book they're the absolute best dogs, and they love me too}, I squatted down, held my arms out wide and hollered "**PITBULL DAWG**." This "vicious beast" leapt into my arms, flipped over on his back and start furiously licking every piece of exposed flesh on my body that he could reach with his tongue.

The ferocity of this attack knocked me ass-over-teakettle in the front yard. I was laughing so hard I could barely breath. Every direction I moved there was a huge wet tongue with an eighty-two pound brute behind it trying to keep me pinned for a good lickin'.

Kona {not the same Kona in the dedication} finally relented and I got to my feet "ya think he likes me" I asked.

"I think he likes you better than me, I never get a greeting like that." As Hemet said that he looked at Kona, who grinned and wagged his tail even faster. As we walked into the house Kona fell in behind us. When we got inside he got a drink, flopped on the floor at my feet, heaved a big sigh and passed out. Hemet watched all this with a grin and laughed at the big sigh. "I knew there was a reason I trusted you, and I was right, he's a far better judge of character than me," Hemet said.

The first order of business was to line up a couple 'a big fat rippers. After that a big nugget of Skunk Bud was burnt to a cinder in the bong. With our minds in the right part of the galaxy we got down to business.

While Hemet showed me around his property we talked about all manner of things, but seemed to skirt the reason I was there.

I finally asked pointblank "why me?"

Hemet said he could tell I was "cool" the first time he met me at Chicken Delight, when we happened into each other again a couple 'a years later and could sit down and bullshit he knew I could use what he had to teach me. After the long lost friend greeting I got from Kona he was convinced I was the right man for the job and now it was time to get to it.

I didn't know exactly what "it" was yet, but I had a good idea and was getting ancy to find out and get the show on the road. At the back of his property was a ramshackle building that looked like it'd been there since Christ was a corporal and would fall down if you looked at it too long. This was originally the pumphouse for the first well on the property. The well was an old cistern type. Basically just a big deep hole in the ground. The well'd dried up and the pump'd been moved when the well was redrilled leaving an empty shed with a deep dark hole in the floor.

Sometime later the house was hooked up to city water and all the wells were abandoned. This particular shed was overgrown with Tamarisk, Prickly Pear, Palo Verde, Jumping Cholla and several other types of trees and cactus and situated on the property in a way that traffic to and from was hidden from prying eyes and nosy neighbors.

After entering the shed and closing the door, you could lift the cover over the well and climb down a ladder made by strategically removing bricks from the sides of the shaft to afford hand and foot holds and step across the well shaft into an underground room set up like a laboratory with glassware everywhere.

This entrance was more than a little awkward at first, but after a few times it was as easy as walking up and down the stairs in your home. The lab was complete with a fresh air system and a waste disposal system that pumped all the toxic, caustic waste into the old well shaft making the place pretty much undetectable.

Once I'd taken in all the equipment and the ingenuity it'd taken to create this underground chemistry set, I could begin to ask some intelligent questions. By the end of the first day I had a firm grip on a whole new meaning of the word cook and was vibrating with excitement at the thought of learning to cook meth for fun and profit.

We partied the rest of the day and early into the next morning, but by 8:00AM we were back in the lab and my education was well underway again. Hell I was already counting my chickens and the eggs hadn't even been laid yet.

At this time the original base ingredient Benzedrine grit was still available and that was what we were using. It'd already been outlawed, was becoming hard to get and was being replaced by ephedrine as a base. Benzedrine was still readily available in Mexico if you had the connection and Hemet was hooked up so we didn't have any worries, for the moment anyway.

On the ride back into L.A. visions of $$$$$$$$$$$$$$$$$ danced in my head and I felt like a kid at Christmas time. I was buzzed from the fumes, the weed and the anticipation of the good life ahead. If I could do half as good as Hemet I'd be sitting pretty in no time. He'd been cooking for about ten years, had kept it all together and low-key enough to fly under law enforcement's radar. This was really pretty easy to do at that time because the cops didn't know what crank was, it wasn't the mainstream drug it is now.

As long as you did it in a rural setting with no neighbors around to complain about the smell, kept the traffic down, kept your mouth shut about it and went to work every day, you wouldn't get a second glance. If they caught you with it on the street {never carry more than a small amount} they'd test it with bleach {the test for cocaine}. If what they tested didn't turn blue, they didn't know what it was unless you were stupid enough to tell 'em.

It'd be a few more years before the cops figured out what it was and how to detect it in a suspect. In the meantime it was "make hay while the sun shines" and bottom line, I hadn't even begun to think there was a down side let alone how bottomless it could be.

The next weekend I was sitting out in Hemet before the outbound weekend traffic even started. When I got there no one was home, so I sat on Christine and smoked a cigarette. Before I was done with it I heard a scooter idling down the drive. Hemet came around the curve into sight {the drive was curved just enough so you couldn't see the house from the road} and grinned when he saw me. He rolled up, flipped his bike onto the kickstand, shut it off, threw his leg over it and stood up all in one fluid motion.

This motion ended facing me with his hand out. We shook warmly and headed for the house. Sticking his key in the door he looked at me and said "hold on!" The door opened and Kona exploded onto the porch like he'd been shot out of a cannon, his tail wagging his whole body, he knocked Hemet ass-over-teakettle into the driveway and wrestled, licked, nipped and stomped all over 'im. He and I laughed until we were both coughing from the dust cloud they were kicking up, then Kona saw me and the scene was reenacted right down to choking on the dust cloud.

After we were both beaten into submission by the watchdog we dusted ourselves off and headed into the house to line up for the weekend. After a big fat ripper and a couple 'a bong loads, we'd attained the right altitude and were shooting the shit. I asked Hemet where he was coming from when he rolled in and was kinda' shocked when he said "work."

"What the fuck are ya workin' for" I asked. He was kinda' mad when he found out that I'd lived off the dope I took home with me, but there was more than enough to stay high on all week long and still make almost $1000.00 cash. Hell I still had some of that dope in my pocket.

Hemet explained that the way to get caught dealing dope out there was to be seen out-n-about all hours of the day and night, never going to work, but having plenty of money, people coming and going at all hours, new toys {cars, bikes, boats shit like that} and the people you're seen with. He explained that if you're on a scooter out there you're already a suspect for any crime that happens around you. I'd never lived in a place like L.A. and really couldn't imagine the lengths that the cops would go to to secure a bust, but I'd eventually find out.

When Ma and I'd lived here I was more of a family man and was home every night, never out running the streets, so that wasn't even something I'd've thought about anyway. Back then if we were out, it was to go to the store or run a legitimate errand of some kind and I can't ever remember getting fucked with except one time and that was all we'd needed.

Ma and I were on the way home from Mark and Debbie's early one Saturday morning after partying there on Friday night. We were on Imperial Highway in the city of Southgate when we were suddenly surrounded by cop cars and run to the curb. With drawn guns the cops charged the car screaming and made us both exit the driver's side of the car.

This was almost impossible for Ma because she had a cast on her left leg from her hip to her toes; it was hard enough for her to get in and out the passenger side. They wouldn't let her have her crutches and kept up the stupid fuckin' screaming till I'd had enough and screamed **"WHAT THE FUCK'S THE PROBLEM?"**

Everything stopped as fast as it started and one of the cops said that a car that looked like ours'd been involved in an armed robbery.

"Do we look like robbers" I asked.

He looked at Ma still struggling to get outta the driver's side, then at me, said "not really" and left so fast it was like they were never there. Ma and I looked at each other, I helped her the rest of the way out of and around the car and back into the passenger side and we went on home wondering "what the fuck" that'd all been about.

Hemet went on and pretty much told me that I'd have to get a job and keep a low profile or he'd have to sever all ties with me because he couldn't afford to have any attention called to himself or his property. He didn't want any stupid thing that I might do to be traced back to him and jeopardize his operation. This I took to heart immediately and another lesson was learned. I didn't realize at the time how deeply into my life this rule would penetrate.

During my time with Hemet he taught me how to cook the best dope in Southern California. How to sell my dope to avoid getting busted and how to cover my trail to stay under the radar and avoid the scrutiny that most cranksters bring to bear on themselves and others around them.

What usually gets cranksters into trouble is some type of abnormal activity performed in the wrong environment. One thing leads to another and jail is almost always the end result. If the crankster doesn't freak out and squeal on everybody, they release him with a tail and find his entire circle, bringin' 'em all down.

This is why as a cook you're better off to have one customer that your entire product goes to. This simple practice'll cut your chances of being busted to almost nil. Sometimes this limits the money you make on a batch, but you can't make shit sitting behind bars.

Dealing to the street is the most dangerous part of dealing. The spun motherfuckers ya gotta' deal with are dangerous to your health because ya never know what they're gonna do and ya never know when or what's gonna spin 'em right off the edge and start 'em ratting on everybody they know. If you're cookin' and one of these lunatics knows about it. When they have a meltdown you become a leverage point if they get busted. Many a scumbag is still on the street today because they ratted on everybody they knew to keep themselves from doing time for whatever stupid shit they got caught doing.

These people suck because the only effective way to deal with 'em is ta kill 'em. If ya shut 'em off they aren't smart enough to go bother somebody else or just straighten-up and fly right. They high dive off the edge of reason and commit felony stupidity, throwing a searchlight on everyone around 'em. This always marks the beginning of the end of what was a good thing. Bottom line "**trust no one**," alone with a minimal amount of social contact is the safest way to live as a cook for more than one reason, another plus to being a loner.

Along with learning to cook I'd gotten a driving job hauling gas around Southern California during the week. I was still sleeping on Mark's porch because partyin', ridin', keeping my scooter runnin' and livin' like a vagabond was working pretty well for me at the time. I rarely knew where I was gonna wake up or if I was even gonna sleep. The only place I had to be was work, but that was always getting in the way of the party and come the weekend I was in Hemet.

The day came when I finally had to take my road test to get my motorcycle endorsement on my drivers' license. Finally I'd be one hundred percent legal.

I started my day off with a good breakfast, speed-n-weed, breakfast of champions and headed down to the brand new Compton DMV to take my test. Everyone told me to take my test on a dirt bike because the course was too short for a Harley. Of course no one I knew had a dirt bike, so I took Christine. Flying down the freeway that morning I didn't know what to expect, but I never would've thought this would happen.

I arrived at the DMV, parked in the area under the awning and went inside. A middle-aged Mexican man waited on me. He grabbed his clipboard and walked outside, stopping to glance at Christine as he walked by and tell me to meet him across the parking lot by the orange cones. I fired up the bike and was sitting there when he got there.

The first part of the test was the controls, he asked me where the throttle was, I showed him, next the brakes, I showed him, then the clutch, I pointed to the left foot pedal, he said "no that's the shifter."

I said "no *that's* the shifter" and pointed to the lever sticking up out of the transmission. I reached down and showed him the action of the pedal and the lever so he'd understand, because he sure looked confused and later said that in thirty years with the DMV he'd never seen anything like that {that's because everybody used dirt bikes}.

He looked at me and the bike for a second and said "okay start it up, ride around the cones and park back here when you're done."

I kicked the beast to life, sat down, put it in gear and he motioned me to shut it off. I thought he was gonna fail me because the bike was too loud {they can do that}. Instead he leaned down and said "fuck this, if you rode that thing here like that, then I guess you can ride it anywhere else you want, meet me inside at the picture desk," then walked back inside.

I rode up to the building, parked under the awning and walked inside, had my picture taken and finished the paperwork. When he handed me my temp I asked him why I'd passed so easily. He told me that in thirty years at the DMV he'd never seen a motorcycle set up like that. He felt that if he couldn't even understand how the bike worked, he really didn't have any right to judge my performance on it, even though that was his job. He figured that if I'd ridden it there he really couldn't question my ability. Since I obviously knew how to handle the beast he figured I could ride it anywhere else I wanted to go without a problem. I don't think he quite believed me when I told him that they all came that way years ago. He didn't really have any ammunition to argue with so he just accepted it.

Totally legal now I headed off to the bar. The week flew by as I partied my way to the weekend. I was gone with the wind after work on Friday. I didn't even notice the traffic as I blasted down the Dave Lane on the Riverside Freeway.

I got a subdued greeting from Kona {odd}. Hemet seemed a little preoccupied as he said he was outta grit and there wasn't any sense in going to the lab because that was the first process.

Okaaay, my skin prickled, what the fuck? It passed as we decided to ride down to a local watering hole and shoot some pool and drink a few beers. After a few beers Hemet told me his ex'd been fuckin' with him pretty hard all week and that everything'd be back on track by the next weekend. When the bar closed we rode back to the house, after a tune up and a couple 'a bongs I decided to head for the city.

I was sitting out back of the Stagger Inn smoking a joint when Preacher opened the door at 6:00AM. I was wired and ready for a hard day of drinking. By 9:00AM no one else'd shown up. I took off in search of the usual bunch of merrymakers I'd come to know. Couldn't find a soul anywhere, no one was home, but no one was out-n-about either.

I spent the weekend bouncing from empty bar to empty bar. Finally a little after noon on Sunday the familiar roar of some well-known choppers drowned out the jukebox momentarily and in strode a pack of red-faced highway heroes to tell me I'd missed one helluva party up in Whiskey Flats {damn it, Old Miner's Days was always a good time}.

I listened as everyone shouted their accounts of the three day party in the streets of Whiskey Flats and the Kern River in the gravelly voices ya get from too many lines, joints, cigarettes, beers and of course the whiskey {for me anyway}. When the bar closed at 4:00AM I rode over to the Pegasus in the Port of Long Beach and had breakfast before I started my work week at six. When I got to the shop my boss made me take a shower before I started my shift, he said he didn't want me around any customers smelling like booze and dope. What a way ta start a week.

The week flew by like they always did. Along about Wednesday I got around to Mark and Debbie's and it's a good thing I did. They were all in a panic because they hadn't seen me in a while and they still had my stuff. They'd been trying to find me for a week and a half Mark said. It hadn't seemed that long, but time flies when you're having fun. The problem; they were moving to Reno that Friday after Mark got off work. The house was all but packed and they'd been staying at Mark's in-laws house most of the week. I hadn't a clue what to do at the moment so I took a shower, packed all my little bit 'a shit and got it ready to move when I found a place for it.

Turned To Stone

Mark and I talked for a minute or two after I got my shit together, then I hauled ass for the shop. Right after I parked I was talking to some friends out front. Another friend pulled up in his cage, out of the passenger side stepped a gorgeous blonde that I knew wasn't his ole'lady. She smiled radiantly as she walked towards me. When she was almost to me her foot scuffed a uneven brick and she fell right into my arms laughing. As I righted her she said her name was Grace.

"Yah right!" I said with a laugh. We were both hooked.

We walked into the shop just in time to be elected to go get beer, the collection was taken and we walked out to Christine. I let Grace walk out the door ahead of me so I could check out the most perfect ass I'd ever seen in my life. I couldn't wait to unwrap this little sweetie.

The hardest thing I've ever done was kickstart Christine with an eight inch hard-on {hard as fuckin' steel} sticking three inches up over the top of my pants {it had to go somewhere}. It was clamped there by my belt and poking me in the stomach like a broom handle. Each time I tried to stomp down on the kicker pedal it bent the poor thing so backwards it felt like it was gonna break.

Once on Christine Grace melted against me like she was born there. Both hands gently encased the whole length of my dick, it was hard to drive with two heads and only enough blood to run one at a time. When I slowed to turn into the liquor store she breathed "next one" into my ear. We took a quick blast through traffic and returned to the liquor store. Standing in line with her everyone in the store was staring at her as if they'd never seen a woman before. She didn't even seem to notice as she gently held my elbow and chatted quietly in my ear.

Her breath was warm against my neck and smelled faintly of cinnamon. I had to get outta there before my dick exploded and the proximity of this gorgeous creature wasn't making things any easier. When she reached into my pocket and got the money out {I was holding the case of beer, mostly to hide my raging hard-on}, the cashier was lucky I didn't blow a load all over his face.

Starting Christine wasn't any easier this time, especially with every dude in the store watching us. Trying to ride back to the shop with the case of beer balanced on the gas tanks and the head of my dick wasn't the easiest or most comfortable thing I'd ever done either. I'm glad the liquor store was only a few blocks away I don't think I'd've made it too much further in that condition.

Back at the shop, I threw the case of beer on the counter and we ran for the office accompanied by a chorus of laughter {they'd all bet I'd never even get the bike started}. She was naked before I could get the door open, we turned each other inside out and every which way but loose. The taste, the scent, the feel of her perfect, perfect body, better than drugs, better than riding. That's right, I said it, actually better than riding while on drugs, get the drift?

This was the first and to this date the only time I'd ever been fuck-struck like that. My world was rocked, I felt like fuckin' jello inside. She was the one, if there ever was or would be a one, she was it, honey blonde, perfect everything. And the way we clicked, like we were one, I've searched for that again my whole life and never even come close to it. Why are the good ones always taken?

When we finally left the office it was almost dark. Fuck, I had to go to work in a little bit. We walked out to cheers and laughter even though everybody was pissed because all the dope was in the office. Once everybody was lined up and smoked out I found out that tonight was a friend's birthday blowout. That's where everybody was going after the shop closed except me, I had to work. Oh I tried to call off, way too late to get a replacement, so I had to go.

I dropped Grace off at the party and rode to work, got there two hours late, rushed through it and arrived back at the scene of the crime right at daybreak. The carnage was unbelievable, there were bodies everywhere, just dropped where they'd passed out. Some of 'em were covered with makeup, mustard, ketchup, spray paint and all kinds of other stuff identifying the lightweights that passed out early.

I was still picking my way through the human wreckage when Grace came outta the door with two cups of coffee in her hands. I dropped a small rock of crank in each and took one. We stood in the driveway and surveyed the damage while she described how each partier'd met their demise. The talk and the laughter caused some of the corpses to stir, there's something hilarious about watching waking drunks first thing in the morning. They didn't stir for long, but once the sun started cookin' 'em they'd be movin'.

As she talked I stared, I wanted to spend the rest of my life listening to her. Fuck, here comes that dick again, peeking over my belt. That nosey little peckerhead had to start shit first thing in the morning and she put him in his place straightaway posthaste. I could get used to this very quickly {I already was, what a sap, huh}.

After our breakfast of each other we were ready to face the day, I had to find a place to live today, the deadline was tomorrow and we were burning daylight. We were almost out the door when the cause of all the problems staggered outta the kitchen door and fell into a seat at the picnic table with a stupefied grin on his face that looked like he'd picked it up off the floor somewhere on his way out the door.

He looked rough enough that I felt that we needed reinforcements, I got out my bag and laid out three rippers. Grace declined saying she'd do her's later {I fuckin' loved her}, the birthday boy and I divvied up the lines. A few minutes later Grace and I were roaring east on the Artesia Freeway on Christine, who was running better than she had been before I picked Grace up, this led me to believe she liked Grace as much as I did {more about Christine's likes and dislikes later}. We stopped at the shop first. I'd been able to find everything else I ever needed there, just by asking "hey, do you know where......" and this was no exception.

While talking to Bird about my predicament his ole'lady Kat came in to do the books. He asked her about taking in strays, she pointed at me and said "who him, no fuckin' way," giggled, kissed me on the cheek and went back into the office. That was easy, Bird gave me a key and Grace and I spent the day moving my handful of nothing.

First we went over to Bird's and moved some stuff around in the garage. We got so dirty doing that, that we took a shower so long that by the time we were done ice cubes where coming outta the shower nozzle and evaporating to steam when they hit our skin. We then fucked on every piece of furniture in the house, out in the back yard, everywhere until we'd spent all of our bodily fluids and could barely move.

Finally in the early afternoon Kat came home and was astonished at how much we hadn't gotten done. Well we'd just have to get lined up and get two men on it right away, which we did in record time. When we got to Billy Goat Acres no one was there, we used the time to try and drown the one-eyed prick again. We were in the bedroom when I heard a truck pull up out front and familiar voices coming toward the door. I said something, she hadn't heard 'em and had no intention of stopping, she jumped up slammed the door shut, threw herself down in front of me and jammed me back inside her.

With three redneck fuckers in the living room hollering stuff like "what's goin' on in there," then giggling like children we finished. Grace went into the bathroom and I walked out into the front room. When she walked into the room all conversation stopped. This was the first time Mark and them had ever seen a woman of this caliber except in a magazine.

I knew just what their tongue tied silence was all about. Mark said "now I know why I couldn't find you for the last two weeks." After the blast of laughter from the boys and a shining smile from Grace, Mark's father and brother-in-law were tripping all over themselves and their tongues trying to be gentlemen. While Grace kept 'em occupied I packed my stuff on Christine. When I was done Mark and I exchanged phone numbers, gave each other a hug, I shook hands with Donnie senior and junior and we roared off into the sunset {literally}.

Back at Bird's we partied in the back yard till the wee hours of the morning. The next day we had the house to ourselves all day with nothing to do but each other and we did that all day long. Early in the afternoon with my heart on my sleeve I was shot down in flames.

Grace was married and lived in New Mexico, outside of Espanola. She'd married her childhood sweetheart when they graduated high school, who'd immediately turned into a jealous psycho fuck and moved her into the middle of nowhere. They'd moved to New Mexico because he was a jealous fuck and he wanted to get away from all the people he thought were interfering with his relationship. He became abusive and possessive, which compounded when he started using heroin sometime after the wedding.

The abuse continued as the drug use escalated {downs make ya crazy, they do me anyway} to where Grace was afraid for her life and she ran. That was where she was when I met her. She was contacting him every day by phone and he'd beg and promise, her mixed emotions would tear her apart while she was on the phone. When she hung up and came back to me all was forgotten momentarily, till the next time.

I didn't wanna pressure her away from me, so I just kept my stupid fuckin' mouth shut and enjoyed every possible second with her. When she got around to the part where she was leaving next Tuesday, I jumped up and called work and said I wouldn't be in till next Wednesday and if they didn't like it to find another driver I didn't care.

I didn't wanna lose her, but I had no idea what to do or say that'd keep the inevitable from happening. This new turn had placed an iceball in the pit of my stomach that I couldn't shake.

We got high and took a ride to San Pedro. The whole time I was preoccupied with how I could prevent losing her to her psycho husband. I couldn't help feeling a space growing between us that I couldn't make go away and it was fuckin' killing me. What the fuck was I gonna do?

Sitting next to her in the park at Point Fermin I turned to her and said "don't fucking leave!" A look of relief washed over her face and she threw herself on me, the iceball was gone and my baby was back.

When I hadn't immediately put up a fight at the mention of her leaving she thought it didn't matter to me and I was just out for the good time we were both having. Far from it, I never wanted her to go anywhere without me and visa versa. Maybe her husband felt the same way, if he did I could see why, I didn't think about that at the time. How could anyone love her more than me and if he loved her so much why'd he treat her so bad?

We left the park and walked along the rocks to Sunken City, as soon as we got outta sight she stripped off her cloths all in one motion and attacked me. My God she was unfuckinreal! Her body was perfect, lightly tanned, almost the same honey color as her hair. Her light blue eyes always sparkled. She just seemed to glow all over. I couldn't keep her outta my thoughts for a second and didn't want to, she never even wore makeup {didn't need it}. I was completely overwhelmed by her and I didn't even know if she could cook, not that that mattered in the least {she was incredibly edible}.

After she thoroughly beat me into submission we lay on the rocks and soaked up the Southern California sun. I rolled a joint and we got high sitting so close together that we were inside each other, only one of us had to hit the joint for both of us to enjoy it.   When we were done as if she'd read my mind she said "lets go to Ralph's {a grocery chain in Cal.}, I'm gonna make us a nice dinner." I watched her dress and was amazed at everything about her, when she tried to put her jeans on she fell right into my arms laughing. I promptly stripped her naked and beat *her* into submission this time, very easy to do since she melted like butter and always tasted faintly like cinnamon.

I had to ask her if she'd ever felt like this about anyone before. She said she hadn't and as an afterthought she explained about her husband being her high school sweetheart, that they'd married almost right after school. As soon as that happened he changed and got real possessive. This got worse every day till she couldn't even see their friends anymore, the same friends they'd both grown up with {they'd known each other all their lives}.

They'd both been mild partiers, socially, no major hang-ups, then he started using heroin and this only made his problems worse. She loved him because that was how she was and stuck by his side. He came home one day with this big plan to move to New Mexico, saying it'd make their lives better and he'd get off the drugs there because there wouldn't be any pressure and they'd make a new life.

Espanola is a very hardcore town with gangs and serious drug and alcohol problems. It's very much a wild west town, psychotic behavior runs rampant fueled by alcohol and many different types of drugs. Heroin was probably the most prevalent of these drugs at the time and speed wasn't very well known around there at all then. I'd be willing to bet heroin's been replaced by crank today. It seems that crank or crack have replaced heroin as the number one addiction today in most markets.

When they got there he stuck her in a trailer in the middle of nowhere with no transportation, left for days at a time, came back it seemed just to be shitty to her, wreck the place and take off on another bender. She'd finally had enough and called a mutual friend of ours {he kinda' introduced us the day after we met}. He bought her the ticket that brought her to me and that was where we were right then. When I heard this my heart soared, she's not gonna go back to that asshole on Tuesday, not after the fantastic week we're having, I was sure of it.

Back on Christine she melted into me the way only she ever has and we were one, Christine, her and I as we flew to Ralph's and then home.

Once there she made me go in the living room and mind my own business while she made one of the best dinners and desserts I, we, all of us'd ever had. Dinner was on the table and the kitchen was spotless when Kat and Bird rolled in. Kat's initial reaction was "I don't like other people in my kitchen," but when she saw the spread and condition of her kitchen she didn't mind.

After dinner the girls cleaned the table and Bird and I went in the living room and rolled a joint. He looked at me and started to say something, I couldn't contain it I said "dude she's the one, the only one." That was all I had to say, he smiled his understanding. He had his one in Kat and he knew it, that made his understanding all the more complete.

When the girls came in Kat said "girl you're welcome in my kitchen any time." When the joint was gone Grace said she wanted a shower and the girls headed to the bathroom. After Kat got Grace a towel and what not she rushed in and wanted to know all the details, she liked Grace {who wouldn't}. I gave her a quick rundown {she and I always had that kind of bond, could talk about anything with each other}, she didn't want her to go either, she saw the change the last few days'd made in me.

I would've done anything Grace asked me to without question I loved her that much. I trusted her with my life, hell I trusted her with Christine. I'd kill for her or die for her. I'd do anything but lose her. I couldn't let her go back to that fuckin' asshole in New Mexico. Kat swore to help me all she could.

When Grace came outta the shower and curled up in my lap, I forgot anything that had to do with disturbing that moment {I needed a shower too, but it could wait}. It wasn't a minute before she was asleep, pretty soon our hosts wandered off to bed, I picked her up {she was light as a feather}, put her on the couch, covered her up and went to take my shower.

When I came back her cloths were folded neatly on the coffee table with a note on top "wake me." How could I not, each time was better and better. This time was a slow comfortable screw that lasted what felt like hours and was excruciatingly wonderful. I wouldn't believe this could ever end.

The next morning I remembered Hemet, a quick call and it was "see ya would-n-wanna be ya" till next weekend. We spent the weekend ignoring the plans we'd made and took a few short rides here and there like to a payphone once a day so she could check in with dickhead. I hated this part of the day {I wished she'd just forget that nightmare, but she said he'd come looking for her. I thought good I'd rather deal with him here on my terms, I'm sure I could find a dumpster with his name on it somewhere}. Thank God it wasn't ever for very long. The rest of the time we partied in the back yard, bar-b-qued some tri-tip and relaxed in great company.

Monday came and we were alone all day, it was fun playing house, but Tuesday hung over our heads like a huge weight. All my thoughts were summed up by three words "don't fuckin' leave" it rolled through my head on an endless loop all fuckin' day. Finally it spilled outta me in a flood of tears, we both cried for a long time and she finally said "I have to go back and end it with him before we can do anything more than this. When I leave him it'll be for you, for life. That means marriage, the whole deal, understand?"

Of course I understood, that's what I was hoping for, I'd die for her and I did. "Come and get me in two weeks, I'll be ready when you get there and we'll just go." Of course I agreed. She said she'd go home and pack the few things she wanted and ship them to our friend out here and be ready to travel light when I got there. We'd even go for a real motorcycle ride, see the country, go to Sturgis. She'd always wanted to do something like that and I'd always wanted to do something like that, with someone like her.

I'd've agreed to anything to keep her in my life, this sounded like a dream about to come true. The making of these plans took the weight off the rest of the day. I don't think I could've survived another minute without exploding if I hadn't said something. The relief was tremendous, knowing that this was as important to her as it was to me. The day was beautiful with a cool breeze coming through the house and we just lay on the couch completely entwined in each other not speaking and dozed off until we heard the roar of StrayKat coming down Lemon Avenue.

We all spent the evening together getting high after Kat and Grace made dinner and cleaned up the kitchen. Kat would shoot me this funny little smile every time no one else was looking, kinda' like she knew something I didn't. She never had a chance to do more than that before she stood up and dragged Bird off to bed, which is what happened to me as soon as the bedroom door closed behind Kat, I think it was planned. As we were falling asleep that night Grace breathed "I love you" in my ear, my brain and my heart caught fire simultaneously.

The next morning the house was empty when we woke up, we never even heard 'em leave. We took full advantage of the situation until the very last possible moment and then flew across town to her sister's house to get her stuff and the taxi that took her to the airport. When I got back to the house the silence was deafening. It'd be hours before she called to say she'd landed in Albuquerque. I decided to go to the shop. As I was walking out the door a plane flew over that'd just taken off from LAX. I wondered if that was the one she was on, it was headed in the right direction.

That evening right on time she called from Albuquerque. By that time I missed her so fuckin' much I was ready to go get her right then. She agreed, but said that this was the right way to do what we had to do to be together always. Two weeks was a speck compared to a lifetime and after these two weeks we'd have a lifetime. It couldn't happen soon enough for me though.

It was impossible to do anything for the next two weeks, no matter what I was doing all I could think of was her. In the middle of a stinking refinery all I could smell was her light cinnamon scent. She was the only thing I could keep my mind on and that wasn't good. I needed to work all I could because I wanted to have plenty of cash in two weeks. During the week Grace called every morning right after I got home from work. We'd talk about everything and always leave each other with "I love you." This was never enough, but it helped take the edge off the waiting.

When the week was finally over I jumped into the Dave Lane on the Riverside Freeway and headed east. A good dose of Hemet'd clear these cobwebs of love and make the next week go by a lot faster.

When I got there Kona's greeting was kinda' halfhearted. Hemet wasn't his usual chipper self either. He handed me about an once and a half of dope and said he was outta grit so there was no sense in even going down to the lab. We did a couple 'a rippers, smoked a couple 'a bongs and sat there in silence. Fuck, what a couple of morose bastards we were. I was mooning over Grace and who knows what the fuck had Hemet off kilter.

Finally Hemet suggested we ride downtown, have some burgers, drink some beers and shoot some pool. I agreed and off we went. When we got to the bar, we sat at the bar drinking ourselves into the right frame of mind to shoot something even if it wasn't pool.

Hemet said his ex'd been fuckin' with him all week long again that was why he was outta chemicals and outta sorts. He hadn't had the chance to see his guy because he was dealing with her all week. He then admonished me to never get tangled up with a woman it only leads to no good. I guessed this probably wasn't a good time to begin mooning about how wonderful Grace was and how she made me feel so good with just a look or a touch of her hand.

We closed out the bar, rode back to the house, did another line and smoked a bunch 'a bongs. I said fuck this and headed for the city. By the time the sun came up I was sitting at the back door of the Stagger Inn smoking a joint expecting to hear the familiar roar of about a dozen scooters whose owners where coming to drink breakfast with Preacher.

The door unlocked and I walked into the neon darkness of the bar. The first thing Preacher said was "where's Grace?" This immediately put me in a funk, I missed her so fuckin' much I could hardly stand myself. Even dope didn't make me feel better, it was like a part of me was missing. I couldn't wait I called her, her husband answered the phone and I hung up. One more week motherfucker! Everyone I saw that weekend asked "where's Grace," it was making me nuts.

That week dragged by, she called every day, finally it was Friday. I'd be headed east in a few hours and with my sweetie in another day or so. I'd never allow us to be separated like this again.

Finally I got my last check cashed and with a pocketful of dope and money, a fresh oil change and a full tank of gas I jumped into the Dave Lane and got this journey underway at full tilt. I stopped in Hemet ta say "see ya," when I got to the top of the drive there was a **FOR SALE** sign on the fence. As I idled down the driveway I got a funny feeling {not funny ha ha either}. I stopped in front of the house. It was empty and a realtor's lockbox was on the door.

Well at least I didn't have to ruin Hemet's day by telling him I was throwing everything away for a girl. He'd've had a field day with me over that, if he was in the same mood as the last time I saw him. Riding outta town that day I was five feet eleven inches tall and weighed one hundred and thirty-two pounds.

Oh well, I jumped back on the freeway, grabbed a handful of gas and headed for my personal paradise {anywhere my sweetie was}. The traffic was unbelievable. I-15 was packed with Vegas weekend traffic. I didn't even slow down till I got on I-40. The first chance I got after that I stopped to do a line and smoke a joint. As soon as that was done I gassed up and pushed on. By the evening of the next day I was in Albuquerque, after a quick bite to eat I headed north on I-25.

It was just starting to get dark as I hit the freeway. In a few minutes I thought I was going blind. I couldn't see a fucking thing. I pulled to the side of the road and pulled my shades off, everything was fine when I took my glasses off. It was the lack of ambient light that I wasn't used to. In L.A. it's always almost like daylight, even in the middle of the night because of the high pressure sodium streetlights they use to burn off what would be a nightly blanket of heavy fog so thick you couldn't see your hand in front of your face without 'em. Because it's always lit in L.A. you never need clear glasses at night, so I didn't even own any.

I took off again without any glasses this time, which didn't work very well. In the desert the wind always blows because there's nothing to slow it down. The radical temperature changes always create convection currents and the prevailing westerly winds never stop. There really isn't much for the wind to blow around except sand, tumbleweeds and every other thing that isn't nailed down or anchored to the ground in some way.

All this means that you won't last long without eye protection riding in the desert. I-40 is a busy east/west freeway with constant traffic. The wind is more or less always at your back when you're headed east, so I didn't really notice the darkness or the wind the night before. I-25 on the other hand is not near as busy and has an almost constant crosswind. When it gets dark out there it's fuckin' dark and the blowing sand doesn't make things any better.

I finally had to settle for easing up the shoulder sans shades. The occasional traffic, especially the trucks that flew by made this a scary and dangerous choice, but the only one I had besides stopping completely and that could only've been worse out there in the middle of nowhere on the side of a freeway. It seemed like an eternity before I saw an exit sign and I still had five miles to go before I got there.

I finally got to the Cerrillos Road exit and boy was I thankful. There wasn't shit all the way from Albuquerque to Sante Fe. Cerrillos Road was the first exit I'd come to since passing Bernalillo. I jumped off and rode up through Sante Fe to Highway 285 and headed for Espanola. We'd already arranged for me to stop at a bar a short distance from the turnoff for Grace's trailer and call her.

When I got to the bar there was a party of some kind going on and the place was packed. I tried calling, no answer. I got a beer and sat at the bar, this didn't last long though. Before my beer was half gone I was invited to join in the festivities. As the beer flowed and the weed was smoked more than one partier commented to me that a line would sure be a nice right about then. I must've just looked like I had dope or something. Maybe it was the California license plate on Christine that naturally led 'em to assume biker, California, crankster I don't know.

It took a few more beers before I was ready to do any myself. When I did there were a whole bunch of noses looking over my shoulder and I was buzzed enough to be too generous. Everyone that wanted one got a line that night and the party rolled on till the break of dawn. I'd forgotten why I was there momentarily and become caught in the moment. Something that was always my downfall throughout my life.

The next day when my hangover was assaulting me from all sides I regretted dishing out any of my bag to total strangers. When I pulled it out to do a blast and get my head back in the vicinity of my body I was pissed at myself when I saw how much I'd given away.

The bag I'd brought with me would've lasted me a month at the very least and I probably could've stretched it out twice as long if I had to. Instead I had about two thirds of the dope I brought with me left and that wasn't gonna do shit for me for very long as burned out as I was getting.

I did a line and headed into the bar {I'd passed out on Christine under a mesquite tree at the back of the parking lot sometime around sunrise} to throw my face at some water, pound back some hair 'a the dog and of course try Grace's number again.

After I felt almost human I grabbed the phone and the sweet voice at the other end made my day. When she heard my voice, she said she had a feeling I was there and had wanted to be home, but her husband had actually been nice last night {he even bought her a car} and taken her out to dinner to make up for being four hours late picking her up at the airport. He'd been mister wonderful the whole night long, so there was no way she could get away without causing a big fight. She gave me directions and I took off.

Five minutes later the ache in my arms was replaced by the warmth of her perfect body and we smothered each other with kisses.

She knew exactly how to take care of a man, when we walked into her trailer the smell of breakfast cooking made it feel like home, I wished I really was home. Immediately after breakfast she led me to the bathroom, started the shower, stripped off my sand blasted, road-grimed clothes and took them with her when she left. The warm water of the shower felt great, while I was still washing my hair I felt her hands washing my back and after I was squeaky clean we made love right there in the tub.

When we were done she disappeared down the hall while I tried to get my long hair and beard brushed out. Before I could say anything she was back with clean cloths that she'd gotten outta my saddlebags. She finished brushing out my hair and beard while I tried to get dressed around her. When I walked out into the living room she had a joint rolled and lit. After we smoked the joint we relaxed on the couch enjoying the quiet and comfort of each other. We spent the day lounging together while she washed my filthy clothes and packed 'em back in my saddlebags.

When I pulled out my bag of crank she gently took it from me and put it away "you need to sleep, you look wrung out." I gave in to her touch and while she scratched and rubbed my back I fell off to a deep sleep.

I don't how she got me there, but I woke up early the next morning in her bed with her breathing softly next to me. I rolled over, melted into her back and fell back asleep. The next time I woke, it was to the smell of bacon cooking and sun streaming in the windows.

After breakfast she told me her husband'd probably be back sometime today. He'd take off for days at a time and come back in foul moods pass out for a while then leave again for God knows where or what. I told her we should just leave and let him come home to an empty trailer; he'd figure it out eventually.

That was what she intended to do, but she had a big check coming in the mail and she wasn't gonna leave that check to him, besides we could use the money. She'd counted mine while I was asleep and figured we wouldn't get too far on what I had left. I agreed, but I didn't like hanging around like this.

About midmorning she heard his truck coming up the road and started to panic. I told her not to worry if it came down to it I'd simply kill him and dump him out in the desert for the coyotes and bugs to eat. She shot me a disapproving look and said "he is my husband you know!"

I apologized.

She made me promise not to do anything to him no matter what and to meet her at the bar I called her from if anything went wrong.

He came raging into the trailer and immediately got in my face, I did as I promised and went to the bar without lifting a finger {big mistake}. She told me to wait there and she'd call me when he left again. I sat at the bar nursing beer after beer until early into the next morning. I finally went out and slept on Christine under the mesquite tree until the sun came up.

I snorted a line with the bartender when the bar reopened and began nursing beers again waiting for the phone to ring. Around 10:00AM the phone rang for the first time that day and I almost leapt outta my skin, it wasn't for me.

The next day found me in the same place waiting for the same call. I finally couldn't wait any longer, fuck that promise if I had to break in and kill the motherfucker with my bare hands to get her away from him, so be it.

When I got to the trailer there was nobody there and by the dust blown over the driveway there hadn't been anyone there for a couple 'a days. I walked over to the mailbox and checked it, Grace's check was there. I walked over to a window and looked in, the place was a shambles, nothing like the tidy homey place from a few days before. I immediately thought the worst, there was really nothing I could do except go back to the bar and see what happens, but how long could I hang around waiting for what to happen?

I rode back down to the bar, got a beer and for the first time I asked somebody from the area if they knew Grace. I didn't like the answers I got, the picture of Grace painted by the bartender was not the Grace that I knew and I had a hard time getting my brain around what I was being told. I finally just closed my mind to what was being said, finished my beer, fired up Christine and headed towards Sante Fe.

As I was pulling out onto the highway a tow truck hauling Grace's husband's wrecked truck drove by and a few miles down 285 cop cars and tow trucks had the southbound lane of the road blocked. Sitting as low in the saddle as I did I couldn't see over the vehicles to see what was going on and the state trooper controlling traffic quickly gave me the evil eye when I tried to slow down too much and sternly told me to keep moving.

An iceball formed in my stomach that day that didn't take long to move up to my heart. I tried telling myself that he'd probably had one major hissy fit, wrecked the place, probably slapping her around some in the process, took off in a lather, wrecked his truck and she being the woman she was, was in the hospital with him. She knew I'd stick around till she contacted me and we could take it from there.

Every chance I got until I left New Mexico I rode back up there and checked out the trailer. I even left Judith's {you'll meet her in a minute} phone number in the front door hoping she'd call. I didn't give a shit about Judith, she was just a place to hang my hat until something happened anyway.

Finally one weekend the trailer was gutted and every wrecked thing was in a pile out in the yard, all of her things that'd made that trailer so her's was just a pile of wreckage to be scooped up and thrown away, the front door stood agape ripped half off it's hinges as if to taunt me. I had to go in, even after all this time I could still smell her faint cinnamon scent or was it just in my mind? I hadn't had any crank in weeks bordering on months so I wasn't hallucinating it or was I?

I walked all around inside and out. Sitting down on the porch in the warm sun I didn't understand how I could feel so chilled in the warm New Mexican sunshine, like someone'd walked across my grave. I remember thinking I didn't even know her last name. Then I remembered the check in the mailbox, I sprinted to the empty mailbox driven by a morsel of hope. I never would know her full name, maybe it was better that way. Who the fuck was I kidding, there was only one way this could get better and I really didn't see that happening.

I picked up a lace curtain tie that had her scent imbedded in it and jammed it in my pocket and kicked Christine to life. As I took one last look I didn't see the wreckage, I saw the place as I had at first. With the most beautiful creature on earth ever, smiling at me just like she was the day I arrived. I knew my hopeful assessment of what'd happened was bullshit. How little did I know.

Downbound Train

It'd be more than three years before I found out what happened to Grace. Long before the ice had turned to stone, sealing my fate and dooming me to be alone even in the most crowded of rooms and a lifetime of loneliness, ruining every relationship before they ever got started. No one I've ever been with since has come close to giving me the feeling I had the moment we met. While the emptiness and pain got pushed into a hole so deep inside me it'd never see the light of day again, I was disabled emotionally forever.

This is the first time in my life I've allowed it to see the light of day. Twenty-three years later it hurts just like it did when I was living thru it. I was numb from the neck up then, unable to do anything but wonder what happened for three years. Now I can't describe the anguish in my heart that wants to consume me each time I let the memory loose in my head. It could've been so different if handled a different way. If anything could ever cause me to go back to using, it would be that. The worst part is knowing that I was the cause of it.

I think I'd've been better off to never know the irreversible God-awful truth and to assume she'd had a change of heart and stuck with her ole'man, but the physical evidence at the time and the eventual crushing truth have been a world of painful weight every millisecond of my haunted life. I've never forgotten her, I can see her in my mind today as clearly as if she were right her with me now.

I have to say right hear that the loss of Grace tainted every relationship I've ever had right up to and including my last failed marriage. I've never felt that mutual attraction to any other woman in my life and at this late stage in my game of life I don't think I ever will.

When I arrived in Sante Fe there was some kind of celebration going on. The streets were filled with people and a fiesta was going on in the town square. I backed my scooter into the curb in front of the only bar on the square with motorcycles in front of it. I sat back on my pack, kicked my feet up on the handlebars and watched the festivities with my eyes while my brain tried to make sense of the last few hours. I finally tired of speculating, but I knew in my heart that the things the bartender up north'd told me just couldn't be true.

Within a few minutes of parking the owners of the other scooters came outta the bar to introduce themselves. They were up from Amarillo for the holiday weekend and were camping out in Pecos. After introductions all around, we hung out on the sidewalk drinking beers and enjoying the show going on around us. While we were standing there a woman walked up and started quizzing us as to whose scooter was whose, she guessed Christine and I right away and started flirting with me, she suggested we go up on the balcony and watch the action from up above.

On the way up the stairs Judith lifted her skirt to show me she wasn't wearing any panties and once on the balcony she took my hand and put it in her crotch. It's said that the way to forget one woman is with another, I'll try anything once. If the woman you're trying to forget was the one, you'll never forget her and the memory will destroy every relationship you ever have so that's bullshit! Judith definitely wasn't gonna make me forget her, on her best day she couldn't hold a candle to Grace. Later as the party was winding down in town the Texans suggested that we adjourn to their campsite and continue the party there.

Judith said she'd have to get some jeans and a jacket because it got pretty cold once the sun went down. We all rode to her house down off Cerrillos Road and waited while she changed. When she came back out we all cranked up and roared off down the street, at the end of the street Christine coughed and died. When I tried to start her again it was like there was no compression. Without taking her apart I couldn't diagnose the problem.

I motioned for the Texans to go on, Judith said she knew where they were camped and when I figured out the problem we could ride out there. She and I pushed Christine back to her house and into the garage where I started to take her apart immediately. Within minutes I knew the problem. The screws that held the throttle plate in place had come out and been sucked into the motor {fuckin' great}.

I continued to dismantle the motor to find the screws, they'd lodged in the front intake valve and gouged up the valve seat. There was nothing I could do until I could get parts, but where in Sante Fe New Mexico was I gonna get throttle plate screws for an M74B Linkert carburetor? This particular carb'd only been obsolete for about thirty years at that time.

Nothing I could do today so Judith and I went in the house, got stoned and had sex later that evening. It definitely didn't hold a candle to sex with Grace, in fact it sucked, no sex would've been just as good if not better. We just hung out for the rest of the night and the next day I went out and took the front head off my motor. I got the screws outta the intake valve, went down to the auto parts store and got some valve lapping compound. Using the valve I repaired the valve seat with the lapping compound. Fluid checked the seal with some WD-40 and put the whole mess back together once I got the valve to seal. I still had to find some screws to replace the ones that got destroyed though.

Judith knew all the scooter people in the area so we toured all their haunts to try to scrounge up the screws or something to replace 'em with. Finally someone had a clue where I could get a complete carb. He didn't know how much and because of the holiday the dude was outta town. No one knew when he'd be back. We got his phone number, did a little partying with these folks and went back to Judith's house to kick back and wait for the next day to come.

The next morning was the start of a new week and with any luck new life for my broken ride. After a phone call made by Judith, we hopped in her cage and headed to the old part of town. We pulled up in front of an ancient adobe building {a real adobe, not the bullshit frame and stucco that contractors try to pass off as adobes to unknowing snowbirds and city folk}.

Upon entering the dimly lit interior the first thing I noticed was how cool it was inside, I didn't hear an air conditioner running. When I commented on it, the guy behind the counter said that that was the thing about adobes, somewhat like a cave the temperature stayed very consistent inside making them easy to heat and cool. Seems that the building maintains its temperature without much help at all. When I asked about the screws, he said he only had a complete carb. Visions of dollars I didn't have danced in my head, but when he said ten dollars I just about shit. That was a hell of a good deal to a total stranger.

Within a few minutes of returning to Judith's I had my old ride roaring again. The first thing we did was take a ride out to Pecos to see if the Texans were still there. Of course they weren't, but it was a beautiful ride. It was the first time I'd taken a ride that wasn't some type of mission in a while and I was beginning to appreciate the wide open beauty of the real west.

Being from back east originally and living in or near cities all my life the only things I knew about the west was the bullshit that was slung by the old Hollywood B movies. Actually being in places called Pecos and Sante Fe was beginning to seem kinda' cool to me.

The fact that I'd been using less crank for the last few days, was resulting in a more relaxed attitude and the ability to slow down and look around a little bit, something some brothers from Texas have advised me to do many times.

After I told Judith about this she did a good job introducing me to the wonders of The Land of Entrapment. For the next few weeks we toured The High Road to Taos. Attended several of the Pueblo Days in the area. In the summer months in New Mexico the Indian Pueblos open their doors to the public and provide a first hand look into the way life used to be for the Pueblo Indians, complete with full costumed dances and all the traditional foods and clothes, a must see for anyone on any weekend in the summer.

We swam in Nambe Falls, camped in the Pecos Wilderness and visited friends of hers that lived the old way in the Llano Valley. By the old way I mean these people's idea of running water was the ditch out front. It being a diverted mountain stream that ran past everyone's cabin, maintained every Saturday by the men from the entire valley.

Working as a community the ditch was diverted again into and thru each cabin, resulting in naturally running water. The lighting was candles or oil lamps, the heat came from wood. At night when you went outside the glow from the stars was just phenomenal because there might've been two electric lights glowing in the whole valley, it was like stepping back in time a hundred years.

There was a whole valley of people who'd dropped out of the world as we know it and gone back to a simpler time. While the entire world around them went slowly, but it now seems irreversibly off the deep end of reason and became the infested, infected, injected, neglected, politically corrected society of dumbed down, hurray-for-me-n-the-hell-with-you assholes that flock through the highways and byways of this land intent on whatever personal mission they're on at that nanosecond. Their only concern being their cell phones and their cigarettes. Oblivious of the damage they do to everything they touch, including each other. Self righteous enough to proclaim they're doing it all in the name of God. A concept they have no real grip on, its just something they downloaded off the internet one night by accident while they were looking at the latest porn. How dare you say anything either. According to them they have the right to be as stupid as they possibly can.

I wish I could go back there right now and see how far the world has intruded on and polluted that beautiful, near pristine valley that displayed the awesome grandeur of the truly wild west, all you had to do was open your eyes, breath the air and look around.

The view from anywhere in that valley was of the Pecos Wilderness. The mountains where the Pecos River was reborn every day by high mountain runoff and eventually flowed into the Rio Grande way down by the Mexican Border, the same runoff that provided the valley with its running water. Ya know I've been pretty fuckin' high in my life, but nothing beats sleeping under the stars, with coyotes howling all around you and the occasional scream of a big cat. Waking up to the pure air and sunshine of those high mountain mornings.

If I'd had one correctly working brain cell in my head at that time I'd've stayed in New Mexico and the story would've ended there and wouldn't even be worth telling. At this time in the story I'd been clean of crank for about two weeks give or take a few days, my brain'd cleared and I could think about anything I wanted to without the overwhelming need for speed screaming thru my head like a freight train, drowning out any other thoughts.

Instead of thinking that the nearest dope is in Albuquerque and I'm a hundred miles away in the middle of nowhere, oh my! I could see, smell, taste and almost touch the power of The Wild West. It has a definite effect on you that is very tangible. I could clearly see why these people'd chosen this place to call home, given the remote location. If a plane didn't fly over once in a while you'd think the world'd just gone away.

I should've stayed and made a place for myself in those mountains, but I again chose the wrong path and returned to the world I knew speed, weed, bikes and chicks. Not for awhile yet and not with the vengeance and self-destructive dedication I acquired when I finally returned to California. Let's get back to the New Mexico story though, cause it's far from over and it has its moments.

A week or so after our first visit to the Llano valley we returned for a weekend long mushroom party. The party was held in a high mountain meadow about a mile and a half or so off the highway. By following a four wheel drive rut through the woods to an easy slope about twenty feet long that dumped you into a river about nine inches deep and twelve or fourteen feet wide, you'd find on the other side of the river a meadow full of campers and partiers. Getting into the meadow on Christine wasn't easy, she wasn't exactly made for boonyhopping, but with a lot of luck and a little skill I was the only biker there that'd rode his bike.

When we got there I was immediately stuffed with Magic Mushrooms and sent out to play, a high mountain rain sent us to the campsites and fires shortly thereafter. Even in the summer without the sun the high mountains are a chilly place. When you add the ice cold rain that falls from time to time a nice warm fire is a good thing to have. Around the fire this big Indian dude named Denny and I started swapping lies about how tough we were. With the power of the shrooms propelling us we commenced to spend the next twelve or so hours rolling around in the mud locked in a psilocybin fueled death match in which we completely flattened one gal's campsite, tent, kitchen and all. She just gave us more mushrooms and we went right back to it after the break.

Finally we tired sometime in the middle of the night. That was when I rounded up Judith and we took off up the slippery as ice, mud layered four wheel drive rut. Not before we crossed a river that was about twenty feet wide and almost up to the carburetor now and negotiated the twenty foot slope that was slicker than owl snot on a brass doorknob did we even get to the four wheel drive rut though.

Did I mention that without the meager glow of the junk six volt system's headlight it was so dark that you couldn't see your hand in front of your face {literally}. Each time the bike stalled out {and that was frequently} it was a blind ordeal trying to find the kicker peddle or any other control for that matter. You couldn't let go of the thing or you wouldn't find it for what seemed like a panic prolonged eternity.

Being so fuckin' high on mushrooms all you can do is laugh hysterically to keep from freaking out completely in the pitch blackness and fighting a loosing battle with water and mud was exhausting. Before long all three of us were covered with mud, I lost Judith somewhere on the trail and finally gave up because Christine was unbelievably hot. I flipped the kickstand down and stretched out on her to wait out the night.

As I lay there watching brightly colored specks of light drifting around in the blackness I noticed the sky lightening through the trees {false dawn; happens every day about an hour before dawn}. About sixty-five minutes later, after Judith caught up with me we were standing on the paved road. I'd stopped about ten feet from the road, but hadn't known it because of the darkness. When we got back to Judith's we were so filthy from head to toe that the cleanup procedure started with the hose out in the back yard.

Gettin' Out While Gettin's Still Good

I'd been broke for a while and it was time to get some money. I started hanging out at the unemployment office in the morning trying to get some day labor to at least scrape some gas money together to get outta town with. Judith was wearing on my last nerve and any time away from her was welcome.

After a few days of unsuccessful hanging around I was sitting in the lobby one morning waiting for anything to happen. Two guys walked in, spoke to the lady at the counter for a short minute and walked out. A second later the lady asked if anyone was an experienced carpenter, everyone but me raised their hand, the lady made note of this and sat back down. Seconds later she psssted me and motioned me over. When I walked over to her she told me to go see the men in the white Ford van outside.

As my eyes accustomed themselves to the bright Sante Fe morning I spotted the van and strode over. A dude motioned me in the side door. I climbed in and sat down on the spare tire laying on the floor. The guys introduced themselves as Don and Chris. They asked if I knew anything about carpentry and when I said no Chris laughed and I told you so'd at Don. Handing me an ice cold Bud, they both said "you'll do," laughed and we all took a long pull off our beers.

They explained that when they walked in and cased the lobby they recognized everyone else there but me and I didn't look like I knew shit from shineola about wood. They were right and that's why I got the job. They didn't want someone second guessing their work. They just wanted a grunt to carry wood and move shit no questions asked, my favorite kind of work. I had three and a half weeks of work at two hundred dollars a week cash for the full weeks and forty dollars a day for the next three days.

I followed their van up to the jobsite in Tesuque and met the contractor they worked with. An immediate argument ensued as to whether or not I could smoke pot on the job. Gene {the contractor} won, conditional on my performance. At least for now I could get stoned at work {only during breaks though, that really hurt, ha,ha,ha} unless I started fuckin' up, then that would be the end of it. How can you possibly fuck up being a grunt I wondered?

The job was simple, do what the three of 'em needed me to do for the next three weeks without fuckin'up, pretty easy. The three of 'em were gonna be busy framing the house, setting vigas and latias {whatever that meant} for the living room ceiling and they needed a grunt who'd just do what he was told.

Vigas and latias are barked and limbed, unfinished Lodgepole Pine trunks and limbs that are set in a pattern. Vigas are the long trunks of the trees and span the room, latias are the smaller branches that are laid between the vigas to form a specific pattern and complete the entire ceiling. The overall look is awesome and so western, but the cost is phenomenal and the wait time is worse because the whole ceiling has to be cut to fit and then shipped, if anything {God forbid} happens to any of the pieces before the ceiling is set, everything has to wait until the pieces are replaced, stopping progress on the house for maybe months sometimes depending on how strategic the piece was.

The vigas and latias aren't usually delivered to the site until a day or two before they're due to be set in order to try to prevent theft. They're a very hot commodity in New Mexican construction. If you can provide them to a customer without any out of pocket expense, you'll easily nab a hundred and fifty to two hundred thousand dollars more profit from the sale of the house without shouldering any of that expense. After outlining the job to me and conferring on some points amongst themselves we spent what little of the afternoon there was left getting stoned, drinking beer, swapping lies and getting to know the crew we'd be for the next three weeks.

A little before 7:00AM the next morning I bumped Christine to a stop outta the way at my new place of employ. I swung around in the saddle and laid back on my gas tanks to await the bosses who were long in coming. I didn't care the sky was bright blue and the fresh desert breeze had so many sweet scents on it I was amazed that I'd ever want to leave there.

About a quarter past eight the bosses straggled in all hung over n-slept in their cloths lookin' n-shit, damn. I sat on my bike and watched as they tottered from their vehicles to the closest patch of shade {there wasn't much out there till the roof went on}. They kinda' rolled to sitting positions on the ground, shaded their eyes with their hands and groaned almost in unison.

They sat there drunkenly rambling on about their fuckin' laborer that probably got pissed because they never showed up and took off. They chuckled about that {they were still drunk}. Then one by one mid-mumble, they started to nod off. When they were obviously oblivious I walked up to 'em and screamed **"WHAT THE FUCK'S GOIN' ON HERE"** at the top of my lungs right into their ears and stood back. They looked like The Three Stooges bumping and staggering their way to their feet. When they realized it was me we all had a good laugh.

After that subsided, I looked at Gene and said "I've been here since seven." He just nodded and we moved on to the important stuff like the party at Gene's neighbor's house the night before that I had, not too regrettably missed {I hated feeling like they looked}.

There was ice cold beer in the van and Gene broke out his pipe, before long we were all in a better frame of mind, a little work might get done today after all. Some kinda' job, the bosses broke every one of their own rules the first minute of the first day. I knew I'd like it here just fine.

On a rainy afternoon, the third of July, Judith and I were in a bar {the name escapes me, but it was on Agua Fria st.} in Sante Fe. We'd been there for a while with some friends and had had a few beers. As I bellied up to the bar to get another beer I casually replied to a girl's question that was standing next to me. Outta the blue a beer bottle smacked her right in the side of the head and knocked her bleeding to her knees.

I looked in time to see Judith storming outta the bar in a huff; she jumped into her pinto and sped off. I followed as quickly as I could on Christine. When I got to Judith's house she'd already been there a while because she had most of my stuff thrown out on the wet lawn in the rain. My pistol, reloading equipment, clothes, things that really shouldn't get wet and she was throwing even more as I rode up the driveway.

She was standing in the overhead door between the door casement and back fender of her car throwing my shirts like they were confetti out into the mud and crap in the side yard. More of my stuff was already all over the front yard. I aimed right for that psycho bitch's legs and nailed the gas {I was gonna run her down}.She stepped back just far enough that Christine got wedged in between the door frame and the car fender before I could do any damage to the lunatic in front of me.

I jumped off the bike and tried to get at Judith. The only way to get her was over the car. By the time I got into the garage she was in the house with the door locked. I went back out in the front yard to get my pistol outta the rain and the rest of my other soggy stuff as well. I never got to the other stuff because the cops pulled up, saw the pistol in my hand and freaked. The next thing I knew I was cuffed and stuffed and taken downtown.

A bond was set and a bondsman finally showed up early in the morning {2:30-3:00AM early}, the bond was only a thousand dollars, but I didn't have the hundred bucks to cover the bondsman's ten percent, that was the rub. After explaining the situation and an assurance that he'd be paid the following Friday. With some directions to the job site so he could collect his money and the fact that he hated to see anybody in jail on a holiday, he signed the papers and I was free on bail.

He gave me a ride to the end of Judith's street and I walked down to her house. All my shit was still laying all over the lawn {even my pistol}. Now it was a dried up mess and not worth repacking without washing first {ain't gonna happen there though}. As I was throwing, cramming, stuffing everything in my saddlebags Judith came outta the house and stood there so I could ignore her. I just wanted to get the fuck outta there. I couldn't stand that bitch. I pulled Christine out of her resting place between the car and the doorframe {Judith hadn't touched anything once the cops dragged me away}. That was when I realized the ignition switch'd been on all night and the battery was dead as a doornail.

Fuck! That means I'll at least have to talk to this bitch one more time before I'm gone. She opened the hood of her car after I had Christine ready to go. I ran some jumper wires from my battery to hers, fired up my trusty steed and got the fuck outta there.

My first stop was a laundromat where I washed, dried and repacked all my clothes, my sleeping bag and anything else that had to go in a washing machine. While I was doing that I cleaned and oiled my pistol out on the sidewalk like I did it every day. Nobody seemed to even notice.

Once I got all this done I had no place else to go, so I headed out to the jobsite. By the time I got there it was pitch black except for a little bit of star light. I unpacked after my eyes got used to the lack of light. Made a little camp on the slab. Bed down for the night and slept like the dead.

The next day was a Sunday, no one showed up all day. I had the whole place to myself so I did some exploring. The road to the house dead ended at the Rio Grande River. I took a quick dip to cool off and headed back to the site. The solitude was exhilarating. It was the first time I'd ever been completely alone in my life, I loved it.

Finally late in the afternoon hunger drove me into town to this little bar that served food and ice cold Bud. Don and Chris told me about this place because it was right on the outside of town if you were coming from our end. Bottom line the food was good and fast and the beer was cold. What more could you ask for?

Around dark o'clock I headed back to the site. As I idled up what will be a driveway someday a huge rattle snake crawled into the pinion trees that surrounded the site, reminding me to shake out my sleeping bag before I crawled into it. This was a good thing because another one was curled up right on my bed when I walked over to it, he didn't feel like moving either. He was especially pissed when I deftly flipped him out into the yard with one yank on the bag.

That night I slept on Christine using my sleeping bag as a mattress and my poncho liner as a blanket. Again I slept like the dead, waking as the sun lit the sky. I rode to town to get a quick bite for breakfast and was back at the site long before anyone else got there.

Gene got there first and cared not in the least that I'd camped on the slab. If he didn't care I didn't. He did tell me to keep the place clean in case the investors came by to check on the progress. That morning the plumber came by and got the water working. Not long after that the electrician came by and hooked up the juice, now we're cookin' with gas!

That night after work instead of riding down to the river for a cold dip I stood right there on the side porch and took a shower with the garden hose. When I got back to the site later that night it was only dark till I turned the light on, which will attract all the kissing bugs in the area {not a good thing}if left on too long. The bite of a kissing bug is at least ten times more annoying than a mosquito, but if you're allergic it can throw you into anaphylactic shock and you can die in minutes. You don't even know if you're allergic to 'em till you're bitten, better to never find out. Kissing bugs are attracted by light , but like dark places to hide in, like the folds of a blanket or sleeping bag, always a good idea to shake out any bedding before you crawl into it indoors or out .

By the end of that week most of the roof on that part of the house was framed and sheeted so we'd have a place to take a break outta the sun during the work day and I had a roof over my head at night.

One night while I slept a thunder storm snuck up on me. It woke me with a thunderclap so loud I thought the world exploded. That was pretty scary 'cause it seemed like I was right in the middle of the storm. Sante Fe is seven thousand feet above sea level and the site was a couple hundred feet above that. Those storms don't have much ground clearance at that altitude. When the lightning lights everything around you with that eerie bluish green glow in the wee hours of the morning and rain whips you from all directions at once with the force of a load of buckshot {at least it feels that way}, you begin to envy people's warm, dry houses.

Just as quickly as it comes it's gone, then you're left with a stillness like the world is saying "holy shit what was that?" When the sun came up that morning everything that wasn't packed in a saddle bag was soaked including my bed, which I wasn't too happy about.

The sun'd barely broken the horizon when I heard the now familiar sound of Gene's pickup flying up the road. He slid to a stop out front, jumped out and hollered my name. I answered him with an annoyed sounding "what" and walked out into view.

He asked if I was all right.

I said "yah, why wouldn't I be?" He just shook his head, laughed and packed a bowl, by the time Don and Chris got there we were so wasted I didn't wanna work and it took me most of the morning to get my ass in gear and wanna get something done.

By nine all the soaked stuff was bone dry again. Everything was back to normal including me and work was going as always. Lift this, move that, stack this, set this up, tear this down, the usual stuff a laborer does at a job site. I liked the job I'd lucked into and living on the site was pretty cool too. Especially when we had a storm like last night. I wondered what the rich folks that buy this multi-million dollar home will think the first time something like that rolls thru that little valley, up the hill and blasts 'em outta bed in the middle of the night. At least they'll have walls to keep that buckshot like rain off 'em.

One afternoon during that same week my bondsman showed up to inform me that the charges'd been dropped by the court because Judith wouldn't sign a complaint, but I still owed him a hundred dollars for my bond. I told him I got paid on Friday around 3:00PM. Gene verified this and he went away. He was back on Friday, took half my pay for the week and went away happy. I wasn't so thrilled, but I was free without any future worries. I probably should 'a thanked Judith for that. Fuck that she started the shit.

Life was going pretty good. I hadn't used any speed for almost months now and felt great about it. My energy was back; the major reason to continue using is that speed wrings all of your natural energy outta ya. In order to be able to continue with everyday life you have to continue using. Like heroin there comes a time in a speed freak's life when crank becomes a maintenance drug and use is necessary just to get through the day, the longer the use, the longer and harder the recovery.

I enjoyed my job, worked with some pretty good guys and everything was going along right on schedule. Around the end of the first week {Thursday I think} the vigas and latias were delivered. They're usually not delivered until a day or two before they're set because of their value and the amount of time it takes to replace 'em if they're stolen, which was a very common practice amongst the contractors in the area, something I didn't learn until later.

The next day dawned with the clouds laying right on the ground and a damp chill permeated the air. About the time we started working it started raining and continued all day. By now my little corner of the slab was pretty well enclosed so the only thing getting wet was Christine. We hung around the slab most of the morning waiting for the rain to break, but it never did. By late morning the towel was thrown in and the beer and the bowl was broken out, we sat around and got high for a while, then everybody split and I was left by myself for the weekend.

I enjoyed the solitude and the beauty of the site. That weekend I hung out at the site reading, relaxing and getting high. Only going into town to eat and socialize for a little while each day. I brought a girl up to the site for the night that week. That was a hassle; I had to go into town too early to take her home instead of sleeping in. I never did that again.

I spent most of the time at the site because I didn't have much money and didn't feel like blowing what I had. Pretty soon I'd be moving on and I'd need all the money I could get for that.

Saturday dawned with blazing sunshine and a cloudless sky. I packed up early and went to town to do laundry and have some breakfast. After that I got enough canned stuff to last until Monday afternoon so I wouldn't have to go anywhere the rest of the weekend once I got back to the site. Along with food I got a couple 'a magazines to read and headed up the hill.

Sunday was even prettier than Saturday. All I did was lay around and read. About midmorning I heard a pickup truck rattling up to the site so I got up and walked into the shade of the sheeted garage and stood in the shadows.

The truck pulled up, two guys started to get out that I didn't recognize. About the time their first foot was reaching the ground I stepped outta the shadows and they scrambled back as if they'd seen a monster. I stood there pistol in hand reading their license plate number over and over to myself as they tore away from the site. I went back to reading and nodded off in the sun.

Sometime later that day the same rattle woke me up. This time I had some fun. When they were a couple 'a steps from the truck a piece I shot the hood ornament off the front of the truck from my hiding place in the garage. You'd think I shot one of them the way they scrambled. The driver took off without his passenger completely in the truck. The guy held onto the door until the truck's momentum and a prickly pear cactus took his feet out from under him. He fell smack on his face in the prickly pear and rocks around it. That was when I shot the back window outta truck. The driver floored it and almost ran over his buddy. The fishtailing pickup careened wildly outta sight with his bleeding buddy running for what he thought was his life screaming at the top of his lungs for him to stop. I had a good laugh as I walked back to my camp and sat down to clean my pistol.

Later that evening I rode into town for a beer, instead of going to my usual haunt I went to a place where most of the woodworkers in town went, out of curiosity. Sure enough in the parking lot was a red windowless Ford pickup with the hood ornament missing. I entered and ordered a beer. Sitting across the bar from me were two guys. One with a nose brace on, his face and chest all torn up and scabbed over like he'd been drug over a cactus by a pickup truck or something.

I absently eased around the bar to get closer and listened in as they talked to a third and forth dude about their near death experience. The driver swore up and down that he was being shot at from all sides and nose brace was complaining because he had to let go right into a prickly pear cactus and he still hadn't been able to get all the spines out. Sometimes it takes years for 'em to come out I still have some in my elbow from 1991.

I couldn't help laughing out loud when I heard this and saw how torn up he was. The four looked at me like they were ready to fight. I broke that ice by telling 'em that for a thousand dollars I'd go wherever they said and take care of the assholes that did that to 'em. They immediately felt the need to recount the entire story to me including the gunfire coming from all sides and the hail of gunfire they escaped from as they left.

When I said the gunmen couldn't've been very good shots if all they got was a window and a hood ornament. They looked kinda' sheepish and explained that they were carpenters not killers, so they didn't know if it was good or bad.

When they asked me what I did, I told 'em I was a hired killer for a motorcycle club and was on my way to Colorado to kill a chapter of the same club for fuckin' up and pissin' the rest of the club off. They just about shit their pants right where they stood, they turned as white as sheets. When I asked if they belonged to that club or knew someone who did, I thought I was gonna have to catch the closest one when he nearly fainted.

I finally got around to asking what prompted all the gunfire.

They said they had no idea; they were just driving by {the road dead ends at the Rio Grande River} the place on the way to church {not one church anywhere near there} that morning when they were opened up on. I expressed my sympathy to these God-fearing church goers and told 'em if they changed their minds I'd be there a few beers longer and drifted away.

The next morning I told the crew about the fun I'd had. Turns out that the would-be thieves were actually Gene's neighbors {the ones who had the party I mentioned earlier}. He'd seen the shot up pickup truck and spoken to the owner on the way to work that morning. We all had a good laugh and went to work setting the vigas and latias. By the end of the day the hardest part of the framing job was done and I was sucking up bees with the shop vac for something to do.

After work that day we were sitting around getting high and laughing about the day before when Gene told me about the problems contractors faced when building with vigas and latias. Something that rich homebuilders almost always want in the million dollar homes that he builds.

Jokingly I said I should start a business as a lumber guard and keep the Lodgepole pines safe for the industry. Maybe I should've, life in New Mexico sure was nice and I bet it'd've been even nicer with a house to live in.

With the vigas and latias set I could take off all weekend long now. I just had to be back at the site on Monday. I thought I could handle that little bit of responsibility. The following weekend Chris invited me down to his house for the weekend. Of course I accepted. When we finished work on Friday I threw some things in Donnie's van and followed 'em south through town past the state prison and on down Highway 14 into the heart of the Tijeras Mountains.

Madrid

Madrid {pronounced MADrid} was originally a conscription mining town. The owner had discovered a rich coal deposit in a little valley not much bigger than two football fields {a real blink-n-ya missed it kinda' place} in the middle of the Tijeras Mountains between Sante Fe and Albuquerque on Highway 14 {The Turquoise Trail}.

A conscription town meant that the owner of the mine and his henchmen'd go to the bars in outlying towns like Sante Fe, Las Vegas N.M.{the deadliest town in the old west}, Albuquerque, Raton, Sonora, Trinidad, Sante Rosa, Tucumcari and put mickies in peoples drinks, when they woke up they'd either already be in Madrid or chained to a wagon taking 'em there.

Once there they were held as captives and forced at the end of a whip to work the mine. They were paid in mad money that could only be spent at the general store or the local saloon. Escape was next to impossible, first off cause you had no idea where you were. Next if you did get outta town you most assuredly died in the desert surrounding it. Life as a slave was far more preferable than burning up in the desert.

Another reason was Madrid Dogs these dogs where like the proverbial Hounds of the Baskervilles, they were huge, the size of a Great Dane with the build of a Mastiff, solid black with golden eyes and they wandered the streets at will. These dogs were particular to the town. I've never seen 'em anywhere else. The first time I saw one was the day Chris brought his to work, he and I hit it off instantly and by the end of the day we were big buddies, that was just a few days before I was invited for the weekend.

I was told by several of the town's people that these dogs'd been bred by the original owner of Madrid to hunt down runaways back in the conscription days and now they're a permanent fixture in the town. Nobody owns one they adopt you and keep everything on your place safe including your other pets and kids from coyotes, cougars and anything else that might seek to do you and yours harm. You could sleep with your doors open at night, wander the town in the dark, drunk, always protected by these dogs if they liked you.

Chris had a pack of Blue Healers as pets and a Madrid Dog for protection. I couldn't tell his dog from the others in town, but it seemed to me once you were in with one you were in with all of 'em.

One night I drank way too much in the Mine Shaft Tavern and passed out in the parking lot on Christine. I awoke in the darkness in the middle of the night because I had to piss like a race horse. When I put my foot down to stand up I bumped something big and black as the night itself, a pair of golden eyes looked up at me from the dark, I reached down and patted a massive black head and said "sorry bud." The eyes blinked their acquiescence. When I walked a little distance into the bushes he followed me, stood guard while I did my thing and flopped back down next to Christine when I flopped down on top of her. We both heaved a sigh and passed out again.

The next morning we woke with the sun. When I stood up he did too. I sat down on Christine and pulled him close in a bear hug, kissed his huge black head between the eyes and scratched and petted him all over. He soaked this up like a gigantic black sponge and gave me one big lick on the face with his pink and black tongue. "Let's go home big boy" I said as I kicked Christine to life and pointed her towards Chris's.

When I rolled into Chris's driveway a few minutes later a huge black shape laying in front of the door raised it's head and a thick black tail thumped a greeting on the stoop as I walked up. Chris's dog'd been in that spot all night. I could tell by the warmth of the stoop and believe me I checked as I was repeating the greeting that I'd given to whom I thought was he a few minutes earlier in the parking lot of the bar.

If he'd been there all night, who had my bodyguard been that night? Anyone of the dozens of dogs that roamed at will and adopted whoever at will, for life or just a few hours. That would have to be my guess.

When I walked through the door I got slapped in the nose with the smell of breakfast on the stove and coffee in the cup. I sat down, Chris looked up and said "too much fun?"

Bleary eyed and still half drunk I replied "not enough." We both laughed, then I told him about my bodyguard.

He looked at me with a "yah so" look on his face and when I was finished his ole'lady said "you're in" from the stove and that was the end of the discussion.

Modern day Madrid was a wild little place in itself, with five witch sects and a curious group of inhabitants. Passing through as a tourist you don't get to see the crazy shit that goes on there. Unless you happened to be sitting at the Swiss Miss Café when a coven of witches walked by and disappeared right before your eyes, only to reappear a little ways down the street. I was so engrossed with the place that I spent my last two weekends there before I left New Mexico.

My first weekend in Madrid I converted some real money to mad money, kind-of-a when in Rome thing and proceeded to get to know the town one beer at a time. New Mexico has some of the most gorgeous weather of anyplace I've ever been. So much so that you hate to be indoors at all. Very soon I found myself drinking out on the veranda, watching the tourist traffic go by and the whole town come and go {the Mine Shaft Tavern is pretty much the hub of Madrid, almost all the locals pass thru there in the course of a day}. As they came and went some would stop and talk, but others would hurry past this wild lookin' thing sittin' there sippin' a Bud on the porch.

Pretty soon a battered VW van pulled into the far end of the parking lot, set up a table and put some rocks of all different sizes on display there. Being the nosey bastard that I am it wasn't long before I was down there talking to the hippie that was attending the table. His name was Chris {another Chris} and the rocks were geodes. Geodes are spherical rocks that when cut open reveal almost perfectly formed crystals inside, some are amethyst and some are quartz, all are unique and beautiful.

Chris had a partner named William. We never had a conversation because he had what they now call social anxiety disorder, back then he was just unbelievably shy. After several weekends of hanging with Chris and being in William's general vicinity he'd smile and nod to me and mumble hello under his breath, but that was pretty much as far as we ever got. Chris was a fountain of information on the other hand and the salesman of the pair.

Chris explained that he and his partner would scour the desert for geodes, bring 'em back to their shop, saw 'em in half, polish the face of each half and sell 'em to tourists. That was the normal side of Chris's life, the other side got more and more bizarre as his story unfolded.

I have to explain here that in order to learn about life from life itself you have to keep a more than open mind, you have to accept the unacceptable and comprehend the incomprehensible. Real life is not what you learn in books. Reality is what you see with your eyes, feel with your hands, hear with your ears and process with your brain. If you limit yourself to conventional thought and never look outside the box you miss the things that make this world the truly spectacular place it is.

I consider myself one of the most fortunate of human beings to've experienced all the things I have and still be here to tell you about 'em. I have to remind you that during this period I'm writing about I was using no heavy drugs of any kind and all the experiences that I'm relating are as real as you getting up and going to work in the morning with no embellishment of any kind whatsoever. When I get to places that are hallucinations I'll let you know. For now everything that happened in Madrid is fact and reported to you exactly as my eyes, ears and senses reported 'em to me.

Chris was the one who pointed all these things out to me. He showed me the witch covens and all the otherworldly things that went on in Madrid as a course of everyday life, both white and black {good and evil}. Life in this sequestered little wild west town was wilder than anything you could ever imagine or hallucinate.

The first day I met Chris we hung out outside the Mine Shaft Tavern and talked about the little town we were in all day. It was fascinating hearing the history of the town and all the places in it. While we were talking a pack of Madrid Dogs walked by and gave Chris the evil eye, they bristled as their lips curled back to display huge fangs that could rip anything to ribbons in seconds. He warned me to stay away from 'em for fear of my life. I told him we were buddies, walked over amongst 'em and began to pet each one and talk to 'em. Their tails wagged as we talked and they each licked my hand or arm and then one by one they wandered away.

The main street through town was Highway 14. From where I was standing I could see a long ways in each direction. As they wandered away Chris said something and I looked at him. I looked immediately back in the direction of the dogs and they'd vanished from sight. I was at a loss; Chris saw the dumbfounded look on my face and that began the tale.

Chris was a novice white witch, he wasn't accomplished enough to be accepted into either one of the white covens in town and the black covens hated him simply for being white and a novice at that. Seems they'd have brought him into their folds novice or not if he'd chosen black, but he'd chosen the white road. The display I'd just witnessed was their daily disapproval show, seems none of those dogs'd been dogs. They were witches projecting the illusion of being dogs to get a point across to Chris. A point that they pushed at him each day he was there.

He told me that the baseball diamond on the north end of town wasn't really a diamond at all, it was a pentagram that all five sects used in their rituals. Part of the reason he was hated was that he also had to use that same pentagram for his rituals which interfered with every other sects use. Certain rituals had to be timed right and if he was there when they needed to be, it posed a problem. Basically being the novice he was also the trespasser.

He said the way they kept him from going to the ball field was with the Madrid Dogs. Every time he'd start in that direction on foot the dogs'd take out after him appearing from nowhere and chase him back to the VW. To prevent this from happening he taught himself to disappear. As he was telling me this I noticed that I was beginning to see thru him until he was completely gone. He was still talking, but he was fuckin' gone. Slowly he materialized just like he'd disappeared all the while continuing with his explanation.

Now even back then I considered myself pretty open-minded, but that was more than the most open mind could handle or maybe not. Chris explained that he actually hadn't gone anywhere. Through a form of hypnosis he'd projected the illusion of disappearance into my consciousness. I'd seen the illusion not the reality. He went on to explain that, that was pretty much the basis for all magic {white and black}.

After his display I needed a cold beer and the time it'd take to drink it to absorb all that'd just transpired. I didn't disbelieve him, this was all just news to me is all.

When I came outta the bar with a beer for each of us Chris was helping a tourist pick out a geode and some dude was checking out Christine from a respectful distance. I put Chris's beer in the shade by the VW nodding to William at the same time. He smiled slightly, that was better than the first time anyway. I walked over to the bike and its onlooker. As I walked up he said I needed a set of saddlebags. The ones I'd been given by a friend when I left California were pretty raggedy and falling apart. I agreed, he handed me a card that read Mineshaft Leatherworks on it and we started talking.

By the time we were done I had the measurements for the hides I'd need to get at the tannery in Albuquerque the following Saturday. We'd decided on a price and I'd already paid the cash part, the rest was weed and beer.

When I got done with the leather dude I went back to Chris, who was sitting in the shade drinking his beer. As I walked over I noticed five Madrid Dogs standing up the street staring intently at him as if they were choosing their steak for lunch. I asked him what was up. He said in about an hour he was going to the pentagram to perform a ritual and they were there to stop him.

I asked what he was gonna do. He said he couldn't say because he had to keep his mind clear so they couldn't read his thoughts. All of this sounded just a little farfetched to me. Chris looked at me and said "its not farfetched, you have to keep an open mind or you'll never learn." I hadn't said a fuckin' word. Beyond stunned I shot Chris a look. He laughed, rose and said he'd be back soon. With that he walked behind the bar.

I sat down in his chair to watch traffic go by. A few minutes later I felt someone next to me. Expecting Chris I was surprised to find William there. When I looked up he nodded up the street. I looked and way up the street was Chris walking toward the ball field. The Madrid Dogs were still staring intently at the back of the bar waiting for Chris. I started laughing and turned to speak to William. He was gone. The dude was fuckin' creepy that's all I can say about him, cool, but creepy.

I went in and got another beer. Came out and sat back down in Chris's chair to watch the cactus grow. I had that feeling again, started to turn and there was William's hand with a Jamaican styled spliff in it {a spliff is a joint shaped kinda' like a cone}. I took it, nodded up at him and he walked away.

I don't know what was in that spliff, but I woke up some time later with Chris nudging my shoulder. William was standing behind him grinning, my beer was warm as piss and undrunk and only one hit smoked off the spliff. We had a good laugh about it as we lit it and passed it between the three of us. I have no idea what I did at the bar that night.

I woke up on Christine sometime in the early morning hours with a Madrid Dog lying next to me like before. I wandered to a bush, got rid of some beer and laid back down. The next time I awoke it was to the smell of bacon cooking and the sun was almost all the way up over the mountains that rimmed the little valley that Madrid was in.

I followed my nose into the bar and found the bartender at the grill cooking a huge breakfast that looked like it'd feed a dozen. When I staggered in, she looked up and said she was glad I was still alive. When she said that I checked my pockets to see how broke I was. Surprisingly enough I had more money than I started with {don't ask me how that happened} and another pocketful of wooden mad money.

I went in the men's room and threw my face at some water. It took three tries to hit it, but it sure felt good when it finally got there. I looked in the mirror and found out why the water felt so good. I was sunburnt to beat the band from passing out in Chris's chair the day before.

I walked into the bar and the bartender laughed when she saw my face, "I bet that stings" she said and chuckled. She motioned me to a table and brought me out a platter not a plate, a platter of chorizo and eggs, fried potatoes, bacon and toast with a gigantic Bloody Jerry {beer and V-8 or tomato juice} to wash it all down.

I felt a whole lot better after I finished breakfast. In fact other than my broiled face I felt pretty good. When I walked my dishes into the kitchen there wasn't a soul in the place, but the back door was open. The bartender was out back cutting the tip of a leaf off a cactus. The leaves of this cactus looked like giant spikes with little spikes down each side.

She came inside and squeezed some faintly greenish goop onto her hand and wiped it on my forehead immediately cooling the fire. This was my introduction to the Aloe Cactus, one of God's little miracles.

With the fire out and a cold beer I went outside to enjoy the morning on the veranda. It wasn't long before the old VW was coming down the street and Chris and William were set up for another day. Chris suggested we go over to the Swiss Miss for coffee. The Swiss Miss is an outdoor café right on Main Street and a very cool little place to relax in the New Mexican morning air and socialize.

I was sitting facing the street, so I was the first one to see the five white robed figures coming down the street. I nodded in their direction and Chris looked. He turned back to me and said "watch this."

As they neared the corner of the white picket fence that bordered the grass patio we sat on they began to fade into invisibility as Chris'd done the day before. Everyone coming out of the general store across the street, walking around on the sidewalks and sitting at the Swiss Miss was as dumbfounded as I was the day before and stood as if glued in place by what they'd just seen. In a minute or two just beyond the other end of the fence, they all began to materialize back into view and continue solemnly up the street, never breaking stride or acknowledging the public around them.

It almost looked as if they were levitating not walking {they probably were, according to Chris}. The looks of wonder on all who saw this, slack jawed and bug-eyed made me laugh out loud, breaking the spell on everyone around us. The buzz from the people around us was the only thing you could hear as they quietly exchanged their disbeliefs on what'd just occurred.

Chris took that moment to tell me not to party too hard that night because something spectacular was in the offing for the night to come. I asked him repeatedly throughout the day what was gonna happen, but all he'd say was "you'll see"....."you'll see."

The rest of the day I hung out with Chris, talked to the leather guy and turned down every offer of another spliff from William. At each refusal he'd just smile to himself and walk away. No wonder the guy never spoke, he had to be paralyzed from the neck up smoking that shit.

I asked Chris what it was. He told me it was something that William grew himself and it was very rare that he shared it with anyone, but he liked me and that was his way of showing it. I told him a handshake would be less dangerous and when I said that a roar of laughter came from the front of the van where William was tinkering with something. A second later William walked up, wiped his hands on his camo trousers and stuck out his right hand. We shook hands heartily like old friends, both of us grinning like long lost buddies. Not a word was spoken by either of us, but the smiles dancing in our eyes bespoke a bond that time or distance would never erase.

That evening after the tourists had gone for the day the real show started with a procession of black and white robed groups seemingly flowing up and down the main street of Madrid in an arcane waltz of good and evil.

As the groups flowed past each other, bolts of colored lightning would shoot out from the faceless hooded forms into the opposing faction. Returned in kind by the recipients. Individual combatants would peel off from sects and engage in macabre dances simulating combat, yet never physically touch each other. Lightning would pass between them like blows being thrown by boxers. Each recoiling and retaliating until they would disappear and blow away on the wind like colored wil-o-the-wisps.

Chris explained to me that this whole battle was over the right to be the first to use the ball field, which I thought was just a little bit on the childish side. I wasn't a witch so I didn't really grasp the importance of the ball field, I was just enjoying the show.

After all the combatants had melted away in wisps of smoke the real battle started in earnest above our heads. From the mountain tops that rimmed the valley containing Madrid, bolts of lightning of all different colors shot across the valley from all different sides to all different sides. Sometimes they collided in the middle with a deafening boom, showering the valley with colored sparks, lighting the whole valley with an eerie glow momentarily, then plunging the whole place into a darkness that seemed to swallow all the light in the valley like a black hole.

The spectacle culminated at exactly midnight with bolts of red, blue, green, yellow, orange, purple and pink lightning colliding in the air over the center of the valley with a thundering boom that shook the ground we stood on. Then a column of light comprised of all those colors like an electric rainbow shot straight up into the air like a psychedelic comet until it was outta sight.

With that a stillness crept over the valley that seemed like it'd be a crime to break by making any sound at all. I sat stock still for quite some time as did everyone around me. The phone in the bar broke the silence. It was a dude named Richard who owned Poor Richard's Camel, kind-of-a restaurant but it was in his house just a ways up Main Street almost to the ball field {you could see the ball field through the trees from his front yard}. He called to say he was cooking breakfast for everyone who showed up.

En masse everyone wandered up the street in little groups quietly mumbling amongst themselves. When we got to Richard's the whole place was dark on the outside. As we neared the door, it was thrown open and a subdued light from regular old incandescent lights shot out into the drive which was somehow kind of relieving after the spectacle I'd just seen.

Once inside no one placed an order. It was kind-of-a chow line deal you walked by and stuck your plate out for whatever you wanted which me being me was everything and lots of it {too much is never enough}.

While I was eating, the hair on my neck stood straight up like it was full of electricity and my skin started to crawl. I looked at Chris who was bent over his plate shoveling, it was like he felt my gaze cause he stopped and looked me dead in the eyes. At that moment his eyes were black holes, like a dead mans. Our eyes locked for a moment then he went back to his plate.

I inexorably left my plate and went to a window facing the ball field. From around the edge of the blanket that blacked out the window a bluish white glow was getting brighter and brighter. When I went to move the blanket aside the person closest to me quietly said "don't do that."

I left the window and sat back down, took a few bites and swallowed. I wasn't interested in food anymore, like a moth to a flame I had to see what that glow was. As I walked to the door everything inside stopped. When I walked thru it outside I got a weird feeling, like electricity coming in my ass and traveling up my spine. When the door closed behind me the darkness wasn't the same as when we arrived. I walked around the corner of the house to get a view of the ball field.

In the center of the pentagram that made up the diamond a number of glowing white robed figures were seemingly levitating a few feet off the ground and spinning slowly in a circle. All robes flowing in the same direction. Under the glowing hoods there were no faces, blackness as deep as the cosmos was all I could see. A droning chant was coming from everywhere and nowhere. As the drone increased in volume the altitude of the circling figures got higher and higher and the light got brighter and brighter. The drone rose in a crescendo. At the height of this each white robed being shot in its own direction from the circle into the sky and seemingly took a place amongst the stars overhead.

When the circle broke the silence was deafening and the darkness absolute. I stood like I was made of stone for I don't know how long. Suddenly I felt someone at my elbow. Chris said in an odd kind of hollow voice "you have a power in you." I turned to him and his previously black hole eyes had a faint glow to them that quickly faded when our eyes met. I turned to go back inside, but the door was locked.

"Come on" was all Chris said. As we walked down Main Street the sky was lightening with false dawn. Neither of us said a word all the way to the bar, we didn't even look at each other, we just trudged along side by side. I felt like I weighed a ton and my feet felt like blocks of lead. When I got to Christine I flipped my lead weighted leg over her and flopped backwards into the seat, laid back against the gas tanks and was out like a light.

When I awoke it was full daylight and Chris's van was gone. I'd never even heard it go, the doors to the bar were locked. Nothing moved on the streets, not even a dog. I stood in the bright New Mexican silence wondering what the fuck had happened the night before and what the hell was going on now. The place was like a ghost town, not even the usual tourist traffic was moving. Birds weren't even singing which was really odd because if you knew anything about Magpies, you'd know they never shut up and they're everywhere out west. Darkly iridescent green and white flashes of yakking activity from sunrise to sunset, hell they even mumble in their sleep.

After I don't know how long I turned and spoke to Christine, scaring the shit outta myself with the sound of my own voice. I kicked the old girl to life and got the fuck outta there as fast as she'd take me, tearing the silence in two like a jet through the sound barrier.

I tore up 14 towards Sante Fe like the devil himself was on my back fender. Not even slowing down till the state prison outside of town came into view. I stopped at the little bar on the north side of town closest to the jobsite and had a beer or two to wash the dust outta my throat. I got a sixer to go, stopped and got a couple 'a burritos to go and headed to the safety of the jobsite.

When I got there some people were walking around looking at the site and the construction so far. As I idled down the road towards 'em I could tell that they weren't there to steal anything because they'd've had to get their hands dirty and you could tell by looking at 'em that never happened.

When I got closer, one of the men walked out to the road. I idled by him nodding to him as I did and parked Christine in the shade, dismounted smoothly {kinda' showin' off} and sauntered over to him all in one motion. He stuck out his hand and said "Dave?" I nodded and shook his hand. He introduced himself as one of the investors that was building the house. I thought oh boy here it comes, the we don't want you staying here anymore speech.

He took me over and introduced me to the rest of the folks in the group. One was his wife and the other couple was the people that were buying the house. They were very cordial to an obviously untamed looking thing like me. When we walked inside and I took my shades off, they caught a glimpse of the casual intensity in my eyes and stepped back a little bit especially the women.

The first guy began explaining to the buyers how I'd saved 'em several hundred thousand dollars and a major setback by keeping the vigas and latias from being stolen. Without going into all the details of shooting up the would be thieve's pickup {I don't think he knew that part}. He explained to 'em how that kind of theft happens all the time and really puts a screeching halt on a job, causing all kinds of problems and setbacks.

Tiring of all the palaver I excused myself and went to the other side of the site and busied myself with some useless thing on Christine. I'd parked her amongst some pinion trees and when I walked around on the opposite side of her I heard the now familiar rattle of my closest and most trusted neighbor, a five foot long diamond back rattler.

He was coiled under the base of the closest pinion tree in the shade and was just telling me he was there {most rattlers are pretty good about that, except for the Mojaves, they'll chase ya}. He hadn't even raised his head yet, I think he'd gotten used to me. We encountered each other almost every day once or twice a day. He was the one I flipped off my sleeping bag when I first moved up there.

I was tired of these folks hanging around {I wanted to take a shower in the hose and well you know}. I got an idea and my diamond backed buddy was gonna help. With the help of a forked stick I soon had him by the neck, his body coiling and uncoiling around my arm, rattling like the pissed off snake I knew he'd be.

He was a beauty, I'll give him that and he was putting on one hell of a show. I walked out from behind the trees into the sight of the group. The women gasped, one dude said "oh my God" and they all headed for their cars.

As they were flinging gravel to get outta there before the snake got 'em I set him down in the driveway, where he promptly coiled and struck as to if to say "we had a deal motherfucker." I was well outta reach, but the chickens in the cars driving away got an eyeful of pissed off striking snake as they retreated.

I said my thanks to my neighbor as he headed back to his pinion tree and took my nice cold shower. After that I put on clean cloths, had a burrito and drank my beers as the sun slowly sank over the Jemez Mountains in the west.

The next day Donnie and Chris were first at the jobsite. When Chris walked up all he said was "had enough yet" and walked on by. Donnie looked at me quizzically and laughed at something he thought was funny.

I was looking forward to Gene showing up and packing the pipe, but by the time he got there I was hustling scaffolding, plywood and lumber. That went on all morning without a break; we only took as much time as it took to eat lunch and then back to work. Chris'd been in a foul mood all day as he was want to be at times. About two o'clock I found out why. He and Donnie had to leave because he had to go to a hearing about his driver's license. He'd gotten a drunk driving some time earlier and now that it was time to get his license back the state was giving him a hassle. I hate it when that happens. I've never had a DUI, but I've had my license suspended for all kinds of other shit and there's always some last minute bullshit to deal with before they'll give it back.

After Chris and Donnie left, Gene and I sat down in the shade and got high. He told me about the buyer's reactions to my neighbor and I the day before. We had a laugh because the buyers didn't think there were any snakes in the area.

This was wild desert before the slab got poured, with coyotes, rattlers, lizards and scorpions everywhere, they still were. For the most part they stayed away from the heavily traveled areas, but a few feet away from those travel areas there was a rattler under every few bushes. All different kinds of lizards scurried everywhere, a couple 'a different kinds of scorpions were around; coyotes visited the place nightly and were always howling in the distance.

That's why I liked it; it was high desert camping with running water and electricity. You couldn't really use the lights much at night otherwise you'd be inundated with kissing bugs in no time, their bites hurt at the very least. I liked that about the west, everything out there bites or stings even the plants, but it's all on the ground. No mosquitoes flying in your face and biting the shit outta ya all the time {Ahhhh hates musquitoes}.

The week flew by as work on the house was nearing completion; the biggest part of my job now consisted of hustling scaffolding around the site, which was definitely a pain in the ass. Friday came soon enough and bright and early Saturday I was headed to the hide exchange in Albuquerque, I got my hides and rode up to the square near the university.

Every old west town has a square, in the horse travel days that was where you parked your wagons and watered and fed your stock when you got to town. Everything was built around the square and all roads led to it. That made it easy to find no matter where you came from.

I had a beer and a burger and headed for Madrid. When I got there the leather dude was in his shop and we went to work. I didn't have much to do but supervise, so I drifted between the leather shop and the bar.

For whatever reason the barmaid wasn't as friendly as the weekend before, so I didn't linger, not to mention the summers in New Mexico aren't conducive to staying indoors for long, it's just too nice. I wandered from the veranda back to the bar, to the leather shop, back to the bar all day.

I'd paid the money and beer part of my bill at the leather dudes, but the weed part would have to wait until the next weekend. I just couldn't find any, Gene was the only other smoker I knew besides William and he and Chris were nowhere to be seen. I wouldn't give anybody any weed that I got from William anyway I'd be afraid the shit'd kill 'em. It did a number on me and I ain't no lightweight, not that I'd even ask him.

Leather dude was busting ass on these bags, they were huge. You can see a full on side shot of these bags if you can find a copy of EasyRiders, In the Wind # 19. Christine, myself and a young lady {at the time she was 19} whom you'll soon meet are the ones on the cover, the only ones. The picture was taken outside Sturgis S.D. less than a month after the bags were made.

I kicked around the Mine Shaft Tavern all weekend, took a ride up to Chris's house to see how his hearing turned out. As usual worse than you can ever expect with something like that, a shitload more money on top of the shitload of money he'd already paid and he'd be driving again. This really sucked, that's why I consider myself more lucky than smart, it's not that I've never driven drunk or not been caught driving drunk, I've just never been prosecuted.

I've been stopped when I was so drunk that I had to hang onto the cop and his car at the same time to keep from falling on my ass and they let me go. One time I fell right over my motorcycle just trying to sit down on it, they still let me go. They probably figured I'd kill myself and they wouldn't have to deal with me anymore.

That was then and this is now, with the penalties the way they are and the wisdom of age being what it is. I have a hard time doing anything that stupid anymore. Life doesn't have quite the kick it used to, but I don't wake up in jail anymore either.

I kinda' got off the track there a little bit, anyway I didn't hang around Chris's very long he wasn't in the best mood and I couldn't blame him. I headed back to the bar and the leatherworks. When I got there he had one side done and was hard at work on the other one, he was gonna have 'em done in one weekend. I needed to get some pot to seal the deal with, but where?

Sunday afternoon the bags were done. I ended up giving him another case of beer to seal the deal because I couldn't find any weed. I sat and drank a few of his payments with him and headed north to the jobsite early in the afternoon. On my way outta town the old VW rounded the corner headed into town as I was headed out. I turned around and followed 'em to the Mine Shaft; I didn't wanna leave without saying goodbye. I wouldn't be coming back, the job'd be done this week and I'd be movin' on in the opposite direction.

Chris and I talked for a bit, William gave me half a spliff, we said our goodbyes and I was off again. This time there'd be no reason to turn back.

At the jobsite I got all my shit together and sat down to smoke my half a joint, as the sun went down over the Jemez I took a hit. Sometime in the middle of the night I came to freezing my ass off and crawled into my sleeping bag. The next thing I knew Donnie was taping my foot to wake me up. It was nine in the morning. They'd been there for two hours hammering and sawing and fuckin' with me until they began to wonder if I was dead. No matter what they did I hadn't stirred till then.

I jumped up to a chorus of laughter from my three bosses, after a few minutes I was on the job just a little bit more than dazed. To this day I've never smoked anything that did that much damage after just one hit. At lunch I showed Gene how much of the spliff I had left, he said we should try some after work. I didn't reply one way or the other. I had to sit on this idea for a bit, this isn't anything you'd smoke and then try to drive on. I was pretty daring when it came to doing stupid shit like that; I'd driven all over the place when I didn't even have any business walking, but there's no way I'd attempt to drive on this stuff. I don't think you could stay conscious long enough to get in a vehicle, let alone start it anyway.

At the end of the day I asked Gene if he had some papers. The only way I could think to share it with him safely would be to roll a couple 'a pin joints n-give him one to take home. That way at the end of his day he could take a hit, hit the dirt face first like I did and not have anything he still needed to do.

We accomplished this and sat down to smoke a bowl of some less dangerous weed and drink a few beers in the shade of the roof we'd recently finished sheeting. We lingered a little longer than usual because there were only a couple more days of work left. Then I'd be goin' down the road a little reluctantly to whatever lay ahead of me while the other three would move on to their next project after finding another laborer. For the past few afternoons and during the work days the three of them'd tried to talk me into staying. I'd almost considered it more than once, but I was young, dumb, n-fulla cum. I figured I had to move on.

The next day Gene showed up at 11:00AM looking like he'd been drug through a knot hole backwards. I laughed my ass off when he climbed outta his pickup, cause I knew the reason he had that "shot-at-n-missed-n-shit-at-n-hit" look.

It'd happened to me enough times to read all the signs. At least he'd had some warning. When it happened to me I'd walked into it blind and got broadsided by the stuff. When he walked up I couldn't contain myself. All I could say was "I warned ya!" We had a good laugh over it and went back to work. He was about useless the rest of the day, which didn't matter anyway the job was done. All we were doing was cleaning up the site and loading the scaffolding and stuff.

This was done by two in the afternoon and we just hung out for a while socializing. Just about the time we were done working Gene's wife Debbie and their little girl showed up. Quite often Debbie'd stop by in the afternoons to attend the daily cast party, this afternoon she was attending the wrap party.

While we were sittin' there smokin' and drinkin' the four of 'em tried to talk me into sticking around a little longer {hind sight being 20/20, that probably wouldn't've been the worst thing I could've done}, but Sturgis was calling and I was feeling the need for speed.

Being a Taurus I'm as stubborn as they come and once I get an idea in my head you can't drive it out with dynamite. They gave up and we enjoyed the company one last time.

After everyone left I took a shower and put on clean duds. I gathered up everything, went to the laundromat, did laundry and just kinda' rolled around Sante Fe one last time.

It was a good thing I had some of that spliff weed left or I'd've never gotten to sleep that night. The billions of stars in the western sky made an unusually bright display that night as if they too were asking me not leave. I took a small hit off my pin joint, enough to put me to sleep, not paralyze every brain cell and was gone for the night.

Goin'

I woke with the sun and had most everything packed by the time anyone showed up. Donnie gave me the number of a friend of his in Denver that would possibly have some work when I got there. Chris gave me $50 as a bonus. Gene paid me for a full week, even though all we did was fuck off most of the time and a half ounce of weed as a bonus.

While this was going on the investor from the snake incident showed up and expressed his thanks for keeping the job on track with an additional $200. He asked one last time if I wouldn't stay and do the same at the next few places they were gonna build.

I thanked him, pointing to Christine patiently waiting for her queue to skidoo and said I really had to go. We all shook hands. I walked to Christine, kicked her to life and eased out onto what would be a street someday. We got out onto the main road which passed by the back of the site and I cranked on the gas. As I passed by the site we all waved one last time and after a little trip through Sante Fe I was on I-25 headed north.

On the way north I stopped in Las Vegas New Mexico just to see the place. During the days of the wild west, Las Vegas was the most dangerous town in the west. The life expectancy of a stranger who couldn't handle a gun was about three minutes if he had something somebody wanted.

It was a little tamer in the early `80s, but the wild west feel was still there. When I rode down the main drag heads turned and some stared like I was being sized up. I didn't care, back in those days when I was traveling like that I was locked, cocked and ready to rock. My piece was in a shoulder rig under my leather and I'd just as soon shoot you as look at you, especially if you wanted to press any kind of issue. I favored the "shoot first, fuck the questions" approach to personal safety and never giving a sucker an even break kept you alive and healthy a lot longer than being a nice guy. "Nice guys finished in a box" or worse, coyote bait.

After my little detour I jumped on the interstate again. Next stop Raton N.M. for a little gas and a joint. I jumped on the freeway again after the break and hit a little freezing rain going over Raton Pass. That shit feels like thousands of needles hittin' ya in the face simultaneously and the only thing to do is keep on rolling thru it.

When I came down the other side into Trinidad Colorado it was bright sunshine and summertime again. If you don't like the weather where you are out west just ride ten miles and it'll be totally different. For almost the rest of the day I rode in sunshine.

Around late afternoon, when I was getting close to Pueblo Colorado my mirror came loose. As I got closer to Colorado Springs it started to rain. The closer I got the harder it rained. I finally pulled off the road at Fountain Boulevard, into a Seven Eleven parking lot. I tightened my mirror and rolled another joint kinda' waiting for the rain to pass in the gathering darkness.

As I was sitting on Christine smoking my joint a good lookin' little blonde {Valerie} walked up saying "you got problems too?"

"Nope only solutions" I said as she walked past me to the payphone.

She tried a few calls, evidently got no answer, slammed the phone down and walked away in disgust.

As she walked past me I held out the joint and said "problems?" She took a hit, passed it back and explained that her company pickup had died on the freeway just past the Fountain Boulevard overpass and she'd walked down here to call somebody. Being Friday night nobody was home anywhere, not even her folks.

I told her to hop on back we'd go check it out. When we got to the truck the first thing I smelled was fried alternator and the battery was stone dead cause it'd been running on it for quite a while.

I told her I couldn't do anything for the truck, but since it was Friday night we oughta forget the truck and go out partyin'. She said to take her home so she could change and we'd do just that.

While I was in Sante Fe Judith had introduced me to quite a few of the scooter people there during the quest for a carburetor. One in particular was a dude named Jorgee; I'd seen him a few times since our introduction with and without Judith.

Seems there was no love loss for Judith amongst any of the scooter people there. I don't know why, don't care, she was a flake in my book and probably considered worse in theirs. Anyway after the blowout with her I'd visited Jorgee and the guys that hung out at his shop a few times. My northbound attitude had been brought up in a conversation or two and he'd told me that if I stopped in The Springs, to look up a tramp named Puppy, a friend of his who had a shop there.

I asked Valerie if she knew where his shop was.

"On Wasatch" was her answer so we headed there first.

When we were almost there a group of bikes coming toward us lead by a tall redheaded dude motioned to us. Valerie said she thought that was him. They pulled over and I did a Uee and rode back to 'em.

Puppy asked if I was looking for him.

"You Puppy" I asked.

He was, we followed the group to Denny's and grabbed a corner booth so we could all fit.

Once seated I asked Puppy how he knew I was going to his shop. He said no scooters ever came to that part of town, except to see him. We made some introductions all around. There was Puppy and his ole'lady Sheila, Knucklehead Larry, Joe Dandy and of course Valerie and myself in the booth.

When I told Puppy that Jorgee was the one who referred me to him, he asked after him and immediately got even friendlier than before. They thought it was pretty cool that Valerie and I'd just met a few minutes earlier and proceeded to start figuring out where she and I could spend the night after the partying was over.

As soon as that was all worked out we arranged to meet at the Bank Shot, the only bar in town that didn't hassle scooter people. Almost all the bars there had signs saying **"No Motorcycles"**, **"No Leathers"**, **"No Harley stuff"** a real scooter friendly town. I've seen prisons that were friendlier than that. Anyway I took Valerie to her folk's house, where she lived and a few minutes later she was back out and ready to ride.

We met everybody at the Bank Shot and had a pretty good time that night, the best I'd had in a while. I hadn't done much socializing since I'd left California. That night I met pretty much everyone who was anyone in The Springs and had a great time with this gorgeous little blond.

Once the bar closed we all rode over to Joe's, where we were gonna spend the night. We met his roommate Benny whose place it was. We were given the VIP suite and sent to bed.

What Valerie lacked in experience she made up for with great looks and a willing nature. She was naked and ready before I even had my boots off, my kinda' gal. She wasn't quite the caliber of Grace {no one ever has been}, but she was working on it and I had to give her an A for effort.

While we were warming up the wet spot for round two I asked her when she knew she was gonna fuck me {a question on every guys mind during a one night stand}. She said when she was walking up to me at the Seven Eleven. Best answer possible. At that moment I was fuck-struck and pussy whipped all in one fell swoop. All thoughts of Grace vacated my brain and I was living proof that the way to forget one woman was with a hot blonde. This didn't last long though and I kinda' felt like a traitor the next day.

Other than the time I took her to her folk's house to get some cloths we spent the weekend together.

My plan when I left Sante Fe was to work for the two weeks before Sturgis in Denver, get some money and crank in my pocket and up my nose and head for Sturgis. I'd do bike week and blast all the way over to Maine after that. Visit my family and be headed back to California before the weather got cold.

The One-eyed Kidnapper

That'd been the plan Grace and I'd made when we were still in California. I wanted my mom and sister to meet Grace. She had that easygoing one of a kind class about her that my family would've liked. I should've stuck to that plan, had a weekend of fun with Valerie, parted friends and left it at that. No way, the one-eyed idiot in my pants started doing the thinking and before I could stop it, things were coming outta my mouth that shouldn't've.

Sometime that weekend I told Valerie about my plans. She said she'd wanted to go to Sturgis for a while. That was when the wrong head started talking out *my* mouth and I couldn't shut him up. The bad {or good} thing about being a tramp is that all plans can easily fall to the wayside when confronted by a pretty girl and I was the consummate tramp.

All thoughts of the good dope in Denver got pitched and I ran around like some fuck-struck teenager with my dick in my hand thinking of ways to stay up this little blonde's ass.

I should've known better. She had a boyfriend that lived with her in her parent's house that they thought the world of. That weekend he happened to be in Chicago with her brother-in-law, whom he worked with {did I mention that he had a good job and a bright future, unlike me} at an optometrists convention.

When he came home on Tuesday Valerie'd moved in with me at Benny and Joe's and left him high-n-dry {I should've immediately wondered when that would happen to me, cause it wasn't long before it did and more than once in our three years together}.

I'll never understand why God gave men two heads and only enough blood to run one at a time. It seems that the wrong one takes over at the worst possible time and fucks everything up. Happen to you? It's happened to me, hell I used to have pictures of it with captions on the back.

Instead of following my plan I hung around The Springs with my head happily up her cute little ass, pissing away my money until we went to Sturgis on a wing and a prayer. If it hadn't been for meeting Puppy up there hanging out in front of Coast to Coast Hardware we'd have starved to death and never gotten back to The Springs.

The record of this event is on the cover of In the Wind #19 and scattered across a lot of the pages inside, along with the special `84 Sturgis edition of EasyRiders.

We were almost instant celebrities in The Springs. These editions flew off the racks so fast that we almost didn't get copies ourselves.

Three years later when she left me for the bigger better deal she refused to give me any of our memorabilia. She'd become the same selfish bitch that most crankwhores become eventually. The little girl had grown up and become the worthless piece of shit that I knew she'd be the first time she stayed gone for three days and gangbanged the entire construction crew she worked with.

I should've packed up and gone back to California then, but I didn't. I stuck around for a couple more years of abuse, dishing out my own paybacks when the mood struck me. It was a stupid game that I shouldn't've played, but when you constantly think with the wrong head you fuck up a lot.

Back to the story, after Sturgis we got back to The Springs and I figured it'd be easy to get a job, ha! I couldn't buy a job. Try as I might no doors opened for me any time soon. Valerie got a construction job at the Falcon Space Center out on the prairie east of town. One day she didn't come home. Then two days. On the third day I rode out to the site. After hanging around for about forty-five minutes she came walking over and asked me what I wanted. I asked her if she was coming home.

She said she'd be home that night after work; she had to go and walked away.

She finally came home the next night after not going to work the next day along with the half dozen guys she worked with. When she walked into our bedroom at three in the morning. She was drunk, naked, didn't know where her cloths were and had cum running outta her front and rear, around her mouth and down her thighs. I knew then I'd made a big mistake by not movin' on after that first weekend, but I didn't have two nickels to rub together to leave town with by then.

A few weekends later something happened that I hate to this day.

When I met Joe Dandy he was riding the raggedyest Sportster you've ever seen in your life. I immediately nicknamed him Pushstart because of this rattle trap of a bike. This thing had to be seen to be believed. It leaked a small pond of oil every time you parked it, so much that Joe put everybody's used oil in it to keep it lubed. He said it was a waste of money to buy oil for it and I had to agree. It had a notched 4 x 4 wooden block bungee corded to the handlebars for a kickstand. Every fuckin' thing on it was so worn out that it flopped around or wobbled going down the road. You never rode behind him because stuff like exhaust pipes would just fly off at any time.

When this happened we'd all just stop. Joe'd run back and get whatever it was that'd escaped momentarily. Beat it back into shape with a rock or whatever. Pry it, pound it, slip it, slam it back into place and off we'd go until the next piece escaped.

He was always riding along kicking or pounding on something to keep it on the bike or to keep the bike running. This thing looked like an accident that'd found a bunch of places to happen, Joe just wouldn't let 'em. The wheels wobbled. The lights flickered or went out altogether. It flung oil everywhere, it smoked, it backfired, but Joe rode it everywhere he wanted to go and back every day.

We lived on Circle Drive just past Fountain Boulevard in a brick house with a steep downhill driveway about a car length and a half long. He'd launch this thing down the driveway, jump on it and have it running at the bottom of the drive in time to stop on a dime before shooting out into traffic every fuckin' time we left the house. That was the only way the bike could be started, push starting it.

I told you that to tell you this. Valerie hadn't come home one weekend for some reason. By then I was used to it and didn't care, I was just playing her for all I could get by then. We used to go to this country bar on Garden of the Gods Road Sunday afternoons. This girl that hung out there named Terry used to flirt with me when Valerie wasn't around.

This particular afternoon she was looking long and hard in our direction and Joe finally asked her to dance. After a couple 'a dances she got her drink and came over to the table with Joe. He asked her if she wanted to go for a ride. She accepted. We took off and rode up to Castle Rock. She was hanging on to that wobbling fuckin' Sportster for dear life all the way up there. I could tell by the look on her face, this wasn't her idea of fun.

We stopped in Castle Rock and had a few beers. When it was time to leave she followed me outside ahead of Joe who'd bought her the few beers she drank while we were there. She told me she didn't wanna ride back with Joe because she was scared of the bike. I couldn't blame her, but I told her "you'll have to tell him yourself." As she was telling him, he looked at me over her shoulder like "you motherfucker." All I could do was shrug my shoulders, point at the Sporty and shake my head no.

On the way back she started humping my back and nibbling on my ear, things I know Joe wanted to have happening to him. The Sporty died at the Monument exit and we coasted off the freeway into a gas stop there. While Joe was beating the Sporty back into submission and teaching it some new cuss words, Terry was whispering in my ear that we should leave, she was horny, Joe could get the bike running, he'd be alright.

Joe found the magic cuss word or rock or something and got the wayward Sporty running like I'd seen him do a hundred times before in the short period of time I'd known him. I had no intention of leaving him there with a broken scooter, I'd leave her there first no matter how horny she was. We hauled ass for the house and didn't stop for anything till we got there.

Once there Joe busied himself with the Sporty out in the garage and I took Terry in the bedroom, stripped her naked and had my way with her. She was plenty good looking and I had fun with her that night.

The next day I was just riding away from the house with her on the back when Valerie's Continental was turning the corner onto Circle. I took Terry home and never saw her again, I can't remember why. That incident put a riff between Joe and I that I tried to fix by telling him to fuck Valerie sometime. I don't know if he ever did, I sure hope so, if not he was one of the few that didn't.

Sometime soon after that Benny told me if I couldn't pay my rent I'd have to leave. I can't blame him for that, Benny didn't know me from Adam and didn't owe me a fuckin' thing. See what happens when you think with the wrong head? I'd hung out with this little slut until I was stuck with no money and no job basically living on her handouts which weren't enough to get to Pueblo on. I'd fucked myself big time, might as well take advantage of her as long as I could and rake her over the coals as long as possible. I didn't have anything else to do and snow would be flying pretty soon.

Valerie lost her job at the space center almost as soon as she got it because the government shut down The Star Wars Project almost as soon as it started. She got one immediately after that delivering auto parts at a place out on Academy Boulevard. After the bullshit with the construction crew and her taking off for weekends at a time with no word at all, I could give a fuck about her. Now I was just out for all I could get and to make her as miserable as she made me.

We moved outta Benny's to a basement apartment on her parent's side of town. I hung around with Larry, his brother Lance and their friends during the day until she got off from work. Then we'd hit the bars till around nine or ten. Getting fucked up every day was my priority; I could give a shit what she wanted me to do.

Life sucked in that basement. It was definitely made for people that had no intention of bathing. The shower was chest height, at its best just a fast drip. The bathroom was like a refrigerator, especially where the shower was. I had to walk around stooped over or bang my head on pipes, door frames and ceilings in some places.

The other tenants upstairs were college kids and assholes training for the Olympics. These idiots acted like the only thing that mattered in the world was them. At three every morning one of the jerks upstairs would start lifting weights, dropping them on the floor after every set was completed. His weight room floor was our bedroom ceiling.

When I told him this his answer was "tough shit, if you don't like it move. I'm in training for the Olympics and that's part of my training schedule."

After that, every night about a half hour after his bedroom light went out I'd blast the stereo. When he started banging on the floor for me to stop I'd turn it up until I couldn't hear him pounding any more, put the tape player on repeat and go to the bar until 2:00AM.

When I'd finally come home every light in the house would be on and the assholes upstairs would be a bunch of pissed off assholes. "Payback was a bitch" for 'em. After about four days of this he finally confronted me crying about how it was disturbing his training and he couldn't get his proper rest and bullshit like that.

When I asked him about my rest his answer was, that my rest wasn't important because I wasn't training for the Olympics like he was and I'd just have to deal with it.

My answer to him was that I was in training to be a selfish, arrogant, self-centered, asshole like him and that he was my new training buddy and if he couldn't handle the pressure or didn't like it, he could move.

One of the things myself and everyone I knew had grown very tired of in The Springs were the trainees blocking traffic on their bicycles and in their wheelchairs. Instead of riding on the sides of the roads and allowing traffic to flow like any normal person would. They'd ride in packs, five, six, eight or ten abreast blocking whatever street they were on like they owned the street and the taxpayers that supported them were a nuisance for them to bear.

Not to mention they'd do this crap constantly during rush hours and hold up traffic. Making people late to work. Expecting the public to accept that their training was far more important than the mundane lives of the people they inconvenienced on a daily basis.

The jerks that lived above us were prime examples of that mentality. I eventually got sick of them and their crap. When they couldn't handle a taste of their own medicine, like the spoiled babies they were, they complained to the landlord, conveniently forgetting to tell him about the weightlifting at three in the morning.

This was all happening at the same time that Valerie met some guitar playing fruitcake and moved in with him. After being gone a little over a week she showed up at the apartment on a Sunday afternoon complaining that the landlord had called her mother and complained to her about my attitude.

I asked her if she told him about the weightlifting. She said that was too bad for me. I'd have to stop harassing the trainees or leave. I told her that both her and Roger {her new boyfriend} could fuck off and die, fired up Christine and rode off to the party I was going to.

At the party I met for the second time that week another little sweetie and we started to hang out. Her and I were out at the curb sitting on Christine smoking a joint, when guess who drives by in her own car alone this time, Valerie.

Once it got dark we all moved up to the Bank Shot for the rest of the evening. Sometime during the evening a friend said "I think someone wants to see you" and motioned towards the window. There was Valerie outside looking in, right where she belonged.

I went outside and asked her what she wanted. She said she wanted to come home.

I told her "fine, I'll see you when I get home."

"Oh I can't come home tonight; I couldn't hurt Roger that way."

I thought you don't care if you hurt me that way, but all I said was "fine" and went back inside.

A week later she showed up. She'd come home was her comment and I guess I was supposed to jump for joy or something. We never said a word about it. I wouldn't've listened to it anyway. She was a slut, I'd already faced the fact that I'd made the worst decision possible and that was that. Now I was just gaming her for all she was worth.

Sometime in the midst of all this I'd gotten a job with a plumber repairing all the screwed up plumbing in some new condos that'd been built behind the IRS offices of all places. There were a few finish carpenters, electricians, the maintenance man and Bird {different Bird} and I on the site and that was it.

We had no real supervisors. All we had to do was make continual progress every day and we were cool. Bird was as big a fuckoff as I was, but he was a journeyman fuckoff and a wannabe scooter person.

People around talked shitty about Bird to me, but he always treated me square. I got paid every week {cash}. The money was right and on days that the weather sucked he'd pick me up and bring me home. We got high every day, all day and we even did a little of the garbage they called crank around there.

The crank around there came in through one source, a bunch of so-called "outlaw bikers" who played at being tough, but were really just a bunch of hillbilly hoodlums. Some of their patchholders didn't then and never did own bikes as long as I was in town. I thought it was pretty pathetic when I picked one up hitchhiking with his patch on.

A couple of 'em fit the mold and I got along fine with 'em, but for the most part they didn't like me because of Valerie. At one time or another they'd all tried to get her on the back of their bikes. The ones that had bikes anyway. It pissed 'em off that this tramp that blew in on a thunderstorm had her from the first minute in town {not that I had much}.

By the time the dope they imported from the west coast got to the streets of Colorado Springs it'd been whacked five or six times and wouldn't get a fly high. This just added to the boredom of life in The Springs. If I'd had the dope to do it with, I could've become a raging crankster. If I'd had the glassware for a lab I could've gotten rich. There's nothing that cuts the boredom quicker than a big fat ripper of glass that blows the top of your head off and lights your hair on fire.

By now spring was springing in The Rockies and a plan was formulating. My job would be ending soon. Our lease on the hellhole would be up about the same time and the Yuma Prison Run was coming up. I mentioned all this to Valerie. That was when she informed me of the new place we'd be getting as soon as her sister and her family moved into their new place. That evening we took a ride down the street to where her sister lived and checked it out.

With something to look forward to, life was beginning to be a little more bearable without dope. We worked and packed and counted the days till we could get outta the hellhole and on the road to Yuma. I was still five-eleven, but weighted one hundred and fifty-five pounds the day we left.

The day finally came when we packed our shit both on the bike and in the hellhole. We threw our stuff in the door of our new place and got on the road for Yuma. The first day wasn't any picnic. We froze our asses off, got caught in three hail storms and ended the day in a snow and ice storm in Sante Fe.

A motel for the night ended that misery, but didn't end mine. It reminded me of how I'd come to meet the blonde laying next to me. I spent the night wondering about Grace and what'd happened to her. I was so close to Espanola, that if the weather'd been better we'd've taken a ride up there the next morning just to see what I could see.

When we woke up the next morning everything was covered with a sheet of ice. With about three inches of snow on top 'a that. We weren't gonna get very far on that so we had breakfast and hung around the room till they started bugging us about check out time. When we got out on Cerrillos Road there were just two bare tracks in the ice, but it'd warmed up considerably.

I-25 was in much better shape and once there we hauled ass. We'd have to if we were gonna make the run. It was only a weekend event and it was already Friday morning. I stopped in Socorro New Mexico to get gas because I was going through Showlow Canyon to Phoenix, across I-10 to 85, down 85 to Gila Bend and west on I-8 to Yuma. This all changed when we got to the gas station and saw the snow on the mountains west of us. The dude at the gas station said the canyon was closed because of the ice storm the night before.

We ended up going all the way down I-25 to The Deming Cut Off and hitting I-10 from there adding quite a few hours and miles to our trip. We stopped in Lordsburg to get some gas and smoke a joint and were on our way again. It was getting dark when we stopped outside Tucson for more gas and another joint. We were both stiff from the time on Christine and still had a long ways to go. It was midnight when we made our last stop in Gila Bend for gas.

This was Valerie's first truly long ride. I could tell it was getting to her. She didn't wanna get back on the bike and kept dilly-dallying around. We hung out for about an hour or so until driven by the need for speed I got us on the bike and we got going. I knew when we got there all my friends would have a bag of crank and the lines would get laid like a truck stop whore.

Once on I-8 I rolled on the gas and held it open. The last thing the dude in the store said was to watch out for coyotes. Running wide open thru the desert at night on a bike wasn't a very smart thing to do because a coyote'd put a definite cramp in our style if we encountered one.

Screaming through the darkness, as loud as Christine was I thought for sure nothing'd even think of coming anywhere near us. I barely had time to let off the gas when my headlight picked up the flash of brownish grey coming at us from the right at a high rate of speed. I shut the gas off completely and the coyote passed about a foot in front of my front wheel.

It takes a lot less than a coyote to put you down on a bike, especially in excess of 100 mph. Hell a good gust of wind'll do the job quite nicely. I-8 isn't very heavily traveled. If we'd survived a crash at that speed we probably wouldn't've lived through the night scattered all over the road like we'd've been.

I don't think Valerie even felt me let off the gas. I think she was asleep. It was better that way because I was freaked out enough for both of us. I slowed down for God only knows what reason. If we were gonna die we'd already be dead. It didn't last long though and before long we were rocketing towards Yuma wide fuckin' open again. At last the lights of Yuma came into view and we were exiting at the fairgrounds exit.

I stopped in a parking lot next to the offramp and rolled off the bike onto my feet. Valerie had a much harder time of it. I had to pull her feet off the passenger pegs to help her straighten her legs and then pull her off the bike so she could walk it off. We both staggered around like drunken sailors. We were moaning and groaning and in Valerie's case crying, our bodies especially our legs hurt so bad.

We'd just spent a little over fifteen hours in the saddle of my old rigid frame ground pounder and it took more than a few minutes to walk this off. I got my land legs back before Valerie and could actually stand up straight while she was still staggering around stooped over and crying. I know it wasn't nice, but I couldn't help laughing once I got over the pain.

We both finally recovered and got limbered up. The blood was flowing again and the crying had stopped. We still had about a mile to the fairgrounds, but neither of us wanted to get anywhere near Christine. She just sat there on her kickstand quietly mocking us, daring us to get back on.

After about a half-hour, forty-five minutes or so our sleeping bags and the end of the road was calling us too loudly to ignore. We hesitantly and gingerly got on Christine and headed for the fairgrounds.

When we got to the sign in area we could barely get off the bike to sign in and get our run pins. With that done we could barely get on the bike to find our campsite. As we idled through the fairgrounds I saw all kinds of people that I knew from L.A., but not the folks I was looking for. Then I heard a shrill whistle that I'd recognize anywhere and there they were, sitting at the picnic table right in front of us.

I wobbled Christine to a stop, glad I wouldn't have go near her for at least a few hours. After introducing Valerie all around, she and Kat took off. I on the other hand had only one thing on my mind, getting high, really high. The mirror was broken out and we all lined up. The rush of the dope felt so good, this is what I'd ridden thirteen hundred miles for if nothing else. Seeing friends that I missed terribly wasn't even in the car with getting some crank in me, but it was right outside the door.

It'd been almost a year since I'd done anything that resembled real dope. It'd worn on me to the point of making me crazy. There'd been days in that past year when I didn't think I'd make it through the day and there'd been days when I wondered what kind of a weakling I was that a little bag of crystalline powder could have such a profound effect on every bit of my life. During occasional moments of clarity I appreciated the chance to get away from the shit and realized the grip it had, but then I'd think it can't have much of a grip because I wouldn't pay for the garbage they called crank in The Springs. I'd only do it if it was free.

Now I was in heaven. It was just starting to drip down the back of my throat and the rush was coming over the top of my skull making my hair stand on end. In a nanosecond I'll be blasted into the state of consciousness that was my personal paradise. When it came it was like a huge orgasm and well worth the ride. The flood of dopamine flowing through my brain was better than sex or riding or anything other than more dope.

After a quick trip to the shitter {that's the measure of good dope, if it makes you shit when you snort it you can bet it'll be a good buzz. It almost always makes you shit when you slam it unless it's bunk, but not snorting it, that takes good dope} I was back for more. After a couple more lines and a joint I was ready to put up the tent and lay down till my ears stopped ringing.

One thing about any addiction, No matter how long you're away from it, when you go back, you pick up right where you left off. There's no getting back gradually you jump right back into the deep end you got out of. As good as that first line felt it only made me want more,

more, more. It's almost as if you're making up for lost time. Once I got a little bit it wasn't enough until I snorted so much it put me to sleep {first sign of an overdose}. That whole weekend I probably snorted twice as much as my friends that used every day {too much is never never enough}.

When I got to where I'd parked the tent was up and Valerie was sleeping like the dead, atta girl. As I climbed into our sleeping bag the sight of her naked got the other head to thinking. One thing about crank is that it takes longer to get it up, but once you do it's a fuck fest because it gets so hard you can't stand it and stays that way for hours and cumming feels like a minor explosion. Against some mild protest my one-eyed witless wonder took over and the sky was getting light when I rolled off Valerie and closed my eyes.

Dickhead Central

I awoke to the sound of wrenches tinkling outside my tent about an hour after my eyes closed. I say awoke, but I wasn't really asleep I was kinda drifting in limbo, wired but relaxed, mind racing, body immobile. I pulled on my pants and boots and crawled outta the tent to see a royal pain in the ass named Papa Smurf fixing a motorcycle that wouldn't be broken till he got done with it.

Years earlier I'd built a Sportster for Papa Smurf {I knew him as Steve} when I worked at Chicken Delight. The day the bike was done and dialed in I took it for a ride {one of the few Sportys I've ridden, I don't like 'em, too small, I always feel like I'm gonna fall headfirst over the handlebars} and really liked the way it performed for a Sportster. That afternoon Steve picked up the bike. He rode off like an old lady going to a funeral {he didn't need a hotrod Sporty, he needed a tricycle}.

The next morning when the owner got to the shop, Steve was sitting in the driveway with the bike in the back of his pickup truck saying it wouldn't run, that it never ran right and he wasn't paying for a piece of junk that wouldn't run. Of course the boss was immediately up my ass for fucking the bike up. I wheeled it around back into the shop. The battery was dead as a doornail, brand new less than twenty-four hours earlier. I put it on the charger and proceeded to start checking the timing, the carb settings and the pushrods.

The timing was out in left field, I reset that. The carb was in right field, I reset that. The pushrods were so tight the valves wouldn't even close all the way. I readjusted those. After this with the battery still on the charger I started the bike. It fired immediately. I unhooked the battery charger and the bike still ran so I knew the charging system was working. I rolled the bike out into the alley, dialed in the carb and took it for a test ride.

I went past the front of the shop doing a wheelie in second gear. Pretty good for a bike that wouldn't run! I rode around for a while to make sure everything was alright and working like it was supposed to. When I got back to the shop I parked the bike near the door and put the battery charger back on it until Steve came to pick it up that afternoon.

When he came in I fired up the bike and did a few wheelies and burnouts to show him and the boss how good it ran. The dipshit went away happy and I cleared myself with the boss, who thought that everything was my fault {of course}.

The next fuckin' morning I happened to be the guy that got there first and who the fuck's pickup truck was out front? You guessed it, Steve's! He wouldn't even talk to me about the bike. He even went so far as to roll the window up and smoke himself out with his own stinking pipe.

When the boss got there he looked at me and said "what the fuck's this?"

I didn't know and told him so. Steve saw him in his mirror and jumped outta the truck screaming about his fucked up bike. He wanted his money back bla, bla, bla. The boss was a pretty big dude {he made three of Steve} and when he told him to shut up he did.

He asked him if he'd seen what his bike'd done yesterday in front of the shop like everyone else had.

He said he had, but when he got home {he rode the bike home} he shut the bike off and it never started again and the battery was dead this morning when he tried to start it.

The boss told me to roll the bike around back. At this Steve had a fit and said he didn't want me anywhere near that bike, the only one he wanted to touch it was Wrench. With that he wheeled the bike around back himself and started to hang around in the shop waiting for Wrench, like he was guarding the bike till he got there. When he didn't come up front in a few minutes the boss came and got him, telling him he couldn't hang around in the shop area. He said he didn't know when

Wrench would be there and he had other shit to do when he got there, so he didn't know when the bike would be done. He'd call him later.

As soon as Steve left he asked me about the day before. I told him that everything on the bike had been fucked with and everything was the same way today. The reason the battery was dead was from him trying to start the bike after he had everything on it so screwed up there was no way it was gonna start. I showed him just what I meant by trying to start the bike, the battery'd been allowed to sit long enough that it had recovered enough to roll the bike over slowly a few times before it quit again. This indicated that the battery was in good shape simply discharged from unsuccessfully trying to start the bike.

I reset everything he'd screwed up. This time I marked it and took Polaroids of the settings before and after. After I did all that I showed the marks to the boss and gave him the pictures. The bike sat on the charger until after lunch when I took the bike out for a long ride. Long enough that Steve was there to pick the bike up when I pulled in. Seeing Steve there I did a donut in the drive until all you could see was a cloud of smoke which I shot out of in a wheelie, riding it through third gear up Lakewood Boulevard.

I came back to the shop, flipped the kickstand down and said "yur turn!"

Steve bitched to the boss about me working on the bike, but paled when the boss told him Wrench had told Steve to go fuck himself. He really hadn't, he hadn't even come in that day. Steve rode off like an old lady going to a funeral again and I bet the boss my paycheck he'd be back the next day. A bet he wouldn't take.

Sure as shit the next morning he was back with his son in tow, threatening to sue the shop if the boss didn't hand over all of his money. He wasn't paying for a piece of junk that wouldn't run, bla, bla, bla. The boss got out the Polaroids of all the unfucked settings. Showed the before and after pictures to Steve. Gave him a bill for the last two tune-ups and rolled the bike in the shop telling Steve he'd get the bike back when he paid for all three tune-ups. I tuned up the bike again for the third and final time, telling Steve if he fucked with it this time, he was on his own.

That afternoon his son brought him to the shop to pick up the bike. Steve rode off like an old woman again and his son hung out for a bit to talk to me about building him a bike in the near future.

My first comment to him was "you're not gonna to be like your dad are ya? Cause if you are, find somebody else to build it."

He told me that wouldn't be the case and why his dad did that shit. I already knew why, he was an idiot.

Well anyway this same jerk-off was outside my tent fuckin' with his new bike. A Wide Glide that according to him had to have the pushrods adjusted four or five times a day.

He fucked with the pushrods so much the locknuts were all rounded off and you could barely get a wrench to grab 'em. For those of you that don't know what the hell I'm talking about, The pushrods are between the lifters and the rocker arms and open the intake and exhaust valves on a Harley, you "set 'em n-forget 'em," just like the carb and the timing. You don't fuck with this stuff every time you stop the bike for five minutes.

The only good thing I could say about Steve is that from a shop owner's standpoint he was an excellent source of revenue. You could build a new bike for him one week and have to do at least a top end job on it twice a month because his type of hands on approach to motorcycle ownership caused burnt pistons, that was usually a complete motor job if the pieces ended up in the crankcase, burnt valves, lots of broken parts and stripped threads to repair. The problem there was you got sick of looking at the idiot's face every day knowing he'd be back in two days or sometimes two minutes with the thing you're fixing today broken again.

To say I hated this idiot was an understatement. The sight of him made my blood boil! I'd had all of him I could stand with the Sportster incident. He was so stupid that he couldn't even understand why I hated him, even after I explained it to him more than once. As gently as my rage allowed I grabbed his bike and him and hustled him about fifty yards away.

On the way back to our tent Kat "hey'd" me from hers and motioned me inside. She had some lines on a mirror and handed me a tooter. As I snorted my line she said she was glad I hadn't killed him. It's not that I didn't want to, it's just that it would be a waste of time to kill the stupid fuck. My time that is, he certainly wasn't worth going to the joint over. There are people on this planet that are here only because it's against the law to kill 'em n-he was definitely one of 'em!

He just needed to take his stupidity elsewhere. After we all did our lines Kat very diplomatically explained to Steve how near death he was when I grabbed his bike and moved it. After that he moved the rest of his shit and stayed outta my way the rest of the weekend. Everywhere we went that idiot was there fuckin' with his pushrods and believe it or not as much as I wanted to be, I wasn't done with this dumbass yet.

In my little tirade about Steve's messing with everything on his bike I neglected to add that there is a time you need to adjust your carburetor, when you change altitudes. Colorado Springs is 6975 ft. above sea level and Yuma is at roughly sea level. I'd ridden from Colorado to Yuma and never touched my carburetor. Meaning my engine was running lean which would cause it to cough out the carb and die once in a while. Mostly when you were taking off from a light or a stand still of some type.

I told you that to tell you this. Being the tightly unwound, newly reanimated crankster that I was that tweakend, I was always way ahead of myself and forgetting shit before it ever happened. Every time Christine'd cough and die I'd think "I need to adjust that." A second later when it started I'd ride off without doing it, all wound up with everyplace to go.

A bunch of us had been riding around Yuma all day. We'd gone to the prison during the morning after our breakfast of champions {speed-n-weed}. When we left the prison we stopped for lunch, lines, joints and beers. From there we decided to go to the Harley shop. On our way there at a traffic light Christine coughed and died. It'd happened so much that Valerie slipped off the back to give me room to kick her back to life automatically. I reared up from the wrong side of the bike, without testing the peddle and with all my weight and momentum jumped as hard as I could on the kicker peddle {the stupidest thing you can ever do to an old kickstart Harley}.

The kicker peddle shot all the way through it's stroke like it wasn't even connected to anything. When the peddle stopped at the bottom of the stroke, my foot didn't. It shot off the peddle sideways, landed sideways and continued bending sideways until my ankle bent ninety degrees with a pop that sounded like a gun shot and made everybody, even the other people on bikes look in my direction.

Crank being the painkiller that it is, we limped me and Christine to the side of the road, got her going and took off for the Harley shop. When we got there my foot was making my boot look like it was pressurized and it was all I could do to sit down. Walking was outta the question.

Bird kicked Christine to life for me and we went back to the fairgrounds. It was only a couple miles, but it was all I could do to get there. I had to get this fucking boot off it was killing me and I didn't want my foot to start busting the stitching on the boot. Too late. When I undid the ankle strap the stitching on both sides of the vamp busted immediately. It only took about a half hour to get the boot off and once it came off there wasn't any getting it near my foot again.

Another partner from L.A. at the run had family there. His ole'lady was from there and her mom and dad still lived there. In fact I'm pretty sure that's where my bum foot and I ended up, at her folk's house. I don't remember how I got there. I remember being helped into a bedroom, Valerie and other people being there, no one being there and everyone packing me up and getting me ready to ride to L.A. after the run was over.

I don't even remember why I don't remember which is pretty weird for me. I remember some of the ride back to L.A. mostly because I was driving, but I don't remember, remember the ride. Anyway Valerie and I ended up going back to L.A. with friends. There was no way I'd've made it back to Colorado like that.

We couldn't afford to just do nothing while in L.A. This was only to've been a weekend run, we should've been home the following Tuesday. We didn't have the time or the money to hang around and do nothing. I had a traffic case in Colorado Springs that Friday. We had a new house to move into and Valerie was supposed to be back at work.

The very first thing I did was call the court and get a continuance for a month. With that outta the way, I had to learn how to kick start Christine with my left foot so that I could make it to work at a friend's bike shop. Getting the job at the shop was a lot easier than learning to kick the bike with the wrong foot.

At first it seemed almost impossible to start the bike from the wrong side. Kicking with the right foot was natural, your weight was centered over the bike and when you rocked back on the kicker peddle your weight held the bike to the ground at all three points {the two tires and the kickstand}.

When kicking with your left foot, all your weight's hanging off the far right side of the bike, putting your center of gravity and all your weight out in space. Which means as soon as you start to rock back on the kicker peddle the bike wants to fall to the right, which is the unsupported side. As the bike continues to fall, the kicker rolls toward the ground. The kicker peddle gets about three quarters of the way through its stroke when it slams into the ground. Then your face slams into your knee because you've done the stupidest thing in the history of kickstarterdom *again*, put all your weight into it. The bike rolls over on top of the last two disasters *and* the hurt ankle following the everything comes in threes theory which is bad enough. Unless to top everything off the bike starts while its falling on its side, adding to the excitement.

All of these things and more happened as I was learning how to do this. The trick was to rock back on the kicker which placed your weight far to the right and hold the bike to the left {on the kickstand} at the same time. This was no mean feet and defied at least one law of physics. If it didn't break any laws of physics, it sure broke a few laws of decency. When the kicker kicked through, you fell on your ass and a seven hundred pound piece of iron rolled over on top of a foot already so painful you couldn't brush your hair without hurting it, the neighborhood learned an entirely new vocabulary of cuss words. I spouted some I'd never even heard before and I was an accomplished cusser.

I'd started getting my mouth washed out with soap for swearing as soon as I was able to talk. At four years old my dad caught me reciting every swear word I knew at the top of my lungs with all the other neighborhood kids listening and laughing, especially after I was caught and was getting my ass kicked all the way home {literally, with both feet}.

The mouth washing I got for that alone would've deterred most idiots from ever opening their mouth again, let alone getting caught cursing about the scrubbing two days later. As you can tell I haven't gotten much better over the years, but I think there are just some things that a cuss word or two best describe and this was definitely one of those things, especially as many times as it happened while I was perfecting the technique.

It took me several weeks to make this rather sideways method of starting my bike a habit. Eventually it was as easy with my left foot as it'd been with my right and I had plenty of powdered painkiller to help me thru the process.

With a wheeled rolly gig for my tools and to sit on as I worked, my new kicker style and a snootful of crank every time I turned around, I was as close to heaven as I was gonna get for a minute.

I'd've never left SoCal again if it hadn't been for that fuckin' ticket in Colorado. I'd've gladly put Valerie on a bus and been done with her ass for the love of my dope and the good shit that flowed like water in L.A. The problem was I'd have to appear for that ticket eventually. Right then I had a month extension which really wasn't much, but something happened to make it feel like an eternity.

As we were approaching the shop for work one morning soon after Yuma I saw a pickup truck in the driveway with a red Wide Glide in the back. As we turned into the driveway it was hard to miss the fact that the idiot driving the pickup had managed to park so as to block the entire drive. You couldn't even walk past the truck, but you could get in-n-out of the driver's door easy enough.

As I sat there looking at the parking job and the bike in the back the name STEVE leapt into my mind. Sure enough who came running out to move his truck, Papa Smurf. **FUCK, FUCK, FUCK** was the only word going through my head over and over as I parked my bike and limped inside. I couldn't stand to have this idiot anywhere around me. Now with his bike here that means he'd be here at least every other day and that wasn't all. He'd put some money into this place making him a silent partner that didn't know the meaning of the words **SHUT THE FUCK UP**.

Did I say heaven earlier, I meant **HELL!** Everything this guy did rubbed me the wrong way. The more he got on my nerves the less he'd shut up. His stupidity was so complete that he couldn't learn the simplest things, because he couldn't shut his mouth long enough for the information to sink in, not that it would've anyway. He especially couldn't learn to keep his hands off his motorcycle, no matter how much money he cost himself.

The reason his bike was in the shop this time was because while he was in Yuma he'd adjusted the pushrods so tight that he burnt the top end up on the bike on the way home. Pushrods are one of those things that you set n-forget for anyone but Steve, he eternally fucked with 'em. I can't count the times I saw him just in Yuma "adjusting" his pushrods. I couldn't imagine going on a run with him, he'd drive me insane and I'd kill him before we ever got to the place unless it was right around the corner.

After the incident with the Sportster at Chicken Delight I had no use for Steve, I never got to know him any further than knowing I didn't *wanna* know him. The exposure I had to him this time showed me he possessed some of the least endearing qualities a human can possess. He was a nosy ass busybody and a snitch, no not a snitch he was a fuckin' tattletale. Like a little kid he'd run and tell the first person he found about whatever he saw or heard that he didn't like or didn't agree with. You couldn't party around him cause he'd call the cops.

He was the kind of person that'd call the police if he caught his mother J-walking, hold her till they got there and sign the complaint as a witness. He was so stupid that he never understood that all the shit he put me through with the Sportster at Chicken Delight, fuckin' it up every night and claiming I did it every morning, was the reason I hated him in the first place. Not to mention the time he wasted outta my day redoing the same things day after day and trying to get 'em done for free. He'd run and tell somebody {whoever he thought was in charge or the nearest cop if that didn't work} about the stupidest shit and couldn't understand why you didn't like him.

Having this dickhead around was like having a cop riding in your pocket and he was gonna be around a lot while his bike was here. The topper was that in a roundabout way I actually worked for this idiot. At one point he even thought he could flex that muscle and get a reaction. He did but it wasn't the one he was hoping for.

One of the things Steve did at Dick's shop was creep up behind ya and peek over your shoulder while you were working on something. It was easy to tell he was there cause he smoked a pipe and it stunk to high heaven {I think he smoked cowshit in it}. One morning when Dick was gone I yelled at him to get the fuck away from me, his retaliatory remark was that he was my boss and he'd do what he wanted. I simply walked away from what I was doing and sat out front on my bike smoking a cigarette waiting for the boss to get back.

I knew as soon as Dick got back Steve would run and tell just like a five year old. When they walked into Dick's office I went back to work. A few minutes later I'll be damned if he wasn't hovering around again. He finally started to say something, I shot him square in the open mouth with WD-40 making it look like an accident. Of course he ran crying to Dick who sent him home to end the bullshit for that day.

I grudgingly started working on Steve's bike, knowing he'd be hanging around incessantly, putting a damper on the day every minute he was there. To me it seemed like a waste of time to fix this idiot's bike. He'd only fuck it up in a week or less, blame it on me and want it fixed for free. This was a pain in the ass to me, revenue security to Dick and I saw his point. That didn't make having this idiot around constantly any easier, especially when his presence made getting high such an ordeal.

Ya wouldn't see him all day, but as soon as ya got the dope lined up on the glass and the tooter in your nose, here he'd come. If he saw what you were doing he'd run and tell the first person he found and disappear. The next day he'd be back unable to understand why you couldn't stand him.

It seemed like within five minutes after ya started working on his bike he'd be there up your ass, wheezing that stinking pipe smoke in your face, asking stupid questions. I'd just put everything away and go work on something else, causing him to run and tell again. The amazing thing about all this, *THE GUY NEVER GOT THE MESSAGE.*

Finally the day came to put Steve's bike together and get him outta my hair for a little while {at least a week, I hoped}. Of course he was at the shop before anybody else, sitting in the driveway when we got there. As soon as I saw him I knew it was gonna be one of those days. I was ready for him today with a whole bunch of rotten tricks to play that would wear him out with all the running and telling he'd have to do.

I thought about dropping a rock in his coffee and watching him spin right the fuck out, but Bird talked me out of it. I thought it'd've been hysterical to watch the idiot chase his tail all day, but like Bird pointed out it'd've been my luck that the stupid ass would OD and we'd all get busted. He was probably right I'm sure Steve'd tell 'em everything he knew {which wouldn't even take a minute} over and over and over again if he was wired.

With more than a few reminders like being squirted with WD-40 and pipe ashes being blasted in his face by an errant blast of compressed air, a couple'a good shots of oil on his shirt and pants, some greasy hand prints smeared on this-n-that he figured out that he should keep his distance. Once we got his perimeter established and he stayed outside it and bothered other people, assembling his bike was just routine and only took a few hours.

The closer his bike got to completion the harder it was for him to stay away. By the time I had the gas tanks back on he was in my way again, Every time I turned around I had to wait for him to get outta my way, trip over 'im or knock 'im down.

Finally in my most buddy like manner I turned to him and whispered "do you wanna know what'll make this bike run like a stripped assed ape for along time?"

He hunkered down next to me and asked "what?"

I leaned in real close and screamed "**LEAVE IT THE FUCK ALONE**" in his ear at the top of my lungs.

Of course he ran right off to tell and I had a good laugh mostly cause I knew it didn't even sink in, but it gave me the time to finish the bike and get some gas in the tanks without tripping over him every time I moved.

When he got back the bike was running and I was fine tuning it. I took it out, got it up to heat, finished dialing it in and parked it out front when I was done. Now he had no reason to be in the shop area at all and I could have some piece and quiet or so I thought.

The next morning roaring up Eastern Avenue giving the neighbors their first headache of the day and setting off car alarms, I saw from four blocks away the gas tanks and handlebars of my personal nightmare sitting in by now an all too familiar pickup truck.

When I got there I rode right by him, parked, went in the restroom and snorted a big, fat ripper. That done I went out front to see what now. The bike was off the truck oil running from under the gas tanks all over everything. Now what?

The first thing I noticed was the odd angle of introduction on the braided steel oil crossover line that I *hadn't* put on there the day before. This was obviously the source of all the oil that covered that whole side of the bike.

The day before when I finished the bike I used the stock crossover line {the oil line that runs from rocker box to rocker box on a shovelhead} that was on the bike. On his way out the door after the bike was done Steve bought a set of braided steel lines to replace the stock ones with and went home to change them himself {I could've simply put these lines on about two hours earlier when I put the top end together}.

When the idiot got home and couldn't get the fitting on the braided steel line to start in the hole in the rocker box by hand, he put a wrench on it and twisted it in so sideways it looked like he'd pounded it in with a hammer. Proud of his work he went out for a ride spraying oil everywhere. He finally noticed it, shut the bike off and called his son to bring the pickup.

This moron manages to do all this while clean and sober. In the period of only a few hours and on an almost daily basis, this idiot does more damage in a few minutes than most tweakers can do in a week. I was amazed when I found out this guy was sober. I always figured he was on some good shit to be that much of a fuckup.

When I found out he was sober, I asked him about it. He puffed out his chicken chest and declared he was proud of it. I couldn't resist telling him he should try drugs, as fucked up as *he* was it might help. After all "drugs are for people that can't handle sobriety" and he never seemed to be doing a very good job. He didn't think that was at all funny. When I told him it wasn't a joke he stormed away in an indignant huff, just like the chicken chested bitch that he was.

As the line was kicking in real hard I rolled his bike in the back and took it apart {I took apart what I'd just put together the day before}. One rocker box had to be replaced he'd fucked it up so bad. The other could be repaired, that verdict got him outta my hair for the rest of the day. He did wanna know if it'd be done the next day before he left though. I was so sick of Steve and his bike I shoved it in the corner and covered it up so I wouldn't have to see it the rest of the day.

My month was coming to an end, but being on my feet all the time and riding every day wasn't allowing my foot to heal very fast. I called the court in Colorado and got another extension. I now had another month for Steve to torture me with his crap in. I don't know how I'd've made it through a day around him without drugs. If I'd had to deal with him sober every day I wouldn't've made it through the first half hour without killing him. Another example of drugs being for people who can't handle sobriety.

It was a relief to work on a bike other than his and not smell that stinkin' fuckin' pipe as he hovered over my shoulder waiting to be in the way when I moved. Sometime during the afternoon I smelled that pipe, looked up and he was just coming into the back. I got up, walked out front and sat on Christine, smoking cigarettes till he was gone. I guess there's just no rest for the wicked and I couldn't be righteous cause I needed a rest from his inane intrusions, but couldn't get even one moments piece.

Finally after having a few days to finish a couple of other jobs, it came time to put Dipshit's bike back together. I got to the shop as soon as I could that morning to get as much work done as I could before he got there. Lucky me, he was sitting in the driveway eating donuts and drinking coffee when I got there. The guy with the keys was nowhere to be found, so I had to listen to how happy he was he was gonna get his bike back and how he couldn't wait to go riding, bla, bla, bla. I finally snapped and told him he'd be riding now if he'd keep his fuckin' hands off the bike and he wouldn't be riding long for exactly the same reason.

Once I blew up at him he went and sulked in his pickup until the keys arrived. As soon as they did he was in run and tell mode, crying about how mean I'd been to him and how he'd just been trying to make conversation and he couldn't understand why I was always such a bastard to him.

I listened to all this shit through the wall as I was doing my second wake up line of the day. I was gonna need all the chemical assistance I could get that day to keep from killing this idiot and beating his bike to pieces with a sledge hammer. I'd like to know where it's written that you have to like everybody and put up with an idiot like that's bullshit every minute and not say something about it. I'll never understand why he couldn't get the hint and leave me alone. If someone treated me the way I treated him, I'd never go near 'em, let alone pester 'em to death every time I saw 'em with the same stupid bullshit that pissed 'em off to begin with.

Steve was kept outta my way that morning, by lunchtime I was done with the bike and rolling it out the door. As soon as the bike was on its kickstand out front I was on mine and outta there. I didn't wanna see the face of or hear one word from the jerk that owned it. I knew I wouldn't be done with Steve till the day we went back to Colorado, but I was done with him that day and that's all there was to that!

A little later, while I was soaking my ankle in ice water, the shop called to let me know he'd finally left. I pulled on my boot and went back to work. It was so nice there with no Steve, no Steve's bike. I got a lot done that afternoon and was hesitantly looking forward to the next day.

Next morning no Steve, a good sign, ten-thirty no Steve, a damn good sign, walking out to go to lunch and lingering a little too long out front before leaving. **FUCK**, he's driving in the drive as we're riding out, bike in the back of his truck, trying to flag us down. I grabbed a handful of gas and hauled ass like I didn't even see him along with everyone else. He could wait till after lunch, he could wait till hell froze over for all I cared.

Seeing him ruined my lunch that day. I had heartburn like there was no tomorrow after my lunchtime ripper, till I got back to the shop. No Steve, no Steve's bike, what the fuck?

He'd ridden somewhere that morning. Whenever he got where he was going he adjusted the pushrods on a hot motor. While he was off doing whatever it was he was doing the motor cooled off. He'd adjusted the pushrods so tight hot, that when the motor cooled off the valves wouldn't close, resulting in no compression. No compression, no start, good thing too because this was exactly how he'd burned up the top end on his way home from Yuma. Now he's trying to do it again before the new top end's even broken in.

The definition of insanity is doing the same thing over and over and expecting different results. Stupidity is doing it after you've been told repeatedly not to. Idiocy is never understanding why you shouldn't do something, no matter how many times its explained to you, after you've fucked it up over and over.

I firmly believe Steve was afflicted with more than his share of all of the afore mentioned things and was so glad that Dick listened to this broken record and not me. He'd adjusted the pushrods and gave him a little pep talk {Dick had the ability to tell you to go to hell, make you thank him for it, then pay him for it, and ask directions from him before you left} and sent him on his way before we ever got back from lunch, thank God. In all my life I can't think of anyone I've ever disliked more than Steve. Hopefully the talk Dick had with Steve did some good, we'd see. Something must've sunk in cause we didn't see Steve anymore for a while, which was a major relief.

Once my foot got tolerable we actually got a chance to do a few things besides work. After all, we were in the scooter capital of the world. No matter which way you go in Southern California on any given weekend there's something scooter oriented to do. There's all kinds of cool little bars out in the canyons of Los Angeles, Orange, Riverside and San Bernardino counties and in all the beach towns. Swap meets sometimes tweakend long and if nothing else you can always go to Hollywood and watch the freak show. That was always good for a laugh.

Since we had to save our money for an eventual return trip to Colorado and I had to stay high while we were there, we only got to scratch the surface of the shit to do in SoCal, but we did manage to have a little fun. We hit a few swap meets {picked up some Purple Hog chaps pretty cheap}, hit a few bars and took a few rides. We were there for ten weeks, that was all the time Colorado would give me. By that time we were both tired of sleeping on the living room floor anyway and wanted to get back to our new house and especially our waterbed. When we left California this time, I weighed one hundred and twenty-seven pounds.

Kingman

Finally the day came when it didn't matter how much my foot hurt, or how much Steve fucked up his bike, cause I wouldn't be there to fix it. We had to go, I had to be in court the next Monday and we both wanted to get home. I just wasn't looking forward to the eleven hundred mile ride. The weather'd be a lot better because it was now summer and there'd only be snow at the highest altitudes, like Wolf Creek Pass.

We left on a Friday morning taking the same route as I'd taken the year before, I was tempted to stop by Hemet's old house just for old time sake, but I rode right past the exit without realizing it until miles later. The traffic wasn't as bad this time, but the dope situation was horrible we had barely enough to get there.

As we were crossing into Arizona the back end of Christine went kinda rubbery, it felt like we were getting a flat tire, I stopped and did a kick test of the tire, hard as a rock no problem there. With about forty-five miles of desert till the next town I wasn't gonna fool with it out there. I'd wait till I got to Kingman just in case it was something major.

By the time we got to Holy Moses Wash the back end of Christine felt like rubber and it was hard to keep her going in a straight line. Valerie hadn't felt the problem as soon as I had, but I could tell when she did. When I gave Christine the gas to pass a truck instead of turning into the lane next to us we kinda shot crab ways into it. When that happened her hands and knees clinched around my waist and stayed that way till we got to the Harley shop.

That was the friendliest Harley shop I'd ever been in, in all my life. The guy behind the counter pretty much told me to go to hell as soon as I walked through the door and the experience went straight downhill from there. What'd happened was the nut that held the backing plate for the old mechanical brakes in place had split and allowed the left side of the rear axle to wander back and forth in the chain adjustment slot every time I gassed or braked. I didn't think the Harley shop'd have one of these nuts in stock cause that type of mechanical brake had only been obsolete for about thirty years and of course I was right as attested to by the rudest counterman I've ever experienced in my life at a Harley shop.

I wasn't the only one that was having a problem with these assholes. Another couple there'd broken down on a brand new bike. Though the bike was under warrantee {they just bought it in L.A. and ridden it this far} the dealer in Kingman told 'em they had to pay cash for the major repair or take the bike back to L.A. for the warrantee work.

When I asked if there was another shop in town, the answer was "why the fuck would I tell you that?" After that they told me I was welcome to leave at any time because they didn't have anything to fix the piece of junk I was riding anyway, wasn't that nice of 'em?

When I walked outside I noticed a puddle of oil under the end of my generator {something that doesn't even have oil in it}. After a closer look I knew the seal in the drive end of the generator'd gone bad along with the backing plate nut. Not that any of that shit's related in the least little bit, other than being on the same bike.

I went back inside for more abuse and was pleased to find someone with a much better attitude behind the counter. I had a much better chance of them having the seal cause they still used it in Sportster generators. I was right, they had one and they were more than happy to let me work on the bike across the street in the Circle K parking lot.

We rode across the street and I got busy taking the bike apart. The bike was still blazing hot, just like it was outside so I was trying to not touch anything and still get the generator out. Before I got too involved I wanted to do a bump cause I was runnin' outta steam. Kinda' hard ta snort a line in the middle of a convenience store parking lot, but I got that job done before I started any other.

Once the blast started working so did I. It was so hot out that the bike'd barely cooled off at all. Once I got the generator out I took it apart and took the drive end over to the shop leaving Valerie to watch our stuff. The shop was really friendly while they charged me seventy-five dollars for a three dollar seal and the installation of it. After paying that much for the seal I was glad they didn't have the nut, I'd've hated to see how much they would've charged for that.

When I got back to the bike an old Datsun was parked next to it with a dude sitting in the passenger seat, he spoke as I walked up and we got into a discussion about the wonderful atmosphere at the Harley shop and the friendly helpful staff. We finally got around to the unsolved problem of the backing plate nut. Seems he had a friend with a machine shop on the other side of town who could make one in no time. When his girlfriend came outta the store we all shot the shit while I put Christine back together and then we followed 'em to their trailer, where they made a phone call.

After a cool drink and a joint we rode over to the house of the guy with the machine shop. He looked at the nut and said he could make one in about half an hour. We unpacked the bike in his garage and I followed him to his shop while Valerie and the other folks kicked back at his house. Half an hour later Christine was as good as new. Once back at our new friend's house it wasn't hard to convince me it was time for a party, so some more people were called and the grill was lit.

We partied till early in the morning and slept way too long the next day. When we finally got moving we really had to haul ass if we were gonna make it for Monday morning. We didn't stop for anything but gas until we got to Kayenta Arizona. We got there shortly after dark. The reason we had to stop was to clean and readjust the points in my old six volt voltage regulator. My headlight was so dim I could barely see the road in front of me which wasn't a good thing in the middle of open range country.

In case you don't know open range means just that. There are no fences and cattle, wild horses and jackasses roam at will, sometimes right out in the road. One time on The High Road to Taos with Judith's fourteen year old daughter on the back, I rounded a curve on the mountain road and had all I could do to get Christine stopped before we plowed headlong into a small herd of cattle wandering across the road in the middle of the day. At night with the headlight as dim as it was we'd be dead before we knew what we hit if I didn't stop and fix it.

Once I had my tools out and the bike apart we were the lucky recipients of some extremely drunken help from one of the natives who admittedly had never even seen a Harley, but was determined to help or at least steal something while he was trying to help. It was pretty funny. The first time I looked up he was tottering in front me talking to Valerie and I about helping with a wrench from my toolbox in his hand. As he's drunkenly babbling on-n-on he slips the wrench in his pocket like nobody's looking right at him and continues on babbling like we both didn't just see him do it.

When I called him on it, he pulled not one, but two wrenches out of his pocket and put 'em back in my tool box and went right on talking like nothing ever happened. He got kinda' upset when I told him to stand away from the bike. I didn't want him falling on it and knocking it over. With all the stuff packed on it it'd be impossible to pick up without taking everything off it first and then repacking it and I wanted to get outta there as soon as possible.

I knew eventually he'd get around to wanting some money by the way his conversation was going. He was already saying that I owed him something for giving back the wrenches. I finished quickly and polarized the system. When Christine roared to life he jumped back about six feet and it seemed to sober him up a bit. We loaded up and headed towards Four Corners in the darkness of the desert night. At first I was really gassing on it, but I remembered the coyote on the way to Yuma and settled into a more reasonable pace.

Somewhere near Four Corners in the middle of the night I spotted a picnic area and stopped for the night. I chained Christine to the picnic table we made our bed on and we slept like the dead until the sun came up. Once the sun was up we were too and on the road. In a few minutes we'd be in Colorado and by the end of the day we'd be in The Springs.

We stopped in Cortez Colorado and got gas and something to eat. Then headed towards Walsenburg through the heart of the Rockies. It was gonna be a long day. In one day we were gonna go from the desert of northern Arizona through the Rocky Mountains, over Wolf Creek Pass elevation 10,900 ft. to the Eastern Plains and on up the Front Range to The Springs. A journey that at one time would've taken months.

It was mid June. We left Arizona in shirt sleeves, Cortez in leather jackets and kept adding cloths every few thousand feet we climbed until we finally got to the top of Wolf Creek Pass where there was still four feet of snow on the ground and it wasn't much above freezing. By Pagosa Springs it'd warmed back up, but we were still more comfortable with leathers on. We reached Walsenburg by midafternoon and The Springs a few hours later. It felt good to be home, even though we had to wade through all the stuff we'd just thrown in the door in our hurry to leave months before.

We slept on the sagging foldout couch that night and both woke up miserable the next morning which was also court day. We were there at nine and gone in fifteen minutes after pleading not guilty. Not much of a reason to fuck up my California vacation if you ask me.

I Make Me Hate Myself

It was my first day waking up without a line in a long time. We had a whole house to unpack and put together especially the waterbed, which was where I wanted to be. Unfortunately I had to work for it, **MOTHERFUCKER** I was in a bad mood. This wasn't gonna be a very good first day back, I could just tell. There was gonna be too much work, not enough energy and the weather was gloomy on top of that!

The first thing I started to do when we got home was assemble the waterbed along with all the other related incidentals. It took us all day, but by early evening everything was done and the waterbed was heating up. I was in an even shittier mood because I'd spent my first day without dope and I didn't like it.

That waterbed was the best thing I'd felt in a long time. If I wasn't gonna get any dope that's where I wanted to be, but no there was always something that had to be done. Like eating or going to the bathroom and when that wasn't the problem there was always the inevitable everything else that people have to do every day of their lives.

I'd only been using regularly again a little over two months and was right back to where I was before I'd left the first time. When we got back to The Springs I weighed one hundred and twenty-six pounds and the depression and fatigue I felt this time was worse than anything I'd experienced before. For some reason when I ran outta dope in New Mexico the year before and dried out I didn't have any real problem with it, but this time it really bugged me and there wasn't a damn thing I could do about it. There was no way the garbage they called dope in The Springs would get me where I needed to be so there was no sense wasting money on it. It was better to go cold turkey and tough it out for a while, but the tough was getting tougher, the while was getting longer and I just wanted to *stay* high.

The first thing you do when you run outta dope is sleep, a lot at first tapering off to a normal sleep pattern eventually. When you're awake you can't get outta your own way and the last thing you wanna do is anything except eat. This coupled with the gloomy weather we had the first week we were back made me a pretty gloomy motherfucker.

Soon after we were home I found out that one of the coolest people I'd ever met had been run over and killed by some lunatic on Academy Boulevard the week before and had been buried the day we got home. The bitch that did it, drove away with just a traffic ticket.

The first day I woke up without dope I hated that I had to come back. Without dope you feel like you're imploding. The first few days you feel hollow, wrung out and you're jonesing hard, generating the foulest mood known to man. Everything made me wonder why I hadn't put Valerie on a bus like her mom wanted when we first got to L.A. I should've done that except I had to return anyway for that ticket and I didn't realize until the day after it was gone how much I'd miss being high.

I don't know why I was still thinking my home was in Colorado when I didn't even like anything there that much or Valerie either. She'd fucked around on me quite a few times by the time we'd left for Yuma and anything I felt for her at first was long gone. I guess I figured I'd ride it till the wheels fell off, which was exactly what I did.

The first day we woke up to sunshine I appreciated Colorado a lot more, you don't ever get air that clear in L.A. The view we had out our front window was unbelievable compared to the view from our last place {a basement} or from a lot of front windows I've had. We had a pretty cool place here. It was a one bedroom bungalow tucked under the foot of a bluff, in the far corner of a church parking lot. We were in a neighborhood five minutes from downtown. It seemed like it was out in the country though because we had no close neighbors, were surrounded by a large fenced yard, a treed lot and a bluff on three sides. A hundred yard walk through the trees put Valerie at the back door of her parent's house.

Our closest neighbor was a nest of Magpies right outside the bedroom window, which was almost as bad as having a freeway outside.

They don't do anything quietly {not even sleep} and they're up and down with the sun. It was a pretty cool little place, kinda' small {the king-size waterbed took up the entire bedroom} with no shop space or cable TV access, other than that it was perfect for the two of us.

One of the first things Valerie checked on was getting cable TV. Regular TV reception sucked right there for some reason, but an installation fee of over four hundred dollars was far more than it was worth.

Having grown up in that neighborhood Valerie had friends that lived right around the corner on the street below us. She was there visiting one afternoon when a cable TV salesman came offering free installation. She signed up for cable and got an appointment for the installation. When they got there to do the job, they had to postpone it for a couple 'a days once they saw the size of the job.

They had to run the cable from the street below up an alley through some trees and across our yard to the house using only the existing poles, a distance of about one hundred and twenty-five yards with a long unsupported span between the last pole and the house.

The biggest issue was doing all that work for free, but corporate told 'em to do it so they came back and finished the installation. At the time they told us that the only way to do it right was to run it all underground, but they didn't have the time right then.

Several months later though, after numerous service issues caused by weather they came back and did just that, all for the free installation voucher. Valerie got a big atta girl for that one.

Sometime during the first few weeks we were back I finally talked my way into a job at one of the best equipped motorcycle machine shops I'd ever seen in my life or so I thought at the time. *CUTTING WOOD*, that's right *CUTTING FUCKIN' WOOD* and stacking it. Along with cutting wood I painted the fences and every outbuilding with buckets and buckets of used hydraulic fluid, built feeders for cows, built fences and mended the same. Basically everything that had nothing to do with motorcycles.

During the wood cutting party days, there were sometimes four of us out there all day long with makeshift tables and skill saws cutting and stacking piles and piles of wood. Valerie'd also gotten a job there as the shipping and receiving person which was pretty convenient on the days that both of us worked together.

I sound like I'm complaining, but it was actually pretty cool working outside all day in the summer. The weather was great in the mornings, but by midafternoon almost every day it was either raining buckets from one torrential thunderstorm after another or spitting snow from one snowstorm after another in the winter and this shit usually lasted till the bars closed.

The reason this happened daily was because Colorado Springs is right under Pikes Peak which is almost fifteen thousand feet tall. The prevailing westerly winds pushed weather systems across the peak and as they gain altitude to go over the peak the moisture in 'em condenses and falls on The Springs in gully washing rain and hail storms or blizzard condition snows while five or ten miles to the north or south you might have beautiful weather all day.

The amazing part of all this is that you could stand out on the eastern plains where this shop was located and watch the weather build, bust and engulf The Springs in whatever was happening that afternoon and maybe never get wet yourself. Then came the not so amazing part when you had to ride home in rain or sometimes hail so strong it knocked your glasses off your face and almost knocked you off your bike.

I've got a tattoo that commemorates an afternoon in the rain just trying to get home from work. This particular afternoon we left out east in a light sprinkle, by the time we'd gotten a mile or two west we hit a literal wall of water. In a nanosecond we were soaked to the bone and miserable. The biggest part of the misery is knowing the only thing to do is go on. We finally got into town where the hardest rain'd already passed and it was just a steady downpour.

I can't remember why he stopped me {probably for speeding}, but a cop had us standing in the downpour for about forty minutes in front of Snake's Tattoo Shop on Platte Avenue while he did his thing in his dry cruiser. After he was done with us I pushed Christine to a parking spot in front of Snake's and had him tattoo "**one cop can ruin your whole fuckin' day**" on my right arm.

After that I always made a point of showing the arresting officer the tattoo I got "just for him" before I was in handcuffs. On more than one occasion I rode away from a worsening situation with just a ticket because of that tattoo, when a little deeper roadside investigation would've uncovered a large quantity of meth in transit or worse.

Dragonland

The first time I walked into this shop I was impressed with the equipment I saw and the potential it had. As I was leaving I thought I'd like to work there. At the time there were two guys working there Donnie, the dude that did the tear down and assembly and Mel, the owner and machinist. That was pretty much how the shop was set up. At the time it was one of the best equipped machine shops I'd ever seen. Good work stations with everything you needed for the job within arms reach. If I remember right Mel had six milling machines all setup to do several different jobs each. He had the machinery to build anything you could imagine, but neither the heart or the knowledge. Mel did everything like he wasn't interested in it in the least, like he had a grudge against it and it was all just a big inconvenience to him.

He had everything broken down to dollars and cents and that was the basis for every move he made. If it wasn't in his catalog he wouldn't do it because he said it wouldn't be worth his time. Later after working for him for a year and a half I found out he wouldn't do it cause he couldn't do it, he couldn't do anything that his brother hadn't programmed the machine for and shown him how to do. He didn't do much of that stuff very well either.

The first time I walked outta the shop with Joe Dandy and Knucklehead Larry was right after I'd gotten to town. I made the comment then about wanting to get a job there and they both laughed. When we got to the Bank Shot they told me about the experiences people'd had in the past with Mel and how people from town wouldn't go out there for anything because of 'em. The more people I got to know around town the more stories I heard about Mel.

It seems that everyone'd tried him when he came to town because there wasn't much there besides the Harley shop, but there were a bunch 'a people that rode. When I got there, there weren't very many shops. Puppy's, which was a few parts hanging on the wall, a tool box and a place to use 'em. I seem to remember a place called Brown's that I might've been to once that had even less. There was another dude named Fu who at the time of my arrival in The Springs was working outta his garage but within a few months had a shop on Fountain.

Fu and I became good friends and though we're not close today I could still get ahold of him if I had to, which is more than I can say for 99% of the people I've known. By the time Fu got his shop we were good enough friends that I'd been partying at his house one rainy Friday night, gotten way too drunk and passed out on Stu's Honda chopper in the rain. Something I never lived down as long as I knew those folks.

I was so drunk I couldn't even move without the whole friggin' world spinning including that Honda. No matter how many times someone fucked with me about being on a Honda I just couldn't move. From there on out when a certain few individuals wanted to get in a shot, all they had to do was mention sleeping on a Honda to instantly top me. Not too many things could top that.

Well anyway everybody that dealt with Mel got burned. By the time I got to town three years later nobody had a good word for the guy. Everybody had an S&S Carburetor or a Phase 3 Belt Drive hanging on the wall of their garage because they didn't know how to jet the carb for the altitude and neither did Mel or they didn't know anything about aligning the engine sprocket shaft and the tranny mainshaft for the belt drive and neither did Mel. He didn't wanna know either, but he had the balls to call himself an expert to anybody that'd listen to his bullshit. This isn't just my opinion, he was known as an idiot throughout the motorcycle industry.

By the time I left The Springs three years after my arrival I didn't have anything good to say about the dumbass either. To me he was just another shit-talking, backstabbing moron from New York City.

Donnie was from Pueblo, so I never got to know him as well as I'd liked to've. He was kinda' quiet and quick to laugh, but the only time I ever saw him outside Mel's was at a party in The Springs before I ever saw him at the shop and there were so many people there all we got to do was nod to each other. Donnie was good people and from what I understood had at one time been the president of a local Pueblo bike club. We always had a few words coming and going every day, but never got to know each other very well.

I'd worked for Mel {cutting wood} for quite a few months when work started piling up on the benches and nothing was getting done. Mel had several people come in and do some of the work, but none seemed to work out, so he finally asked me if I could do it. After hanging around for months doing everything but working on bikes, almost like I was prospecting for a motorcycle club, I finally got a break. Where was Donnie?

Mel showed me the lay of the work areas and the order in which to do the jobs and I went to work. It took a few weeks to get caught up with the backed up work. During the conversation one day he casually mentioned that someone told him that Donnie had lung cancer, that was why he stopped showing up for work. He was *mad* that Donnie never called him to tell him he wasn't coming back; instead of giving a shit the guy was terminally ill.

I didn't have much of a reply for Mel, a practice I should've continued the entire time I worked for him, but wasn't smart enough to do. A few days later Mel mentioned Donnie again and I asked him why he didn't give a shit.

"Ahh he was late all the time and wouldn't call or just not show up and not call. That stuff pissed me off. Like this last time he never came in or called for two weeks. I finally had 'a get somebody else. That's why you're here; fuck 'im."

When he found out that Donnie died a few months later, all he said was "who fuckin' cares?"

I'm a pretty heartless motherfucker, but I couldn't be that shitty about somebody I worked with everyday just cause they were late.

Once again everything came back to dollars and cents, the human equation didn't matter. Nothing ever seemed to matter to Mel, but how much money he made yesterday or last week and that was always the topic of discussion sometime during every day.

Working for Mel was like working for a spoiled five year old. If ya said or did something he didn't like and you never knew what that might be, he'd call an end to the day and tell ya not to come back the next day, he'd call ya when he needed ya. Then you wouldn't hear from him for two weeks. He'd finally call when work was backed up so bad you could hardly walk around in the front of the shop.

Remember I told ya that Valerie worked there too. The whole time I'd be sitting around waiting for the dickhead to call, he'd have Valerie in there every day doing her job. He'd send her home with some kinda' lie to tell me every afternoon *and she'd actually do it*, that was the thing that got me.

Occasionally he'd have other people come in and do my job while Valerie was there so she could come home with that good news, what an asshole.

I need to give ya a little background on Mel before we go much further; as you've probably figured out he owned a motorcycle machine shop outside Colorado Springs. Well it wasn't always that way.

Mel was originally a truck and bus mechanic for Nassau County in New York City. He'd owned a big shop out there too, that mommy and daddy financed and his brother set up for him. For whatever reason {probably to get away from all the people he'd pissed off back there} he bought the land in Colorado, packed every piece of machinery he had in U-haul trucks. I don't mean crating each machine and carefully loading 'em. He muscle-fucked {like so much scrap iron} as many as he could pack into each trip to save on the cost of the move. Then he bounced 'em two thousand miles, subjecting 'em to all kinds of vibration, temperature and humidity changes, muscled 'em into place out in Colorado and never recalibrated one of 'em. He didn't even know how.

After all the trauma he put these precision machines through he couldn't understand why when he tried to relocate the countershaft hole in a blown-out Sportster transmission case it ended up an eighth of an inch off.

When I asked if he'd recalibrated his machines after the move. First he asked what that was. When I explained what it was, he asked why he'd have to do it. When I answered that stupid question he told me I didn't know what I was talking about and blew the whole thing off like everything else. Some machinist huh?

Mel's answer to this problem was not to recalibrate the machine {he couldn't} and redo the job correctly. He honed out the main bearing race until the snap ring groove for the main bearing retainer wasn't much more than a shadow. This groove held the snap ring that held the main bearing assembly {thirty-two loose rollers and their retaining rings} in place, without it this whole assembly would come apart and end up in pieces in the tranny, which is exactly what happened to a customers bike from town right after it was supposedly fixed. Two hundred and seventy-five pound Mel got beaten to the ground by one hundred and thirty pound Jim that day. He deserved a lot worse because of his don't give a fuck attitude, but his girlfriend called the cops when he started losing the fight.

Mel threw the guy's money in his face {his idea of fixing it}, but that didn't make it any righter. There again he boiled it all down to money. The essence of the problem completely escaping his dumb ass. He was wrong but his ego and his ignorance of his equipment wouldn't let him admit it and fix it.

Before I watched this last incident unfold I was a victim of his bullshit myself. I needed to freshen up my motor and had a few performance things I wanted to do at the same time {change from pan to shovelheads, hotter cam, port the heads, big bore kit and S&S carb}. You'd think working in a bike shop this it wouldn't be a problem. He turned it into a fuckin' ordeal for me.

For months prior I talked to Mel about doing this. My bike was my only transportation and I couldn't count on Valerie for shit so I wanted to get everything done as quickly as possible and be back on the road in a few days or weeks tops. Mel agreed repeatedly with this plan.

I'd tear the bike down the night before, bring the motor in and tear it down first thing so that Mel could be doing the machine work that day while I was doing my regular work. The next day I'd assemble my motor first thing, pay for the work Mel did and bring it home that afternoon after work.

As soon as I walked through the door with the motor he got pissy. When I put it on the bench and started to tear it down he asked what I was doing. I told him I was doing what we'd talked about the day before.

"Oh yah" was his answer as he wheeled away. A step away he turned back and said "I didn't think you meant today" and stormed off.

I told him I'd do it somewhere else if he didn't wanna do it {I should've done it at Fu's to begin with, I ended up redoing it there anyway}.

"No, I'll do it" was his reply {he did it all right}.

As soon as I was done tearing down my motor he told Valerie and I with piles of work on the floor to do he didn't need us any more that day and sent us home with an "I'll call ya when I need ya."

I asked about my motor.

"I'll call ya when I'm done and you can come pick it up."

When I said I'd need to put it back together, his answer was "here?"

Well yah that was what I'd planned on and he knew it. Either that or he paid so little attention to the half dozen conversations I had with him about it the last few months that it was all a surprise to him.

He agreed to it by saying "fine" and walking away.

I had a real bad feeling as we left. Halfway down the driveway I told Valerie to turn around I was gonna get my shit outta there. When we got back the door was locked and though I could see him in the shop and he saw me when he turned around, he ignored my knocking and wouldn't open the door.

Later that morning he called Valerie and asked her to come in and she worked pretty much every day after that. She came home the next day telling me how Mel was raving about being used by the people that worked for him and he was sick of it. The only problem was I was paying him to do it like any other customer would, the only consideration I asked for was that he do the job right away. All the other work was mail order; it didn't matter if their work got done today or tomorrow.

I didn't hear from him for two fucking weeks. He wouldn't even answer the phone when I called. I could hear him from the background tell whoever answered the phone {usually Valerie} to tell me he was busy.

When he finally called "your stuff's done, come-n-get-it" was all he said.

It was kinda' weird living, sleeping and working with my enemy's {friends don't treat ya this way} friend. The whole time this was going on Valerie went to work out there almost every day and would come home defending Mel's actions to me while I twiddled my thumbs getting more and more pissed. When he finally called I drove out there in Valerie's pickup wondering what kinda' mess I'd get and if it was together or not.

When I got there it was on the bench in pieces. Mel handed me a cardboard box and told me to get it outta his shop. After it was all packed in the truck I started to walk back inside to find out what I owed him. He met me at the overhead door "no charge" was all he said and yanked the cord that slammed the door to the ground.

On the way into town I stopped in a Seven Eleven parking lot and checked out the damage. After a quick look I figured out that the only thing he'd done right was counter boring the heads and cases for the big bore barrels, everything else was a disaster. I drove by Fu's just in case {ya never knew when Fu was going home}.

When I got there even though it was late evening the place was wide open. While Fu and I were looking at the mess Mel had made, Clay {the only person on the planet besides my mother I'm still in touch with today} came out, looked at some of the obvious shit, looked at me and burst out laughing. He'd told me not to trust Mel for shit.

The motor, if you went by the numbers I got when I measured everything, was actually more worn out than when I took it out of the bike. He'd honed, ground or cut everything into worse shape than it was in before I disassembled it and only half the work that needed to be done was.

Thank God for Fu. He let me bring the damaged components in one at a time and turn them into the motor I wanted to build in the first place. All I had to put up with was the constant ribbing and laughter from Clay, but that was pretty easy because he and I were good friends and still are to this day. He and Fu were the ones that helped me the most to get back on the road as soon as possible.

I ended up having to replace parts that he'd butchered, like my rods. He'd ruined a set of new polished connecting rods by grinding the sides down to nothing; you don't ever grind on the rods. This actually caused me to do a lot more work to repair the damage he did than I would've had to do ordinarily.

It almost seemed like he did everything on purpose, cause no one could do that shitty a job on something by accident. It ended up costing me twice as much to rebuild my motor as it should've because he's such an ignorant egotistical piece of shit, which put me outta money to finish the rest of the bike.

A few months before the motor deal with Mel I was hanging around Fu's when a big dude walked in looking for Fu. I didn't recognize him from around town anywhere and I'd been around long enough to know pretty much everybody {at least by sight} that rode in The Springs. Fu was out back at the time. When he came in the door it was like old home week instantly. Obviously this was somebody Fu'd been waiting for, just by the greeting he got I could tell he wasn't somebody walking in off the street looking for motorcycle work. He and Fu went into the office and came out a few minutes later. When they came outta the office we introduced ourselves and I went home shortly afterward.

By the time I brought my injured motor to the shop we'd been friends for awhile. In fact I'd gotten the shovelheads that went on Christine from Clay. The wreck that Mel made of my motor confirmed what I'd always suspected. All the bragging he did and the line that he fed every new person that walked through the door including me was bullshit. His entire pitch was filled with how talented he was and all the shit he could do with all the machines he had in his shop. He couldn't even do a good valve job. The worst part about it was he'd slung that crap to the public for so long he believed it himself.

Months after the motor ordeal with Mel and Christine was all done and running. I was working out there one day when some tourists on bikes came through the door. Mel seeing strangers immediately came up front and started his spiel with an added twist. Christine was inside because it'd been showering earlier and was in full view from the front counter. Mel was rattling on about all the stuff he bragged he could do. Midbrag he turned around, pointed at Christine and told the tourists he'd built her.

Right after he said it a 9/16 box end, open end wrench slammed into the wall next to his head, I'd missed. He laughed it off like it was a joke. It wasn't funny and he was the only one laughing.

I told him in front of the tourists "you didn't build my bike, in fact everything you did you fucked up and I had to redo." He got pretty red-faced, but continued his bullshit anyway.

About the same time I was rebuilding Christine I finally made a connection for some descent dope that did the job. It was a good thing because pretty soon I'd be burning the candle at both ends and in the middle trying to make a buck, get my motor repaired and get the rest of the bike rebuilt so I'd have some wheels again.

I spent the first few weeks after the motor meltdown with Mel at Fu's shop working on my butchered parts. Having to buy new parts to replace the ones Mel had destroyed was eating up all the money I had and being on the outs with Mel pretty much meant I wasn't gonna have any more money any time soon, so the rebuild got stalled for months after I ran outta money. At first Valerie'd drop me near Fu's on her way out to Mel's in the morning and either she'd pick me up or Clay'd drop me off on his way home. Valerie picked me up one afternoon a few months after the fiasco. On the way home she told me that Mel needed me to work, I should call him when we got home.

As much as I hated doing it, I needed all the money I could get. I called him and we agreed to meet at the Denny's across town. After Valerie dropped me there, I'd ride out to his place with him in the morning after we had breakfast. He'd drive me back there when he went into town for dinner after we were done for the day.

The day went as planned. Nothing was said about the motor, I did my time, collected my cash and that was that. When we were about to leave I tried to call Valerie and got no answer. We drove into town and I tried to call her from Denny's still no answer. I wasn't gonna hang around Denny's so I started walking. When I got home the house was dark and Valerie's things were gone. She'd taken off on another one of her flings and left me high and dry like she'd done more than once before, but never when I was without transportation.

It's a good thing I'd found some doable dope, cause I was gonna need it. Without wheels to get around it was gonna be pretty hard to get much of anything done. I'd have to find a way cause I was the only one that was gonna get my bike built and solve the transportation dilemma I was in. I didn't have time to think much about Valerie leaving {I was getting used to it}, I had other crap to deal with.

In order to keep all the balls I was juggling in the air I had to get up at 5:00AM walk across town to the Denny's to meet Mel. Work there from nine to three. Get dropped off at Denny's walk halfway back across town to Fu's and work on my stuff there till 10:00PM. Get dropped off at home, work on the rest of the bike until about 2:00AM, snort a line and lay down till five. Then start the whole thing all over, day after rainy, shitty day. Unless Mel didn't need me, which was quite often because he didn't have me work on the days Valerie worked for him.

One thing about Mel he always took a perverse delight in starting and continuing trouble or misery in other people's lives. He always acted like your buddy to find out what was going on so he could gossip about it with anyone who'd listen. He loved to cause trouble with his gossip and sit back and watch his handiwork unfold while claiming to be your friend the whole time. Thanks to his bullshit a simple rebuild that should've only taken a couple 'a weeks ended up taking six months.

I was working on the bike in the living room late one night about two weeks into that program and started to feel kinda' weird. At the same time the dude I was getting my dope from called to see if I needed a reup. I told him I did, that the door'd be open in case he was gonna be real late cause I might quit early that night.

He drove a taxi and worked all kinds of weird hours cause he was an owner/operator and a crankster. He'd run until he couldn't see straight, go home for a little while and be right back at it a few hours later. Kinda' the same thing I was doing except he did a lot less walking in the rain than I seemed to be doing lately.

The schedule of the last two weeks. The lack of food and rest was finally catching up to me. I'd felt kinda' puny like I was getting sick or something all day. I'd gotten soaked walking across town that morning to meet Mel and worked in my wet cloths for six hours, chilling me to the bone that morning and I never got over it. When I got to Fu's that afternoon I was glad I didn't have that much more I could do that day. I got dropped off earlier than usual at the house and thought I'd actually take it easy for the rest of the day.

I was sitting on the couch looking at everything that'd been done so far and realized I'd overlooked a very important part that needed to be taken care of before I went any further on the rest of the bike. Figuring I'd get the work done and be back on track by midnight I snorted a line and started to work. A little while later I was thinking that the line I just did wasn't working as well as it should so I did another and went back to work.

The only problem was that I was getting so spun from everything that I wasn't getting anything done. I was wandering around in circles looking for the part that was in my hand cussing a blue streak because I'd just seen the part, but couldn't remember where. When I finally realized it was in my hand I was pissed because I'd just wasted the better part of two hours looking for it.

After I got over that I couldn't remember what I was gonna do with the part I was looking for and got mad about that. Then I remembered what I was gonna do and couldn't find the part because I'd laid it down while I was storming around the house trying to remember what to do with it. By the time I thought I'd be done I'd actually set myself back a couple 'a days and was really getting pissed about that.

When the phone rang I was starting to feel real weird, lightheaded and weak, the easiest way to put it is, I felt transparent. When I was talking to the dude on the phone it sounded like he was in a far off bucket and I could hardly hear him. I told him about the door and don't really remember hanging up. I started to make a sandwich cause I thought if I ate something I'd feel better and don't remember anything after that.

The next thing I knew I heard someone way off in the distance say "he's awake." I opened my eyes to see who was talking about whom. I thought I'd died and was at The Pearly Gates the light was so bright. It took a few seconds for me to figure out it wasn't jail and was shocked to see I was in a hospital.

Once I was alone for two seconds I scoped the place out, found my cloths and got the fuck outta there. When I walked out the door I had no idea where in town I was or which way was home. I walked in the wrong direction for about fifteen minutes until I recognized something and then headed back in the right direction.

As I neared the hospital I got a flash of blinding paranoia and scared the shit outta myself, what if I'd been under arrest and just escaped? I calmed myself down by saying to myself "you've already done that once and survived, you can do it again." To avoid detection I walked a few blocks outta the way around the hospital instead of walking directly in front of it.

I walked home, found the door closed but not locked and everything the way I'd left it {a disaster area}. A bag of dope was in the fridge hidden under my last beer, everything was as it should be complete with a half made peanut butter sandwich on the counter. I finished making the sandwich and ate it as stale as it was from sitting out all night. It was Saturday so I had no place to be, which was good because if I did I was late and whoever I was supposed to meet was shit outta luck.

I looked at the mess I'd made of my usually tidy work area and tried to remember what'd prompted the tirade that created the mess. As it was coming back to me I panicked and started searching the house for the part that kept eluding me the night before. This time the first place I looked was both hands. After searching the whole place over I found it on top of the refrigerator {don't ask me how it got *there*}. With it in my hand I figured I'd better go ahead and do as much as I could to Christine today and rest all day tomorrow to be ready for the grind of the next week.

Walking towards the back door I heard car tires on gravel. Sounded like a taxi, I knew he'd be around soon. I hadn't paid for what was under the beer yet. By the time he was gone I knew how I ended up in the hospital. He'd found me lookin pretty bad, thrown me in the car and dumped me out in front of the hospital just like we used to do during our extreme sport drugging days of the past. How I got from the curb to the bed neither of us knew and I wasn't going back to ask.

After my taxi left, the lines we'd snorted while he was there started to kick in pretty hard. This time the brain cell I was working with started out a lot clearer and I actually made progress until around one the next morning. I was as done as I could get until Monday when I'd have the lower end of the motor to set in the frame. I had a good thirty-six hours to do nothing in and I was so wired I could hardly stand myself. Thank God and Valerie for cable TV, without it I'd've gone nuts that night, but this was back in the days when MTV played music videos, J.J.Jackson was the head V-jay and the big sound, hair bands ruled the airwaves.

A friend'd shown me how to hook up the cable TV coax to the stereo too so the sound would come thru the speakers. I put on MTV and kicked back with a few bowls and my last beer until around sunrise when I woke up on the couch and went to bed.

Once I got in bed I laid there looking at the backs of my eyelids for hours until I couldn't take it any more. I threw my eyes open and looking in the bedroom window was Valerie. She came in the house crying, hugged me, said she missed me and wanted to come home.

Why should this time be any different, sure come on {the place was in her name anyway, why shouldn't she}. Fuck me around some more at least I'd have transportation again. I acted like I gave a shit, we hugged and kissed it all better, but like the last time she couldn't hurt her new boyfriend so it was still another two weeks before she moved back in.

About a month or so after Valerie returned, Christine and I were back on the road. Valerie's return was timed just right. After all the other work was done I had to load the bike up and take her to Denver to have the exhaust pipes made, Valerie's pickup came in handy for that. Once the pipes were done I had to glassbead and paint 'em and I was a free man again. Not havin' your scooter is like bein' in prison cause you're not very free without it.

Once Christine was done I told Valerie the first two thousand miles had to be solo for breakin purposes. What a dick huh, payback is always a bitch though. Actually it was to give me some time alone with my scooter and I really could give a shit if the little bitch ever rode with me again anyways. That way I didn't have to put the rear seat or foot pegs on. I've always enjoyed that real clean uncluttered look and a passenger seat and pegs don't fit my idea of clean. Besides after I got the bike dirty and scratched it a few times myself I'd be far more tolerant when she or someone else did it.

That was why I painted it flat black rustoleum. I could fuck it up one day and have it lookin' brand new in a couple 'a hours. The most easily fucked up surface was the white header paint on the pipes. I loved the look of the white pipes on the mostly black bike, but all it took was one boot scuff or scratch to start the pipes lookin' like shit and it was much better if *I* did the first damage. By the time Valerie started riding again I'd fucked the pipes up and repaired 'em enough to be sick of it.

My First Sportster

Sometime between tearing Christine down on Thanksgiving and the Addams County swap meet in January we were at a friend of Valerie's apartment. The dude managed a music store off Academy Boulevard. While we were talking he mentioned that someone had parked a Harley in back of his store and left it sitting there for months. I was immediately interested and this dude became my new best friend, for the next few minutes anyway. I tried to find out what type of Harley it was, but he didn't know so we had to go find out pretty much right away.

We checked the bike out as soon as we left their apartment. The bike was an early '70s Sportster. It'd obviously been sitting there a long time, rust from the front rim had stained the asphalt under the tire. The two of us couldn't get the bike into the truck by ourselves so we went over to another friend's house close by hoping he was home. He was, an hour later he was back home and we had a Sportster in our shed that I didn't know what I was gonna do with yet, but the day was still young.

I never had much use for Sportsters, even though they were the backbone of the service industry. That probably had something to do with it right there, you worked on five Sportsters to one Big Twin when you worked in shops. Some people liked 'em and rode the shit out of 'em. My first Harley was a Big Twin and I never got used to the skimpy feeling of a Sportster. Now I needed to figure out how to turn a Sportster into a Big Twin, at least the parts for one.

The easiest way was to dismantle the bike, bring all but the number bearing pieces to a swap meet and part it out. The only flaw to the plan was that it was a Sportster and everybody there that paid for a vendor's space had at least a shitload of Sporty parts he was trying to get rid of too.

I took my time and had the bike completely dismantled in about six hours. All the number parts disappeared and everything was ready for the next swap meet which was right after New Years. Valerie gave me the big bore barrels that I needed for Christmas that year, which was a big expense in the conversion, but that was still only a small part of the whole project.

Several times during the build the project stalled for lack of money. Hopefully the proceeds from the Sportster would be enough to finish the bike. I couldn't count on steady work from Mel, he was such an infantile egomaniac that you never knew when or what something would set him off. He'd send ya' home in the middle of the day and not call for two weeks or a month.

Working for him really sucked sometime, in fact all the time, kinda like living with Valerie, but it was all I had at the time and all I could do until I had wheels again. It seems like life always gets you by the balls at the worst possible times, especially when you're a drug addict. It always comes down to a choice between drugs or the rest of your life when money gets low.

If you're hooked on something like crank that you can't function without, the wrong decision seems like the right one at the time and the dope tells you it'll all work itself out while your high. Come the next day or so later, you have less money than before, haven't done a thing you were supposed to and now you need more dope. That was pretty much the description of one complete loop in the downward spiral of a crankster's life. Repeat that for days, weeks and months on end and it doesn't take long before the vacuum of meth has sucked you dry.

The hardest thing for an addict is balancing being sucked dry by meth with everything else in life. You have to love the other things more than dope to accomplish anything besides getting high. I justified spending bike money for dope by saying I needed it to keep me awake to work on the bike all night and go to work the next day, which was true to an extent. The money I spent on dope would've been better spent on the bike instead of furthering my trip down the road to the bottom. Hell I was just taking the first real steps into the abyss by rationalizing drugs over life. First time I'd ever placed drugs over my bike when there was a choice, but not the last.

In no time the biggest swap meet in Colorado was next weekend, there were all kinds of last minute rushes to get through before we had everything loaded and were headed for Denver. The remains of the abandoned Sportster was in the back of Valerie's Toyota pickup along with crates of Fu's parts for the swap meet. In the back of Fu's truck was a freshly restored `51 Panhead. In eighteen days four of us'd gotten together and taken something that'd been buried up to the top triple tree in chicken shit and turned it into a show winning vintage restoration.

It was around this time that I ran into my taxi driving connection and began getting some pretty decent dope. I kept my use to myself so I wouldn't have to share my dope with anyone including Valerie {I'd be willing to bet that had a lot to do with her leaving in more ways than one}. She'd had a time with coke before I met her. From her description of her life with coke I didn't want her sucking the life outta my dope bags prematurely, so I kept it from her as much as I could.

Anyway we got to the Addams County Fairgrounds, delivered the Panhead to the show pavilion, found our spots, unloaded the parts and got ready for the next day. It was early morning by the time we got to our motel rooms, thank God for better living through chemistry.

I was up and had my line done before Valerie ever stirred the next morning. One of the things about using crank that you discover very early on is that you can extend your up time by little catnaps. When you start to run down, if you do a little bump and lay down for a little while, you never actually sleep, but somehow when you rise you feel rested.

I used this tactic along with forcing myself to eat and taking vitamins to keep myself from becoming your typical wasted speed freak and prolong the high I got from crank. It also kept away the crystal creatures and meth monsters, something I hadn't had enough experience with to name yet, maybe that was because I hadn't fried enough brain cells.

My drug budget was such that I couldn't afford to snort all my dope up in two days and not have any for the rest of the week. I learned how to stay high all week on the amount of dope that I could afford. As long as the quality of the dope remained good I'd get through an entire week on a minimal amount of dope undetected by Valerie or anyone else.

I was teaching myself how to be a very sneaky and undercover dope user. For the first time in my life I was deep enough under the spell of crank that I was actually analyzing my actions and reactions in order to develop some type of science or method to my use that would conceal it from whoever I wanted to, but allow me to be high all the time.

We all had breakfast and went to the meet. When we got there Clay handed out some little purple microdot hits of mescaline and the day was officially underway. Within a few minutes I felt the first stages of uncontrollable laughter coming on that signaled we were gonna have a good day no matter what happened.

We had a large area right in front of the stage and every one of us was all fucked up on mescaline. Before long we were the lives of the party and people were walking by just to see what was gonna happen next, this included the security personnel and the cops. Several times that day I turned around to see that we were surrounded by cops watching nothing but us. This wasn't paranoia; we were having one hell of a good time and were very loud, drowning out the events on the stage in front of us several times during the day while we did it.

One dude walked up, picked up a part outta Clay's pile and asked the price, Clay told him "ten bucks." When he asked what it was Clay and I exploded with laughter, Clay told him to put it down and go away in between bursts.

As he walked away two cops standing behind him turned in our direction and focused in on us. We separated like kids caught smoking in the boy's bathroom at school. They walked right up to our area and stood there watching us like we were the only ones in the whole fuckin' place. The only way not to blow it and start laughing in their faces was to turn away and act like something'd grabbed our attention. When I finally turned back to that side of the room they'd drifted off thru the crowd, probably to watch us from a distance.

One of the contests they had on the stage was a panty give away. The catch was that to keep the panties you had to put 'em on, on stage. Clay being the instigator that he was talked Valerie into going up, putting the panties on over her jeans and walking away.

The whole crowd cheered when that fine little blonde switched her ass onstage and took the panties. When she slipped 'em over her jeans and walked away smiling and waving they hit the fuckin' roof.

Everyone in our section busted out laughing so hard I'm amazed none of us had an aneurysm, even the cops that were never far away by now had a good laugh over it.

After giving away one set of panties without seeing skin the stipulation was made that the panties had to be **CHANGED** on stage.

The next girl more than made up for the prank Valerie'd pulled when it came to showing skin. She got up on stage took off all her cloths, threw them into the crowd and started her own little sex show with the Harley panties. That went on so long they carried her off the stage still masturbating and moaning, out the back door and probably out to a van or somewhere and gangbanged the shit out of her.

The reason I say that is because about an hour and a half later a dude grabbed the mic onstage and asked people to bring her cloths up front. From where I was standing I could see her standing just behind the stage naked waiting for her clothes with a freshly fucked half to death look all over her.

Sometime during the afternoon the same "what is it" guy from earlier stopped and looked at the Sportster parts I had laying on the floor. As soon as I saw him I burst out laughing like a madman, telling him to just go away in between gasps for air and sidesplitting laughter. Valerie looked at me as though I'd lost my mind, as much as I wanted to sell those parts I was driving away the only person who'd even looked at 'em all day at laugh point.

I couldn't stop laughing to save my life. That mescaline was probably the best I'd ever done. Enhanced by the line in the morning I couldn't get a coherent thought into or out of my brain edgewise to save my life. I had a mind like a steel trap, nothing got in and nothing got out!

When I wasn't laughing at something I was fuuucked up. Inside my head was like a big traffic jam of sound that made it impossible to pick one sound like a voice and hear it. When people spoke to me I saw their lips move, but couldn't pick 'em out of the cacophony to understand 'em. I'd just look at 'em, smile and laugh insanely not having any real clue what the fuck was going on or what'd just been said.

After a while I was starting to get a little freaked out by my newfound super power, as soon as I convinced myself it was only the dope and I'd come down eventually I started to. A little while later I was down further than I wanted to be and was kinda' pissed at myself for killing my own buzz. It was a good thing though because the festivities of the day were coming to a close and it was time to leave until tomorrow. Where'd the day gone? Time sure flew while we were having fun.

The next day we started packing up just before noon. We were all wrung out from the party the day before. I was glad I had a line to get me going that morning; otherwise I'd have lain in bed until someone physically threw me out.

By the time they gave out the trophies for the bike show we had everything else packed for the trip home. The Panhead had been entered in the antique restoration class where it took second place. It would've taken first place if the spokes in the wheels had been cadmium plated instead of black. In that class attention to detail is the name of the game. The bike has to be restored to exact factory specs including cad plated spokes if that's how that model was originally sold. Hey second place isn't bad if you consider only a month before that it'd been buried to the top tree in shit.

Fu got the trophy and before we could load the bike up made a deal to sell it. I can't even remember if we brought it home with us, but I do remember that it was a long drive home. It felt about twice as long as it was going up.

We went straight to the house when we got into town instead of going to the shop. I unloaded all the Sportster shit back into the shed, not one piece of that fuckin' thing did I sell. Hell I only had one person look in the direction of it all weekend and I ran him off at laugh point before he could even ask me what something was. Christine wasn't gonna get built that way, that's for sure.

I was relieved to hear that there was another swap meet in the Denver Coliseum in a few weeks. Maybe I'd have better luck then. I know I won't be as fucked up as I was at Addams County. I didn't get anything but a lot of laughing done at that swap meet and that didn't pay even one of the bills for that weekend, but it sure was fun.

The next day we went down to Fu's and unloaded his parts out of Valerie's truck. After that we went home. I was outta steam and needed to talk to the taxi driver after Valerie went to work the next day. Wouldn't ya' know Mel called and wanted us both to come in. It'd be late the next night before I could get any dope.

I woke the next day in a foul mood that got worse as the day progressed. It was one of those moods where you'd love to tell everybody just what you think of 'em and end it with a deeply heartfelt "go fuck yourself!" You just can't afford to so you end up biting your tongue and walking around stewing in the mess you've made, mad at everybody else involved when actually you were the one that fucked yourself.

I was so sick of hearing Mel tell anyone that'd listen how great he was, when everything he did sucked {he'd already fucked up my motor and thought he got away with it because I didn't say anything about it. I didn't see the point he'd just reduce it to money} because he put no heart in it. He didn't have any to put there was the problem. All he thought about was money.

The good part about working that day, I had more money for dope that night. I guess we all become one kind of whore or another for our drug of choice. In that context the word whore has a much broader spectrum than more commonly thought of in society.

The day was finally over, late that night I met a taxi at the end of the alley and I was back to normal the next day. All night long I felt like a kid on Christmas Eve. I couldn't wait to get up and do some dope. I was up and high before the sun came up. As soon as I was high I could think of a quite a few things that I could do to get Christine further down the road to being together.

I went to work quietly at first, but before long I was in the midst of a frenzy of work and was making more and more noise till I woke Valerie up. I was in a great mood and she was fuckin' pissed {I would've been too if the situation was reversed}. I refused to see the problem which was grounds for a knockdown, drag out screaming match first thing in the morning {probably another reason why she left}.

Working for Mel was sketchy at best. Just like I knew it would be for the next few weeks because I needed the money. I only managed to do a very little bit to Christine every day, the lack of any real money was putting a serious damper on the progress and it was pissing me off a little more each day.

Finally the next swap meet was here. I didn't really wanna go through loading all the shit up, dragging it to Denver, unpacking it, packing it back up and dragging it home again. After a little prodding I got over my basic laziness and loaded it up {nothing ventured, nothing gained}.

The Coliseum was much smaller than Addams County, so I pretty much had myself talked outta everything before it even happened. I was just going through the motions halfheartedly. I figured I'd sell even less than I did at Addams County. I was almost convinced to start packing up stuff for the second time while another part of me was saying just leave it. A dude walked up, picked something up and actually gave me money for it.

In a few hours time Sportster parts turned into Big Twin parts and at the end of the meet I had nothing to load for home. I got about fifteen hundred dollars outta that bike that day. More than I'd've gotten if I sold it all together with a title. It wouldn't be long before I was back in the saddle once again. I thought it was more than I'd need to finish the bike and the last major hurdle in the race to get the bike done.

It wasn't long after this that Valerie left. A few weeks after The Coliseum swap meet Valerie woke up to an entire house covered in flat black overspray from painting the frame in the living room in the middle of a cold winter night with all the windows open. I still don't think it was the drugs that made me do something that stupid. I just had no other way to do it, so day or night it had to be done.

Once it dried I vacuumed it up just like any other dust, but until then everything in the house was flat black. Not long after this I came home to an empty house again. I was used to this and the only real thing I cared about was the lack of transportation. At least now I could do my dope without having to hide from anyone. Anyway we already know she came back and after that little back story we'll get on with the main mess.

While I lived in The Springs I fed on a pretty constant basis three addictions; pot, I'd been smoking regularly since age twelve, alcohol, I had my first drink at nine and speed, I'd been using more on than off since I was thirteen. I'd started smoking cigarettes when I was six. Maintaining these habits was costly in more ways than one; one of the expenses was time both in court and jail due to incidents like this.

One evening four of us were sitting around partying and ran outta whiskey. This dude Keith and I made a liquor store run in Valerie's pickup. The liquor store was only a few blocks away on the other side of the freeway. While we're standing at the counter checking out, Keith pointed out a four wheel drive Toyota up on the sidewalk and then up on an embankment trying to run over a girl that was walking.

Being two drunken lunatic idiots we took the liquor back to the house. Left the truck at home and walked back. On the way back the Toyota was parked in a parking lot near the sidewalk so we performed a little drunken vigilante justice on it, on the way to the center ring of this three ring circus. A little further up the sidewalk in the corner of the wall of a building and the end of the retaining wall for the bridge over the Arkansas River I spotted this dude with his hand up ready to smack a girl that he had pinned in the corner. I ran up and drilled him in the side of the head, knocking him down while Keith kept the other guy and his girlfriend busy. The gal in the corner jumped over the dude that I knocked down and ran off across the bridge.

An ambulance that'd been sitting at the traffic light radioed the cops and then tried to break it up. It was already broken up was the problem. The dude that I hit got up running and never let me get within twenty feet of him to continue the fight. The fat ass ambulance dude got out with his maglight like he was gonna do something and ended up running for his ambulance about the same time the first cop showed up.

This guy was just getting everything under control when another cop showed up. The second cop was a white guy with an obvious afro perm in his hair, in my disablingly able state I immediately started calling him hairdo which was a big yank on his chain every time I did it.

Anyway the first cop transported me and hairdo transported Keith. On the ride to the jail I had to piss. Being the caring and sharing individual that I am I decided to share this with the cop. I slipped my cuffs around in front of me and pissed all over the front of the cop's car and him through the cage that separated us.

He tried to rough me up when we got to the jail. I was so preoccupied with making hairdo's life a bundle of joy that I didn't really notice it. I found every reason in the book to say hairdo, hairdo, hairdo as much as possible until he screamed **"DON'T FUCKIN' CALL ME THAT"** and slammed me face first into the steel door of the sally port.

I bounced off the door and screamed **"OKAY HAIRBAG!"** The door opened and we were inside.

One cop was covered with piss and the other one *was* pissed, truly a match made in heaven. I felt absolutely wonderful about bringing these two together too. To make matters worse for the pissed on and off cops, the deputies running the intake area were getting a big kick outta the shit I was doin' to hairbag and his buddy.

During the processing I was lucky enough to have a female deputy. As soon as I told her the story she was sympathetic and between her and the other deputy that processed us we got pretty lucky. Keith got released on an OR because he hadn't really done anything and my bail was only a hundred dollars which Keith just happened to have in his pocket. The booking process probably took a half hour or so and we were released. As we walked out, there were my two cop buddies doing their paperwork. When we walked by I said "see ya hairdo, uh hairbag" and walked out both of us roaring with laughter.

Keith and I walked back to the house. The whole thing only took about an hour and a half and the girls didn't believe our stories until we showed 'em our bail slips. I did a weekend in jail for that stupidity, the price ya pay for the life ya lead.

Another time a bar had recently opened right up the street from where Clay lived in Fountain called the Cuckoo's Nest. One Friday evening we knew we wanted to do something, but we didn't know what. Checking out the Cuckoo's Nest sounded like a good idea so we headed up there early in the evening. We were there long enough to drink almost a whole bottle of Jack between four of us along with some other drinks like Amaretto Slammers and that kinda' stuff.

We decided we'd head to Denver for some real fun. It was pretty dead in Fountain and we had all weekend. A few blocks after leaving the bar my right side gas cap fell off. I was pissed but we could stop at the shop on the way to Denver and stick a new one on, not a really big deal. I tied a bandana over the fill hole to keep the wind from siphoning gas into my lap and off we went.

Just before we got to the freeway the same thing happened to Clay's bike. This was no coincidence now, we'd both filled up on the way to the bar and neither of us forgot how to replace the gas caps in the time it took to fill our tanks.

We could only assume someone at the bar had fucked with the bikes as a prank or something. Prank or not you just don't fuck with a scooter that isn't yours and everyone in the bar was gonna understand that when we were done or die trying. Before we went back in the bar I gave Valerie my 25 auto. Pistol so I wouldn't be tempted to shoot somebody with it.

As Clay and I stormed into the bar he roared **"WHO THE FUCK.........."** The rest was lost to me as I hit the first dude that stood up in arms reach and continued across the room after anything or anyone that moved. Clay was doing the same thing and in a very few minutes we'd wrecked the entire bar and the customers were either on the floor or running out the door.

One dude wouldn't stay down. As he headed for the door I chased him. Outside he was across the street and gone about the time a cop on each side of the door grabbed me and put me up against a car. The ruckus inside had subsided because the cops were inside by now taking control of the situation. By the time Clay, Peewee and Valerie came outside I was cuffed in the spirit of public safety and the dude I chased outta the bar was giving his story to a cop. When they got outside we all got lined up to play the usual twenty questions. I guess when ya go off like that somebody is bound to wanna know why.

One of the usual questions for those of you that don't know is, do you have any weapons or drugs? Rather than having the cops find my gun on Valerie and have some real trouble I told 'em she had the gun. They took it and that was that for the moment.

When they asked Clay I could tell by the look on his face that he was lying when he said "nope." As he was saying it he was raising his hands to be patted down and with the slickest move I've ever seen, he tossed a 22 long, five shot derringer over one of the cop's heads to land on the windshield of one of the cop cars slide down it and the hood and hit the asphalt right at the same cop's feet.

After a second of incredulity on the cop's parts we all busted out laughing while the cops freaked out about the gun. After all it was one of the funniest things we'd ever seen in our lives. The "I didn't do that" look on Clay's face was pretty fuckin' hysterical, even the cops got a good laugh about it eventually. It was a good thing, instead of turning it into a big time felony bust they kept their sense of humor and we got processed and released within the hour never spending any time in cells and not that much time in cuffs.

Once released we walked back down to the bar about a hundred yards away, got on our scooters and headed back to Friday night. First stop was to get some gas caps. By the time we got that done it was after ten o'clock. Too late to ride to Denver so we stuck around town and if I remember right at the end of the night the crank wore off before the party did and I didn't have any more. When that happens all the alcohol that didn't effect you before when you were drinking it like water kicks in and if you're conscious you do the stupidest things you can possibly think of in rapid fire succession.

I'm pretty sure at the end of *that* night on the way home we got stopped and I was so stupefied I told the cop I couldn't read so I didn't know I was speeding or maybe it was because I was so drunk I couldn't remember the alphabet, let alone recite it. Well I might not have known I was speeding, but he knew I was a drunken idiot and made me park the bike. He had Clay take me back to the house a few blocks away, get Valerie's pickup, come back and get the bike and the girls that were watching it and bring 'em home.

By the time Clay and I got to the house, I was five times drunker than I was when the cop stopped us and started raving about him taking my bike cause I couldn't read. I panicked when I couldn't find the keys to the pickup right away and destroyed one of Valerie's sister's end tables she was coming back from California for in a few months.

That wasn't the end of my bullshit yet. When we all got home and Valerie saw the table she hit the roof. My idea of fixing it, was to gather up the evidence and throw it thru the picture window into the driveway. Problem solved, right? Well it wasn't until I jumped out the window behind it and disappeared into the night. Like my buddy Doc Holliday used to say about me, "instant asshole, just add alcohol!"

Our gun man in Old Colorado City turned us on to a young attorney who took care of everything and Valerie and Clay got slaps on the wrists for the guns. Sometime during the fracas the girls'd given the barmaid {whom Valerie knew} twenty-five dollars for the damages, so the bar didn't press any charges. However I don't think it ever opened the doors again.

Weeks later Clay and I stopped in the Bank Shot one afternoon for a beer. When we walked in I noticed the dude that I was chasing outta the bar when the cops grabbed me, standing on one side of the bar talking to someone. The bar itself was shaped like a big U. Clay went to the other side of the bar and I slid in next to the dude from Fountain to hear his story. When I got close enough to hear I realized he was telling the story of how twenty-five Hells Angels had overrun the town of Fountain and completely destroyed the Cuckoo's Nest.

I got Clay's attention from across the bar and in a loud voice asked him if he heard about the Hells Angels wrecking a bar in Fountain. He burst out laughing and looked at the dude telling the story. The guy recognized him immediately. He then turned to me, paled and ran for the door like he'd seen a ghost. Clay and I burst out laughing. I turned to the guy the storyteller was talking to and said "it wasn't Hells Angels, it was he and I" pointing to Clay. We all had a good laugh and eventually the storyteller returned when he figured out we weren't there to kill him.

Christine was reborn in the middle of May of '86. Just a few weeks later we were evicted by the church. Something about having the devil in that close a proximity to its parishioners. Having their Sunday morning services ripped in half by a pack of roaring Harleys screaming up the alley out back didn't do too much to endear them to their tenants either. With the El Paso County Sheriff's Department backing 'em all the way we were told to move as soon as humanly possible {immediately, if not sooner}.

Valerie's sister was moving to California. She lived in a house owned by their father's business, which was also conveniently located behind the offices of said business {did I ever mention that Valerie's dad hated me with a passion from the moment he laid eyes on me. Can't blame him though I was probably the worst thing that ever happened to her in her entire life} and right next door to his business partners flamboyantly gay son.

Valerie's dad labeled me as a no-good drifter the minute he laid eyes on me and he wasn't wrong in the least little bit. I'd had the label of no-good since I was a little kid and wore it with pride like a union member. Having me on any property that he owned was grounds for an aneurysm in his book. Just the thought of me had him red-faced, spitting foam from his snaggled teeth as he practiced every curse word he knew in short bursts under his breath.

We'd made Sturgis a yearly happening since I'd come to The Springs and this year wouldn't be any exception. We moved into the house on Bijou sometime in June. I can't remember exactly when it was. I know we were living behind the church when I finished Christine in May and I know we where living on Bijou when we went to Sturgis in August of that year.

I probably can't remember exactly when because sometime during those few months my taxi driver'd gotten busted when he fell asleep at the wheel and had a minor traffic accident downtown early in the morning. When they searched him of course they found some dope and that ended my run because I wasn't gonna buy the dope around town.

His dope came from outta town and did a very respectable job, the price and quality was consistent and he was always just a page away. Service with a smile, any hour of the day or night, every cranksters dream, the only thing better is to cook your own dope. But we can't all be chiefs now can we, there have to be some Indians to make the world go round.

Felony Stupidity

This year was gonna be our best Sturgis ever. We'd saved and finagled for quite a while to have as much money as possible. We were gonna go for the whole week instead of a few days at the beginning or end of the run. That meant we had to have money for drugs, alcohol, food, gas and all the other miscellaneous expenses that a week at the largest motorcycle run in the country entailed.

Valerie had scammed this dude out of a quarter ounce of coke, we had plenty of weed and all the other ducks were in a row and quacking merrily when we stopped at Fu's on the way outta town.

Having coke not crank was a little different. I never liked coke, it was a waste of time and money. The shit was expensive and the high so short that you spent more time chasing a buzz than anything else, but when it was free and you were jonesing for crank the buzz was better than nothing. We had quite a bit and my hope was that we'd find somebody that would trade some coke for crank once we got to Sturgis.

We each did a line before we left the house and only rode as far as Fu's shop before I wanted another one. While I was doing what I was doing, Valerie laid us out some lines on the top of the toilet tank in the bathroom. After we did our lines I walked outside and left her to pick up and restash the dope. While she was doing her thing the sleeve of her jacket accidentally brushed the coke, bindle and all into the toilet {the truest easy come, easy go I've ever heard of}. She never told me about it cause she knew I'd be mad as hell. I was mad about everything those days, I'd been jonesing pretty hard since I'd lost my connection and the unsatisfying buzz of coke was only a tease that frustrated me even more.

We hauled ass outta town headed for Sturgis, all the way I was fighting the desire to pull over and do another line and I bet Valerie was praying that I didn't. We got to Mule Creek Junction around ten that night. My plan was to get a bite and a beer, snort a line and ride on into Sturgis. We had the bite and the beer, as we walked back to the bike I said something about a line and Valerie got a scared look on her face as she told me about the coke. If there'd been a roof over the parking lot I'd've hit it, I was fuckin pissed.

We camped there that night and in the morning while I was storming around raving about the lost coke a patchholder that was camped near us came over and said he didn't have any coke, but he could help me out with some crank. I didn't like buying from unknowns but the dope looked pretty clean and the price was right.

Valerie and I did a line, packed up and headed into Sturgis. That was the first thing that went wrong that trip, but far from the last or worst. In fact after we got through the week it ended up being so fucked up I had to get a tattoo over it.

We got into town about midday. We always camped at a little ice cream and burger joint on Junction Avenue a few blocks from downtown. When we turned onto Junction we didn't see any campers at our usual place. This was kinda' odd because the same people camped there every year and it was always like old home week when we first pulled in. As we set up our site and for a little while afterwards everybody was catching up with everybody else they hadn't seen in a year.

We pulled in the driveway and was greeted by a **FOR SALE** sign and a sign twice its size saying **NO CAMPING!** That fuckin' sucked. The property had a snow fence around it and a chain across the drive with **NO CAMPING, NO TRESSPASSING** signs every few feet. While we were sitting there figuring out what to do some of our old neighbors pulled in too.

We were sitting there talking when a cop stopped and told us to move along. I told him we were trying to figure out where to go. He came flying outta the car like I'd told him to go fuck his mother or something. Thru gritted teeth he said he didn't give a shit where we went as long as we got going right then.

We fired up the bikes and went downtown to the Fireside Lounge to have a drink and make a new plan. Not only was this a logistical problem it also hit our pocketbooks too. We camped for free at the diner and kinda' paid for it by eating there. Now we'd have to pay to camp and the only place that was open and required no reservation was the Buffalo Chip Campground.

Our little diner was surrounded by shade trees, a big relief in the hot South Dakota sun and good protection during the helacious hail storms. The Buffalo Chip was a huge field with no shade and no protection. During the day it was pretty much empty, but at night when the party was going on nothing was safe from the hoards of drunken bikers that staggered from one end of the place to the other.

During earlier years I'd seen a dude stabbed to death because a prospect tried to rape his ole'lady and he tried to stop him, people beaten near to death for looking at the wrong dude at the wrong time, women jerked outta the crowd, gangbanged and beaten till they were an unconscious bloody mess and left for whatever else could happen to 'em. Plus the place was a couple 'a miles outta town which made you a sitting duck for the cops if you liked to party in town instead of a dustbowl or mud pit depending on the weather. If I'd believed in omens then the smart thing to do would've been to go home *then* and call it a week, but we ended up at The Buffalo Chip.

We found a spot up on the hill overlooking the stage far enough away that we wouldn't get trampled during the party. There was a bunch of people from San Angelo Texas there and it wasn't too long before we all knew each other. Once we got our tent set up we partied for a while with the Texans. Around dark o'clock we did the last of the dope that I'd gotten that morning {it turned out to be no better than the garbage in The Springs}. I kept the dirty baggie cause there was at least one good line left in it, but instead of leaving it in the tent I brought it for later.

We were going into town to call the folks in The Springs that were coming up later to tell 'em where we were, get something to eat and hit a few bars. I figured I'd probably need that line later. This was Monday night. It was amazing how many people there were in town already, the run had just started the day before.

Around midnight it felt like a good time to call it quits. We rode up and down Main Street then headed for The Buffalo Chip. Just outta town we were stopped by two of Sturgis's finest for speeding. I'd been doing forty-five mph they said. I had a pretty good buzz but I wasn't so fucked up that I didn't notice the forty-five mph speed limit sign right behind him as he was reading me the riot act. When I pointed out the sign to him he said it didn't matter now because he smelled alcohol and shoved a pocket breathalyzer in my face. I tried the old trick of spitting when I blew, didn't work.

I was pretty fucked up, but I remember I was sitting in the front seat of the car uncuffed and had the urge to smoke a cigarette, forgetting that the dirty baggie was in my pack. There was one cigarette left in the pack and the dirty baggie clearly visible inside the cellophane on the side of the pack. With a cop sitting right next to me, pretending to be fishing around in the pack for a cigarette, I snuck the baggie outta the cellophane and hid it deeper in between the label and the inner foil. I stuck the cigarette in my mouth and lit it, crumpled up the empty pack and threw it out the window.

The cop sitting next to me looked at me, but didn't say a word. The cop outside went **"OH NO YOU DON'T"** and grabbed the pack. He started ripping it apart till he found the baggie, handed it to his partner and started raising hell with him for not paying attention. I remember how unreal the scene looked during the bust and while we were sitting there with the red and blue lights flashing off everything around us. Through it all every time I looked at Valerie she looked terrified. Twenty-one years later as I write this I can still see the look on her face as we're driving away with the strobing lights enhancing that look.

I can't remember how she got Christine to the campground I wasn't there, she mighta' rode her for all I know. I was in the gymnasium of the high school being booked for drunk driving and possession of a controlled substance while she was dealing with all the outside shit. Deal with it she did and was at the jail the next morning looking worn out, you could tell she'd been crying.

There was a window to the outside right in front of the cell we were all in. My first recollection of the cell was that there were a lotta motherfuckers in there. Then I started to recognize some faces. While we were setting up our campsite and getting to know the Texans a couple 'a dudes from Virginia set up right next to us; they partied for a while with us before they headed into town and we never saw 'em again. That was because they'd both been arrested for drunk driving and had spent the night in jail.

I went to court sometime that morning and my bail was set at fourteen hundred dollars, we didn't have that kind of money so I was stuck. Valerie said she'd do the best she could, left to make all the phone calls she could and to find a bondsman. When she came back and said there was only one bondsman in town and he wasn't dealing. The only thing I could tell her was to see if he'd trade Christine for me. Better her in jail than me, at least she didn't have to worry about the crappy food.

It was touch and go there for a while, but Valerie talked him into the trade. When I was released I had to go out to The Buffalo Chip, get Christine and bring her to the bondsman's office. The bondsman was also a local realtor named Jerry and was actually a pretty nice guy. When we arrived at his office we put Christine in a large building next door and locked her up. He kinda' explained how the case was gonna go and what I'd have to do to get Christine back before Friday morning's court date, otherwise I'd be without wheels the rest of the week. This was Tuesday evening.

After we got done at the bondsman's office the Texans who'd helped Valerie through all this crap took us out to the Buffalo Chip and partied with us the rest of the night. We'd been lucky to meet 'em, they'd traveled so far and so many people had gone that they brought along a chase car just in case. They probably never figured on chasing a stranger's case though.

It felt good to be outta that jail, but I felt like just as much of a prisoner without my bike and no matter how hard myself and everyone else tried to cheer me up I was fuckin' miserable. I was wrung out and depressed with no dope in sight, which made me even more miserable.

I crapped out early and moped around like I'd lost my best friend {I had, when I needed it most}. I had no interest in anything. I thought for sure I was gonna end up a South Dakota citizen for a couple years anyway. At the very least I thought I'd lose Christine. Visions of gray bars danced in my head and cold ass South Dakota winters haunted my thoughts.

After a shitty night of lying awake quietly freaking out we got up and took showers, got as buzzed as we could get and headed into town. During bike week all the merchants in Sturgis clear out their stores and rent the space to outside vendors for the week except for the lawyers. They do a booming business keeping idiots like me from becoming unwilling citizens of South Dakota.

Believe me every day there's a new crop of derelicts locked up and bailed for every kind of "too much fun in a no fun zone" offence on the books and this keeps the attorneys in town plenty busy. If we'd been staying in town, not having Christine would've been a lot less a problem, but we probably wouldn't've been stopped either. We could've spent the nights in the bars, where I wanted to be and staggered to the lawyer's office in the morning smelling the way I felt without having to get a ride from anyone.

It was convenient how the town was laid out. The bars were at one end of the street and the jail and courthouse at the other with the lawyer's offices right in front of the courthouse.

When we got to town we went straight to a lawyer, after talking to him I felt better. He handled the case for a couple hundred dollars. He was just gonna plea bargain it down to a fine and a license suspension for a month that wouldn't affect me in Colorado.

The only problem was coming up with the money to pay the fine so I got Christine back instead of forfeiting her in place of cash. That was the deal I'd signed with the bondsman. If I didn't come up with the cash within thirty days of the completion of the case I'd loose Christine. I wasn't leaving South Dakota without her and that was it, whatever that took.

The first person we called for money was Mel. Hell we both worked for the guy, it was only eleven hundred dollars that I needed. I'd just work it off no big deal. First he stalled us, then he lied to us saying he'd sent his girlfriend into town to send it Western Union and the money should be there now. In between calls with Mel we called Fu's and talked to Clay. Valerie'd called the day before while I was in jail. We called to see when they'd be there and let 'em know everything was handled {we thought, but Clay didn't}. Once we were done at the lawyer's office we walked the two blocks to the Western Union/bondsman's office to wait for the cash and spring Christine.

No cash ever came. When we called Mel he said his girlfriend wasn't back yet so he had no idea what the deal was. By the end of the day we knew he'd lied to us about the whole thing. If he didn't wanna do it all he had to do was say so in the first place instead of pulling that juvenile bullshit.

We got a ride out to the Buffalo Chip and I spent another night in an even worse mood, raining on all the parades around me. I spent most of the night in the tent laying there listening to the wildness going on around me, pissed at the world for having fun without me.

The next day we were back in town and on the phone first thing, Clay wasn't surprised that Mel pulled that shit {neither was I really}. He was as much of a stand up person as a limp noodle was, the lying fuck! Clay said they'd all be leaving in a little while and they'd be there in a few hours. He told us where their campground was and we wandered that way when the time came. This was Thursday, court was the next day, we'd spent the week in Sturgis alright. The only way it could've been more miserable was if one of us'd been killed, as shitty as I was feeling I'd have felt lucky if it'd been me.

Later on that afternoon we hooked up with Clay at their campsite. Fu was running a little behind. It seems he'd fitted his pistons just a little too tight when he built the motor in the Panhead he rode to Sturgis. Clay'd left him and the rest of the crew in a rest area a ways back with the sticking pistons. A little later Fu rode in on the Panhead and shut it off. That was the last time that motor ever ran until it was rebuilt, in fact a few minutes after he shut it off you couldn't even turn it over.

Once everyone got there we went out to The Buffalo Chip and got our stuff and set up with Fu and them. The next morning we all went to court to hear the verdict. I pled guilty and received my fourteen hundred dollar slap on the wrist and my license suspension starting the Tuesday after bike week ended. When it came time for the cash part Fu stepped up and paid it for me saying we'd work it out.

As soon as I had the receipt for the fine in my hand I hotfooted it to get Christine outta jail and get the fuck away from all these suits and uniforms. I didn't really think about it at the time. That was my first felony drug conviction, the only one for meth and the beginning of four before I finally wised up.

For the rest of the run Clay and Peewee and Valerie and I rode thru the Black Hills taking in the sites while Fu spent his time at the campground getting drunk and throwing sticks at his Panhead. We'd spend the evenings doing what scooter people do on motorcycle runs and every other time they get together, partying.

I can't remember whether we left on Sunday or Monday, but we left in a hurry. Clay and I flew south toward The Springs, We passed packs of bikes, cars, everything that got in our way, me down the shoulder and Clay down the yellow line in excess of or near a hundred mph all the way.

The day we left was pretty hot, so all I was wearing was a leather vest, no shirt. Flying through Wyoming at outrageous speeds every piece of exposed skin was getting pelted by bugs, these particular bugs burned when they splattered all over my skin till I thought I was gonna catch on fire.

We finally stopped for gas in Lusk Wyoming. Before I gassed up I found the hose and was gonna wash the bug splat off and hopefully put out the fire. As soon as the water hit my skin it was like I was made of gas and someone had thrown a match on me. I started jumping around and hollering like a lunatic. I kept spraying the water for a few minutes figuring that it would eventually wash the bug splat off and it'd stop burning.

The more I sprayed the worse it burned till I thought my skin was gonna fry right off my body. I got these blotches of fire engine red skin that felt like they were actually on fire everywhere the bugs'd hit me and they burned as bad as they looked. Everybody in the gas station looked at me like I was insane as I hopped, hollered and sprayed water everywhere until I realized it wasn't working and quit.

I gave up on the hose and gassed up and we got outta there. We passed everything we'd passed previously and then started in on a whole new mess of traffic exactly the same way, wide fuckin' open. We had to've really been moving. It was four hundred and one miles from our house to downtown Sturgis and we made the trip in four hours and fifteen minutes, that included gas stops.

It never felt so good to get mauled hello by a pitbull as it did when we walked into the house that afternoon. Our psycho killer pitbull Knucklehead'd been babysat by Valerie's mom and sisters while we were gone. At one time when I was sitting in jail in Sturgis I wondered if I was ever gonna see him again. I suppose I should tell you about him, he's a story all in himself, a more vicious dog you've never seen.

Knucklehead

Knucklehead's real name was Chauncey. He was two or three years old when we got him. The reason we got him was because he was a vicious killer. We lived up behind the church when he came to us one Saturday.

Valerie and I were at the Bank Shot early one Saturday afternoon. There were quite a few people there, mighta' been a pool tournament or something. Anyway I was talking to this dude named Steve at the bar and he was talking about having to shoot this pitbull later on.

When I asked him why, he told me the dog belonged to a friend of his who'd gone to the joint. When he went to the joint his ole'lady inherited this dog that'd been chained outside in every kind of weather, starved, beaten, fought and generally abused until you couldn't even get near him to feed him.

She had a new boyfriend up in Divide I think it was and he had coon dogs. She eventually moved in with him, when she moved she brought Chauncey with her and stuck him in a cage. Every chance he could he got outta that cage, into one of the coon dogs cages and killed the dog. He'd killed two or three of the guy's dogs and he was gonna have to go.

I told Steve I'd take the dog as soon as I heard the story. We arranged that he'd go up, get the dog and meet us at our place with him. After he left we had a few more beers and I told Valerie about our new dog.

We headed to the house after a while to wait for Steve. It got later and later and no Steve. I'd about given up on him when the phone rang. It was Steve and the reason he was so late was because they'd just now gotten the dog chained into the back of his pickup. The dog put up such a fight they had to club him unconscious with a 2x4 to get him in the truck. He said he'd be there in a few minutes and about forty minutes later I heard this snarling, growling, raging beast getting closer to the house.

I walked outside as Steve was pulling into the driveway. When he got outta the truck the dog lunged at him, but the chain he was on stopped him just short of biting a chunk outta the back of Steve's head. Steve ducked, dodged away from the truck and into the side yard when he felt and heard the dog lunge. The dog stood at the side of the truck foaming at the mouth and straining at the leash wanting to get something, anything, especially Steve.

As I stormed up to the side of the truck Steve hollered for me to watch out he'd bite. I got right in the dog's face and screamed, **"SHUT UP-N-SIT DOWN"** which he did instantly with a shocked look on his face.

Steve screamed **"NO"** as I reached over the side of the truck and unhooked the chain.

Steve ran away as fast as he could when I pointed toward the front of the house and hollered **"NOW YOU GET UP THERE N-SIT DOWN."**

The dog jumped outta the truck, ran up to the front of the house and sat down on the sidewalk just like he'd done it a million times.

When Valerie came outta the house he turned to her with the tip of his tail wagging, but he didn't get up. She bent over and hugged him, he licked her face and looked at me with a big smile on his face. Steve walked over to his truck and got in incredulous. He couldn't believe what he'd just seen, but he wasn't gonna get caught out in the open when the dog realized he was free.

I put a chain on one of the trees across the driveway that could reach to the back door so he had plenty of room to move in and put some bowls of food and water on the floor for him in the entryway and he made himself to home. I don't know if he'd ever been in a house before, but he taught himself about the couch first thing. As soon as we took our eyes off him for five minutes he made himself ta home real quick. I looked around the door into the living room and he was passed out cold, stretched out on his back all four feet in the air on the couch, snoring like a chainsaw, looking pretty comfortable.

I was awakened by the smell of dogshit at four in the morning the first night we had him. I was pissed as I snatched him off the couch rubbed his face in it and put him outside on the chain. That's why I don't think he'd ever been in a house before, he didn't try to hide what he'd done, on the contrary he put it in the middle of the kitchen floor like a masterpiece he wanted us both to see.

The next morning when I brought his bowls outside he laid down and put his head on his paws like he was asking forgiveness. I went over and patted his head and Valerie and I left for work. When we got home he was still there {I thought for sure he'd run away} and happy as hell to see us.

I walked over unsnapped the chain and told him "no poopin' in the house" he looked at me like he knew, ran off to the farthest corner of the yard took a big dump and looked at me as if to say "how's that?"

When I said "good boy," he scratched off flinging grass and dirt everywhere and ran in the back door.

When I got inside he was sitting next to Valerie on the couch getting told what a good boy he was. We never had another masterpiece displayed in the house ever and he never displayed a vicious bone to Valerie or I, others weren't so lucky.

The only problem with the dog was he was an **animal**. He hadn't been around people so he hadn't learned all the things house dogs learn early.

One Sunday afternoon we heard a truck in the driveway. It turned out to be a friend from Denver whose nephew raced go carts. The whole family'd been down in Pueblo at the races all day. On the way home at the last minute he decided to stop by and say hi. The family included his fifteen year old niece whose time of the month it was.

As everybody filtered into the house his niece walked by Knucklehead in the kitchen. He immediately found something very attractive about her, I could tell by the way his ears picked up, his eyes widened and he started walking on his tip toes with his nose in the air. Another dude {her dad} who was with Orr told her she had a new friend as she walked through the living room to a chair. When she sat down in the chair, Knucklehead without missing a beat climbed up in her lap, got her in a headlock with his front legs and began humping her face furiously.

It was all I could do to get him off her after I managed to suppress my laughter that exploded from all of us at first. Once off her I had to put him on his chain outside so he'd leave her alone. Five minutes on the chain and he was howling up a storm and wouldn't shut up to save his life. I went outside to shut him up. As soon as I walked away he was at it again. I hadn't even gotten into the house before he started back up.

The poor kid was pretty shaken at first, I would be too. He wasn't the least bit gentle with his advance. After they left we were both pretty surprised by him, he didn't act like that toward Valerie ever, only thing I could figure was Valerie just wasn't his type. Having a rude, crude and socially unattractive pitbull suited me just fine, that wasn't a real problem, but his constant running away was.

Every so often Knucklehead would take a notion and run off. Most of the time he'd stay around the house with you when you were outside. Every once in a while if you weren't keeping a close enough eye on him he'd take off though. We always looked the neighborhood over for him, but never found him. Every time we'd find a card from the Humane Society tacked to our door when we got home from work the next day.

The first time this happened it cost ninety-five dollars because we hadn't registered him when we got him. We went to the pound and there he was sitting there in a cage looking like a common criminal. The tip of his tail started wiggling when he saw us. When we got to his cage we got the "please get me out, I won't do it again" greeting. Pretty much the same greeting I gave someone who was gonna bail me outta jail, without the words.

We brought our criminal home and figured this'd be the end of it cause we'd watch him a little better, wrong! He just got sneakier. If you didn't put him on the chain right away, the first time you weren't looking he was gone. This happened four more times at fifty-five dollars a pop. I paid it three times, but the fourth time I refused.

The fourth time he ran away from Valerie while she was taking him off the chain. Ordinarily when you took him off the chain he ran to the back door and waited to be let in, this time he took off like a shot.

Valerie called me out at Mel's in tears because she thought I'd be mad. I wasn't mad I simply said "fuck 'im." I wasn't gonna spend that kind of money to bring home a dog that didn't wanna be there, he wasn't worth it. I told her it was alright I'd see her when I got home.

When I got home we talked about it and I told her then if she wanted to waste more money on the dog she'd be the one to pay I was done. I voted for cutting our loses with this mutt and getting a puppy that was more trainable than Knuck was. Once a dog starts running like that it's hard to stop 'em and if you let it go for very long {especially with a pitbull} you could end up in a lot of trouble if the dog bites someone, especially a kid.

We knew some of his story, but not all of it, we had no idea about all the things in his life that might set him off and make him vicious. I wasn't worried about Valerie or I. I was worried about some total stranger that happened across him, who might do some everyday thing and the dog attack him for it. We decided to let 'em keep him when they caught him and cut our loses.

Later on that evening we were sitting on the couch watching TV when the phone rang. Valerie answered and in a few seconds was in tears. I could hear someone on the other end with a full head of steam hollering and swearing as I took the phone from her. I waded into the asshole with both barrels. In a few seconds I had him crying and I now knew what the dog's problem was.

The dude on the other end of the phone was his original owner. He'd just gotten outta the joint and returned home. When Knucklehead ran away he was caught hanging around this same house on the other side of the neighborhood each time. This was because it was the house were he used to live. This time when he ran away someone was home and let him in. We'd put one of those tags with our name, address and phone number on him when we got him just in case.

The dude called accusing Valerie of stealing his dog and he was gonna kick her ass and all that shit till I got on the phone. Once I explained to him how we got the dog and that if he ever tried to touch her or even called here again I'd kill him on the spot in front of God and everybody his tune changed.

I told him if he wanted the dog to send the collar back and keep his fuckin' dog the damn thing was a pain in the ass anyway. He apologized and said he'd send the collar back in the mail. That as they say was the end of that and we didn't have to worry about it anymore.

The next day when we got home from work a familiar looking card was on our door. The dog was in jail again. We called the dude who owned him now, told him the dog was in the pound and wished him luck.

An hour later he called back saying they wouldn't release the dog to him because he wasn't the registered owner. I told him it wasn't our problem, we're done with the bullshit with this fuckin' worthless mutt and hung up. Valerie looked heartbroken and moped around almost in tears for a while. She finally looked at me, grabbed her jacket, jumped in her truck and took off. I knew where she was going, so I sat down to wait.

A little while later the back door opened and Knucklehead came charging in the living room happier than I'd ever seen him. Valerie came in and told me to call his old owner and tell him we had the dog and it'd cost him fifty-five dollars to get him back. I called the dude who was happy to hear we had him and wanted to know if he could owe the fifty-five dollars because he'd just gotten out and didn't have the money. I told him when he got the money to call us and if we still had the dog {which I doubted we would} he could get him then. That was when he said "fuck it, keep the dog."

I had to ask him how the dog got away, he said after he'd talked to us he'd taken him out and put him on the chain and in the morning he was gone. I knew instantly what'd happened. He got stuck on that same old miserable chain. Knowing there was something better just over the hill and said fuck this. As we talked I understood why the dog ran away and was almost willing to bet he'd never do it again.

The next day Valerie had to work and I didn't, I decided to do a little test. I let Knucklehead out like I was gonna put him on the chain and never did. The dog spent the day in the yard off the chain and never strayed once for a minute. In fact he actually came to the door and barked to come in a few times and asked to go out the same way instead of having to be taken outside and brought back in like a prisoner. He never ran away again as long as Valerie and I were together. He was smart enough to know when he had it good after he did a little comparison shopping.

The Final Countdown

Like I said before I interrupted myself. It felt good to be home. I thought for a while there it might not happen. Now I had a new debt to take care of, everything is a compromise isn't it?

I don't exactly remember how it happened, but I ended up working out at Mel's some more, not as regularly as before, more on an "I'll call when I need ya" kinda' thing. If I could've told him to go fuck himself I would've. But at that time in The Springs the economy wasn't anything to write home about and I'd never had very good luck finding a job there anyway.

I don't remember the reason he gave for the crap during Sturgis. I really didn't give a damn {it wasn't hard to figure out he was a lying piece 'a shit}. Juggling my three habits was getting to be a pretty full time job in itself and took up a lot of my time. I didn't have time to think about Mel's stupid bullshit. I'd found several people to get crank from that was fairly decent most of the time. I can remember thinking on more than one occasion how I could clean up if I only had a lab.

A few months after we flew home from Sturgis together Clay packed up and moved to the left coast. He'd had enough of the daily drenchings and The Springs in general, I couldn't say as I blamed him. I'd been entertaining thoughts of California for a while. The water of Valerie and I was rapidly flowing over the dam and I needed better drugs and some new scenery.

Valerie'd gotten a job as a cocktail waitress at one of the popular night spots in town and it was fast becoming her new lifestyle. Granted she brought home some good drugs from time to time, but putting a bar in the middle of a relationship {not that we had much of one by then} is the quickest and easiest way to kill even the best couple. Throw a bunch of drugs in there and pretty quickly you've got less than nothing.

My biggest problem with leaving The Springs was moving all the stuff I'd accumulated while I was there, most of it was parts for Christine and things I was gonna upgrade her to in the future and I didn't particularly wanna let 'em go. An answer for this was in the offing thanks to Fu again and the lack of work provided by Mel.

At this time the MMA {Modified Motorcycle Association} in California had approximately one hundred motorcycle swap meets a year. When Clay got out there he immediately tuned in to the swap meet business. In his travels he found a shop inventory of some pretty choice parts for a pretty good price. Fu purchased the inventory and he and Clay started hitting the swap meets out on the coast. This meant a lot of driving and Fu just wasn't the one that wanted to be behind the wheel from Colorado Springs to Frisco or L.A. nonstop, however this was right up my alley.

The first few times he did it with some other friends that either drove him nuts or visa versa. We were talking one day because I still owed him for Sturgis and it sure didn't look like I'd make that kind of money anytime soon working for Mel.

Since I now had plenty of time on my hands, we both figured I'd work off my debt by doing some driving. Fu paid the expenses and I got us from point A to point B nonstop, most of the time, depending on the quality of the dope. We hit swap meets all over California, which was pretty convenient because my stuff needed to go to L.A. in the worst way and what better way to get it there than bring it myself. It wasn't that much, it'd just be hard to replace if I sold or left it and I had almost everything I needed to make the conversions I'd planned.

By this time I was using all the time and made no bones about how much I hated The Springs and how little I liked Valerie and she felt the same about me. Her dad was always on her to get rid of me and she'd met other people at the bar that were promising her bigger and better things.

When we'd go to the coast we'd be gone sometimes a week. I'm sure the piece and quiet alone convinced her she didn't need me around. By the third or fourth trip she was only concerned with how long I'd be gone and wanting to know in advance when I'd be back. As much as she denied it I could tell by the look on her face as she said it that she was already gone and rather than have a blowout she'd just bide her time till I was gone, after all I was leaving anyway, right.

Bandits

Though Valerie worked for him a couple days a week I hadn't heard from Mel in months when the phone rang one freezing winter morning. Mel asked me if I wanted to work. Of course I did, he explained that he'd woken up to a motorhome parked outside his shop and when he opened the door a group of bambinos had come in and wanted a motor built while they waited. He tried to put 'em off and talk 'em into dropping off the motor and he'd ship it to 'em when it was done, but that wasn't their plan and the plan wasn't changing. He said "now I got these bambinos standing around in my shop and I can't get 'em to leave, would you want to come out and build this motor for 'em?"

I told him I'd be there in a while and hung up the phone thinking "what the fuck are bambinos?" He'd told Valerie to come in with me so we both got ready and headed for Mel's. In the summer it was a nice ride out to Mel's, but during the winter the drive out there seemed twice as long and on dreary, cold days like this with the wind howling across the prairie the drive sucked, even in the pickup truck.

When we got there, there was a motorhome parked in the yard with a huge rottweiler chained to it. The dog was so big he looked like he could pull the motorhome. He was probably the biggest rotty I've ever seen. We went inside expecting a shop full of people and only found Mel. Valerie knew her job, so she went right in the office and got to work. Mel and I walked out into the shop.

The last time I'd worked for Mel he'd gotten his panties in a wad about something and told me he wouldn't need me anymore. That was a few months earlier. When that happened motors'd been laying everywhere waiting to be rebuilt. Both benches had torn down motors on 'em. Each work area was full. That was exactly how I found the place when I walked back in the shop. Not one fucking thing had been touched. It all lay just like I left it the last time I was there, right down to the tools I'd laid down when I walked out.

Before I could do anything on the "bambinos" motor I had to finish the jobs already on the benches so I'd have some room to work. While I was doing that a bunch of guys came in and started standing around with their hands in their pockets looking like Cheshire Cats and talking quietly to each other. Once I got one bench cleared I picked up their motor and put it up there, went to the other bench and started clearing it.

Each bench had all the hand tools you needed to do engine work right there. While I was working on the other bench the guys nonchalantly started taking a rocker cover off their motor. As they were moving the motor around to get a better grip on it they dropped it on the metal bench with a loud bang. Mel whipped around like he'd been shot at and before he could say something stupid, I said "hey, if you let me finish what I'm doin' here I'll have that whole motor apart in forty-five minutes and you can see everything then."

They looked at me, said "ok" and backed away from the motor like they'd just been shocked or something. I had to laugh because they all looked like they'd been caught with their hands in the cookie jar.

That broke the ice and we started talking. They weren't fuckin' bambinos, they were Bandidos from Texas {I told ya Mel gave a fuck about nothing}. I personally think it's kind of insulting not to get that right and only showed his disrespect and ignorance. As I finished what I was doing and got to their motor we talked and got to know each other a little.

The Bandidos are a large motorcycle club that claim Texas as their home state the way the Hells Angels claim California as theirs and rightfully so on both counts.

Although Texas is their home state the entire western part of the country has chapters. These guys were brothers from several different chapters who were particularly close and had decided to do something special for one of the group at hand.

One was from Galveston, that's what I'll call him, three were from Houston I'll call 'em T and F and TW, the last but not least one was from San Antonio, so I'll use that moniker for him. For some reason I think T's ole'lady was there too and of course the rotty Dillinger {I don't think he'll mind if I use his name}.

When I got to their motor I'd told 'em previously I'd have it torn down in forty-five minutes and they called me on it. While we talked my hands went to work.

The reason they'd come all the way to Colorado from Houston was because this time of year in Texas every shop has a waiting list for motor work because they're so busy during the off season. They'd read Mel's add in one of the bike magazines that stated a three day turnaround on motor work. They called him and of course he had to blow his own horn as loudly as he could, never thinking they'd take him up on it.

The reason the motor had to be done right away was because Galveston, whose motor it was, had been sentenced to eighteen months in Huntsville for killing a scumbag that was dealing dope to school children in his neighborhood. I guess the cops couldn't seem to shut this guy down or something, so Galveston solved the problem for once and for all. I think he should've gotten a medal for it. Texas still having a justifiable homicide law saw some justification for what he did and only gave him eighteen months.

The idea was to have a fresh scooter upon his release, which I think was the least that should be done. That way he could pick up where he left off when he got out. I gotta' tell ya it felt good to meet some real people. I'd been too long in the world of wannabees with bikes. In The Springs that was what ninety-nine percent of the scooter people were. It was a town full of losers.

Most of the people that I liked were already gone because they had the same opinion of the place. A couple of my favorite people had been killed in bike wrecks over the years. It was getting pretty lonely in The Springs for me as of late. It was a relief to meet some real people and party with 'em while they were there.

I told 'em forty-five minutes. It only took forty-one that day and the motor was in pieces all over the bench. While some of the parts drained, others got washed until everything was washed and dried on a clean bench. Once that was done one by one every part that needed it was glassbeaded and rewashed till all the parts looked like new inside and out. All deposits had been removed and each piece was ready to be machined.

Sometime during that afternoon I was given the universal "do you get high" sign by one of the brothers and invited to take a break when I had the chance. After I finished prepping his motor was the perfect chance. I went out to the motorhome and met that rotty face to face.

He was huge, the biggest I've ever seen and playful as hell. I knocked on the door. The occupants were amazed to see me playing with Dill when they opened it and even more amazed that I'd walked up to the motorhome and he hadn't made a sound.

On the contrary when I walked up he hunkered down with his butt in the air, stub wagging furiously. He bounded up, licked my hand then my face and started running around in tight little circles with a big smile on his face playing as hard as he could on the short chain. This was what they opened the door to after I knocked.

The folks from Houston and Galveston were rotty people. San Antone was a pitbull person like myself, but dogs are dogs and they took pride in the training of their rotties. All of their dogs had a job and Dill was no exception. That I'd walked up without him even making a sound was a thing of note to them. We all lined up {good dope too}. About the time I started to leave Mel was walking toward to the door. As I stepped out he asked if I'd want to start on the other motors that'd been sitting there since our falling out.

I went inside and started on one of 'em. Before I was done one of the brothers came inside and stuck a little care package in my jacket pocket with a nod and went back to the motorhome. Once I was done with that disassembly and prep we called it a day. Valerie and I walked to the motorhome, said see ya and headed home. That night it got pretty cold and I thought about 'em in the motorhome. I wished I'd asked 'em to come to the house, I enjoyed their company. I'd be sure to ask the next day.

When we got there the next morning we went to the motorhome for coffee before Mel knew we were there, that way he wouldn't be suspicious. He was anyway, for some reason he didn't like that I got along with these guys or any other customers for that matter, not that it was even his fucking business. I figure it was because he didn't want me telling 'em what I knew and thought of him.

A little while after I went inside the brothers started coming in and out. Mostly Galveston and T hung near the bench, watching and talking with me as I started to reassemble his motor. A couple of times Mel said something about being in my way. I said they weren't and he went away. By the end of the day the motor was back together and ready to go on the test stand to be fired before it went out the door.

We all went back to our place to celebrate, looking forward to hearing that badass pan motor roar to life in the morning. They'd brought some good dope with 'em, saying it was just average, they obviously had no idea what kind of garbage passed for dope around there.

Earlier that day while we were talking Galveston said his ole'lady'd left him recently. I immediately thought of this gal that had been one of the local club member's ole'ladies and had been hanging with Valerie lately. I had Valerie call her and meet us at the house once they accepted my invite to spend the night.

When we got back to the house, our guests bought the fixins for dinner and root beer floats, one of my all-time favorites. Someone did the cooking and we all got high. Andrea showed up, I pointed her at Galveston and the night moved on. We partied till the wee hours. Mel said he had something to do in town first thing in the morning and he'd call me to let us know when to come in and with plenty of chemical energy we definitely wouldn't be late.

When the phone rang the next morning it wasn't good news. That fuckin' asshole had put the motor on the stand himself and fired it knowing we all wanted to be there the first time. This had been a special thing to these guys and after getting to know 'em it was to me too. He intentionally fucked that up just to be a dickhead.

He got on the phone "the motor sounds really good, it fired right up," like it was just another motor on the stand. This yanked my chain all the way to overload and beyond. I just couldn't believe he could be that much of an asshole. Then, he never amazed me with what a shithead he could be.

The motor was still on the stand when we got there, he fired it up, I disconnected it and we put it in the motorhome while someone paid the bill. While it was being paid Mel got a couple of other opinions on his "initiative" earlier in the day {if anybody could fuck up a cool thing it'd be Mel, just cause he doesn't give a shit about anyone but himself}. I'd learned a long time ago that it was a waste of breath to say anything about anything to Mel he didn't give a shit about anything but money.

I'm sure everything said went in one ear and out the other, if it even went in at all. He didn't care what anybody said or thought about anything as long as he got his money. We just got in the motorhome and went back to the house; to me it wasn't worth the wasted breath. I'd watched him pull this crap for two years on everyone including his own family members why should he change now or even care, which I know he didn't. He only cared about himself and his money.

A little while after we got there some of their brothers from Denver came down to visit for a couple of reasons. One is because the Bandidos are a very tight organization and it's mandated that you meet all your brothers face to face at least once. All these folks were old timers who knew each other well and took every opportunity to see each other again. Two was because the guys that I met liked me like I liked them and they thought I might be a good Bandido. It was their way of introducing me to some of their heavy hitters for assessment, before they made an offer to me someone else might not like. To be brought into a club everyone in that chapter has to vote yes on your patch. One no and you don't make it, it's a waste of time to cultivate someone that ain't gonna make it.

The folks that came down from Denver were as cool as their brothers from Texas. There were three patchholders that were very high up in their chapters and nationally and a prospect. The first thing that happened after hands were shaken and we'd all lined up was the prospect was sent to the store for root beer float fixins. While all this other stuff was going on Valerie was getting ready for work, about halfway through the first float she said she was going to work and headed out the door. In a second she was back. There was a flat on the front driver's side tire.

I excused myself from the group and went out to change the tire. As I was putting the spare on I heard from inside the house, **"PROSPECT WHAT THE HELL ARE YOU DOING IN HERE, WHILE HE'S OUT THERE CHANGING THAT TIRE?"**

The prospect came flying outta the house and reached for the lug wrench. I told him it was cool, I was almost done anyway. He said if

I didn't let him finish he'd be in a world 'a shit, so I let him finish and went back in the house.

Through the window I watched him finish the job and put the jack away. He even held the door for Valerie when she got in the truck and brought the flat up on the front porch. We spent the rest of the afternoon getting high and shooting the shit. Early in the evening the Denver people left. Before they did they all had a little confab in the motorhome that I wasn't privy to, mostly because some of it was none of my business and some of it was probably about me.

When the folks from Denver left and everybody came back in, the first thing we did was line up, which was always a good thing to do, especially when you're trying to figure out what to do next. That evening F went out on the town to check out The Springs and eventually hooked up with Valerie at the bar. While Galveston and Andrea made the rounds of all four or five bars in town. They all got back to the house around the same time and again we crashed as the sun was coming up.

A few hours later we were all up again, the Texans were headed back south today, Andrea was going along till Galveston turned himself in, so we stuck her car at the head of our driveway until she got back. Along with a care package of the good shit was the phone number and the directions to T's house in Houston and an open ended invitation to show up whenever. They already knew they were welcome here anytime and I made that clear to the Denver folks also. As the motorhome pulled away I felt kinda' empty, but I knew I'd see these folks again. I'd make it a point to.

10, 9, 8, ...

The rest of that year was a pain in my ass {literally}. Due to the pain in my ass I added another drug to the three I was juggling, painkillers. A line, a joint, a few beers, and a couple 'a painkillers and I was in prime shape every day. Add to that the knowledge that Valerie'd made the bar her new lifestyle. A roommate that was as bad an influence on her as the bar was and the knowing that she was fucking around on me. You had one psychotic headcase looking for a place to have a meltdown.

My working at Mel's was almost a thing of the past now. If I was lucky I might get a couple days work a month while Valerie worked almost every day for him. I was beginning to really hate her and the whole town in general.

Anytime I went anywhere with Valerie, especially around the people we used to be friends with, the reception was if not cool, nonexistent. People looked at me like "what the fuck are you still doing here," as if I was a total stranger and didn't belong there. I didn't, I belonged in California with the good drugs and the nice weather.

Valerie'd finally gotten familiar with the local losers and was always trying to get me to go to the clubhouse with her. Why, so I could get ratpacked and watch them gangbang her? Fuck that, I had my own plans for the local boys that would put an end to their bullshit once and for all.

My plan was simple. While they were all in the clubhouse during their Friday night church meeting I'd firebomb it with a few Molotov Cocktails. Since there was only one way in or out, I'd simply shoot each one as they came outta the burning building, that'd put an end to their bullshit once and for all. It was hard to work on this plan with

Valerie around because she'd've told 'em right away. They were part of the bigger, better deal that she'd fallen for.

It was beginning to seem that I'd worn out my welcome and every day made that ever clearer. The bar Valerie worked at closed at 2:00AM. When she first started she'd be home around three. Now she was showing up around sunrise with her cloths crumpled up in her hand wearing only some dudes coat, saying she wasn't fucking around she fell asleep at a friend's house. She was becoming quite the little crankwhore, but wasn't very good at lying about it. I don't even know why she bothered to lie or come home for that matter.

Around Sturgis time The Bandits stopped by again for a visit and invited us to go to Sturgis with 'em. After the fiasco the year before I had no real desire to go anywhere near South Dakota. Christine was down for a little maintenance work and I really didn't wanna be seen anywhere with Valerie if I didn't have to. It was bad enough when I had to go somewhere with her around town. It was embarrassing for me to be seen with her. Everyone in town knew what she was doing and who she was seeing but me. She wasn't shy about her new man; it was just that she had no desire for a confrontation, especially since I was leaving anyway.

She finally got her wish in the form of a court order. Someone had come to visit the faggot next door and had parked right across the end of our driveway on one of the rare days that Mel called me to do some work. When I walked outta the house to leave I couldn't because the driveway was blocked, with a head full of everything I snapped and fucked the car up n-busted the windshield n-shit.

The inconsiderate asshole got the fuck outta there in a hurry then and of course called the police. They didn't see me do it so they couldn't arrest me, but Valerie's dad saw a perfect opportunity to get me outta his house and pressed charges.

I didn't have the money for a lawyer so of course he won. I had to pay restitution {which I never did} and be outta the house in ten days. Without a pot to piss in or a window to throw it out of I was screwed. Valerie did something that I didn't understand at the time, but do now. She rented a little house in Old Colorado City and moved my stuff in there. There were two reasons for that. To finally get me out of her life so her and her new boyfriend could play house the way she and I'd done when we first met and her new friends could rob me of Christine and anything else they wanted.

Every few days she'd come by and visit casing the place for her friends. One day when I wasn't there she came in and stole all my leathers. I would assume to give 'em to her new boyfriend. Restraining order or not I went right over to the old house, she wasn't there but the roommate was and I got all my shit back.

Her roommate made up some bullshit excuse for the theft that I blew off as I retrieved my things and walked out the door. I stopped for a few minutes to see Knucklehead who was confused all to hell. I hated leaving my dog but I'd come to town on Christine and that was gonna be the way I'd leave, not much room for a dog in that plan.

It was at this time that Mel got his ass kicked for fucking up the Sportster that I mentioned earlier. When Mel wouldn't do anything to fix the mess he'd made of the guy's bike except get his ass kicked the dude asked me if I'd help him with it. Through this travesty I made a new friend that didn't care about all the bullshit with Valerie and her new friends.

Without any income and needing money to leave town with I wasn't gonna spend money paying rent on a place that I didn't want and Valerie had a key to. After no word from Valerie for a couple of weeks she showed up one night acting like nothing'd ever happened {typical junkie move}, being all lovey-dovey. She stripped got into my bed, spread her legs and said "fuck me."

I was immediately suspicious and refused. I threw her cloths at her and told her to get the fuck out and leave me alone. She flew into a rage and stormed out. When her pickup truck passed under the kitchen window there was another truck right behind her that'd been parked in the alley by the garage doors with the lights off.

I found a cigarette lighter cause I didn't have a flashlight and went out to check the locks on the garage where Christine was housed. The lock was still intact, but one end of the door'd been pried away from the frame. If I'd done Valerie like she wanted I'd've been in the wrong part of the house to hear or see anything that happened in front of the garage and would've come out to no scooter in the morning.

I knew Valerie had become pretty fuckin' scandalous, but I didn't think she'd stoop low enough to help someone steal my bike. Crank like most drugs takes your morals and chucks 'em in the ditch like they were so much garbage.

Valerie wasn't any different than any other junkie now and was about as trustworthy as a fart in a wind storm. The only thing I knew for sure was that I had to get outta that house if I wanted to keep my shit. Now that her new friends knew where to look it was only a matter of time before Christine and maybe even my life'd be gone.

I'm sure her friends felt the same way about me as I did about them. The only thing that kept me from killing 'em was the law against murder, they seldom knew where I was unless I was in sight, but I knew where they were most of the time. When the time came it'd be easy to fuck 'em all up at once. Maybe I could even get Valerie when I got them, after all "birds of a feather," let 'em all fly to hell together.

While all this was going on I was trying to help Jim with his Sportster that Mel fucked up. The only thing that could be done was tear it all back down weld up the countershaft hole, relocate said hole and reassemble the whole mess. The hardest part about this plan was the only guy in the area that could do the machine work had already fucked it up once and had no thought of repairing the problem. His cure was to throw Jim's money in his face and tell him to get off his property, resulting in an asswhippin', but neither of these things fixed the problem.

There were machine shops in Denver that could help us with the problem, all we had to do was the assembly and disassembly, which becomes more difficult the less equipped for the job you are. The little bit of stuff I carried with me on my scooter {everything else had been moved to California months earlier} wasn't near the tools we needed to do the job and Jim only had the most basic of hand tools.

I met Jim right about the time I was moving into Old Colorado City. Along with him I met a gal named Angel. The only thing I can say about her is, I've never seen anyone that stuck on themselves in my life. She was one of a kind all right, a kind I'd never seen, nor ever want to see again. She came in handy in the grand scheme of things, but turned out to be a scandalous little bitch in the end and Christine hated her.

Her and I stayed at Jim's for a couple 'a weeks until Valerie's new friends found out where I was and I moved outta town for good. Angel's folks lived way the hell out on the prairie east of The Springs. I had a few things worth a few dollars to get rid of for the cash to get outta town. Seemed like that was all I was gonna have. I hadn't worked for Mel in months, not since the early spring and it was early fall when Angel and I landed at her folk's place.

The place was a trailer out in the middle of nowhere, the only neighbor they had was the wind, which always blows out there. All the bushes and grasses grow at a permanent angle because the wind blows 'em that way, it never stops. We had to be getting outta there real soon. I didn't particularly want to be sleeping in a heatless fifth wheel trailer when the first snows flew in Colorado that year.

After a couple 'a weeks at her folk's house we headed south on Highway 287 toward warmer weather. The day we left was one of the last days of Indian summer, kinda' warm with a frigid breeze coming down outta the mountains. I was glad to be leaving this place. I never should've spent more than the weekend there when I first met Valerie. The only good thing to come outta there was meeting Clay. Other than that it was just time wasted. But that's been pretty much the story of my life anyway, wasted time, a life wasted, in more ways than one.

We made it to a picnic area outside Dumas Texas the first night, made our bed on a table and got outta there right after the sun woke us up the next day. I don't think Angel had ever traveled quite like this in her life and I don't think she particularly enjoyed traveling like this now. This was budget travel at its worst. Sleeping under the stars or in the rain. Eating as little as you can the one time you do eat that day. Smoking a cigarette every hundred and fifty miles whether you needed it or not. Wringing every mile you can outta every line snorted. Yup this is the life!

Just as we were getting on I-40 in Amarillo we had a flat tire on the rear. We got off onto the feeder road, did a flip under the first overpass and into a 76 gas station lot. They did tires there so I knew they'd have a tube to fit this sixteen inch tire. The only hassle was I had to unpack the entire motorcycle to do it and of course for all the cold and bluster up in Colorado it was ninety plus degrees in Amarillo that day.

About an hour or so of hard work and we were headed outta town at a high rate of fuel consumption. At that time it was a beautiful panhandle day with not too many grasshoppers. They hurt like hell when you catch one in the middle of the forehead at seventy mph, but there were clouds on the horizon and the further south we went the closer and thicker they were getting. It only stood to reason though we were headed toward the Gulf of Mexico at the end of hurricane season, when tropical storms abound.

Early in the evening we were on the south side of Wichita Falls Texas when a DPS officer stopped me for speeding. In the ensuing search for contraband {he was positive I was an incognito Bandido smuggling drugs into Texas from God knows where} an Arkansas Toothpick was uncovered in my things.

This particular knife is a double edged fighting knife now known to me to be illegal in the state of Texas, after a lecture and an hour and a half delay we were back on the road.

We got to the south side of Dallas late that night and stopped around one-thirty in the morning, just as we got onto I-45 from I-20. We found a dark corner in the back of a gas station with a little wooden platform like thing to throw the sleeping bags on and crashed for the night.

We were awakened before dawn by the beginning of a light drizzle. Everything was soaked before we got it packed on the bike and headed down the road, which really didn't matter much because the further south we went the worse the weather got. By the time we were halfway to Houston from Dallas it was raining and blowing so fucking hard there wasn't a dry spot anywhere on me. Every bit of leather I was wearing was soaked and water was running down the crack of my ass into my boots like a river.

We were finally on the outskirts of Houston when I stopped to get my directions to T's house outta my wallet. I called the number, it was disconnected. He said it might be if he's outta town, if he is that'll suck. The only thing left to do was follow the directions to his house and hope he's there.

When we made the last turn on the directions I was relieved to see a bunch of motorcycles at a house up the street. It looked like they were just pulling in whoever they were. Some had just parked and others were still backing to the curb. When one turned around I saw the unmistakable patch of the Bandidos on his back and knew someone was home.

As I turned into the street and found a spot at the curb all eyes were staring "who the fuck" at us pretty hard. It hadn't been any day in the recollection of all these Bandidos that a nonpatchholder ever parked in front of this house and dismounted, but that was what this motherfucker was doing right now.

As I walked toward the group of brothers forming near the garage door, I was pulling off soaked goggles and a drenched flyers cap. Once these things were off someone said "heyyy" and stepped outta the group, walked up with his hand out and asked how I'd been. It was San Antonio and he was as wet as I was. He had a grin from ear to ear, after he recognized me F came outta the bunch too smiling. As he got to me the overhead door at the front of the garage opened and there was the guy that ran the show around here T.

When the door got to the top San Antone got T's attention. When he had it, he pointed at me. It took a second for T to realize that I wasn't one of the crew that'd just pulled up. At the same time he realized that, he recognized it was me and almost wrung my hand off with a grin.

I was glad to see T; he was a pretty happy go lucky motherfucker for the office he held in the club. I'd liked him from the minute I'd met him up in Colorado and it was evident by the welcome I got then that the feelings were mutual.

Houston And Points West

It was pretty hectic around T's house for the first few hours we were there. The group that was backing into the curb when we arrived had just got back from a funeral in Mississippi. If we'd gotten there ten minutes sooner we'd've knocked on the door of an empty house and our only alternative would've been to head west, like we'd do sometime in the future anyway.

I probably mentioned this before, but I didn't find it out until after I'd been there a while and to you as the reader maybe it doesn't seem all that important. I was the first nonpatchholder that ever entered T's house and without revealing his office within his chapter suffice it to say that this to me was an honor equal to being given the key to a city or something.

That day as I walked among his brothers shaking hands and learning names it felt like the most natural thing I could be doing at the time and though some of 'em were wondering "what the fuck" {except the few that'd been guests at my house in The Springs} they took their queue from T and were friendly. Believe me when I tell you this isn't usually the case when an unknown tramp appears anywhere a group of club members is gathered, especially at one of their homes outta the blue like I did. Hell if I didn't know me, I'd want to know what the fuck I was doing there myself.

Everyone there was as wet as the next person so everybody split pretty quickly. At times like those the only thing that feels better than a hot shower and dry clothes is a big fat ripper, a hot fuck in the shower, some dry clothes, a big skunk bud in the bong and washing it all down with a couple 'a Lynchburg Lemonades. Now that's feeling good.

Within a few days Angel'd been put to work with T's ole'lady, where she proceeded to do every wrong thing you could possibly do including telling people she was T's *new* ole'lady, good move, smart girl. I'm not gonna waste my time even describing her to you cause she just ain't worth it. Let's just say Christine hated her and I have proof as witnessed by at least a half dozen Bandidos one Sunday afternoon.

We were all going out to The Battleship Texas for the yearly celebration there this particular afternoon. I rolled Christine out to the curb and fired her up on the first kick like most of the time {first kick or the first hundred}. She sat and idled for a minute. When she was warm and ready to go I sat down blipped the throttle a few times, everything was fine, she was feeling and sounding good. Angel sat down on her and she died.

We went through this three more times until she finally agreed to run but she didn't agree to how well. All the way out to Baytown she coughed and farted and spit and sputtered acting like she was gonna die one minute and kill me the next. When we finally got off the ramp for the memorial in Baytown she died a horrible choking death worthy of any Hollywood B western.

Angel got off; she started right up like there wasn't a problem. Soon as Angel sat down she died. I looked at F who stopped when I did, he said "she can ride with me." Angel rode with him the rest of the day and Christine ran fine. Later on in T's kitchen after Angel'd been shipped off to F's lock, stock and barrel. We were having a laugh about that finicky old bitch of a motorcycle and I made the comment that she was possessed. TW added "yah and we know by who." That was the best way you could sum up that old thing "possessed."

When we got to Houston Christine was feeling a little wishy washy. Especially out on the freeway, she was getting hard to hold in a straight line, wanting to wander from side to side in the lane. I never could see anything wrong with just the quick glances I was giving her.

We were always on the go while I was there "taking care of business." One evening we'd gone out to one of the bars that members from another chapter hung out at or it might've been their clubhouse, I can't really remember. It seems to me I remember sitting outside for a while drinking more than one beer waiting for church to get out {nonmembers aren't allowed in church}.

Anyway on the way home that night Christine really cut loose, she was all over the road, it was all I could do to get her back to T's in one piece. Once we got there T had a pretty good bench to work on a scooter with. The bench brought the bike up to near chest height, but T rigged up a deal that you could hang the back or front of the bike from and raise and lower it to any height you needed, making it real easy to work on or see the underside of the bike.

After getting the bike in the air it was easy to see the center post was broken completely away from the frame top and bottom. The transmission gusset and a frame rail were cracked as well. Well anyway this looked like a job for Superman. The next thing to do was a big fat ripper and get two men on this right away. Before the sun came up the next morning Christine was torn down and ready for a trip to the welder. While she was down I found a leaky main seal in the transmission. Now was a perfect time to fix stuff like that, I had a new seal in my saddlebag and tearing down a transmission is easy as 1 2 3.

Like all jobs that are easy as 1 2 3, this turned into a trip to the machine shop and replacing broken parts and of course way more than the original leaking seal would've been. If you aren't gonna do the job right from beginning to end why bother to do any of it?

After a couple 'a days everything to finish the job was right there in T's garage. A couple 'a hours after we did the first line Christine was coming down off the stand and I was ready for another line. She was like a new bike again, especially now that she was free of Angel and all her crap.

That'd been a pretty interesting evening, the night that that conniving little bitch got found out and run off. Angel'd gone to work at the same club as T's ole'lady. Immediately she started telling people she was T's *new* ole'lady and a bunch of other shit, all this stuff was getting right back to T of course.

I can't believe how stupid this bitch was to come to someone's town, be a guest in their home and try running a game on everyone around her. How long did she think it was gonna last? The more I knew Angel the less I liked her and if Christine didn't like her that really spoke ill of her {how can a motorcycle not like someone? Mine didn't like Angel, I have witnesses}.

It was becoming increasingly evident that she was pack ratting the money she was making at the club. Her and T's ole'lady would work the same shift. T's ole'lady would come home with four hundred dollars. She'd come home with forty dollars and a whiney bullshit story.

I didn't particularly care what she did with the money, just don't lie to me about it. All this came to a head one night after I blew up at a smart ass remark that she made. She went storming out in the living room looking for help and sympathy from T and ended up getting put in her place and shot at for her trouble. The result of me not wanting her and no one else wanting her around was she got shipped off to someone that did and quick, within the hour after she'd started the shit. Thanks F.

With her bullshit outta the way life was much more laid back around T's. Shortly after her dismissal T got a wild hair, shoved all the stuff in the living room outta the way and started building a little flat fendered T-n-T bike right in front of the couch. We worked on that bike for seven days and nights thanks to the marvels of faster living through chemistry.

At the end of the seven days we got geared up and headed for Galveston for the tweakend. We got down to the waterfront about dark o'clock and were gonna eat at this seafood place. As we were sitting there T noticed someone messing with our bikes, which were under a streetlight. They were a long ways away if you were gonna do something in the way of prevention, I'd venture to say they were even outta pistol range, they were that far away.

I can't remember why the would-be vandals were messing with the bikes {they knew whose they were is why and were trying to get a rise out of us}, but they started coming inside. When the leader came through the door it was none other than the dude I'd built the motor for up in Colorado. I didn't have to check my watch to know it hadn't been eighteen months yet, hell it hadn't even been a year. I was glad to see him, his answer to my first question was "good time." After that it was a party the rest of the tweakend.

Since my arrival we'd done lots of good dope. This last week in particular we'd burnt the whole candle to a cinder. By Sunday afternoon the good dope we'd been doing all week wasn't doing the job we needed it to and I was beginning to think nothing could do the job until I got some sleep. T and I were sitting at a picnic table outside the Galveston clubhouse commenting on how wrung out we were, when a brother from Louisiana came walkin' up and sat down. He could tell that our candles were burnt to a crackly crunch and weren't gonna be lit much longer.

He laid out three little piles of powder, just a glorified matchheads worth a piece saying "this'll do the trick," drug 'em out to lines and passed the glass and a straw. The dope smelled like a burning tire and we didn't really do enough to start a bad drip. When the drip did come it tasted like burning tire, but it was a smooth burning tire.

In not very many seconds at all I felt like I could've flown to Houston from there without any help from my motorcycle at all. That right there was the best fucking dope I'd ever done in my life bar none. In a matter of minutes I felt like my hair was standing on end, even though it was tied down in a ponytail. That shit was great. Do you think the genius that cooked it would even claim to knowing the recipe so I could get it out of him? Nooo. Damn it!

We made it back to Houston that night no problem. It was trying to go to sleep when we got there that I couldn't do. I wasn't alone in that and we ended up working on the T-n-T bike till Monday afternoon.

During my stay at T's we made the rounds of most of the local chapters. There were quite a few in the area and I met a lot of the brothers. All of 'em where pretty cool people and I'd've liked hangin' with 'em if that'd been where I'd been headed at the time.

The only time I ever felt uncomfortable was at one dudes anniversary party out in Baytown. I don't do well in crowds, never did and this was a huge blowout, this dude was a long time member, thirty-three years if I remember right and there was at least a hundred or more people there.

Around any group that size I just clam up and that's what I did, I got so spun I couldn't get a thought to sit still long enough to make it into a word and the more people tried to talk to me the worse I got. For a while there I thought I was gonna explode, I finally got up and went outside. The fresh air slowed my thoughts to were I could at least read 'em as they flew by at light speed.

Before I knew it T rounded me up and we took off. I felt better the further away I got from the crowd. It wasn't that crowd in particular it's all crowds. I've been avoiding that kind of scene since leaving my teenage years behind. I guess now they have a name for that, "social anxiety disorder." I call it not liking people enough to wanna be around that many at once. I've never been a joiner for that reason, I'd much rather do my own thing quietly with only a few people even knowing I'm around. Life's much less complicated that way.

Anyway a few weeks went by and I was in so many words made an offer that I had to refuse. I didn't think I'd've been a good Bandido at the time. California was calling me louder and louder every day and I had to go. I couldn't ignore it or put it off any longer.

I had one more stop to make before I pushed for the coast. It was about two hundred miles west and right on the way. I woke up one day and decided today's the day. By the time I got my shit packed it was threatening rain in the most serious way.

On my way outta town I made a couple quick stops at other brother's houses to say so long and hauled ass. By the time I got to Katy a town just west of Houston it was raining like a cow pissing on a flat rock. There was four or five inches of water standing on I-10 and it was coming down in buckets. If you tried to travel with or behind traffic the spray was just unreal. I jumped into the Dave Lane and started running down between the cars to get out ahead of 'em onto open road.

One of the cars I passed was a Texas DPS {state trooper} in a pack of cars poking along in each others wakes and spray like a flock of ducks. As I passed him he turned on his lights and blipped his siren, like I was stupid enough to stop for him. When I cracked the throttle and shot about five cars ahead of him he turned that shit off. When I got outta the pack of cars I cracked it again and in minutes was completely outta sight of 'em.

Near Seguin I finally ran outta the rain and a few minutes later I was in downtown San Antonio at the Alamo. A few weeks earlier one of San Antone's brothers had been in Houston for a couple 'a days and had given me a message from San Antone to stop by on my way west. When I asked him how I'd find 'em when I got to town his answer was "ask the cops," which is exactly what I did.

I was sitting on Christine smoking a cigarette looking at the Alamo when a cop drove past. I stopped him and when he rolled the window down asked him where the Bandidos hung out. He didn't know but he got on the radio and in a few minutes he had the name and number to one of the bars they hung out in, in a few more minutes he had some directions for me and I was off.

A little later I was at the bar talking to the bartender and in a couple 'a more minutes was talking to the dude that I'd met in Houston. The brother I was looking for didn't belong to his chapter so he'd have to make a few calls to get his number. He told me to hang loose he'd call back and to give the phone to the bartender. I handed the phone to the bartender and in a minute he brought me back a Bud on the house.

About the end of my second beer the phone rang. It was San Antone, he gave me directions to his place. It was kinda' on the other side of town from me, but in a half an hour or so I was turning up this long driveway that I hoped was his. If it wasn't, the yuppies that owned the place'd have a shitfit when they saw what was pulling up to their house.

I rode up the driveway and around to the back of the house, parked under the carport, shut off Christine and dismounted. As soon as my feet hit the ground I heard a pitbull barking at me to get outta her yard. I turned as she ran toward me, squatted down, stuck out my arms and went **"PITBULL DAWG!"** She leapt into my arms, flipped over on her back wriggling from the tip of her nose to the tip of her tail and started furiously licking my face. The patio door flew open, San Antone screamed **"TABOO NOOO"** and came running thinking the dog was eating me alive.

When he got to us he stood there watching her lick and yip in my arms like a little puppy and was amazed when it was all over and Taboo was trotting along at my side as we walked to the house just like she was my dog.

When we got inside he turned to me and said "I don't fuckin' believe it, she doesn't even give *me* that kind of greeting. She attacks everything that comes up this driveway. I forgot to tell you that on the phone. She even attacks my brother's truck every time he comes here and that's three or four times a day."

As he was saying this to me I was looking at her over his shoulder outside the patio door. When her gaze caught mine her tail started wagging furiously and she started yipping for me to come out. I had to get some of my gear off Christine anyway, so I walked back outside.

Once I got outside she gave me another greeting like I'd been away for a month.

After the greeting she ran off into the darkness and returned with a ball for me to throw before I even got to Christine. She laid the ball at my feet and I threw it into the darkness. A few minutes later she was back dropping the ball at my feet again. We did that until I'd gotten all my stuff in, then that was it for the night. When I was done and we were sitting at the kitchen table getting high San Antone looked at me and said "you want that dog? She likes you better than she does me."

I laughed and said "I don't have any room in my saddlebags for her."

He said "I'm serious,"

I just said "no thanks" and left it at that.

The week I spent in San Antonio went by too fast. I liked the weather a lot better it was much drier. It's just too fucking humid in Houston for me. If I'd just been drifting I wouldn't've minded landing in San Antonio for a while. It beat the hell outta The Springs if only because there were Bandidos there, let alone all the other cool shit that I saw while I was there. We went to a shop where some of his brothers were doing some pretty trick shit in the fabrication department for the times.

Taking in strays like me isn't the norm for patchholders from any club. T's brothers in Houston probably thought he'd gone crazy. He ran his own show and more than one of the Houston brothers'd been my guests once, so I was a little more known to them than I was in San Antonio.

I remember sitting around the kitchen table, when one of San Antone's brothers who didn't trust me only because he didn't know me {which is the wisest position to take in a situation like that} asked him point blank if he trusted me with all his shit.

Without hesitating he looked his brother square in the eye and said "yah he did."

His brother in turn asked him why, especially since he didn't trust *him*. His answer was immediate and the defiance in his tone went up a notch as he said "because my dog loves him for one reason, I can't say that about you!"

Earlier when he'd been driving up the driveway Taboo'd been standing on the hood of his pickup truck ripping the wipers off the windshield and snarling like a wild animal. San Antone had to go outside and restrain her until everybody that arrived was in the house.

This went over like a popcorn fart in church. One of the bylaws of all outlaw clubs state that a brother is never wrong. If he is you still back his play until you can get him aside and raise the issue in private. Another one is, citizens {in that case I was a citizen} never come before brothers. That exchange right there broke those rules and pissed his brother off enough so that he left with his business unconcluded. San Antone was putting himself at risk with his brothers on my behalf, not just once either, several times. I got to know another of his brothers pretty well also and he was of the same mind as San Antone and letting it be known as well.

That was why I only spent a week in San Antonio. When he walked in after restraining Taboo while they left, he looked at me and said "fuck that motherfucker, this is my house, and you'll stay as long as you want!"

I reminded him of the trouble he'd get in with the club if he went against 'em head on like that.

He kinda' wound down and said "yah I know."

Bottom line the difference between meeting someone that you know from the gate you can trust and someone that you grow to tolerate because you see 'em every day and they wear the same patch, but never trust is one hundred and eighty degrees different. True friends don't need to be told they're friends and just because you belong to the same club doesn't always mean you're friends or they can be trusted. That's another reason why I never joined a club. I'd much rather have a few friends or only one friend for that matter that I can trust, than be surrounded by motherfuckers I've gotta watch every minute and don't necessarily like.

San Antone and I were friends because we were, it's a kinda' chemistry. He was a brother because he belonged to a club. The best thing I could do for my friend was remove the catalyst before he got himself into trouble with the club. He wasn't nicknamed Iron for nothing. As much as I hated to go, it was time before this whole thing blew sky high and there was some real shit that came down over it.

In the middle of the night with a care package up my nose and another in my pocket I followed San Antone's Vette to the I-10 west interchange. Once there he honked and waved, then peeled off and headed for home. I on the other hand had a long road through the West Texas desert in the middle of the night, better not forget the coyotes.

The next day I called California from El Paso to let 'em know I was on my way. Once I was off the phone I hit the men's room at the gas station for a tune up before I rolled out. Once everything was topped off and tuned up, I blasted off again. Since it was wintertime in the rest of the country the weather was perfect for riding all day long. It only got into the high eighties, low nineties which is perfect for crossing that long expanse of desert between El Paso and L.A. You can ride all day and through the wonders of modern chemistry all night too.

My next stop was in Lordsburg New Mexico. The ripper that I'd done in El Paso was about to blow the top of my head clean off if I didn't stop and do something about it. I pulled off the freeway and got gas, rolled a joint in the men's room and found a place outta the way to smoke it.

Next door to the gas station was an abandoned store, I pushed Christine over there, sat in the sun watching traffic on the freeway go by and smoked my joint until another bike coming east got off the freeway.

The dude riding the bike was wearing a helmet, so I knew I didn't wanna talk to him right off the bat. I knew he was gonna come over there just by the way he looked at me when he was coming down the offramp.

I put the joint out and stuffed the roach in my pocket quickly. As I walked around Christine I wondered if she was gonna be the bitch she always is whenever I wanna move fast and she doesn't. I glanced over my shoulder at the exiting bike, he was just turning onto the frontage road, I eased the kicker thru till I felt compression and jumped on it. **BA BOOM** Christine exploded to life. I slipped into the saddle, stomped the clutch, slammed her into first and got the hell outta there just as helmet was rolling into the parking lot of the abandoned store. I guess she didn't wanna talk to him either.

I knew that dude was gonna come over there and ruin a perfect day with some inane prattle about something I could give a shit about.

As we were going under the freeway overpass I patted Christine on the gas tank, thanking her for cooperating and not making me talk to this guy.

As I was flying down the onramp I glanced across the freeway, the dude had stopped exactly where I'd been sitting and seeing me look {which meant he'd been watching me} waved as I grabbed another gear and cracked the throttle. I'll bet that dude could ask some real lulus for questions, most guys that wear helmets can. Why would you wave to someone who so obviously blew you way the fuck off anyway like I just did? I could see flippin me off, but not wavin'. Oh well I'll never know why, nor will I care, I'll just be glad I didn't have to talk to him.

A few more gas stops and tune ups and I was gonna be in L.A. whether I wanted to or not. When I crossed the Colorado River into California I got that same energy rush that I always get when I enter California. Once I left Blythe I knew it was only a matter of hours before I'd be whitelining my way through L.A. traffic. Hell once I hit traffic it'd still be about two hours before I'd roll into Bird's driveway in Long Beach.

Dropping into Indio off Chiriaco Summit I got my first glimpse of L.A. smog in a few years. As I rolled through Cabazon and Redlands I remember thinking how nice it was of them to have a third stage smog alert to welcome me home. What a fitting way to arrive, on a day when the smog was so thick you could barely see the car in front of you.

Luckily it was only the inland valleys that were smogged in, the further west you got the clearer it became. By the time I got to Long Beach it was early evening and clear as a bell. I got off the 91 at Cherry Avenue and took the surface streets to Bird's house.

As I rolled into the driveway both Kat & Bird came out and we all had a hug fest in the driveway. Bird went in and opened the garage door, Christine got pushed inside and we both sat down for a rest. Unpacking my little bit 'a shit could wait till later. It just felt good to be home.

Downhill On Greased Skids

Meet you at the bottom and we'll get high, if you survive the ride. This return to L.A. was the beginning of the end. My "just say yes" attitude'd been finely tuned by now and was the operating system at the core of my existence. The major reason I went back to L.A. was because I knew the drugs I wanted were everywhere, partying was a way of life out there and the fuel to do it was as available as the sunshine. The climate was another reason I was there. I could be essentially homeless and get by ok crashing here, there and everywhere basically living on my scooter if need be. That way I could keep my cost of living down as far as possible, so I'd have the most money for drugs every day.

The only thing as important as the dope was Christine. If your scooter doesn't run it's just an anchor. If you're adrift in the sea of L.A. with just an anchor it's an awful quick trip to the bottom. Working in bike shops was the way to satisfy all of my joneses. The customers were my contacts and I had immediate access to parts and repairs when I broke my ride.

Getting high and riding was my only concern. Southern California was the best place to do that I'd ever found. I was looking forward to the endless emptiness of searching for the eternal buzz on the streets of a city where one wrong move could mean death or worse and you never knew what that move was, when you're gonna make it or where.

One of the first little bits of information I received when I got there was that Valerie and her new boyfriend were there too somewhere and had already been out to Bird's a few times to visit. The other one was that the shop I'd figured on going right to work in no longer existed and the owner'd moved away from the area.

I had a little money and dope left when I got to Bird's. I could afford to take a day or two off to recover from the ride out there at least. I figured in a day or two I'd start hitting all the shops in the area and by the end of the week I'd have a job. That'd be soon enough for me.

A couple 'a days after I got there I was laying on the couch checking my eyelids for cracks when I heard a freight train going by right in front of the house. I jumped up and ran out the front door to see what the hell was making that noise and everything in the house vibrate. All I saw were the palm trees swaying wildly in all different directions at once and people trying to keep from falling over because the ground was vibrating like the top of an airhocky table. By the time I got outside the train was outta sight down the street, but the noise of it was still plenty loud, that was when I figured out it was an invisible train.

Once the noise subsided I could hear the neighborhood chorus screaming "earthquake" almost in unison. I stood on the porch as the train rolled out of earshot and was amazed at how quiet it was right then. It only lasted a few seconds maybe a minute tops. Then the neighbors started busting outta their houses onto their lawns panicked or pissed whichever the case may be.

So this was an earthquake? It didn't seem that bad to me. It didn't seem too bad to the drunken old pervert across the street and down a ways that was standing on his front lawn half naked jacking off and yelling obscenities like he did in the morning and afternoon while the kids walk by from the school right down the street. He must've been confused by all the noise, probably sounded like school kids to him.

I walked thru the house out the back door into the yard to see if anything had fallen like power lines or poles and then into the garage to check to see if Christine had heard the train too. While I was there I snorted a line from the dope stashed on the bike and listened to the neighbor's dog I'd newly renamed Gunpowder slam himself up against the wall of the garage and rage like he'd've eaten me if he could 'a got at me.

Other than the train roaring down the street at nine o'clock in the morning it was a beautiful day. The sky was blue and the sun was bright, not the usual overcast that doesn't burn off till noon. I went inside and turned the TV on while I waited for the line to kick in and give me the motivation to do something more than that. About a half hour later I still didn't feel like doing anything more than snorting another line. I was kinda' shootin' for getting up, taking a shower and goin' for a ride, but turning on the TV was as far as I could get.

I was getting low on dope and gas money. Maybe I'd see what I could see about getting a little work or a little dope whichever came first. The day ended the next day with both. Now I had to be at work in a few hours and I'd been up partying all night. Should I stay up the rest of the night or should I get some sleep and risk being late on my first day? I checked my dope bag and determined that staying up would be the best bet. I'd close out the bar I was at, go home get a shower and be at my new place of employ at seven on the nose.

Usually on my second day up I get pretty laid back and it takes a lot to even get a rise outta me, but the dude I went to work for this time had his shorts in a wad so tight that he was vibrating at seven in the morning. He lived on his sailboat parked on the concrete apron in front of his shop. The boat and the shop were the only things his ex-wife left him in a brutal divorce. He was fuckin' pissed about it every minute of his life and he didn't care who knew about it. He was so fuckin' straight it was like working for a cop and he was such a dick about everything he'd've made a good one.

He had the most primitive motor shop I'd ever seen in my life. Everything he did was plug fit except the pistons in the cylinders. He didn't have the equipment to do any different a job either. This dude's shop was supposed to've been a happening place at one time. I can remember seeing his bikes in more than one of the bike rags of the day.

He had a drag bike in the front window of his shop that he supposedly built and raced. If he put the lower end of that drag bike together with the same surplus military axle grease that he had me putting lower ends together with at his shop, I bet it didn't run for very long.

That was one of the most glaringly obvious signs of not giving a fuck I'd ever seen in my life. Even Mel used oil soluble assembly grease on the motors we built. If you don't use oil soluble grease when assembling a motor the grease won't break down when it comes in contact with oil and wash away without a trace. Instead the two slippery substances cause clots of the nonsoluble grease to flow into an oil hole eventually and get stuck in the first oil passage it can't get thru. Because it'll never dissolve it shuts the oil off in that passage, ending up with a seized motor somewhere down the road.

When I started with this guy there were sixteen motors on the floor to be rebuilt. My instructions were to get 'em done as quickly as I could so they could go out the door.

From the look of this Flintstone style shop this was gonna be like pulling teeth. It was easy to tell he hadn't bought a tool except from Sears in a long while. Technology had marched a long way out in front of this place and was still marching on unnoticed by this establishment.

To make matters worse I was five feet from the radio and the boss was twenty-five. I got to listen to the worst fifteen oldies songs of all time {most of 'em by Elvis, I fucking hate Elvis} over and over again all day long on the shittiest AM oldies station in L.A. Early during my employment there I made the mistake of putting some real music on one morning when I couldn't take it any longer.

The little fuckhead I worked for came charging back there vibrating all over like he was gonna do something, telling me to never change that radio again. I could turn it off when I got sick of it, but I couldn't change it for any reason. He acted like it was the only station in L.A. and once changed it'd never be found again. Who'd wanna?

After that he'd come back in the morning and turn the radio on. As soon as he walked away I'd walk over and turn it off. From there on out every time he turned that crap on I turned it right back off. It was the only way I could get anything done. Those same fifteen songs playing over and over drove me nuts after a very short time and I was sick of 'em years ago. I didn't need to hear 'em again to be reminded of that. I guess that would be an indication that my road to nuts wasn't that long to begin with.

I'd worked there a week and a half or so, when while walking out the door at the end of the day I got into a conversation with the boss about deadbeats that don't pay their bills. At one time I'd done a little collecting and enjoyed that kind of work. It paid cash, at least 50% of the bill at that and I liked having a reason to fuck somebody up.

He handed me the hard copy of a work order with the dudes name and address on it. He owed like four hundred bucks or something. I went to the payphone outside and tried the phone number on the bill. It was disconnected. I tucked the bill inside my leather and headed for the house figuring I'd take a ride over to this dude's house after I had some dinner. I had to go pick some dope up later in that same general area so I'd kill two birds with one stone.

On my way up Main Street toward the freeway I stopped at a traffic light. Opposite me at the same light was an L.A. County Sheriff's car. When the light turned green I took off in my direction and they in theirs. Halfway thru the light the cops flipped on their lights, did a Uee in the intersection and ran me to the curb. The two idiots jumped outta the car, guns drawn screaming at me to drop the gun and get on the ground. I got off the bike, faced 'em with my hands in the air and asked 'em what gun they were talking about.

One holstered his gun and started to pat me down while the other one held his gun on me hammer back, all jacked up on adrenaline. After the other one got done searching and found out I was clean number two holstered his piece. When he reached for cuffs I asked why I was under arrest.

He said I wasn't, it was for his protection.

"Protection from what" I asked.

He said the reason they stopped me was because they'd seen me reach for a gun that they suspected I'd hidden on my bike and until they found it I was gonna be cuffed. I chuckled and asked if this was the gun he'd seen me reaching for as I pointed to the chrome gearshift lever sticking up outta the transmission.

He walked around to that side of the bike and took a good look, he said "sit on the bike and grab that lever." As soon as I did I saw the light go on in his head. He walked back around to the sidewalk smiling at his partner, turned to me and asked the question that they always get around to eventually "do have any drugs or weapons on you?"

I looked at him and said "your partner already patted me down."

Like he didn't even hear what I said he ordered me to empty the contents of my pockets out onto the hood of the car and assume the position.

I didn't have anything on me to worry about so I obliged the officer without any more talk. As I removed things from my pockets one officer examined 'em and put 'em back on the hood making a comment about "us bikers caring so much stuff in our pockets".

I told him "it was to make 'em work that much harder for their pay."

When he got to the work order, he read the name and showed it to his partner. I thought "oh boy, now what?"

They stood behind me whispering to each other for a long couple 'a seconds, then one of 'em asked why I had this guy's name in my pocket.

I told 'em I worked for the bike shop down the street and he owed us money on an unpaid bill. I was gonna go see him after dinner and see what we could do about getting the bill paid.

It was then that I learned that this type of hands on approach to debt collection had been called strong-arm collection by the state of California and made illegal in the not too distant past.

I told 'em I was just gonna talk to the guy, his phone was disconnected so I had to go over to his house in order to do that and there wasn't any law against that. Both cops immediately got on their high horse and informed me that murder was illegal and I was now a suspect in a murder case and asked me if I had anything to say.

I said "yah this is bullshit!"

With nothing more than this work order to go on they couldn't arrest me. All they did was take down my home and work address and phone numbers and tell me not to leave town. They gave me a card with the phone number of the detective investigating the case on it, telling me to call him the next day before noon or they'd be at the shop to get me at twelve-thirty.

I had my dope delivered to me that night; I didn't wanna be seen anywhere near that neighborhood twice in one day and never again in particular.

The next morning I told the boss what'd happened, as soon as he heard they kept the copy of the work order he went into hysterics. After he calmed down I told him I'd be talking to the cops in a little while anyway. I'd mention it to 'em first chance I got.

I was gonna call the detective around nine o'clock so I could get this shit over with and outta the way quickly. I didn't want this hanging around giving the cops a reason to jack me up every time they saw me.

At eight o'clock the boss came back and said I was wanted on the phone, the detective wasn't wasting any time. He wanted me to come see him as soon as I could get there. I hung up the phone and told the boss I had to go.

His reply, "don't forget that work order!"

"Yah right, fuck you and your work order" was mine.

I went back to my bench and hurriedly snorted a line. I stashed my dope and paraphernalia, made a quick inventory of everything on me to make sure I didn't overlook something and walked outside to Christine.

I guess she wanted to go as much as I did because she took her sweetass time starting. She coughed and farted and spit and sputtered until I was drenched with sweat and so fuckin' pissed I couldn't see straight.

When I was about to blow a gasket completely she fired with a **BA BOOM**, like she just realized I'd been kicking the shit outta her for the last fifteen minutes {first kick or the first hundred, take your pick} and settled into her usual idle. After I got her situated, I had to wipe the sweat off my glasses and retie my hair, when I was done I took off for the Carson Sheriff's Station.

I was more than kinda' nervous by the time I got there. As soon as I parked I wished I'd stopped somewhere along the way and smoked a joint to take the edge off that last line and get some of the butterflies in my stomach stoned so they'd quit flying around so much.

When I got to the front desk I was almost jumping outta my skin. I almost took my glasses off when I spoke to the cop and caught myself at the last minute, afraid he'd see how fucked up I was. I choked and sputtered the first time I opened my mouth, my throat was so dry. I finally got out my name and who I wanted to see and immediately turned for the chairs when I was motioned to a seat and told to wait.

I barely got halfway in the chair when the detective walked out and called my name. I got up and headed his way, he turned and headed for his office with me behind him. I shouldn't 'a done that last line. I was way too fuckin' high to talk to this guy. I was gonna blow it big time as soon as he looked at me. My mind's eye was playing a movie of me flipping out and getting shot by a bunch 'a cops as I'm trying to start Christine and get outta there. What an idiot! Why of all things would

I try to start that old bitch? I'd be better off running if I was gonna try to escape at all. I'd run down Carson to the back of the Ralph's supermarket and..... What'd he say?

I looked at the cop like a deer in the headlights. I was so busy living in my head that I didn't hear what he said and now he's looking at me for an answer. Good thing I've still got my glasses on I wouldn't want him to see my eyes. They must look fucked up because I sure feel fucked up. I shouldn't've done that last line. I'm way to fuckin' high to talk to this cop. My mind's eye started playing that same stupid movie again. What'd he say? If I don't get a grip he's gonna put me in a rubber room before I can get the first word outta my mouth.

"Thanks for coming down."

I heard him this time. It was all I could do to get "you're welcome" outta my mouth, but the act of doing so focused me on talking to him, not freaking out. I snapped right back to reality as soon as I heard myself speak and the rest of the interview went well.

By the time it was done, I learned the dude was found shot to death on his front porch two weeks earlier. I was in Texas when it happened and I could prove it. I had a receipt from the Harley shop in San Antonio with my name on it dated the same day this guy was killed all I had to do was get the receipt to prove it.

I left feeling pretty good. I could easily prove my whereabouts. Case closed as soon as they see that receipt. Can't be in two places at once especially on a flat tire.

I didn't feel like going back to work and wasn't gonna till I remembered I'd left my dope there. I cussed myself all the way back to the shop. As soon as I walked in the boss asked about his work order.

I threw the sweaty folded mess on the counter as I walked by on the way to my bench and my drugs. He said he wanted the work order back. Not what kinda' shape he wanted it to be in. Fuck that motherfucker anyway.

My drugs were where I'd left 'em. Nobody'd snooped around while I was gone. That was all I'd've needed, Mr. Gestapo finding my dope and calling the cops while I was at the cop shop. I quickly snorted another line while I had the privacy to do it. After I was done I said "fuck it," told the boss I'd see him tomorrow and took off to the Key Largo to do some drinking.

When I finally got home around four-thirty in the morning I'd drank myself sober, snorted and smoked a bunch 'a dope, even took three or four hits off a crack pipe, needless to say I was fucked up. After putting Christine to bed I got into my stuff and got the receipt I needed, stuffed it in my pocket and passed out on the pool table out in the garage.

The next morning I got up not knowing where the fuck I was or anything. I figured it out as soon as Gunpowder started throwing himself at the wall and freaking out.

My head wasn't prepared for all that noise before my breakfast line. I found my dope, a clean T-shirt and stumbled into the house. A note from Kat said my dinner was in the fridge, I sat down and ate it cold. I didn't feel like going through the hassle of warming it up. Everything tasted like beer and cigarettes anyway whether it was hot or cold.

I hurried up and wolfed down my cold dinner for breakfast so I could get to the important stuff, water on the face and crank up my nose, not necessarily in that order either. I was supposed to be at the detective's office first thing in the morning. Good thing I didn't tell him what time first thing in the morning was, otherwise I'd've been late.

It took a few lines to get me percolating that morning. Once the lines got me where I needed to be, I took the time to smoke that joint this time before I even thought about going anywhere.

Once I had the right altitude, I had to remember all over again why I wasn't at work and where I was supposed to already be. Except now I'm so high I'm in my own way. I'd start doing something to get me headed outta the house and in the direction I was supposed to be going, midstride I'd forget what I was doing and be lost in place for fifteen or twenty minutes at a time.

I finally got on the street about midmorning, feeling good too. I pulled into the sheriff's parking lot, parked, got off Christine and while I was walking inside freaked out until I found the evidence that I couldn't remember putting in my wallet less than an hour before.

The detective looked at my receipt, made a copy, told me not to leave town he'd be in touch and that was it. I'd wasted half the day and still didn't have anything in the way of an answer from these fucks. I headed to the shop. Tomorrow was payday and if I wanted a decent chunk 'a change I'd better get some work done.

I finished one motor that afternoon, with a transmission job thrown in for a little extra on the pile. One thing about this job, you could skip the bank on the way to the dope house. Cash was the preferred method of payment in this shop and I never argued with a dead president.

My days were numbered at this shop. I was getting closer to having the work on the floor done every day and nothing but a tranny rebuild had come thru the door since I'd gone to work there. This wasn't exactly where I wanted to be shop wise anyway. This place'd been passed over by time and technology. Much bigger and more innovative things were going on in other shops in this town and I had no intention of wasting my life away in this museum of the not quite dead. Especially with this dickhead for a boss.

A week or so after my last encounter with the cops I walked in one morning to find we had a new welder named Shelley. Having her around was a little more comfortable than the dude she'd replaced. He always gave me the impression that he was watching me.

Whenever he was around the hair on the back of my neck would tingle. He always seemed like he was looking for something to run and tell about. I never felt like I could trust him and I finally found out why one afternoon, he was a reformed cokehead.

There's nothing more dangerous than a reformed cokehead, once they get sober many of 'em go off the deep end in the other direction and begin a crusade for the sobriety of every other human being on the planet. They don't see anything wrong with ratting you out to whoever {for your own good, they're trying to help you} and fucking your life up for the next eighteen months to two years, like they did their own.

Once I found out about this dude I steered as clear of him as I could, only interacting with him on shop related issues. I discouraged any other familiarity with either him or the boss by either obstinate silence or monosyllabic answers and stayed in my own little corner outta sight as much as possible. Only appearing to turn off the radio every time it was on for ten minutes {that was all I could take of that worn out crap}.

When I came in and saw our new welder I could tell she partied by the way she smiled when we were introduced by the boss. We chatted for a few minutes and went our separate ways. A little later I peeked around the corner, got her attention and gave her the universal get high sign. She nodded and headed my way, quickly glancing up front to see where the boss was. When she did that, I knew she'd be a good crimey.

We each quickly did our lines and went back to work before the dickhead got suspicious.

For the first few minutes after we snorted the shit I'd look over at Shelley and laugh. The drip on this shit was so nasty and the smell so strong that for a little while after snorting it your eyes watered and your nose ran profusely. If you didn't have something to wash the horrible taste of the drip outta your mouth with you'd puke after swallowing the shit for very long. But I'll tell you what, that shit lit some pretty long-legged fires.

I could do a few bumps in the morning to get me to the desired altitude and stay there until the next morning without any additional stimulation. This shit was great, a crankster's dream and every time I looked at Shelley she was trying to look like she was doing her job. Tears were streaming down her checks and all you could hear from her corner was a constant sniffing as she tried to keep from drowning her work in caustic snot.

At lunchtime we rode down to a burger stand on the corner. I had a double chilly cheeseburger, chilly fries and a large orange soda. Shelley had a small Pepsi or something and she could barely drink that. She sat there watching me wolf down my lunch like I hadn't eaten in a week all the while hyper-babbling "I don't know how you can eat that, I couldn't possibly eat that, I can barely drink this soda, this dope is so good, can you get any more, if you can, will you get me some, how much is it, I've got a little money in my car, if you can get some, when can you get it, can you get it today before we go home, I'd like to have some for tomorrow, I've never had dope this good, are we gonna do a line before we go back, can you get some before we go home?" This hyper-babbling went on the entire time I was eating, nonstop.

When I finally finished I looked at her over the top of my shades and said "you don't need any more," got up, threw my trash away, and headed for Christine.

She hurried along behind me agreeing with me at first about her not needing any more and then it was maybe just a little bit. Then she didn't need any now, but she'd need some in the morning. Could I get her some in the morning? The verbal flood started all over again.

Before I fired Christine up I turned to her and said "you gotta mellow out before we get back to the shop, the dude we work for isn't in the least bit cool. We'll stop and smoke a joint down the street, but I don't think you need any more dope right now."

She agreed and after I got Christine fired we rode over behind a Ralph's Supermarket and smoked a joint sitting on the loading dock. That seemed to help her get a grip on herself and we headed back to the shop for round two. When we walked through the door the boss gave us the evil eye. We'd taken a little longer lunch than he liked. He started to say something.

I cut him off midsentence with "place was packed" and walked out back without even looking in his direction. Shelley went to the job she was doing without a word {which was amazing}. I went back to what I was doing before we'd left.

I worked along in silence for a while waiting to see if dickhead was gonna come back and say something more about lunch, when he didn't I retired to a corner for a minute and did a bump just for old times sake. I didn't really need one, but I did need to stay in practice for the day I won the Olympic Line Snorting, Twin Tooter Division Contest.

Shelly kept wandering away from her work every once in a while, trying to talk me into giving her some more. As spun as she was at lunch she could wait till tomorrow to do some more around me. One thing you always have to consider when turning somebody on, especially with really good dope is the spin factor. Is this person gonna get so high that they spaz under some imaginary pressure and start babbling about the dope, who they got it from and shit like that? Someone like that can fuck you up in a heartbeat and not even know they did it because they're just running off at the mouth and don't even know what they're saying. She exhibited all that at lunch, so I figured it'd be best to just say "no" until she came down a little bit and had a better grip.

That afternoon at quitting time I told her I'd see her in the morning and got outta there as fast as I could before she had time to corral me into any conversation. While I was blasting away from the shop I made note of the sheriff's car sitting on the side of the street obviously watching the shop.

A car'd been there most every day since my last talk with the cops. They never followed me, they seemed more interested in the shop than me. After we all left the boss used to close the gate and lock it usually till the next morning so I don't know what they were seeing after we left, if anything.

The next morning Shelley drug herself in sipping a coffee, thinking about eating the donut she had in the bag she set on her bench. She looked like she'd been "shot-at-n-missed-n-shit-at-n-hit." I'll bet if she got any sleep at all it wasn't much. I myself had spent the night in the bars till closing. Stopped for breakfast on the way home, took a shower when I got there, did a bump and went to work.

Before we got started I lined us both up and got a kick outta the runny face on Shelley again. This time I didn't give her quite as much and she didn't get so spun. I knew she could handle this dope if she eased into it a little more gradually. That was the secret of being a successful crankster. Knowing your limit and gradually doing bumps till you got to that point, instead of blowing the top of your head off the first time and walking around spun right out into left field after that.

Don't get me wrong left field can be kinda' fun if you bring yourself there and back by manipulating the consumption of your drug of choice to achieve left field status. It's when you've gotten to left field on the wrong bus that things get scary and people begin to freak out. One of the things you have to learn early is to keep a grip on the drugs you're doing and not let 'em get a grip on you.

Meth is a monster that'll jump on your back, ride you into the ground and walk away sneering looking for its next victim if you don't keep a grip on yourself and ride it to ground first. If meth gets a grip on you it'll take you places you don't wanna go and you might not get back from. Sometimes it's hard to get thru to yourself that it's just the dope when you're in the middle of a "warp ten with your hair on fire" ride from some first class glass.

Shelley wasn't there the day I went to lunch with a customer I'd met earlier in the day and got jacked by the Carson Sheriffs again. He and I left the shop headed for Carson Street. This time the cop car that was always hovering somewhere near the shop took out after us, lights and siren blaring. He was blocks behind us as we turned left onto Carson right into the middle of a two car roadblock, just for us.

The entire side of the street was blocked off and traffic diverted around us into the oncoming lanes, first they ran the dogs all around us and then the bikes while we lay face down, cuffed in the middle of the hot asphalt street. A very comfortable position on a sunny ninety degree day, face down on a hot asphalt street that had traffic running over it not five minutes earlier.

Once the dogs didn't find anything. One by one we were stood up, uncuffed and made to empty our pockets onto the hood of a patrol car. Then we stood spread eagle with our hands on the nice hot black fender of the same car until they were done rifling through our shit and told us to put it back.

Next we had to sit on the curb while several officers strip searched our bikes. Everything that wasn't firmly attached to the bikes was removed and scrutinized carefully before being dropped in a heap in the middle of the street. Saddlebags were emptied, their contents thrown in the street and stepped on by the cops doing the searching.

After an hour of this bullshit we were told to pick up our stuff and put it away and be quick about it. During the hour we were being searched the first cop asked a bunch of the stupidest questions you've ever heard. The first one was "why were you running from me?" That was the stupidest question I'd ever heard.

My answer was "I wasn't running from you asshole, I came down here for some lunch."

Then he wanted to know why we didn't stop for him.

I told him we didn't even know he was there, he was blocks behind us. Was I supposed to have such a guilty conscience that I automatically stopped every time some cop in L.A. turns on his lights and siren.

What he was trying to do was show probable cause for all this harassment in front of the other cops. I stood right there and listened to him lie to another cop. He was telling him he was chasing us down Main Street after leaving a bar wide open on our bikes.

I fuckin' blew a gasket when I heard the shit he was slinging. I refuted everything he was saying while he was saying it and when he was done told the dude my version of it. That was when we were told to put our shit back and get outta there.

When I was walking away, the cop that started all this bullshit said I'd see him again. I wheeled on him and told him if I did he'd like the outcome a lot less if he was alone! We got on our bikes and got some lunch after I got all my shit put away in my saddlebags.

The boss was pissed when we got back. We'd been gone over two hours. I was just in the mood to be fucked with about being fucked with. As soon as he opened his mouth I jumped in his shit with both feet and walked around a while I was so pissed. He backed up and ran up front. I took the opportunity to get my stash. He came back a few minutes later with a snub nose pistol in his hand and told me to go home and cool off. I gladly took the rest of the day off and the day after that. The day after that being Friday I collected my little bit of pay and took off for the weekend.

Being short of cash that weekend clipped my wings, I had to stay close to home or I wouldn't be able to afford my dope for the week. That meant hanging out at the Alondra Inn, Antone's, the Fireside and the Stagger Inn all weekend, could be worse I could 'a been in jail.

I started off the weekend at the Alondra Inn. Sometime during the evening over a pool game Mary and I found out we had a lot in common when I turned her on to some of the wicked glass I had.

Later on that evening she and I were headed to pick up some more of that hair straightening glass. We'd just turned onto Lakewood from Alondra, being Friday night I was taking it easy. Christine at her quietest is a cop calling bitch. If you start romping on the gas and setting off car alarms all over the place you better have your dope stashed pretty good cause you're gonna be talking to the cops before too long.

That's what happened to us as soon as we turned onto Lakewood a sheriff going in the other direction did a flip and came after us like I'd taken a shot at his car or something. I pulled over as soon as his lights came on, got off the bike and waited for him to get outta the car.

He took a little bit of time to get outta the car because he was running my plate. At the time I was licensed and registered in New Mexico and outta state plates took a little longer to get a reply from, especially New Mexico since they had a reciprocal agreement with no one at the time, that's why I registered there.

He finally got outta the car and asked the first question "do you know why I stopped you?"

"Let me guess, loud exhaust" was my reply.

"Can I see your license and registration?" The standard next question no matter what answer you give to the first question.

I dug my license and registration out and handed it to the cop. The standard next question is {for me anyway} "why is your exhaust so loud?"

I told him that New Mexico was a nonconformist state that didn't have any exhaust regulation on the books so I ran straight pipes because "loud pipes save lives" and being a true nonconformist at heart my bike was much louder than your average bike with straight pipes.

His answer to that was "sounds like a crock 'a shit to me, but it's the best crock 'a shit I've heard in a long time." When he started laughing I knew I'd walk away from this one. He looked at my registration to make sure it matched, it did and he laid it on the hood of his car. He looked at my license long and hard tilting it in all directions and finally asked "what *the fuck* is this?"

I told him that was my license and asked what was wrong; he handed it to me and told me to look at it.

Back then a New Mexico license had the words New Mexico repeated over and over across the background of the license in gold letters. Under the light of the high pressure sodium streetlights all you could see were the words New Mexico repeated across the front of the license in gold letters that was it. None of the other information was visible at all, you couldn't even tell it was there. I moved the license around like he did and couldn't get any better results no matter what the angle.

I handed him back the license and said jokingly it must be a nonconformist license. He started laughing, handed back my license and registration and told me to get outta there he didn't have any nonconformist tickets and he couldn't write a nonconformist a conformist ticket.

That started me laughing so hard I could hardly see my wallet to get my stuff back in it. I thanked him and we got outta there fast before another cop showed up and fucked up a good thing. The rest of that tweakend and many more are just a haze of riding, drugging, drinking and fucking, the only things in life that meant anything to me then.

That time in my life was either a high point or a low point depending on your perspective. High from the standpoint that I lived on and for dope and stayed as high as humanly possible and function till nothing could make me run any further. I'd wake up in the weirdest places. One time I remember I was sitting on the toilet in the men's room of some bar when Wrench from the old Chicken Delight days woke me up. He tuned me up and gave me hell because if he hadn't been watching Christine I wouldn't have her today.

Low because I'd finally given over to the addictions and was allowing 'em to run me into the ground at a pretty good clip. When I got my pay each week my only thought was how much dope I could afford. Unless I needed parts for Christine, dope was my first and only concern. I'd long since reached the point where the only way I felt normal was when I'd ingested enough dope and alcohol to kill a normal person. I'd been practicing for a long time and was finally coming into my stride as a professional drug addict and alcoholic. With a double major in crank and weed and an alcohol minor at the school of hard knocks, I was working overtime to make sure I wasn't missing anything in the fucking up department.

TCOB, Take Care Of Business, kind of a biker creedo, words to live by or die by depending which end of the pistol you're on and when. My goal in all of this was the same as it was when I was a kid. Get as fucked up as I possibly could and maintain every day. The night Wrench woke me up and reamed me for not taking care of my business was a wake up call for me. I wasn't gonna be a drug-induced scooter tramp {truly something to aspire to} if I didn't have a scooter. Without that I was just another junkie looking for my next high, so I better get my head outta the bag long enough to take care of my shit or I wouldn't have it long.

I remember some things from that time like the night I ran a stop sign and almost got broadsided by a cop. Some barfly and I were headed to the house after the bars closed to continue the party in private one morning. When I was real drunk I used to hold Christine in second gear and wind her up tight all the way down my street. This would set car and home alarms off all down the street. At the last second I'd slam on the old mechanical brakes, downshift into first and hope the fuck I slowed down in time to make the turn into the driveway.

Mechanical brakes were the worst brakes you could have on a hotrod motorcycle. They didn't work all that well on a stock bike. When you build one that hauls ass they're an accident looking for a place to happen. I could adjust my brakes and by the end of the day hollering whoa was more effective than the brakes were for stopping the bike under ordinary conditions. Having a passenger only amplified the shitty brakes.

This particular morning between the extra weight, the bad brakes and not letting off the gas soon enough. Not only did we miss the driveway but we shot thru the stop sign at the end of the street right across South Street in front of a cop transporting a prisoner and about a half a block further.

When we finally came to a stop, we got off the bike and turned around to walk it back to the house. It was a good thing because when the cop finally came back he was pissed and wanted to know what the hell I thought I was doing. I told him I didn't think *I knew* I'd lost my brakes. I then told him that not only did I miss the stop sign I'd also missed my driveway three lots before it.

Like your typical cop he asked how much I'd had to drink.

I asked him how that had anything to do with losing my brakes. That was when his partner in the back seat with the prisoner asked me where I was going.

I told him I was going home.

He asked where that was.

I told him "on the other side of South Street three lots back."

He told his partner to forget about it and get going. As the first cop was about to say something else the second one told me to be more careful.

All I could say was "you see me pushin' the fuckin' thing don'cha?"

I'll tell ya what, that's one of the biggest buzz kills I've ever experienced. For all the fucked up I was when we left the bar right up until the time I hit the brakes and we didn't slow down, I was as sober as a teetotaler when we got to the house. I'd've probably blown a 3.whatever on a breathalyzer, but as far as I was concerned I was as close to sober as I'd been in a long time.

I gotta tell ya about Gunpowder, this was the most miserable animal I've ever seen. One wall of the garage was the property line to the neighbor's yard. A Mexican family lived there and had two dogs. One was the looniest thing on the planet. Every time anyone was out in the garage this stupid thing would slam itself against the wall barking furiously the whole time you were there.

One day after listening to this crap for months I got home early and was out in the garage. Gunpowder was going ballistic as usual. The second dog decided it was gonna help this time. As it ran at the wall barking, Gunpowder wheeled on it and attacked it as hard as he attacked the wall. The fur started flying and the other dog started screaming in pain. This only enraged Gunpowder even more. When the missus and the oldest daughter came out the back door to stop it, Gunpowder attacked them too.

They ran back inside and slammed the door. After that Gunpowder stood on the porch panting, looking for something to go after. An avocado fell off the tree in their back yard and Gunpowder was on it, ripping it to mush, spitting it out and going after it again. For the rest of his life he attacked every avocado that fell outta that tree.

Fifteen or twenty minutes after the women got chased back into the house the dad showed up and went in the house. A few minutes later he came out the back door carrying an old rusty pistol. As soon as Gunpowder saw him the attack was on. When Gunpowder got close enough to dad, **BANG, BANG, BANG**, Gunpowder headed for that big avocado tree in the sky. The other dog recovered and ya know it never came near the wall of that garage again.

A couple 'a blocks back up the street that we lived on was a house full of cranksters. The fearless leader of this bunch of hoodlums was a dude named Rodney. He was a trip to say the least. His mom was quite the bible thumper according to him. He had been too, until a few years earlier when he discovered the wonders of better living through chemistry.

Rodney had kinda' blended the two religions Christianity and crank into a little philosophy of his own where God provided man with crank to give him the power to fight the Devil's Minions during the coming Apocalypse. He even showed me passages in the book of Romans that mention a white powder that drove The Horsemen of the Apocalypse to victory.

I used to get a kick outta getting Rodney going about the subject and listening to him explain in the most precise detail how crank fit into the grand scheme of life. Exactly where it belonged and who should be the ones allowed to use it and who not. All I knew the whole time was that he had the best glass I'd ever seen. This stuff lit your candle at both ends simultaneously and kept you burning for a long time.

Like any crank dealer he had a house and yard full of stuff, all kinds of stuff. The whole back yard was full up to the top of the fence with stuff, everything under the sun with nothing but little walkways down between it all. This stuff was packed into every bit of the yard. Deeper than I was tall, it was like a maze. There were motorcycles and all kinds of things in there that Rodney himself hadn't seen for years because it was covered with all the other stuff.

Along with Rodney was an ever changing population of cranksters that drifted in-n-outta the house with the wind. You'd go by there in the middle of the night, all the doors and windows would be standing wide open, every light in the place on and not a soul to be found anywhere.

Rodney was lucky, his mother owned the house he lived in so he didn't do anything but drugs all day long, he didn't have any rent, all he had to do was keep the lights on.

Rodney had a cherry `70 Monte Carlo that he was pretty proud of. As I rode past his house one afternoon I looked and he had the whole interior of the car removed and spread all over the lawn. I thought "oh boy, I can't wait to here this."

I rode down to the house and put Christine away and walked back up to Rodney's house. When I got there the car was scattered all over the lawn, the stereo was on, the lights were on, the phone was in the sink and there wasn't anyone around.

I whistled a few times as I walked around the house. Finally someone whistled back. It was Rodney coming back from the liquor store on the corner. I flopped on the couch and waited for him to come in. I waited and waited and finally went outside when he didn't come in. He was inside the car taking something else apart. I leaned in and asked him what he was doing.

He said that morning when he was going somewhere he heard a noise and he was gonna find out what it was and fix it.

I couldn't help but ask him if the noise might not've been in his head.

He said he didn't know for sure, but he doubted it.

I asked him if he'd taken a lot of car interiors out before.

He said it was his first one, but he could handle it. As we were talking he climbed outta the car because I'd given him that universal get high sign we all used.

We went in the house and lined up some of that glass and once we were both blasting off for parts unknown we went back outside. As soon as we got amongst the car parts I pointed at something and asked him if he knew what it was and where it went.

He picked it up and studied it for a long minute, put it down and said he had no idea. That's when I asked him if he shouldn't stop before his car looked like everything else in his back yard.

A light bulb seemed to go on and for a minute there I thought he'd gotten a grip. We started to put the car back together and had most of it done when I told him I was going home. It was early in the morning and everyone'd been in bed for hours so I was as quiet as I could be while I checked my eyelids for cracks.

After a couple 'a hours of that, I took a shower and got ready to go to work. The last thing I did before I left was a big fat ripper. I didn't wanna run outta steam for a while and with this in me I'd be like the energizer bunny all day and half the night.

When I rode past Rodney's house I expected to see a complete car in his driveway, instead the whole interior was outta the car again, the wheels were off and it was sitting on blocks. The hood and trunk lid were leaning up against the house and Rodney's feet were sticking out from under the car cause he was under it doing God only knows what. So much for so little, I tried to help him. I didn't have time to stop right then, but was sure I'd hear all about it when I got home that night.

When I got home that evening I could tell ole Rodney was pretty spun. The car was all over the front yard and he'd found his noise. The noise was just a U-joint in the driveshaft, which would've been a simple enough thing to fix if he hadn't spun out and taken the whole car apart. I went inside with him and we did a blast, he asked me if I'd help him put the car back together again.

I didn't know that much about cars, not enough to put this disaster back together. Not without a book, that's for sure. He was worried about getting the U-joint fixed and hadn't given a thought to how he was gonna get the rest of the car back together. I went out and looked at all the parts. The seats, carpet, and body panels would be pretty easy if he had all the clips and screws. The steering column, the shifter and console, the window regulators and all the other electronic stuff was gonna be a bitch, especially since I didn't take it out or even see where it came from before it came out.

Rodney didn't come out when I did and he never came out. I wasn't gonna try to figure this thing out by myself, so I went back in to get him. He was out like a light in the middle of the living room floor. I couldn't get him to move so I made sure he wasn't dead, turned him on his side in case he puked and went home closing his front door behind me.

When I rode by after closing out one of the local bars nothing'd stirred, everything was like I left it. Same for when I went to work a little while later.

That evening when I got home was another story. The cops were there and had all the inhabitants laying on the front lawn in handcuffs. I didn't even look, I just idled on by like the law-abiding citizen that I was at that moment.

After the cops left I walked down to Rodney's to see if they left anyone alive. Rodney and a couple 'a other people were there running around like chickens with their heads cut off, freaking out at every sound.

One of the cranksters that wasn't so lucky had been identified in a local burglary and chased back to Rodney's house by the cops. They busted that dude and two others on warrants and gave Rodney a ticket for having his car spread all over the front lawn.

Rodney was lucky, he had a shitload of dope locked up in a safe in his bedroom and the cops didn't even find the safe. It'd've sucked if they'd found it, no more of that good glass, man I'd've been bummed.

While I was there I got an eight-ball just in case the cops came back. If I was a cop, I'd be wherever it was I needed to be getting a search warrant for that place, it was your textbook shooting gallery. If they looked thru the stuff out back they'd probably solve a thousand burglaries. Hell if they went through that whole mess they'd probably find Amelia Earhart's plane.

Once I got my eight-ball, I casually got the hell outta there as fast as I could without freaking out the locals. I didn't want a bunch of spun-out cranksters running to Bird's house when the cops came again and I was pretty sure they'd be back real soon. Later on that night we were watching TV and I noticed red and blue lights lighting the whole neighborhood. Bird and I went out in the front yard and sure as shit there were cops crawling all over Rodney's house.

In the morning when I went to work the cops were still there, the gate into the back yard was open and a bobcat was going in and out dumping stuff into city dump trucks after it was sifted thru by guys dressed in white chemical suits.

I kept Christine down to a burble as I idled by trying to be inconspicuous. I didn't want my day to end up like Rodney's and I didn't want to be tied to Rodney's in any way. Once by 'em I felt like holes were being stared in my back, but I didn't wanna gas it and give 'em any reason to ruin my day if I could help it.

A couple 'a blocks away and I headed for the freeway as fast as I dared. That was the safest place to run from the cops if I had to. Once on the freeway I can be gone thru traffic and outta sight before they can get to the top of the ramp or call in a chopper.

As I thought all this my adrenaline went nuts and I hit the freeway doing about eighty mph, shot across all the traffic to the Dave Lane and hauled ass. I was at the Main Street exit before I knew it and pulled into the shop like my hair was on fire. I parked Christine and walked inside like I expected Sherman Block himself to come popping up outta nowhere and arrest me.

Rushing inside, I didn't say a word to anybody as I went to my bench. Once I got there I saw myself in the mirror that I did my lines on and laughed. I looked like a scared little kid afraid the bogey man was gonna get him. Just to prove I wasn't scared I laid out a line to do right at my bench. Right in the middle of snorting the line Shelley came walking up and I almost inhaled the tooter and all she startled me so badly. So much for bravery.

I stayed close to the shop that day. I don't know why I was so paranoid, if they wanted me they'd've already had me. Hell they would've nailed me as rode by that morning. I wasn't taking any chances today. I ate lunch in and took the back way home so I didn't have to ride past Rodney's house.

When I turned onto the street I could see the yellow tape around the property. I parked Christine in the garage, had dinner and once it got dark I walked down to survey the damage. The cops were still there sifting thru the debris in the back yard and loading it into dump trucks. Some neighbors were standing on the other side of the street so I crossed over and talked with them for a few minutes.

The cops'd come back just like I thought they would, as evidenced by the splintered front door. The people across the street said it looked like something on TV the way the cops swarmed every inch of the property scooping people up, cuffin' 'em and dumpin' 'em on the front lawn.

I'll tell ya what, they fucked that house up. They knocked holes in the walls. They found the safe and everything else that was anywhere on that property. It took 'em the best part of a week to get all the stuff sorted thru, inventoried and hauled off. When the cops were finally done my curiosity got the better of me one evening and I walked down there.

Man what a mess they made of that house. The garage got it even worse cause they found some stuff out there that'd been used in a meth lab at one time. When they found that, they all but tore the garage down one board at a time. It was nothing but the framing when they were done and the house was in just a little bit better shape.

Oh well, so much for so little. I was just glad I'd gotten to know Rodney's connection before he got busted, maybe I wouldn't lose out on the glass. Question is, is it safe to be buying dope from him right now? There's no way to tell if he's been rolled on till the cops're at his door. The fact that Rodney wasn't out yet was a good sign. I didn't know Rodney well enough to be able to judge though.

When the cops were finally done with Rodney's place it looked like a bomb'd gone off there. The house was boarded up by the city and everything in the front was thrown in the back and the gate locked. They'd done such a job on the house that there was no way anyone could live in it. Once the whole deal was done the place was just a blank dark hole on that side of the street day or night. It looked like most places look when the cops get done searching a meth lab or drug house, destroyed.

Weeks after everything'd died down, I was riding by there on my way home from work and saw a car in the driveway as I was rolling up to the place. I slowed down to see what I could see. It was a middle aged woman and a young dude in a suit. I thought they were lawyers or something.

As I got close the dude turned, it was Rodney all squeaky clean and shiny. I stopped at the curb, Rodney walked up, nodded, leaned in and said "dude that's my mom, I gotta go, see ya later" and he got away from me like I'd shocked him or something.

After seeing Rodney I had a little more faith in him. He looked like someone that was fighting a case, not someone that'd rolled his way outta jail on the give us three names game. I went home from there and called his guy Ray for the first time since the bust. He had some, he'd sell some, but he ain't comin' anywhere near here which meant I'd have to ride all the way out to San Pedro if I wanted glass.

I'd been getting my dope from a couple 'a different places, none of which was as good as this glass. In fact the last two batches of dope I got had left huge canker sores in my mouth that I was drenching with enough Oragel to make me puke a couple 'a times a day. I didn't stop snorting the dope or even slow down, I just stocked up on Oragel so I never ran out is all.

It was worth the ride for the glass, that was good clean dope, my mouth'd have a chance to heal if I bought me some 'a that glass. I could stash the other dope for a rainy day aaand I'm gonna go get some glass. See how easy that was? Just say yes, works every time. I talked myself into that so quickly I was on the Harbor Freeway headed for Pedro before I knew it. It was worth the ride. I got the shit $10.00 cheaper and the dude laid out a massive ripper to help me get home.

Only thing, as I was getting on Christine to leave a cop went by and looked me up and down. I don't know if it was because I was a new face or what, but it gave me the willies. I pretended to be doin' something on the bike till he was way down the street.

The line I'd done upstairs was coming on real strong now. I could feel the sweat starting to run down the crack of my ass and my hair standing straight on end. It felt like something was crawling around in my beard and my ears were ringing so loud that it was all I could hear.

What a place to have a rush like this. It's a good thing that cop went by otherwise I'd have just been getting on the freeway when that happened. It felt kinda' cool but I'd hate to've been drivin' when that baby hit.

By the time my shit got back in one basket the cop was long gone. I was off like a rocket now and it was time to get Christine in the same condition. She agreed, fired first kick for a change and we got outta there.

At the last traffic light before the freeway sat my buddy in perfect position to jump out after me as I went by. I'd just ease thru the light watching my speed and my noise and be on the freeway before he knew I was there.

Once outta sight and on the freeway I got the fuck outta there in a hurry, I was way too wired to go home and watch TV so I headed for one of my homes away from home to drink myself into tomorrow.

Instead of going to one of my usual hangouts I headed across the Vincent Thomas Bridge to a place in the Port of Long Beach called The Wagon Wheel. I'd heard from several friends that they had some hot waitresses and even hotter Buffalo Wings.

When I got there, there were three people there and most of the place was darkened. As soon as I walked thru the door I could smell the wings. By now it'd become as easy for me to eat on dope as off so I was ready to munch on some wings. Hell if I couldn't do it on my own, I had some buds in my pocket that'd fix that.

I spent the night drinking beer and eating wings till the door was locked and the sign turned off. I sat in a dark shadow, snorted a line and smoked a few hits off a good sized roach I had before I headed for the house.

The sky was starting to get light as I rolled Christine into the garage; I was so high I didn't feel like I could make the walk into the house so I lay back on Christine's gas tanks to check my eyelids for cracks for a while.

I must've dozed off, because Kat came out on her way to work to see if I was still alive. I woke up when she opened the door. We spoke for a minute, then she took off and I dragged myself in the house.

I should've been at work two hours ago. I'd take a shower and get going as soon as this line starts working. I ate my leftover dinner cold and sat on the couch in a stupor waiting for the drugs to kick in so I could get moving. This dope better start working pretty soon or I'm gonna be in my own way all fucking day, that means nothing'll get done if I have to do it. I snorted another bump to help the first one along. It at least got me into the shower, which is a good place to be when everything inside you suddenly decides it wants out of every orifice in your body at once.

I hadn't felt right since I'd lain down on Christine, no matter how much I smoked and snorted that feeling only got worse. I figured that a shower'd complete the treatment and bring the needed effect.

It was a good thing I'd been in the shower when all my gaskets blew because I spewed shit, piss and puke in three directions simultaneously with unbelievable force. It was like I'd been pressurized to the point of explosion because that was what happened, for the next fifteen minutes I expelled everything in my body like a gusher.

When I was done I felt like I'd been drug through a knot hole backwards and could barely stand. I got the shower all washed out just in time to repeat the performance. I didn't think I had it in me to tell ya the truth and I didn't, all that came outta me was fluid. The most vile tasting and smelling stuff I'd ever seen, kinda' greenish yellow, it was hard to believe it'd come outta me.

It finally slowed down enough to get outta the bathroom, get dressed and get out to the couch. It was eleven o'clock by now. I called the shop to tell 'em I wouldn't be in today or tomorrow. When the boss answered the phone he was instantly pissed. When I told him I wouldn't be in that day, his answer was "no shit, I've already figured that out."

When I told him I didn't think I'd be in the next day either, he replied with "I don't wanna hear that shit, what the fuck's your problem?"

All I said was "sick" and hung up the phone, that was enough 'a his shit.

The rest of the day was spent mostly in the bathroom, sitting on the toilet, puking into the sink. After every round on the toilet I felt a little more spindly, till I could barely move. I'd actually fall asleep sitting on the toilet leaning into the sink, waking up when another wave hit me.

That was how I woke up late in the afternoon when Kat started knocking on the bathroom door. When I woke up my legs were numb from the waist down. I felt horrible, it took me a few minutes to get my shit together and get outta the bathroom. As soon as I opened the door and staggered out Kat said something about how shitty I looked. All I could say was "you should see it from this side" and kinda' half chuckle. That took more outta me than I could stand.

As soon as Kat was out, I made another mad dash for the bathroom. I didn't see how I could have that much fluid in me, I hadn't even so much as drank a glass of water all day and as much fluid as I'd lost it seemed to me that it had to come to an end soon.

This went on for four days, while I got weaker and weaker. I couldn't even so much as take a sip of water without starting another round of projectile puking and pooping.

Nothing worked to even slow this thing down. On the contrary anything that passed my lips caused the same immediate reaction. Around lunchtime of the fourth day I came to with somebody beating on the door. It took me a while to get to the door, but when I finally got it open Shelley was standing there. She took one look at me and said "fuuuck, what's the matter with you?" I headed for the bathroom while she let herself in.

When I came out she had my cloths on the bed and told me to get dressed she was taking me to the hospital. We took a trip over to Harbor General. The place was an absolute zoo. Like most county hospitals in large cities, overworked and understaffed. Ya could 'a died right there in the waiting room and no one would 'a cared. I was so far gone I didn't really notice the conditions, I just needed the restroom, quick.

When I came back someone'd taken my seat and I was in no mood to stand. That was when Shelley hit the roof. She sat me down in her seat and headed for the desk. In a couple 'a minutes she was back with a wheelchair and an orderly who loaded me up and took me back to the ER.

We spent all that afternoon and most of the evening back there while they did tests and pumped me full of electrolytes, antibiotics and vitamins. The nearest thing they could conclude from the tests they'd done was that I'd perforated my stomach lining and my body had flooded with hydrochloric acid. Without some much more expensive and time consuming tests to actually confirm this, this was their best guess. They couldn't've been too far off, cause their treatment worked.

After hours of having fluids pumped into me, blood taken outta me and a few pills thrown in for good measure I was released. The first thing I noticed on the way home was how hungry I was. McDonald's never tasted so good. At the hospital they'd weighed me as part of the initial examination, before the fluids and all I weighed a hundred and seven pounds. That means I'd lost twenty-seven pounds in four days.

It wasn't any wonder that I felt brittle and transparent when I got to the hospital. That was how I described myself to the doctor during the initial interview. The doctor told Shelley she'd gotten me there just in time, another eight or ten hours and I'd've been dead. In fact he didn't know how I'd made it as long as I did and he was amazed that I'd walked in there on my own power.

Now that I could hold down food, all I could do was eat. The only problem was, three or four bites and I was full, my stomach had shrunken so badly. I'd missed four days of work so I called it a week and figured I'd rest the weekend and be right as rain for Monday.

The nearest thing I can figure is the drip that I was constantly swallowing and the Oragel I was constantly swallowing along with it, finally ate a hole in my stomach {or maybe it was the hot wings, I don't know}. All I can say is I did a lotta dope for many years after that and never had that happen again, maybe it was the glass. By Sunday I was back to snorting, smoking and drinking again almost like nothing'd happened.

When I got back to work Monday I was kinda' pissed and kinda' relieved to find that there was only one and half motors left to rebuild. While I'd been gone the boss had started on one of the motors and a pissed off customer had come and got another after he finally got fed up with being put off for almost a year.

I can't say as I blame him that motor had sat there for nine months before I got there, that's a ridiculously long time to wait without a bike in Southern California. I'd've hit the roof after a month. That only left a lower end and a complete rebuild and I was done there unless something came thru the door before I was finished with those. I kinda' hoped nothing would so I could get the fuck outta there. I hated working for this tight-assed motherfucker and this was the deadest shop I'd ever worked in besides Mel's. There hadn't been a customer thru the door all week at times.

One rainy morning right before Christmas I was called to the phone shortly after I got to work. It was Valerie, the bigger better deal had turned out to be a dud and she needed to see me. It seems she didn't like her new situation and wanted to leave. I know I didn't say what she wanted to hear because although I talked to her a couple more times on the phone I never saw her again.

She'd buy drugs from Bird occasionally, but would meet him at the liquor store on the corner so I wouldn't know or wait till I wasn't gonna be there to come by. I really didn't care about her anyway, that was then and this was now.

I finally finished my time at the shop that same week. Nothing'd come thru the door and we left it at I'll call ya when I need ya. I was glad to be away from that sour bastard. He was such a bitter son-of-a-bitch that it was all I could do to go to work in the morning, but as long as there was money there I'd go. I needed the dope.

The first thing I did was stock up on dope when I left the shop. There was no telling how long it'd be before I went back to work and I could make money and keep from running outta dope if I invested now.

Being outta work for a few days would give me a chance to check out the area a little bit, find some other shops and probably another job as well. It felt good not to have to go to that dungeon any more.

I didn't get much time off because the following Tuesday a dude named Motorman called while I was hanging out in the garage listening to Gunpowder try to knock the side off it. One of his guys had just taken a patch and quit. He'd heard what a tramp I was and asked me to come by the next day.

The next day I had a new job working in a happenin' little place with a bunch of derelicts much more like myself. The boss {Vince} forbade dope use as he was taking the tooter outta *his* nose. The general all around wrench {Slide} was the president of his chapter of a local club. Off in one corner of the shop was a crazy little Irish dude {Pete} that happened to be the best frame man I'd ever met.

The boss and I did the motors and trannies. Mostly I remember him walking around spun wondering what the fuck he was doing all the time. As much as he tried to deny and forbid use. One crankster can see it in another and what's good for the goose is good for the gander. Two could play the denial game.

The shop was in the city of Lynwood just off the corner of Atlantic and Imperial. We had a small overhead door that opened onto the

Atlantic Alley behind a Taco Bell. Another alley ran beside the building to Linden Street that fronted the shop's driveway. The hotrod VW shop next door was as full of derelicts as ours was, so we had a pretty cool assortment of nuts in our little corner of the world.

The view out the small overhead door near my bench was nothing short of amazing at times. The alley that ran along Atlantic was a superhighway for the dregs of society. The homeless, junkies, hoodlums, thugs, packs of gangbangers and families of illegals traveled up and down the alley all hours of the day and night.

The alley that ran to the side street was one of the neighborhood's outdoor shooting galleries. It was a few weeks before I actually took a look down that alley. When I did it was disgusting. The alley from one end to the other was littered with broken alcohol bottles, used rigs, cardboard box beds, old cloths covered with piss and shit, human waste, and once in a while a dead body.

During the day while you were working all types of human waste would stop at the door to case the place on the pretext of bumming change or looking for work. You had to constantly be watching the door to keep 'em from grabbing something and running off with it or the bolder ones from coming in and trying to rob somebody.

Across the alley I watched dozens of drug deals go down all day long in the Taco Bell parking lot, sometimes right under the noses of the cops that were always circling the area or eating at the place.

I eventually got pretty good at identifying the different types of junkies and drug dealers. It was pretty amazing to watch these people do their drug deals right under the noses of the cops as they sat in their cars eating, seemingly oblivious to the action going on around 'em. The junkies there must've been hard up, either that or they were used to having the cops around while they did their deals.

I watched one score his dope with the cops in their car not ten feet from him. Once he got the dope he went into the shooting gallery and fired his hit. The whole time the cops were sitting in their car eating. All either one of 'em had to do at any time was lean his head back a little bit and look right and the junkie would've been busted.

I could set my watch by what illegal alien family was eating outta the dumpster. At eleven-thirty every morning a Taco Bell employee would throw four huge bags of garbage into the dumpster at the corner of the parking lot. About fifteen minutes later an entire family of illegals, father, mother and all the children would stop and feast on all the stuff that Taco Bell had just thrown out, that went on all afternoon.

During the lunch hour that parking lot was a madhouse like no other I'd ever seen. Dealers would be selling dope. Junkies would be using it in their cars or in the alley. Homeless families would be eating outta the dumpster. A few people would actually be there to eat like the cops that sat in their cars eating with all this other shit going on around 'em, making sure not to see.

One chilly, rainy morning a few weeks after I'd started work there, the overhead door was closed because of the weather. I'd just come outta the restroom after snorting a morning energizer and when I was walking up to my bench something slammed against the door outside.

When I walked closer to the door I could hear two people arguing about something. Being the nosey bastard that I am and getting as high as I was on that last line, I slammed the lock back and threw the door up. Two of the most wasted junkies I'd ever seen in my life were fighting over a piece of cardboard box like two pitbulls over a bone. When the door banged at the top they both ducked, ran a couple yards down the alley and turned.

I threw the cardboard across the alley and told 'em to keep the noise down. The next day when I opened the door one of those same junkies was laying under that piece of cardboard a little ways down the alley. As I walked up to him I could tell by the blue fingernails that he'd been dead for quite a while. I went back in the shop and closed the door. I didn't want the cops coming in and asking questions later. Not that I could tell 'em anything. It's just the idea, cops were the enemy and under no circumstance did I wanna talk to 'em.

A little while later I heard the familiar sound of a cop car sitting out back idling for a while and knew they'd found the body. When there was a knock on the door I ignored it and kept on working. I didn't have anything to say to them about anything, especially a dead junkie.

A few minutes later a couple 'a cops were out front talking to Vince for a bit. I just kept on working. The next time I looked up they were gone. A little while later it was getting warm in the shop so I opened the door. The body was gone and everybody was doing what they did every other day.

The Ghost Of P.C.H.

When my buddy Mark worked as a delivery driver for NAPA in Long Beach he used to tell me about this guy he used to see down by the Long Beach, Wilmington line on PCH. He told me that the guy was so dirty he was the same color from top to bottom.

Because he was covered with coke slag dust he was dark gray from head to toe, this caused Mark to call him "The Ghost of PCH."

The area this guy lived in was probably the worst place anyone could inhabit on the face of the earth.

The dividing line for Long Beach and Wilmington was the bridge over the Los Angeles River. This is not your typical river. It's a manmade concrete and steel watercourse that is designed to catch and contain the flash floods that sometimes hit the Los Angeles Basin during the rainy season and spring melt in the mountains; you've seen it many times in movies that are filmed in L.A...

On one side of this watercourse is the hustle and bustle of Long Beach's PCH business district, the very first business encountered when entering Long Beach is an ancient Taco Bell on the north side of the highway. The Wilmington side of the watercourse is the slag dump for the Texaco Refinery, eleven square miles of it.

All there is for miles and miles along PCH in Wilmington is refineries and tank farms, a more nasty and desolate part of civilization I've yet to see. The only vehicles that moved thru there were eighteen-wheelers delivering coke to the refineries or tankers picking up gas at the same and the people that worked there.

This is where The Ghost took up residence. The color of him and the color of the coke slag was exactly the same so I'd guess it was safe to say he called the slag piles home.

In case you don't know coke is a form of coal that is used in the refining of crude oil. Once burnt it makes a nasty, dusty mess that I'd guess can't be good to come in contact with.

When I was hauling gas I'd occasionally load at the Texaco Refinery. On my way in and out of the place I'd always look for The Ghost. It took a few times before I saw him and the first time I did, I couldn't believe what I saw.

I was working the day shift for a change and was headed to the Texaco Refinery to load. It'd been months since he'd been mentioned and I'd kinda' forgotten about him.

I was coming up PCH headed towards Texaco one afternoon. I was almost to the bridge when on top of it I saw someone sitting on the curb at the Long Beach end.

The guy was sitting on the edge of the sidewalk with his feet sticking right out into traffic staring blankly and unblinkingly into the oncoming dust storm created as one truck after another roared past him. So much coke passed thru there that the area looked like coal country. The dust on the side of the road and everything else was the same dusty black color as the coke that poured thru there truckload after truckload day and night.

Once the coke's burnt it has a grey color and as you cross the bridge if you look to the right you'll see piles and piles of coke slag as far as you can see. That whole area is the same dead gray color, nothing grows there. The only inhabitant of the area is The Ghost and the occasional stray dog he'd have on some kind of a makeshift leash, like a piece of old electrical cord or something along that line.

One day you'd see him and he'd have three or four dogs on leashes made of anything he could find and the next day you'd see him and he'd be alone. I always wondered what happened to the dogs. Though you might see him again with more dogs it was never the same ones.

I always asked myself why of all the places in L.A. to be homeless, did he pick that one and what could possibly drive him to stay there and not look for someplace better. I'm sure he'd known better at some time in his life. If he's capable of sustaining himself in that environment, he can't be so outta touch that he doesn't know there's something better just a half mile away.

One day I picked up my load of gas and stopped at the Taco Bell right across the bridge to get lunch. I got my lunch to go so I could eat in the truck parked across the street at the curb.

While I was sitting there eating I noticed The Ghost walking down the Long Beach side of the bridge in my rearview mirror. I continued watching him while I ate curious to see where he was going. As he got closer I could see him better than I ever had. He had stringy, filthy, matted hair and beard that hung below his waist. It looked like he was wearing a suit or sport coat that had no elbows in it. His pants had no knees or seat in 'em and looked like he'd freshly pissed 'em. I couldn't tell if he was wearing any kind of shirt, but he was wearing two different shoes. Every inch of him was the same coke gray color, cloths, hair, skin everything.

He took absolutely no notice of the traffic flying by him, the clouds of dust that blew all over him or the looks and horn honks from people that almost hit him. He walked up to the drive-up window at Taco Bell, standing across the driveway from the window I watched him make the universal I'm hungry sign. He pointed to his stomach, then mimicked taking food off a plate and putting it in his mouth.

He did this for a few minutes till a lady came out the door of the Taco Bell with a cup and a box of something and headed in his direction shewing him away the whole time.

Like a wild animal of some sort he backed off further and further as she got closer. She walked over to the opposite side of the drive and set the containers in the grass, then turned and scurried away as if he was chasing her.

He waited till she was inside, then walked over and picked up the containers, carried them off to the fence by the edge of the bridge and sat down in the dirt to eat.

When he started eating I realized that I hadn't taken a bite of my food in a long time. I finished my lunch slowly, watching him as much as I could. After he finished he got up and walked to the top of the bridge, sat down on the edge of the curb, stuck his feet out into the road and watched traffic go by.

When I got out to throw my trash away I kept an eye on him to see if he even saw me, I was only about fifty yards away and figured he'd at least turn his head my way. Not one muscle moved, in fact once he settled into position on the bridge he didn't stir.

I always told myself that one day when I was down there on Christine and saw him I'd stop and ask him what'd driven him to be there of all places.

The Ghost Up Close

The day after they found the junkie dead in the alley I had to go to Downtown Long Beach to pay a loud exhaust ticket I'd gotten. When I was done, being the lazy shit that I am instead of going right back to work I took a little ride. I was gonna stop at a couple of my old haunts that I hadn't been to in a while and see what I could see. As I burbled up PCH, I saw The Ghost standing on the sidewalk near the Taco Bell.

I didn't think it could be possible that he could still be alive after all these years {it'd been almost four years since the day I saw him at Taco Bell in the truck}. As I approached he just stood there on the edge of the sidewalk looking at the ground. There was a wide enough spot there that I could get all the way outta traffic if I pulled over, so I did.

When I stopped about ten feet from him he didn't even stir. I revved up my motor and he slowly raised his head. Every inch of his exposed skin was an open festering, oozing sore, some places had maggots crawling in them and the stench from him smelled like death. As his eyes met mine my skin crawled. There was nothing in there, no sign of life, nothing. The look was as blank as two holes in the ground.

I was shocked and revolted by the look of this person. Whatever had put him in this place had sealed his fate long ago. There wasn't any way any other human could or would come near him without a biohazard suit and fresh air pack he was so far gone. I still don't understand how he got that way or why he let himself get that way.

I was only there for a split second, I had to get outta there before I puked or he moved towards me, one. There was a steady line of traffic, mostly trucks on PCH, but I wasn't waiting for shit I hit the gas and dumped the clutch. Ducking as I shot in front of him just inches away I found a hole in traffic and hauled ass.

When I got to Alameda I took a right and pulled over, as soon as the kickstand was on the ground I was losing breakfast all over the place. That was the absolutely grossest thing I'd ever seen in my life. Dead bodies didn't look or smell as bad as that dude.

After I was done losing breakfast I headed for the Subs and Suds for lunch and a few beers. When I got there Jan the bartender was the only one there. While she was making my sandwich I told her about The Ghost and my recent encounter with him. The story grossed her out as much as it did me. It made me gag again just recalling his face, if you could call it that.

Nineteen years later the thought of that face still gives me the willies, but I still wonder what put that guy there of all places. Was it dope? Did he ruin his life with drugs and having no family to help him, fall through all the cracks to the deepest bottom of any living person on the planet? I'll never know and like as not, neither will anyone else.

More than likely he died out in those slag piles and no one will know or care, the only mention of it to ever be made will be the people at Taco Bell being glad he no longer came around.

That afternoon I didn't get much done when I finally got back to work. The thought of The Ghost was still too fresh. Every time I started to get into my work the picture of that face would pop up in my mind's eye and make my skin crawl, blowing my concentration right out the window.

If I couldn't concentrate on my work there was always something that got that focus back. I went in the restroom to do a line and get back on track. With my face packed I got on with the rest of the day that I'd pretty much blown, up until then. A little speed in the right place and I managed to get some of the work I'd missed done so the day wasn't a total waste.

That night I headed out to do some drinking right from work. I made the rounds till the bars closed. But for some reason all the alcohol I consumed had no effect. I got to Bird's house early in the morning. As I idled down the street I noticed from a block away that the lights were on in the house. When I got there Bird was sitting up watching TV and I could tell by the look on his face he was pissed about something.

When I walked in he asked if I had any dope.

Of course I did. I laid out some lines in the thickening silence. Once we lined up I asked Bird why he was up.

He said he was waiting for Kat, they'd gotten into a fight and she'd jumped out the bedroom window.

I asked him when that was.

He said it'd been around nine o'clock. Shit it was five-thirty in the morning, she could've walked to Arizona by now.

We sat there until he had to go to work. I lined him up again and off he went. He wasn't gone five minutes when Kat walked thru the door. I didn't ask where she'd been, cause her first question was the same as Bird's. I lined her up and did a small bump myself just to be sociable.

As soon as the line started kicking in she started talking, like I knew she would.

Since Dick had left town things were getting increasingly tighter and tighter. They'd both worked for Dick in their own way. Bird was the shop handy man and go-for and Kat did his books once a week or so, on top of her regular job. For both of these services Dick was very generous to both of them.

Once Dick got a new ole'lady she did the books, that cut that income. Kat still had her fulltime job so that didn't matter much. With what they were making they were still doing well enough to buy a house and a new pickup while I was away.

They were doing fine until Kat lost her job and Dick moved away. Bird got a job as a warehouseman that only paid him a third of what he made at the shop.

The problem was all his time at the shop didn't give him any type of viable skill, so in essence he was starting over in the job world. He was doing the best he could with what he had to work with. Unfortunately it wasn't anywhere near good enough. He couldn't ride his scooter anymore because the frame had broken and he couldn't afford to fix it. Life was closing in on 'em pretty fast.

The fight had come when Kat mentioned to Bird that he could probably get a better job if he looked or at least get a part time job as well till she got back to work.

He didn't think he needed a better job and wasn't gonna listen to someone that wasn't working at all tell him to work two jobs. He went to work every day for eight hours and that was enough, was his position. I sat and listened to Kat as long as I could and left for work with a head full of somebody else's problems to try to help fix. I told her I'd try to talk to Bird about it when I got home that night and left it at that.

According to Bird one of the biggest problems was the lack of transportation from having just one vehicle. We walked out in the garage and looked at StrayKat to see what could be done to fix her and give 'em two sets of wheels to work with again. I told Bird that night to get the bike torn down and come hell or high water, by hook or by crook I'd get the frame fixed for him.

The next day I made a deal with Pete to get the frame repaired, that weekend the bike was torn down and the frame brought to the shop on Monday.

It took Pete a couple weeks to get it done because he was stacked up with work as usual. When he finally got it done, I brought it to Bird's house and said "happy birthday."

It wasn't long after that StrayKat was roaring again or should I say purring. For whatever reason Bird put a real quiet two into one exhaust on it, I didn't agree at all, my motto has always been "loud pipes save lives."

On the other side of that coin though, loud exhaust tickets costed forty-one dollars a pop at that time and if you got four or five of those in a week like I did sometimes it added up quick. If money was already tight, spending a hundred and sixty-four dollars on loud exhaust tickets sure wouldn't help matters and it'd suck to have to spend a couple 'a weeks in L.A. County Jail for unpaid loud exhaust tickets.

I'd maintained my friendship with Shelley even though we didn't work together anymore. One of the first rides we took was to her place in Hollywood to deliver an ounce of dope to her one Sunday.

Shelley lived on Highland just off Hollywood above the Steven J. Cannell offices. Usually the streets of Hollywood are empty on Sunday, but today when we got off the 101 onto Hollywood Boulevard the streets and sidewalks were packed with cars and people. Once we passed Gower Avenue we were in the thick of it. Christine was so loud that whenever I hit the gas she'd set off every car alarm within fifty feet of me.

As we made our way thru traffic on Hollywood Boulevard setting off every car alarm around. I was getting a kick outta everybody scrambling to shut off their alarms once we passed. I had so much fun that when we got to Highland instead of turning right and going to Shelley's we turned around and headed back down Hollywood to piss off the other side of the street, after all I'm an equal opportunity pain in the ass.

We made it all the way down to Gower, turned around in the liquor store parking lot and headed back up Hollywood again. We got about half a block up the street when I heard something that sounded more like a siren than an alarm, sure as shit it was a CHP. Since we were only going five miles an hour we weren't speeding.

I was glad I'd gone to the trouble to stash the ounce in my headlight. That way if we got the usual empty your pockets and pat down routine we were both clean as whistles.

When the cop walked up to us he had a half smile on his face, he knew I'd been setting off the car alarms on purpose. He asked for our licenses and registrations, as I handed him mine I asked him if there was a problem.

He looked at me with a widening smile and said "awful loud isn't it?" Nodding at Christine.

He wasn't at all shocked when I replied "loud pipes save lives."

He smiled and added "and set off every alarm in the neighborhood, did you know you set off several building alarms too?"

When he said that I swelled with fake pride and said "then I'm doing my job."

"And I'm doing mine" he added.

We exchanged a few more such pleasantries while he was writing my loud exhaust ticket, in the course of which we found out that he'd watched and listened to us go all the way up the street and back.

At first he was gonna let it go until we came back down and started to do it again, that was when he decided to rain on our parade and make sure we understood that we were having "too much fun in a no fun zone" and it was beyond the time to stop.

When he handed me my ticket and started writing a ticket for Bird I went off. I pointed out to him that his exhaust system was stock and that I was the only one that was making the noise.

He looked at the exhaust and said he didn't care; Bird was getting a ticket anyway and started writing.

I told him if he had to write two tickets write 'em both for me I was the only one making the noise, but he wrote Bird the ticket.

The longer I stood there arguing with him the more I increased the chances of seriously pissing him off and getting us both busted for dope as well as loud exhaust.

Once he was all done with us, he stood there while we fired up the bikes. I let Bird fire his first just to prove to the cop that I was right.

When StrayKat fired he looked at me and said "you're right," walked back, got in his car and drove off as soon as I was fired and rolling.

We went on up to Shelley's and delivered the dope and had a big laugh about the afternoon's events as we got high. Shelley said she'd heard us coming up the street and wondered what was going on when she heard us go back down the boulevard. She was waiting for me to call for directions when she heard us start back up the street after our run-in with the law. The biggest laugh was that again we'd skated thru another potential mess with just a loud exhaust ticket. I paid Bird's ticket as well as mine.

We didn't stay at Shelley's for very long, maybe an hour if that. When we left the boulevard was almost deserted like it usually is. How nice of all those people to show up n-give me such an exciting afternoon on an otherwise typically boring Sunday.

Helping Bird get StrayKat back on the road was only helping him put a band-aid on a much bigger problem, the denial of drug addicts.

If you asked any one of us if we were addicts at that time, you'd've gotten an emphatic no from every one of us. In our minds the problems that each of us had were from everything or anything else but drugs. When in truth all the problems stemmed from the use of drugs and the money wasted on 'em.

Money problems got worse because the money we did make seemed to go on dope first last and always. It didn't matter how much money I made in a week within a couple 'a days after payday I was always broke. The only thing that took a front seat to dope was traffic tickets. It sucks to be on the side of the road for something you know you'll ride away from and have 'em come up with a warrant for an unpaid ticket {it happened to me several times because dope and partying came first}.

Meth is the most deceitful drug there is. As you run your life off into the gutter and beyond, the dope's always there telling you nothing's wrong that can't be fixed with another line. You'll pay that bill or ticket next week; you need some dope *right now*. Pretty soon those bills and tickets get forgotten and come back to haunt you at the worst possible time.

When you end up in jail your first thought is "how'll I get high?" When the lights get turned off at home your first thought is "I need a line." Everything you do every minute depends on how much dope you have in you and in your pocket. If there's no dope nothing gets done {except sleep} until you get some. Once you get some, life becomes an endless frenzy of activity till it's gone.

While I was busy running my life into the gutter on the streets of L.A., the friends that I was staying with were creating their own little disaster with dope. In retrospect I'd be willing to bet that I had a lot to do with feeding that fire. I've always been a bad influence on the people around me. That's why I was banned from all the neighbor's yards and forbidden to play with their kids by the time I was five.

For the next few months Kat and Bird's problems got worse. Mine had already peaked at as much as possible, as often as possible, as long as possible until I was lost in place and in my own way.

For me every line was an adventure, like the night Shelley and I were going from her place in Hollywood to San Pedro to get some dope. We were flying between the cars in the Dave Lane on the Harbor Freeway. I'd just ridden through a pack of cars at about a hundred mph and was just breaking out of the front of the pack.

We were at the Artesia Freeway interchange which had recently been completed and was six lanes wide. As I gassed on Christine to get in front of the cars and at the same time move into the lane to the right of me we started to wobble violently, almost to the point of a tank slapper. When I gassed Christine and steered left she'd straighten up and run straight.

The only way I could slow down and not have both of us end up on our faces at eighty mph was to ease off the throttle and steer to the left across the front of the overtaking traffic in the fastest lane on the freeway.

Once I got into the number one lane it wasn't so bad. The only place we had to go after that was the narrow breakdown lane next to the center divider, filled with all kinds of debris and crap to pound over before we got stopped. That was far better than doing a face plant in the middle of the freeway at eighty mph and getting run over by five or six cars.

Once we got over the rush from that much fun in a no fun zone we looked across the freeway to where we needed to be and back up the freeway as far as we could see. It was gonna be a long way across those six lanes pushing a seven hundred pound motorcycle with a flat tire and we couldn't really see that far back up the freeway because of a little rise that we'd ended up at the bottom of.

We got our shit together for a couple minutes and got Christine in position to be pushed in as straight a line as possible across the freeway as soon as we had a break in traffic.

When the break came we pushed and ran as hard and fast as we could. We weren't even across the first lane when we saw headlights. At seventy mph it wouldn't be long, we pushed and ran harder. We got to the breakdown lane on the other side of the freeway accompanied by screeching tires and blaring horns and of course once we got there not another vehicle passed us for fifteen minutes.

Once we got across the freeway we were at the bottom of the 91 west to the 110 south onramp. The breakdown lane was pretty wide there and the concrete retaining wall was a safe place to sit.

While Shelley sat there and watched Christine, I walked up the onramp the wrong way onto the 91 eastbound to get to an emergency call box. Once I got there the emergency center patched me thru to Bird.

When he got on the line I told him where we were and how to get to me and walked back to Shelley and the bike to wait.

It's a good thing I smoked at that time. If I hadn't I would've started anyway after that. I just wouldn't have had so much practice and as rattled as I was, I probably would've lit either my beard or my nose on fire.

While we sat there Shelley kept telling me what a good rider I was and how she'd ride anywhere with me. All the while I was thinking "whew that was lucky" and saying "if I never do that again, it'll be too soon!"

Bird finally got to us, which wasn't very easy because we were at the bottom of a brand new spaghetti bowl interchange. If I remember right he had to make a couple different tries to get to us. The directions I gave him only got him in the general area, he had to circle around again-n-again to get right to us.

By the time we got back to the house and called Pedro he was gone, so that ended our search for dope that night. We took Shelley back to Hollywood in the pickup and called it a night.

The next morning the tire was fixed and life was normal for five minutes, till the next near death experience. Almost every time I left the house something to bring on that same type of adrenaline rush would happen, so frequently in fact that I began planning for it.

From the house there were about five different ways to get to this one freeway onramp to head north on the Long Beach Freeway. The streets in our neighborhood were kinda' weird. Some of the intersections didn't have stop signs, but they did have some really deep drainage channels on each side of 'em. Unless you wanted to beat yourself and your vehicle to pieces you slowed down to about five mph, especially if you were on a rigid frame like I was.

There was another way to hit 'em though, wide fuckin' open. When you hit 'em like that and kept the front wheel in the air you caught enough air from the first to sail you right over the second, landing safely and smoothly on the other side. Although this is the smoothest way to negotiate those kinds of intersections, it's not the safest and is far from legal.

One morning right after I started at Vince's I was running late and the street was just a little bit rougher than usual. As I was flying low thru one of those types of intersections I crossed right in front of a cop.

He immediately hit the lights and came after me. Being an avid scofflaw I immediately grabbed a handful of gas, got to the freeway and got the fuck outta there at a high rate of fuel consumption.

A couple 'a days later the same thing happened. Then a few days or a week after that until it became a surprise regular event. I never knew when he was gonna strike, but it became like a game for us. It didn't matter what streets I took to the freeway I'd run into him and off we'd go. He never caught me on the surface streets and he never chased me onto the freeway. I don't care who you are a little high speed chase in the morning after a surprise ambush'll get anybody's blood flowin'. It's a hell of a way to start your day I can tell ya that.

As the months went by the only thing I got done was work and party while things got worse and worse at Bird's. Money got tighter and tighter and he was flippin' out more and more. When he finally hit me with the demand that I pay more a week to live there than he brought home it was time for a change.

Through Bird I'd met a dude named Mex, he was on an upswing on the crank rollercoaster. He had a new ole'lady and they'd just gotten a place, they had an empty bedroom and could use a roommate to decrease their individual expenses. I got the job. The same day I packed my saddlebags, put a couple boxes of parts in his ole'ladie's car and I'd moved in about an hour's time.

Mex had the same basic problem I had. He was a drunken, shiftless, stoned, irresponsible crankster that used every other drug that dropped into his mouth or onto a mirror. We were on exactly the same "stuck on stupid" ride to the bottom, operating on the same "just say yes" policy. He also had sticky fingers, a piss poor work ethic and one drink could turn into closing the bar down, no matter what mission he was originally on. Because of this he could say he worked a lot of places, but he never worked at any of 'em for very long.

His new ole'lady {Tammy} was on the same search for the eternal buzz that he was, she'd left her husband and kids to go get high. The only difference was she had a good job that she hung onto for a little while after she chose dope.

Mex and I were two peas in a pod. I was a lot less sticky fingered and slightly more responsible, other than that we both lived on the same "fuck it, lets do a line" philosophy. I think that was why everyone I knew was getting swept away in the wave I was riding. I had nothing but a motorcycle to lose, my budget was geared to keeping my bike running and myself high. Other than a couple crates of parts that I could leave on a moments notice if I *absolutely* had to, I could pack my whole life in my saddlebags and be gone from anywhere in less than an hour's time.

Most of my friends had far more than that to lose so their fall to the bottom was further and would hurt a lot worse on the way down. I don't care who you are it sucks to watch all the things you had in your life slip away to be replaced by dope, not that you try to stop yourself that much. Everyone feels a twinge of regret as their lives slip away one thing at a time, but they still let it go for the sake of meth.

I don't know any exceptions to this rule, everyone I ever knew that did the shit and sometime not for very long either, destroyed their lives and the lives of those around them.

I often felt like I was an angel of death back then, it seemed that everyone I came in contact with ended up heading for the same place and killing the life they had along the way.

Working for Vince, I met a lotta people. I eventually I met Valerie's bigger, better deal while I was working at Vince's. The place was lively to say the least at times.

Between Vince and Mex I met a whole other group of people. The dude that did our wheels belonged to a small club in Whittier. Not only did he do wheels, he made all kinds of tools that made jobs easier, things like greasing your wheel bearings.

Before Rusty made this tool, greasing your wheel bearings meant pulling the seals, washing the bearings and the hubs, repacking the bearings with grease, reassembly with new seals and then putting the wheel back on the bike.

With Rusty's little invention you simply removed the wheel. Checked the seal for pliability. Inserted the tool inside the seal. Attached the grease gun to the other end and pumped it a few times. Without ever taking anything apart you've greased both wheel bearings and are now ready to put the wheel back on the bike. Seals do over time dry out and crack that's why you always make sure they're still soft. This one little item was a boon to the service industry and bike mechanics everywhere.

Many of Rusty's brothers were as ingenious as he was in their own rights and they all partied pretty hard, I think that was why I became friends with 'em and hung out for a little while, especially with one in particular named Pat. Nicknamed Pat Splat because he could hit you once in the face and splatter it.

He and I hung out together for a while. He was probably the most freewheelin' one of the bunch and every time we went anywhere we had fun. As soon as we got somewhere every lunatic in the place would gravitate toward me and the ones that didn't he would find and send my way. This always made for an interesting evening, being accosted by every nutjob around. Some couldn't even speak English.

When Pat and I would go partying we'd cover a lotta ground. We'd spend weekends in the saddle bouncing from bar to bar to party, ranging all over the inland valleys up into Big Bear, San Bernardino and Riverside counties, all over the place. Everywhere a snoot full 'a dope and a tank full 'a gas could take ya. It was Chad's in Big Bear where I had my first Lynchburg Lemonade. Until that time I always drank my Jack with either coke or straight.

Most of the members of the club, though they looked like your typical scooter tramp had good jobs and made good money. One of his brothers had a weekend house in a little seaside town up near Morrow Bay called Los Osos. I was invited up there that summer for their Fourth of July party. Even though they weren't the badass outlaw club that the Bandidos were they still had plenty of practice in the partying department.

The night before I was gonna leave for Los Osos my updated 12 volt charging system took a shit. I worked thru the night until the alcohol from a few hours before took affect and knocked me out. Before I passed out I snorted a line so I'd wake up in a few hours, finish fixing it and get the fuck outta Dodge before the weekend traffic started.

Well I woke up and started working on the bike right on queue, but the Harley Gods weren't smiling on me that day cause the reason for the malfunction was something that had to be ordered.

Christine was fired by a magneto so the bike would run, I just wouldn't have any lights. I could sit around Long Beach all weekend cutting the tension at Bird's with my Buck Knife every once in a while so I could breath or fuck the lights and haul ass for Los Osos anyway. Bet you can't guess what I did.

Once I got past Calabasas the traffic thinned out quickly, by the time I was rolling thru Ventura I was ahead of the heavy traffic. The light was just beginning to fade from the day as I pulled off the 101 at the Los Osos exit and called the number Pat had given me for directions to the house. It would've been time to use my lights if I'd had any by the time I got there.

When I pulled up everybody was out in the shop standing around watching Dillon while he was putting his shifter ratchet back together. The shifter assembly on an old four speed tranny has six screws that hold the drum together. Five of 'em thread into holes in the ratchet lid. The sixth on the very bottom is a little short one that has a thin nut that slides up into a small space between the tranny case and back side of the shifter drum. This nut is only easy to get in when the tranny's on the bench upside down or the shifter lid is off completely. On the bike it's a pain in the ass to try to get back in unless you know how to hold your mouth just right.

When I pulled up Dillon had been trying unsuccessfully for a while to get that screw and nut to go back together. Once that was done it'd be easy to button up what was left so we could go party. I walked over to the crowd after I parked Christine and watched for a little bit while Dillon got more and more frustrated as the nut hit the floor time after time without ever getting near the end of the screw it was supposed to be on.

I asked somebody what happened. A spring had broken in the lid on the way up there earlier. Dillon had replaced the spring, but this last screw was kicking his ass. I stood with the rest drinking a beer and hitting the joint when it came buy, while Dillon from every position he could think of to get in to get the advantage on this screw taught us some new cuss words every time the nut hit the floor.

I finally couldn't take it any more and asked if I could try. By now Dillon was pretty tightly unwound from trying to get the nut on that screw and was convinced it couldn't be done. I thought he was gonna throw it as far as he could and kick the bike in the primary, instead he handed it to me and expressed his doubt that I could get it either.

I sat down next to the bike, positioned the nut just so in my fingers, leaned in, stuck the nut into the little space it fit into, started the screw into the nut, put the 3/8 wrench on the nut and tightened it up with a screw driver. When I stood up, nut in place and tight, Dillon said "beginners luck."

"You weren't holding your mouth right" I said laughing and watched along with everyone else while he finished putting the bike together.

Once that was done we lined up and gained the right altitude, after that we all headed for a little bar in town that I'll never in a million years remember the name of. Maybe that's because I drank about three gallons of kamikazes that night. The thing that stands out in my mind the most was the paranoia of the bartender.

He musta" got ahold of some bad shit that night, or had a bad reaction to the good shit he was doing cause he kept insisting that the place was surrounded by the FBI and the CHP and every law enforcement agency from L.A. to Frisco. Whenever I'd step outside for some air there wasn't anything out there but the ocean and the only sound was the breakers on the beach a few hundred yards away.

We partied there till the wee hours of the morning. Los Osos at that time was a sleepy little resort town and probably still is, that might've had two cops in the whole place and as long as you didn't hurt or kill anybody they didn't wanna even look at you. To think that a little hole in the wall place like that could have all the cops that bartender was talking about and not be lit up like the set on a location movie shoot was absurd.

When we walked outta the bar after the last hurrah and headed for the house there wasn't a soul to be seen anywhere on the street except us. We got the bikes cranked up and headed for the house. I didn't need a headlight. Everyone ahead of me lit the road just fine, but man I'd've hated to be out there alone, streetlights were few and far between in that town and it was dark when it got dark.

I don't remember sleeping at all that weekend. After being awake for so long, the days just run into each other and become a blur punctuated with periods of lucidity. That weekend was like that. One of the few things that stand out in my mind was something that happened on the way home.

When riding in a pack with a club nonmembers ride in the rear and aren't really kept up to speed on where the pack is going. In a way it's kind of a test to see if you're capable of doing something as simple as following a pack of bikes without getting lost. If you can't it's pretty easy to assume that you're not gonna be able to take care of any other business without somebody holding your hand either.

We were flying south on the 101. I figured we were just heading back to L.A. so I wasn't paying as much attention to the pack as I should've been. It was the first time I'd been to that part of California so I was checking out the scenery as much as I could as well as keeping track of the bikes ahead of me.

I was checking out a girl in the car to the right of me. When I looked up everybody in front of me was slowing and getting in the left turn lane for San Marcos Pass Road. I slammed on the old mechanical brakes that needed adjustment every day, but hadn't been adjusted in three weeks and yelled whoa at the top of my lungs.

I shot past everybody nearly clipping a few folks as I squeezed between all the traffic on the right and the bikes to the left of me and about another fifty yards down the highway before I slowed enough to pull a Uee and return to the pack.

When I got back Tex who was leading the pack was pissed as were a few others, all I could say was no brakes. It was a piss poor excuse, but the only one I had at the moment. I didn't really have any excuse at all, I worked in a motorcycle shop. If I'd get my head outta the bag for a few minutes I could've had disk brakes on my bike in one day's time.

The reason for the detour was a little bar tucked back in the trees on what used to be the old King's Highway Stage Road. I can't remember the name of the place but it'd been there a long time. It used to be a roadhouse for the stagecoaches that traveled the King's Highway at one time. Now it was a bar with live music on the weekends and had long been a stop on the weekend party tour for local bikers.

The first thing I did when we got there was adjust both brakes, then get a hard time about the junk I was riding and the wreck we almost caused. I knew everybody was right and had been gathering the parts to upgrade my brakes for a while, but like I said if I was serious about it I could've had the job done in one day and been a lot safer on the road.

I had no idea how soon this procrastination was gonna come back to bite me and fulfill everyone's prophecy. As soon as I got back to Bird's later that evening Kat informed me that Valerie'd been there all weekend, she'd left her new boyfriend and was living at her sisters in Orange County until she went back to Colorado.

"Yah so what," was all I could think, but I don't think I even said anything in reply.

Rusty's club had what they called their "resort" in Fawn Skin on the other side of the lake from Big Bear, it was just a trailer like all the other trailers in the park about a hundred yards from the lake itself, that was the only thing that made it even remotely resort like. It was ideally situated though, it was a hundred yards from the lake and three hundred yards from the beer store. Leaving the term "resort" open ended and remembering a "resort" is in the eye of the beholder, if you think you have one you probably do.

In Big Bear they have a yearly celebration called Old Miner's Days. It was during the last weekend of this event that I went to jail for failure to appear and Dillon proclaimed Christine "a bucket 'a bolts." I wish he could've told me something I didn't already know. If he thought Christine was a bucket 'a bolts, I'd loved to've heard what he thought about Joe Dandy's Sportster.

Christine was just like my life, a bunch of worn out mismatched parts that were thrown together and run down the road as fast as they'd go for as long as they'd last. The most dangerous thing about the old thing was the mechanical brakes. That was at the top of the list, but the list was long even after that. You just got used to it and it was ok till the day you pushed it too far.

That weekend we got to Fawn Skin just before dark on Friday evening. After that we bounced back and forth from the bar to the "resort" till it started to liven up in town. On one of the trips to the "resort" I was seated next to a fishing tackle box. In this tackle box was all kinds of little rubber spiders and bugs. I found a real wiggly spider and put it in my pocket for later. It was getting late in the evening and Chad's was filling up with bikers from all different clubs, independents, tourists, locals and all kinds of people using Old Miner's Days as an excuse to party just like I was.

Once our business was done at the "resort" we headed back to Chad's, when we got there we parked out back. On the way in I took the little rubber spider and stuffed it up one nostril. Walking into the back hallway I spied a yuppie couple at the bar. I walked in and bellied up to the bar in between 'em shouting my drink order like I didn't even know they were there. All the while I was watching their faces outta the corner of my eye. They both seemed pretty annoyed at my behavior which was about to get worse. As I stood there acting like I was oblivious of 'em I began to work up a sneeze.

When it finally let go that spider hit the bar bouncing all over the place. The guy screamed like a girl, hooked his foot on the leg of his own stool when he jumped backwards and fell into the table of the people behind him knocking the table over and everything on it all over everyone in a five foot radius, but mostly himself. His girlfriend screamed with laughter and was turning purple she was laughing so hard.

I paid for my drink when it came, pocketed the spider and walked away like I didn't see anything happen at all, casually glancing at the drenched boyfriend as I walked away. When I got out on the back porch I almost died laughing. That's all I can remember about that night, the next day was real memorable though.

Early in the afternoon a bunch of us were riding into Big Bear and got stopped just outside of town. It was the usual shit, except that I had a seven hundred and fifty dollar warrant for failure to appear. They cuffed and stuffed me in the back seat of this Blazer that was so tight it made you look forward to the jail cell. Somehow Dillon became the lucky one to ride my "bucket 'a bolts" back to the resort for safe keeping, which gave him the information to accurately access my accident looking for a place to happen.

I was pretty well fucked at the moment I probably had a few bucks in my pocket, but there's no way I'd have seven hundred and fifty dollars. Shit if I had seven hundred and fifty dollars, I'd've spent seven hundred and forty of it on dope and put ten in the gas tank, so I wouldn't've had it long. I didn't want the cops to think I was high, so I went into the cell I was assigned and laid down to check for cracks in my eyelids and freak out quietly about my situation.

It didn't sound good, if I didn't get bailed out, on Monday I'd be shipped to San Bernardino County Jail. Where I'd have to wait for L.A. County Jail to come and get me whenever that was {they had up to thirty days}, because that was where the warrant came from. After I got to L.A. County Jail I'd spend time in there while they set a court date now that I was in custody.

Chances are by the time I got to court I'd've been in jail about six weeks to two months and would get time served. Meaning I'd start the release procedure within twenty-four hours after returning to the jail that night from court, unless they handled it in Metro Court. It takes sometimes more than twenty-four hours from the time you're told to "roll it up" till the time you hit the street in L.A. County. This means I'd spend about two months getting shipped from jail to jail to be released as soon as I got to the one I needed to be in for a fifty dollar ticket.

The very last thing that happens to you in L.A. County Jail before you walk outside is a warrant check. If you've been in jail for two months and had cases pending when you went in, there's a good chance that you'll have a warrant at that very last check. If that's the case you'll be handcuffed and escorted back over to the IRC {Inmate Receiving Center} to be rebooked for that warrant and start the whole process over again. See why I was freaking out? I could end up spending six months in jail over a fifty dollar ticket.

I'd been laying there pacing inside myself for hours while my brain mumbled "oh fuck, oh fuck" over and over again, my mind's eye playing the movie of the next few months of hell in my head, when they brought dinner. A stale peanut butter and jelly sandwich and a half pint of milk, but we could have all the nasty tasting water we wanted.

Just after dinner the deputy hollered and told me to "roll it up," my private eye had bailed me out. My private eye, who the fuck was that? It didn't take long for me to get released from that little jail, hell I still had my own cloths on in my cell. Twenty minutes, a half hour after I was called I was walking out the front door of the sheriff's station.

It was Vince that'd come and got me with another friend's money. The private eye was one of our regular customers and a close friend of Vince's. He was a crazy motherfucker that snorted a lotta dope and made a living spying on people so other people could get the goods on 'em in court. Pat {different Pat} was nuttier-n-a-shithouse rat and a laugh and a half to be around.

He and Vince'd ridden up during the day and were at Chad's when Pat, Dillon and the rest of the crew that I'd started out with earlier finally got to the bar after taking care of Christine. This was one of the few times in my life that I had to pack behind another dude and as weird as it felt, it felt good to be out and not having to look forward to those long weeks of incarceration in L.A. County Hell was a big relief.

When we got to Chad's I started to feel normal again after a few lines, beers and joints. That was when Vince hit me with his version of a riot act. For weeks leading up to this I'd been fucking up big time. The riot act consisted of being on time, staying till it was time to leave and doing it every business day. In the resent past my quests for party and pussy had lead me far astray and caused me to either be real late or not be there at all and he'd had enough. I'd have to work as much as I could to get Pat paid back for the bail money as soon as possible.

Vince's demands weren't that hard to meet under normal circumstances. All I had to do was be at work at seven in the morning, shouldn't be too hard to do I'd done it before, plenty of times. The rest of the weekend was a little subdued. Sunday I ran into a girl named Chris that I'd known before and we ended up leaving Big Bear together later that night. She lived out in the desert in Riverside County and that was right on my way wherever I was going so that's where we headed.

August 16th 1988

I was supposed to turn over my new leaf that day and be at work on time ready to put in a full days work. At 9:45AM I woke up out in Riverside County in the middle of nowhere, I wasn't even sure of where I was. I was sure of one thing though it was two and three quarter hours after the time I was supposed to be at work and I had an hours ride to the shop from here *if* traffic cooperated.

While I rushed around finding my clothes and getting them screwed onto my body, I was doing lines, pounding beers and smoking bowls to get my altitude right for the flight in to the shop.

I entered the 91 freeway wide fuckin' open and held it that way for about a half an hour. At the interchange of the 605 and the 91 traffic started to thicken a little, just after that, probably above Bellflower Boulevard or close to it traffic came to a stop in front of me in the left lane. I was in the Dave Lane still doing at least seventy mph with the gas on. I'd just passed a slowing car to the right of me and there was a black Nissan 300 ZX Turbo stopped about fifty yards ahead in the same lane.

I made eye contact with a dude in a white Chevy sedan in his right side mirror. While he was looking right at me he steered his car to the right and moved forward enough to close the space between himself and the car to the right of him, closing my only clear lane. I slammed both grossly overworked, poorly maintained and horribly inadequate breaks on, yelled whoa as loud as I could and steered into the open lane to the right of me trying to get two lanes to the right in the next few yards.

Neither the brakes nor the yelling did a damn thing to slow me down and I hit that Nissan hard dead center of the back bumper. I flipped over the handlebars even though I was braced and holding on with all my drug and adrenaline induced might.

I landed on the back of the car head first on the uneven surface were the top of the rear window met the body, splitting my scalp wide open. As soon as I hit I flipped backwards off the back of the car onto the ground hitting my head hard enough to see black stars with silver trails in the same spot I'd just hit on the car.

While all this was going on Christine bounced straight backwards off the car bumper about fifteen or twenty feet, landed on her wheels and squared off for another assault on the car in front of her.

Christine had what's called a suicide throttle {the whole bike was suicide}, it had no return spring and unless you turned the throttle off yourself it would stay wide open or where you were holding it when you let go. The advantage to this was that there was no spring tension on the throttle grip to hold against on long trips and there was no resistance whatsoever no matter which way you were turning the grip, just smooth effortless action. Also when you were running from the cops, you could gas it, get outta sight for a few seconds, turn out your lights, close the throttle completely, killing the engine, cut into an alley or any dark side street, coast a few blocks in darkened silence in the opposite direction. When the coast was clear simply opening the throttle would restart your engine and you were off to get in another high-speed chase somewhere else. All this was very convenient for a hoodlum like me.

With this set-up I could also adjust how far the grip had to rotate before the throttle plate was wide open, a little less than half a turn was all it took. The bad thing about all this was that if you didn't return your hand to the grip relatively soon after letting go, the velocity of the air moving thru the 2¼ inch throat of the S&S D series carburetor would suck the throttle wide open and hold it there till you closed it.

That was exactly what was going on with Christine when she landed squarely on her wheels, wide open and launched herself at the back of the car again with the rear tire smoking.

I was still bouncing from the impact with the ground when I heard and saw from the corner of my eye Christine go flying past me rear tire screaming and slam into the car a second time knocking it about ten feet forward. This time when she landed just a few inches from me, it was on her side still wide open, she immediately began spinning furiously in a circle, spinning faster with every successive revolution.

I had to jump up and outta the way to keep from getting hit by the spinning bike. Then jump it when it came around get to the axis of its spin and shut off the ignition switch before it took my legs out from under me on the next revolution.

The first thing I saw when I looked up from the bike was the guy that caused all this getting out of his white Chevy and starting my way. This motherfucker's gonna die in the next few seconds was probably what he saw on my face as I started toward him with a unintelligible roar, Whatever it was it scared the shit out of him cause he was back in his car and gone like a shot.

I stopped running towards him as he peeled away and turned towards my bike. I picked it up and wheeled it backwards outta the traffic lanes into the small median near the center divider. The front rim was bent flat but the tire was still holding air, the front forks were bent into the frame downtubes which made Christine hard to push and she'd only roll in one kinda' curved path, you couldn't steer her at all. It was when I was pushing her backwards to the center that I noticed that everything had a red tint to it.

It was at that same time that I began to hear someone in the distance yelling to me to sit down, that my head was bleeding. I looked up and this woman was holding a clean white towel in one hand and motioning me to come to her with the other. When I was close to her she sat me down on the center divider and pressed the white towel to the back of my head.

While I was sitting there two CHP, a tow truck and an ambulance showed up The Nissan got towed away {good girl Christine} and I got the third degree from one cop while the other took statements from the bunch of witnesses that were standing around and the lady that made me sit down and held the towel on my head.

When the trooper got to me her first question was "how much have you had to drink?"

I told her nothing I was on my way to work and I was real late. A white Chevy had cut me off when I was whitelining. I hit the Nissan while trying to slow down and change two lanes at the same time and the mechanical brakes on the bike weren't up to that kind of abuse.

She looked at me and looked at the bike. As soon as she stopped asking questions for a half second I was on her to call Vince to come and get Christine instead of letting a tow truck take her to some impound lot out on Terminal Island or a police station where a nosey cop might find the drugs stashed on her. It took some hard pounding because she insisted that he wouldn't be there as soon as the tow truck, but I won. I told her that if she'd call him right now he'd be there in no time. She went back to her car and used the radio, came back and said "he's on his way, but he'd better hurry up."

He hadn't arrived when the ambulance took me away, but the trooper was at the hospital a few minutes after I came from getting x-rays of my skull and she told me he'd just picked Christine up. Once the x-rays where done and the bleeding stopped, the back of my head was stitched up and I was just hanging around waiting for something else to happen.

It wasn't long before it did, the second trooper came in and started the same drinking and driving shit as the first. I told him the same thing I told the first one and that started an argument about who was gonna do what when they were told to do it. The noise brought the doctor who told the cop to leave, which pissed the cop off even more. All the noise brought the first trooper who was the superior officer to the second trooper and she shut him up and got him outta there like nobody's business. Once he was gone she made sure she had all my information right, told me not to leave town right away she might wanna talk to me again and left.

The hospital I was brought to was a private hospital and as such reserved the right to refuse service to anyone and on that morning I fit the anyone category better than everyone else there. Not long after the cops left I was told that medical treatment was for customers who had insurance and/or could show proof of payment. Since I could do neither I should hold my breath so as not to waste any more of their air and get out as quickly as possible because I was taking up valuable space as well as breathing their air.

The only person I could think to call was Vince. He came and got me and took me home. When we got there he told me to take a couple days off, give him a call and he'd come and get me for work.

Mex was in the garage working on something when Vince dropped me off. It was a good thing he still had Christine all crunched up in the back of his truck. That way I could get all my shit outta her while she was here at home. It also gave me a chance to get the dope I'd stashed on her, I was gonna need it later.

After Vince left I went upstairs and tried to relax. It was hard because I felt really weird and everything still had a reddish tint to it. I didn't feel like doing much, every inch of me hurt especially my shoulders, elbows, wrists and fingers. I could barely raise my arms to hold a tooter tube my shoulders hurt so badly. Both elbows and wrists were swollen and kinda bluish and all my fingers were twice their size and an ever deepening black and blue.

Besides all that my whole head was starting to throb and all I could think was "you think it hurts now, wait'll tomorrow."

Later on that afternoon the phone rang. When I could finally get a grip on it and get it to my ear with my fat purple fingers it was the doctor at the hospital I'd been taken to. He'd finally had a chance to read the x-rays and had discovered several hairline fractures in my skull radiating from the point of impact, which would explain everything being red. Without more tests he would guess I had at least a serious concussion. Besides that I'd sprained my shoulders, elbows, wrists and fingers. He finished up by recommending that I check myself into a county hospital for observation for at least forty-eight hours.

I asked him what that'd do.

He said it would help them determine the extent of the injury and a course of treatment.

I then made some stupid comment about hanging a mirror on the wall and snorting dope for forty-eight hours to keep myself awake, so I could watch myself for signs of a concussion.

He could tell he was dealing with a real idiot druggie here. He ended the conversation by telling me not to sleep for more than fifteen minutes at a time for the next twenty-four hours and go to the hospital if the red didn't leave my vision soon.

I snorted another line when I got off the phone because the way my arms and fingers were hurting it might be a couple 'a days before I could do it without help. That means having to share my dope, which means I'd run out earlier and bein' off from work I wouldn't have the money to reup any time soon.

That afternoon when Tammy came home she helped me as much as she could until drunken Mex came upstairs and got jealous. I sat and watched TV until I couldn't take it any longer, then I crawled upstairs to my room and lay down. Hopefully to die because the pain of all my banged up places was more than I'd had in a while and I wasn't looking forward to tomorrow.

The next day it took me twenty minutes to get down the stairs, everything hurt so bad I could hardly breathe; I wasn't seeing red anymore, so something was healing. The first line of the day was hard to get up the tooter, it took three tries and I almost passed out from the pain.

After I got my shit together from the first, the second wasn't any better. I spent my day doing as much nothing as I could possibly do and live to tell about it. That afternoon a friend from Venice Beach called to tell me he had a vehicle I could borrow when I was ready.

Al was a brother of the dude that Valerie'd gotten hooked up with. He lived right behind one of my favorite hangouts, the Sunset Saloon. The Sunset was at the end of Washington Street right on the beach in Venice.

Earlier that year he and I'd taken a ride up north, we were headed for Stockton to get some tickets for the Redwood Run but never made it. I'd always wanted to go to the Redwood Run, but never seemed to get there. This year I was going, the only problem was the run's in Ukiah north of the bay area. Very few tickets were sold for the run in L.A... You had to know someone up north that could get tickets for you or get them yourself and they had to be bought in person. There were only a few tickets left in a couple places and Stockton was the closest.

My plan was to leave late Friday afternoon, ride up Route One to Monterey, go up to El Sobrante and visit Clay on Sunday. Be at the Harley shop Monday morning, pick up the tickets and be back in L.A. Tuesday morning for work.

On the way outta town Friday afternoon I stopped by the Sunset for a beer. Al and a few other people were getting the weekend started early or late depending on how you looked at it. Back then for me the weekend began on Wednesday and ended on Tuesday.

Anyway, when I told Al where I was going he wanted to go too. I hung around while Al got his shit packed on his scooter and made arrangements to have his goldfish fed.

When he was ready, we had to have a couple 'a beers for the road and all that shit. By the time we got outta there it was way past dark-thirty. By midnight we'd only made it to Thousand Oaks.

We rode all night though and got on Route One in San Luis Obispo as the sun was coming up. We got gas, snorted breakfast, smoked a joint and headed out, by late morning we were in Cambria. When we stopped to drink lunch there wasn't a soul in the bar, within half an hour the place was full. Of course we stayed way too long {until the place closed if I remember right} and snorted way too much of our dwindling dope supply.

We finally got the hell outta there early {around sun-up} in the morning and it was a long ride to Big Sur especially as drunk as we were. We stopped again at San Simeon and snorted the rest of the dope. I just knew as the wind blew the empty baggie out to sea that the rest of the trip was gonna suck, I just didn't know how much. We spent the rest of the day racing through the straights and winding our way through the hairpins and switchbacks on Route One.

The light was just starting to change to dusk as I accelerated around a hairpin with a shear drop to the ocean on one side and an almost shear wall on the other covered with foliage. At the end of the turn was a little straight stretch with another hairpin at the end of it.

Halfway through the straight while I was still accelerating a white moth drifted out in front of me. From the other side of the moth I saw a small mouthful of tiny teeth coming at me. The teeth hit me on the right cheek right at the bottom of my glasses. Part of whatever it was splattered up the inside of my glasses and into my eye. The other part covered the inside and outside of the lens on my glasses and went up my forehead.

There was nowhere to stop. I was blind in one burning eye; this sticky, fuzzy shit was tickling the right side of my face from my cheek to my hairline. I was trying to get my glasses cleaned off without dropping 'em, get the shit outta my eye, keep the bike from going off the cliff in front of me and keep outta Al's way, who was coming up behind me pretty fast the last time I could see 'im.

It took about five miles of wobbling down the road alternating between cleaning my face, cleaning my glasses and trying to keep Christine on the road to get myself back together and rolling again. As I was riding along I was trying to figure out what the hell'd just hit me.

My mind's eye movie of it played over and over trying to figure it out. All of a sudden it hit me; **IT WAS A BAT!** A tiny bat. It couldn't've had a wingspan of more than a few inches, but it was a bat.

Right after I thought of that, somebody in my head said clear as a bell **"don't bats carry rabies?"**

"**FUUCK THEY DO!**" My instant paranoia screamed and the race was on.

As we came into town The Big Sur Inn was on the left side of the road and it was open. We stopped and ate, then made the mistake of going into the bar. Like the place in Cambria, the place was dead when we walked in, but was packed within an hour after we opened our first beers.

Like idiots we tried to find some dope among the group of druggies and drunks that we were partying with. The only thing these people said they could find was coke, which was better than nothing. The smallest amount they'd sell was an ounce though. Al was just drunk enough not to recognize the scam, their plan was to separate us and rob Al.

As soon as the one who seemed to be the ringleader said that he and Al would have to go out back to do the deal alone, I put a halt to the bullshit and told 'em to either do the deal right there or forget it. As I said it, Al knew what I meant and agreed.

The dude said something about the cops watching him and he didn't feel right and bla, bla, bla.

We were standing in the middle of a dark parking lot in the middle of the night with no one around for miles. If anyone'd been near, it was so quiet that you'd hear 'em a half mile away. How much noise do you have to make exchanging money for dope?

I told Al to forget it; Al fired his bike while I watched the hillbilly hoodlums and visa versa, then we got the fuck outta there. We hadn't gone a hundred yards before I knew this was gonna be a bitch. As drunk, stoned, tired and outta dope as I was I could barely keep my eyes open long enough to stay in my own lane.

We battled our way up the rest of Route One into Seaside. Just as we hit the freeway there was a Waffle House next to a Holiday Inn that looked like the end of the road to me. We got the hell off the road just as the Monday morning traffic was getting geared up. That was the last place we needed to be on Monday morning, drunk, tired and outta dope. We'd both be stars on the morning traffic report within minutes of entering any freeway.

Somehow we'd managed to not even complete in two days what should've only taken one to do. Suck up a weeks worth of crank doin' it. Leave ourselves dopeless before not even completing half the trip and incapable of continuing on without more dope because of all the partying we'd done to screw things up so far. According to Al we could get more dope in Stockton, if we could only get there. Right now we couldn't even get from our bikes to the door of the Waffle House.

When we walked into the Waffle House the waitress/manager was the only person there and I think we scared her just a little bit. Her fear didn't last too long when she realized we could hardly keep our eyes open.

As soon as we sat down we began nodding out. She woke us both up when she brought our coffee and said she could let us sleep in the booth for an hour until the day manager came in, then we'd have to leave pretty quickly because right after he came in four or five CHP came in for breakfast every morning.

I remember nodding off and waking up when I felt something wet on my forehead. I'd wake up and sit up at the same time and feel something running down my face. I'd open my eyes and there'd be Al sitting in front of me with his eyes closed, coffee running down his face from his forehead. I'd mumble something unintelligible, laugh at my own joke and go for another dip in my own coffee.

After my third dip the waitress came to me and shook me awake. Once she knew I knew she was there she said, "I don't wanna make you mad or anything, but you have the grossest mess on your face and in your hair. Could you please go in the men's room and wash it off, it's making me sick!"

I got up and walked into the men's room, it was the first mirror I'd seen besides my tiny rearview since I'd hit the bat. There hadn't been a mirror in the men's room at the bar and by the time we got to the Waffle House I'd forgotten all about everything, let alone that.

I had bat guts, shit, little pieces of bone, everything that comes out of a bat when you splatter it with your face in a stripe from just above my eye to tip the of every hair on the front of my head. The front of my forehead had a hardened wall of bat shit up it that had my hair standing straight on end like a billboard advertising splattered bat. It was without a doubt the grossest thing I'd ever seen on my face, and was the nastiest smelling shit I'd ever smelled as soon as I hit it with water. I scrubbed the bat crap out of my hair and off my face which actually made me feel a little more human than I'd felt in a while.

When I walked up to our booth, Al was face first in his breakfast. As I sat down he jolted upright and started eating like a rubber man that couldn't keep his fork in his hand or his food in his mouth. When he raised his head I started laughing cause he'd tried on more of his breakfast than he'd eaten and was going back for another fitting even as I started laughing.

I didn't remember ordering breakfast, but when I got back to the booth I had breakfast to try on too. As soon as I sat down my eyes closed. As soon as my face hit my plate I was back awake, jerking upright with ill-fitting eggs and stuff running down my face. While I was upright I'd put something in my mouth, pass out, do a swan dive into my breakfast and do it all over again. After about the fifth or sixth high dive into my breakfast the waitress called a halt to the competition, declared a tie between Al and I, took our plates, washed our faces off with a damp rag and sent us to bed without the rest of our breakfasts.

A few minutes before seven she woke us, the place was filled with people by now, all of 'em staring at us like we'd shit in the middle of the floor or something. When we got outside our guardian angel came out and said we were in no condition to drive. If we pushed our bikes around the corner, there were some trees we could park under for shade and the cops wouldn't see us there when they rolled in for breakfast in five or ten minutes.

We took the hint and rolled the scooters out back under the trees and passed out against our packs for a while. I remember waking up once and seeing a line of police cars in front of the Waffle House.

Leaving right then seemed to be about the stupidest thing I could think of doing, so I ignored myself and went back to sleep.

The next time I woke up it was because the sun was cooking a part of my leg. Not wearing a watch in those days I could only guess what time it was, the cops were gone though that was one good thing. I woke Al and said we needed to get moving before the cops did come or worse.

We were moving pretty slowly and to make matters worse being dedicated drug addicts we had to smoke a joint before we left. That joint was the last thing we needed and nearly impossible to roll. We could hardly keep our eyes open we were so stoned and tired, let alone do something as complicated as rolling a joint.

We finally got our asses moving and got on the freeway after hours of fucking around. We were taking the 101 north to the 680 north to 580 east. On the 101 just before the 680 interchange Al got my attention and pointed at one of his spark plugs. At first I didn't notice that it was outta its hole dancing around on the edge of the sparkplug hole in the head. When it was dawning on my last working brain cell what was going on and while I was still looking at Al's bike, the primary drive belt shredded and flew off his open primary onto the highway behind us, ending the trip for Al right there.

He coasted to the side of the freeway and I stopped right in front of him. We got off the bikes and looked at Al's disaster. The belt of course was useless. Without a belt we were completely dead in the water. The bike could've made it off the freeway under it's own power with just one cylinder firing, but not without that belt.

I asked Al if he'd ever been towed on a bike before.

The size his eyes got at the mention of it answered my question before he ever said a word. His answer was "no and I'm not about to either!"

I said "that remains to be seen."

After a few minutes I told Al I was gonna find a way off this freeway and I'd be back. I knew we were in San Jose; the 680 interchange was the next exit up. There were housing plattes next to us. The problem was finding an exit that had something at it like a gas station or convenience store, someplace safer than the side of this freeway.

There really wasn't much around there to indicate where any services were. I took off north and mentally flipped a coin for a direction at the interchange, 680 north won. As soon as I was on 680 an exit came up within a mile. It exited onto a large boulevard. About a mile down the boulevard on the other side of the street was a gas station and convenience store. It'd be about two and a half miles from Al to the store. If I had to tow him, this is probably about as far as he'd make it without losing it.

I was used to towing bikes with mine. One year I towed a friend of mine from the diner on Junction Avenue in Sturgis to the Harley Shop in Rapid City at a hundred mph the whole way, so that no one would buy the last belt and/or the shop didn't close before we got there.

The reason we towed the bike was because it took an impact wrench to remove the retaining ring from the front pulley so you could slip the new belt on. When Ferret talked to the shop about the belt, which we were lucky to find at all cause it was an old 8mm Primo and had been obsolete for more than a few years. He asked if they had air to put it on with, they said yes but they didn't tell him it cost sixty dollars to use it and there was a two day waiting list.

We flew to Rapid City passing everything on the freeway like it was standing still. One wrong move and we'd've both ended up dead under a heap of twisted metal and I'd've had it the worst cause he'd've been on top of me before he could 'a said shit.

We got to the Harley shop in time, they had the belt, without hesitation Ferret snapped it up. The cost of the belt meant he'd have to tighten *his* belt. When they told him the cost of and the waiting list for the air he cringed and looked at me. We walked outside and I told him, fuck it I'd tow him back to Sturgis and have the gas station down on Junction Avenue do the impact part.

The ride back was at a far more normal speed; still close attention had to be paid all the way back. One wrong move at sixty-five mph and well, you know. When we got back to Sturgis I towed him straight to the gas station. The dude said he was too busy with the pumps, if we could do it ourselves we were welcome to it. The belt was on in five minutes and the night was saved.

I rode back to Al who'd walked back and gotten the old belt for whatever reason, while I was gone. I pulled up in front of him and parked, there wasn't a cloud in the sky and it was already hot. I gave Al the soda I brought back for him and we smoked a joint. When I mentioned the tow thing again Al countered with hitchhiking every pickup truck that went by.

I said "fine give it a whirl and good luck with it."

While Al stood there with his thumb out I started thinking about getting hit by the bat the day before. It's teeth had broken the skin of my check just under my glasses, it was only a glorified scratch, but how big a wound did it have to be to get rabies.

Watching Al do the absurd and thinking about getting rabies was driving me quietly outta my mind. The more I tried to put the bat shit outta my head the more batshit it was driving me. I had to have something to do before I went nuts thinking about rabies.

After about an hour of stewing in that juice I jumped up and got the snatch cord outta my saddlebag. While Al wasn't looking I tied it around the steering head of his bike's frame, backed Christine up a little bit and tied the other end to the luggage rack on the back fender.

When I was done, I "hey'd" Al.

When he turned around and saw that cord his head started to involuntarily shake back and forth and a low "nooo" escaped him.

I told him it was a piece 'a cake. All he had to do was steer and brake like normal and stay right behind me, cause if he didn't he could pull me down and run over me before he could say "boo." Of course this made him even more nervous, hell he acted so nervous it was making me nervous too.

He couldn't stall any more. I was sick of sitting on the side of this freeway baking in the ever increasing heat of the sun and we were leaving that was all there was to it. He was the most difficult person I've ever towed. He kept putting on the brakes like we were going too fast. I doubt we got much over thirty mph the whole two and a half miles.

It sure pissed off anybody trying to use the left lane on that street. As soon as we got off the freeway it was clear all the way to the left. We went that way when we could, instead of waiting till the last minute and trying to change lanes in front of twenty cars all trying to get into the same lane we needed at the same time.

We finally got to the store and outta the way in a corner of the drive behind some jersey barriers. The only plan I had was to call Clay and have him come down after work with his trailer and pick us up. When we got to the store Al paged somebody from the payphone. When they called back it told me that this payphone still accepted incoming calls and Clay was our only hope.

When Al got off the phone I called Clay's house and left a message for him to call me at the payphone when he got the message and left it at that.

This wasn't any real emergency, not enough to bother him at work anyway. We spent the rest of the day trying to stay outta the sun and waiting for the phone to ring.

Late in the afternoon the phone rang. Clay was laughing before I could tell him the whole story. He said he was gonna have dinner and head out.

A few hours later he called again for some final approach directions. He was in the neighborhood' but wasn't real sure about how to get to us. This wasn't anywhere near his house and was in a pretty countrified and new part of San Jose, which made finding a way around a little more difficult than usual.

In spite of that a few minutes later he was pulling in; we put one bike in the truck and the other on the trailer and got the fuck outta there. By the time Clay'd gotten there we'd been there for a long time. We were both exhausted and disgusted. Al had no idea how he was gonna get his bike back to L.A. and if I didn't get some dope I didn't know how I was gonna get back to L.A. either.

The next morning Al got ahold of his sometime girlfriend, full time cokewhore and gave her instructions about his stash and directions to Clay's. It's a six or seven hour drive from Venice to El Sobrante depending. She finally showed up two days later half naked and couldn't tell Al where her cloths were. All she could say was she met a friend in an eighteen-wheeler on the way up and they'd partied a little with Al's coke as the party favors. She was supposed to've brought an ounce with her. By the time she got there three quarters of it was gone and so was she.

Al quickly hustled her back into the car and headed back to L.A. as soon as she got there. After they were gone Clay and I had a good laugh about the whole mess especially when we started wondering what they were gonna talk about for the next six hours.

Al looked plenty steamed when April got there in the condition she was in. Especially after taking two days, a lotta dope and a lotta money. All we could say was "the price we pay for the lives we lead".

For days after the rescue I could hardly get outta my own way. I had to get moving though, I was two days late already and the way I felt it'd take me at least two more days to get to L.A. if I was lucky. Clay'd quit doing crank and didn't know where to find any so I was shit outta luck. I'd have to get myself back to L.A. on a natch, which was gonna suck there wasn't any natch left in me and hadn't been for a while.

I left right after it got dark on Thursday; I'd only been riding for an hour. The whole time contemplating going back to Clay's and waiting a few more days for some energy to appear outta nowhere. Instead as soon as I got on I-5 headed south I found a dead end road at the first exit I came to, pulled off into a dark corner and tried to sleep.

Even though I couldn't sleep when I stopped, I couldn't stay awake when I started riding. I was so fuckin' wrung out it took me all night to get twenty miles. As soon as I got on the road I'd get so sleepy I'd pull off at the first place I saw. Once I stopped I couldn't even close my eyes.

Once morning came I got on the road in earnest. By late afternoon I was dropping down the L.A. side of Tejon Pass into Castaic. I got to the shop about an hour before it closed. I talked to Vince for a while, drank a beer and when Vince wasn't looking got some dope from Pete and did a line, man did that feel good.

I learned my lesson on that one; always take twice as much dope as you think you're gonna need when you go anywhere.

When I got to Bird's house the first thing I had to do was get some dope so I'd make it to work the next day. I was treading on thin ice with Vince and I needed to get in there and bust out some of the work that'd been waiting for me for the last few weeks. I had to get some money in my pocket and get my job outta the ditch.

Well enough flashbacks let's get back to the story, I don't really remember how I got out to Al's from the apartment in Buena Park. I do remember sitting on his front porch while he was taking his stuff out of his car, talking about the wreck. I know I only used his car a few days, then he traded me for a pickup truck he had sitting around the streets of Venice collecting parking tickets.

The old Ford had seen better days, it now spent most of it's time sitting on the street getting broken into and ticketed on sweeper days. The old beast was a gas hog to say the least. It'd get me back and forth to work and that's it. Any more than that'd cut into my dope and Christine money.

Now that I had all my ducks in a row. I had time to sit down and think about my predicament, I was a scooter tramp without a scooter. An acquaintance named Blue that I'd met through Mex had been in a bad wreck down in Orange county not long after I met him. He was a tramp like me except he was a little ways further down the crank spiral than I was when we met.

Blue lived on his bike {literally}, sleeping wherever he could when he absolutely had to and partying the rest of the time all over the streets of L.A. and Orange County.

The only thing he had was that bike and a girl named Terry. Neither of 'em ever looked like they saw much soap and water, ever, and when Blue had the wreck she was lucky enough not to be with him. Pat and I were at a bar out in some canyon when Blue and Terry got out of a car that they'd hitched a ride in.

A few hours later when we left the bar Blue was nowhere to be found and Terry was packin' behind Pat. Better him than me I didn't have the budget to get two people high all the time and didn't particularly want the hassle of an ole'lady, especially since I didn't know where I was gonna lay my head most of the time let alone worrying about someone else.

I remembered how the next time I saw Blue he was bumming anything he could get in the parking lot of the same bar. A few hours later he was passed out in a heap in an outta the way corner underneath the patio we were partying on. I wondered then if this was gonna be the place he'd end up spinning out in like The Ghost of PCH.

It didn't look like he'd been anywhere since the last time I'd seen him. He was wearing the same cloths only filthier and he had no idea what was happening to his bike. It was impounded at the scene because he was drunk when he wrecked and he never got it back. Right after the accident he talked about getting it back all the time, but the talk faded as time went by and was replaced with the "hey, have you got" greeting.

I don't know whatever happened to Blue, but unless somebody rescued him I doubt he's even alive. The last time I saw him he was in rough shape. I couldn't see myself getting as bad as Blue. I had a job, a place to stay, and friends that were helping me; I'd be back on the road in no time.

Although in some part of my mind I knew that this wreck was a long fall down into the abyss of addiction's destruction of life. At the time I was already far along the road to ruin and completely refused to see that my addictions were the cause. The only thing I blamed for the wreck was alcohol. Since I never liked alcohol a quarter as much as I liked the drugs I did, that was the thing I blamed for the wreck and the thing I quit using, completely! It was twelve years before I ever had a drink of alcohol and I never did enjoy the buzz from it again.

I wish I could've done that with all my addictions as easily as I did alcohol that day, my life would've been very different and I'd probably have something today.

Instead I dove headlong into an abyss that most people don't return from and though I lived through it physically and mentally and survived remarkably well compared to most, parts of me died that a person needs to make it in this world and be happy.

For me there is never real happiness, just days that are slightly less depressing than others. A few moments of laughter amid months of repressed depression isn't living and certainly isn't happiness.

As ok as I thought I'd be, my troubles were just starting, ever since leaving California four years earlier I'd maintained a New Mexico driver's license and registration mostly for the anonymity it brought during traffic stops. Back then the states weren't plugged into each other like they are now and quite frequently the cop that had you on the side of the road at the scene didn't have fast access to all your information. As long as you weren't wanted for anything in a four or five county range you might skate away from the stop before the officer ever got any information at all.

When I got in the wreck I was issued tickets for expired license, registration and insurance. This was the beginning of a court battle that stretched over a few months and ended up with me either complying then or doing ninety days in jail then complying. It was easier to comply and keep packing my face with dope than it was to even think of going without dope for ninety minutes, let alone ninety days. Before I even got a chance for the first appearance on the tickets I got a much bigger case to contend with.

During the week following the wreck I did a lot of drugs and that was it. I milked the wreck for all it was worth time off wise and every other way possible. All I did was hang around with Mex in the garage and do drugs. Sit around and watch TV and do drugs or sit around doing drugs and do drugs. I didn't have to be back to work till the next Tuesday so until then I was gonna be as fucked up as I could be every day.

Monday morning, a week after the wreck I was smoking cigarettes and watching Captain Kangaroo after getting a huge head rush from a great batch of fresh dope. Mex came in and after having a head rush of his own asked if he could borrow Al's truck that I was borrowing to go get a bike that he was gonna work on.

Mex had pretty much worn out his welcome as a wrench in all the area shops because believe it or not he was as shiftless if not more so than me. If it was for me to judge {which it isn't}, I'd say he was worse just because of his sticky fingers. He couldn't be trusted around things you wanted to keep or didn't wanna keep for that matter. He'd steal anything from your last beer to the t-shirt off your back, nothing was safe.

Because of this he worked on bikes in his garage, once you've worked in a few shops and built up a little client base it's easy and much more laid back to work out of a place of your own. If you were a drunken druggie like Mex, it was perfect. Not to say I was an angel I just hadn't completely worn out my welcome yet, but I was working on it.

I told him I couldn't loan him a borrowed truck, but he and I'd go get the bike if he wanted. That sounded like a plan so he called Jerry, the dude that owned the bike and told him we'd be there sometime hopefully soon after they hung up. After snorting and smoking a little more we started out the door for the truck. About forty-five minutes and a few more bong loads later we were headed out the driveway to the city of Paramount.

It was well known buy everyone on the street that the Paramount Sheriffs were as crooked as the day was long. When I first came to California that was one of the first things I was warned about. It was well known that the Paramount Sheriffs would plant dope on you to make a bust if they couldn't find any. I never rode thru Paramount at night and avoided it like the plague during the day.

Well today that was exactly where we were going. When we were waiting to make our left turn onto the street that Jerry lived on a sheriff's car went by going in the opposite direction and he eye fucked us pretty hard as he passed. If looks could kill both Mex and I would've been dead on the spot.

After he passed we made our turn and eased down the street. He must've done a Dukes of Hazard in front of all the traffic behind us because he was behind me with the lights and siren blaring before we made it a block. I let him follow me one more block to Jerry's house before I stopped.

As usual "do you know why I stopped you?"

I honestly didn't, the only law I was breaking was being ugly in public.

And as usual again "can I see your license and registration?"

I gave him the paperwork he asked for.

"The reason I stopped you is because you have a cracked windshield. What are you doing around here today?"

I told him I was doing Mex a favor and picking up a customer's bike for him so he could repair it. That turned his attention to Mex for a minute.

Mex went thru the same ID drill that I did and it was back to me again after the cop got the same story outta Mex that he got from me.

By this time Jerry had walked outside and was standing near the back of the truck. Seeing him the cop wanted to know who he was first. As soon as he knew that he told him to go back inside, which he kinda' did.

He told us both to get outta the truck and sit on the curb between the two vehicles. While we did that, he ran our wants and warrants.

In a few minutes he was back asking to search the truck. There wasn't anything in it, the first thing I did when I got home with it was clean all the trash out of it from everywhere and blow all the dirt out with compressed air.

I told him to be my guest and sat back to watch the show. There aren't too many places and not a big area to search in the cab of a Ford pickup. He rooted thru the cab for about fifteen minutes, ten minutes longer that it takes to search every nook and cranny twice.

On his way back to his car he stopped to tell me that it'd go easier on me if I told him where the dope was. We'd left everything at home; we didn't even have a roach on us.

All I could say was "what dope?" Like I'd tell him if there really was any.

After he talked on the radio for a few minutes he went back to the pickup and began all over again. By now I was getting an uneasy feeling about this.

He rooted around for another fifteen minutes, went back and talked on the radio some more, went back to the truck and was rooting around for the third time when another car pulled up.

As soon as the car got there he walked back to it. The other cop got out; they walked back to the trunk of the second car and opened it.

I thought "oh no."

The two cops stood behind the trunk talking for a few minutes; suddenly the first cop walked to the passenger side of the pickup. While the second cop slammed the trunk down and started walking towards us.

The first cop leaned into the pickup, reached into his shirt pocket, pulled a baggie out of it, turned around and went "ah haaa, look what I've found!"

The second cop was already on top of us telling us we were under arrest about the same time the first cop pulled the baggie out of his pocket. Tell me that shit wasn't staged.

We were taken to the Lakewood Substation for processing after our arrest; it was there that I learned we'd been in possession of Magic Mushrooms. I always like to know what I'm being held for, just in case I have to talk to the press. The substation is just a staging area for the central jail. A place no one in there right mind wants to visit.

Mex being from the area, having family and proof of residence was released on an OR {own reconnaissance} from the substation. My situation was a little different, since I was licensed in New Mexico and had no proof of residence that I could show {showing any proof of a California residence at that time would've had me in violation of other laws, I figured one crime at a time and prayed for bail} I'd have to post a traditional bond that I didn't have.

My only hope was Al, when I called him it was no problem. All Mex had to do was ride out to Venice Beach when he was released. Pick up the paperwork, bring it back to the substation and I'd be released within a few minutes and escape the next morning's bus to the central jail.

This all sounded easy enough, but then there was the Mex factor. Mex was as responsible as a fart in a hurricane. All he had to do was smell a beer and he'd end up God knows where at the end of the night not doing what he was supposed to be doing and having no recollection of what that even was. Before he left I gave him all the directions I could to get him out to the bar to meet Al. After he left all I could do was pray that he'd stay on course and make it back before the bus got there in the morning.

He actually did better than I expected, even though he met Al at a bar, he only had a few beers and actually got back to the substation in a pretty short time. The sun was just going down when I walked outta the substation with my release and arraignment date in hand.

When we got back to the apartment of course the first, second and third thing we did was get high, then I got a ride over to Jerry's and continued on where we left off when we were so rudely interrupted.

It took almost fifteen hours to do a simple thing like pick up a bike for repair, thanks to the bullshit created by the Paramount Sheriff's "if you can't find it, plant it" policy. It was a good thing the truck wasn't towed. For whatever reason they left the thing sitting right where they found it and never did give me a ticket for the broken windshield.

For the next few weeks things calmed down some. I didn't think it was a very good idea to have too many things going in too many courts at once. I already had three traffic cases going in Bellflower. Now I had a drug case in Compton for drugs I didn't do, at least not in the recent past. The last time I'd done shrooms was with Valerie in The Springs one spring day.

We rode over to a friend's house right after we did 'em and by the time we had to leave it'd started snowing. We rode home in the middle of a snow storm tripping our brains out on shrooms, the roads covered with snow and the bike feeling like it was made of rubber. When I turned the handlebars it seemed like it took the front end five minutes to catch up to the rubbery handlebars. That's a bad enough feeling on blacktop, never mind on ice and snow. We made it home just fine, when I shut Christine off in front of the house I told myself never again and I hadn't. That'd been at least two years before the bust in Paramount.

Because I wasn't out running the streets as much. I was actually making it to work more frequently and in better condition. I had to, I had to pay Pat for my bail and rebuild my bike. I was no longer a scooter tramp. I was just a junkie with a twisted pile of junk and a bunch of addictions that'd run wild in his life to the point that they'd taken precedence over everything else.

Even though my act had cleaned up some after the wreck: due to numerous past transgressions, the last few weeks, the drug bust and the upcoming multiple court cases and appearances. As soon as everything settled down Vince called me outside to have the "I really like you, but" talk, resulting in my termination. I really didn't mind except that since I hadn't paid Pat he was keeping Christine until I did, which means I couldn't just drift around getting high and working only when I had to, I had to get another job as soon as possible.

About the same time I got fired Mex and I had our first court date; neither of us had ever been to Compton Court in our lives. **HOLY COW, WHAT A FUCKIN' ZOO!** That was the first courthouse I'd ever seen with metal detectors and police in riot gear standing ready.

Our first appearance was just an arraignment, where you plead not guilty and get set up with a dump truck to plead your case. This being a busy court took most of the day; in the meantime we had to hang around on this or that bench waiting for our names to be called to fill out paperwork and then move on to the next bench.

While we waited for the next thing to happen it was amazing to see the shit that went on in the hallways of that courthouse. While waiting for one thing or another we watched a woman knock four of her boyfriend's teeth out and get hauled away in handcuffs screaming. Another dude got drug out of a men's room hogtied because he got caught smoking crack in there by a deputy and tried to jump out the window and those are just the highest of highlights.

As Mex and I sat on our various appointed benches and watched all this shit going on we'd occasionally glance at each other with a "holy shit, did you see that" look and wonder out loud how the hell we got so lucky as to come here for a court case.

We finally met our dump truck around two in the afternoon, after being there since eight-thirty in the morning I was more than ready to get this over with and get the hell outta there before we got shot right there in the hallway.

When we met our attorney the first thing I asked him was how he could stand the place, he glanced around at the chaos churning around him and said "you get used to it."

He didn't even seem to care that the dope we got busted with was planted. His answer for that was "so what, everybody claims to be innocent. Why should you be any different?" Our own lawyer was convinced we were guilty and he'd only known us for five minutes. I knew then we were fucked, I just didn't know how badly.

After a few more questions he said he knew all he needed to, gave us each a card and said to call him in two weeks and he'd have court dates for us. We told him to make 'em as far in the future as he could and got the hell outta there.

We had to drive all the way home before we could get high cause I didn't feel right carrying dope into Compton in a vehicle that I'd just been busted for dope in. When we got home we made up for the lost time between the courthouse and there though.

In recent times the shops that I'd known for years had dropped out of existence for one reason or another. I hadn't really kept up with all the changes and was shocked to find most of the shops that I knew at one time were gone.

One afternoon I was thumbing through the latest issue of EasyRiders. When I got to the classified section there were a couple 'a ads for wrenches, one was out in the San Fernando Valley which was on the other side of L.A. from me {about an hours drive}, but if that was where I had to go to work who cares? I called the ad and talked to a dude named Micah, by the end of the conversation I was going to The Valley the next day.

Micah and I hit it off right away, by the time I walked outta his office I had my next future firing in the works. While he showed me the shop I met the other two mechanics who turned dreams into nightmares for the scooter people of The Valley. One was a tall lanky character named Hugh; the other was a real character, a little Mexican dude that had about as firm a grip on English as you'd have on a greased pig, named Carlos "Chopper" Ortega. The radio station was the FM version of the AM station at the shop in Carson, fifteen songs, twelve of 'em Elvis, played endlessly from morning till night.

The shop itself was on Sherman Way in the middle of Canoga Park's business district, which is a very busy place during the day. It was strategically located one block from a tittie bar and fifty feet from a tattoo shop. I left there glad to have a job and looking forward to the scenery change The Valley offered, but I wasn't looking forward to that fucking radio station.

The next morning was the first time I had to fight my way to The Valley during rush hour. Why is it called rush hour when everybody moves so slowly? This truly sucked. If I was gonna do this six days a week I'd need a lotta dope just to get me outta bed in the morning. The drive from Buena Park to Canoga Park every day thru downtown was unbelievable. It wouldn't've been too bad on a bike, but in a pickup truck with no radio it was the most boring hour and a half of my life. What a way to start a day, especially every day.

The first days in a new shop are always frustrating for me. I don't know where anything is and it seems to take twice as long to get anything done for that reason. You don't know what kind of people you're working with either; they could be cool or snitchin' little shitheads, jealous that you're stealing their thunder and looking for any reason to fuck you up so they can go back to being top dog.

It always sucks to be the new kid on the block, but if you've got your shit together the new kid thing doesn't last too long and in a week or so you're one of the boys.

For the first few months you're always on good behavior at a new job. I always made sure not to get too high and give myself away. From what I understood Micah'd had his own battle with having "too much fun in a no fun zone" and had just recently gotten back on track with the help of his family.

Micah's place was pretty busy, with a constant traffic of regulars and not so regulars that I got to know pretty quickly, especially the ones that had to do with the dope industry in The Valley. Before long I had a whole new network of dope connections to deal with and a bunch of new places to hang out.

Meanwhile back at home shit was beginning to hit the fan in Buena Park, more and more frequently I was coming home to an empty apartment. My roommates were going off the deep end and tanking their relationship. When Mex did make it home he was usually so fucked up he didn't have a clue he was there. Shortly after entering the place he was either having some kind of drunken fit at Tammy about something or he was passed out cold. Tammy was gone until late usually and left early like I did. Mex who'd gotten a job at Van Nuys H-D after I got the job at Micah's came home less and less.

After not seeing him for a few days I heard that he was in jail for DUI and since he already had the drug case pending in Compton couldn't get out on another OR and no one would go his bail. Tammy seemed pretty glad about it when she told me; her and her kids had been staying with friends to keep Mex from drunkenly harassing her every chance he got. Now that he was in jail she started coming home to the apartment again, but that wasn't gonna be for long.

Now that I was working in The Valley my life started to slowly morph in that direction. As I got to know more people in The Valley I spent more time there. Going all the way back to Buena Park after partying in The Valley was getting old and of all the places in L.A. I was beginning to like The Valley the best. If things continued to work the way they had been I was gonna have to move out there pretty soon.

A few weeks maybe months after going to work for Micah I had enough money to get Christine outta Vince's and close that chapter of my life for good. I picked Christine up on the way to work one morning and dropped her at Micah's so that I could begin working on her in my spare time.

I'd already set it up with Pete to repair and customize my `57 straightleg frame, so the first thing I needed to do was get the bike apart and get the frame to him. That was the most irreplaceable thing that got the most damage and needed the most amount of time to be fixed.

Once Christine was on the dolly in Micah's shop I felt a little better about having her in sight again and was looking forward to getting started on her ASAP. A couple 'a times I caught Micah looking her over casually. One day he asked me if I was gonna put the same shitty brakes on her that'd almost killed me the last time.

When I told him I was just concerned with getting her back together and shit like that could wait till another time.

He snapped "fuck it can, you oughta know better than that," turned on his heel and walked away, I went back to my bench and went back to work.

After lunch Micah came out and asked me what the hold up was with upgrading the brakes.

I told him I couldn't afford the parts and I didn't wanna hassle with setting up a different type of front end right then. Micah stood there looking me in the eye for a long second, stuck his cigar in his mouth and walked away.

A little while later Micah walked up and set a pair of stock disc brake lower legs complete with caliper on the bench next to me. When I looked up he said "don't say I never gave you anything," turned around and walked away mumbling "mechanical brakes, bullshit."

That right there was almost everything I needed to hook up disc brakes front and rear. It was all the major pieces at least. The rest was nickel and dime stuff that I could get any time.

So as not to tie up too much space in Micah's shop, I rented a small storage space in a place on Canoga Avenue, a few blocks from the shop. That way the only stuff that was taking up space was the stuff I was working on at the moment and the rest of it would be safely locked up outta the way.

Along with the drug case in Compton I had the traffic cases in the Bellflower court that were going further and further awry every time I had to appear. I'd been late to court and had to have the date changed so many times that the judge was ready to lock me up and throw away the key. Immediately after the wreck I'd written New Mexico for renewals on my license and registration, which I'd gotten no problem. After that I'd gone to Orange County and gotten some insurance to cover that part of my ass too.

The problem with that was after all the missed appearance dates and the crap I did to stall while I was gathering all my ducks together, the judge wouldn't accept the New Mexico renewal. "In case you don't know it, you're in California Mr. Fuller and as such, I expect to see a

California license and registration the next time you show up and don't be late or you'll see the inside of my jail!" With that I was given a new court date forty-five days later and sent on my way.

Leaving court that day I ran into the dude that dropped Grace into my arms almost four years earlier, coming out of another courtroom. We saw each other at almost the same time. My first question was "gotta line?"

"No, I" was all he got out.

"Want one?"

"Yah, I guess."

We walked down the block to the pickup talking about whatever.

When we got in the truck he asked if I knew what'd happened to Grace. I'd hardly thought of her since I left New Mexico, but I hadn't forgotten one thing about her then and I still haven't.

While I laid out the lines he told me the word he'd gotten was that her husband had flipped, chased her car down and ran her off the road with his pickup truck. When the vehicles stopped he jumped out with a 357 magnum, put five rounds into her head, the sixth he stuck under his chin and blew the top of his own head off with.

I did my lines and handed him the glass and the tooter. I didn't know what to say to that, it all seemed pretty final at the time and didn't sound any better then. I'd died for her the day I saw the wrecked trailer four years ago, there was nothing left that wasn't stone. She'd been "the one" that was it, cut and dried. No one else has mattered since.

We shot the shit a little more about our cases and shit like that, said adios and I headed back to The Valley. I was glad for the long drive; I did it in as much silence as you get on an L.A. freeway.

For the next few months things drifted along without any direction at all. In limbo because of court cases, wrecked scooters, ever increasing drug use and essentially drifting away from my core self, evolving into a more dedicated drug addict and a less dedicated biker. As the months passed I got to know pretty much everybody in The Valley that dealt in any kind of quantity of crank. The higher up the chain you get the better the dope is and I was climbing that ladder like my boots were on fire.

The time after the wreck began a self-perpetuating downward spiral that increased in the rapidity of the descent with every successive loop made. Forced to make the choice between dope and getting my bike back together quickly, the dope was winning more and more frequently and the ratio of money for Christine vs. money for dope was tipping further in the dope direction with every payday.

I'd spend most of my money for dope with the intent of selling most of it and buying bike parts. I'd become my own best customer, selling very little of the dope and as a result could afford less and most of the time no parts. Sucking myself ever deeper into the bag I rationalized these actions internally by saying next paycheck, next week, next, next, next until something inside me set the need for my scooter adrift, while I set sail for the deepest bottom of addiction I could find.

The traffic cases ended when I went over to the Canoga Park DMV one afternoon and transferred my New Mexico registration to California. When I did that they gave me a title that said my bike was a 1964 which was very important. Having it titled and registered as a `64 meant I didn't have to have all the safety equipment that became required in 1966 and subsequent years, like turn signals {my theory was, you'd know where I was going when I went there} and a horn {the loud exhaust would've drowned out anything but an air horn}.

That afternoon at the DMV was the most fun I've ever had fucking with anybody in my life. When I got my California title the clerk let me keep the old New Mexico title, just as a kind of souvenir. My drug-induced {I snorted a ripper in the pickup behind the shop before I left and had smoked a joint on the way to the DMV. By the time I walked thru the door of the place I was wasted} brain cell grabbed that idea about my license as well and ran with it.

After I finished my tests I stood in line waiting to have my test corrected and move on to having my picture taken. Between the correcting and the picture taking I had a forty-five minute dispute with the clerk about keeping both my New Mexico license because that was the license I wanted to keep and my California license which I didn't want but the court ordered me to have. The clerk was an extremely overweight middle aged man that smoked too much and couldn't stand the stress of having a pointless argument with a drug-induced lunatic that refused to make the simplest of choices.

By the time I decided to keep the California license and have my picture taken the clerk's whole head was a reddish purple color, his short blondish hair was standing on end and he was huffing and puffing like an old steam engine struggling up a hill. His glasses had fogged up right before he turned purple so he couldn't see the foam on his lips flying off and landing on the counter when he spoke.

I finally stepped in front of the camera, intentionally leaving on my sunglasses {maybe he'd blow a gasket when we started arguing about taking the glasses off}. Without saying another word he snapped the picture, gave me my temporary and put up his "next window" sign. A few days later that license came in the mail believe it or not and from then until I got a new license I had to put my sunglasses on at every traffic stop day or night.

With all the required proper documentation I appeared in the Bellflower court at eight twenty-five in the morning on the appointed day. I'd arranged to have an attorney present and he was supposed to meet me in front of the courtroom doors at eight thirty. it was a little after when the bailiffs came and unlocked the courtroom. I'd been there so many times in the recent past {back then I was pretty unforgettable, especially to law enforcement} that the deputies recognized me and we said hello.

By nine o'clock when court started my attorney still wasn't there. I spent the morning in and out of the courtroom looking for the guy. At the midmorning break I knew I was screwed when the bailiff asked if there was anyone in the courtroom who hadn't heard their name called. When I stood up the judge said "of course, Mr. Fuller."

He called me down front, read me the riot act forwards and backwards and threw my ass in jail for contempt of court. I stood there freaking out inside while trying to tell him I'd been there all morning, it was my lawyer that hadn't shown up. I was simply outside the courtroom looking for him when the bailiff called my name.

If this'd been the first time I'm pretty sure I'd've been alright especially since I'd complied with all the court's requirements and was ready to finish the case, but this being my fourth time late I don't think the judge even cared what I said, it was personal now. His answer was "BULL, bailiff" and I was brought back to the cells.

I really wasn't looking forward to the bus ride later; sitting in this cramped cell with the inmates bussed in from the central jail was bad enough. It was hot, overcrowded and I was high and wanted the fuck out.

When they brought the stale, green-meated sandwiches that the county passes for an inmate lunch I really began to sweat. That meant that the morning session was over and I hadn't seen the judge. Was I going downtown until the next court date or what? Now I was really freaking out. As much as I wanted to pace I couldn't move but a step or two in any direction and the only way to have any fresh air was standing by the bars at the front of the cage.

The front of the cage was the best place for me to be and that was where I was when my name was called. As soon as I heard it I was at the door, ready. The deputy let me out and didn't cuff me {always a good sign}. He took me to the desk and gave me back my valuables {even better sign}. While he was doing this he explained that the bailiffs that I greeted at the door in the morning {himself included} had gone to the judge during lunch and told him I'd been there in the morning when they arrived and was not only on time but early.

When the judge finished his lunch he had me called out before the afternoon session began. He gave me the lecture about being on time and told me he couldn't, as a judge maintain control in his courtroom if he let people show up when they felt like it. He could and did choose to let it go with a lecture three previous times and he felt that was sufficient leeway. He looked at all my documentation, thanked me for finally complying after this months long battle with the court and dismissed the cases.

With that done he asked why I just couldn't have done that to begin with, I told him I was a nonconformist and complying with anything was just against my nature.

He smiled as he said I'd chosen a hard row to hoe and bid me good luck.

The drug bust wasn't going away quite as easily. Our dump truck wasn't gonna do any more than he had to to get this case off his books and collect his hundred dollars. The only thing he did that I agreed with was get the case postponed for as long as absolutely possible.

At the same time I was flushing my life one line at a time I was on my way to becoming one of Micah's all time best wrenches. I could fix anything scooter or not.

Remember I told ya about the radio station. Well the stereo on the wall above part of my work area was an older analog type dial with the station indicator needle that was driven by a string.

Micah insisted on playing nothing but the same fifteen oldies on that one oldies station day in and day out that was it. Any changes and he'd flip and change it back like his ears were on fire and his fingers were catching. Once that was done he'd wheel around and dare the whole shop to touch it again, all the while looking dead at me.

It was all I could do to keep from exploding with laughter every time he did that. After he'd leave Hugh'd tell me to knock it off cause Micah'd have an aneurysm if I kept fucking with the radio, it made him so mad. I couldn't help it, I could only listen to "Hound Dog" so many times in one fucking day before I had an aneurysm myself, fucking with the radio relieved the pressure.

Carlos didn't really understand what was going on until it happened a few times. He just stood there taking everything in and smiling like it was just the thing to do. I had some things for Carlos to try out too when we got around to it.

On morning I'd heard "In the Ghetto" too many times. When Micah walked thru saying he was going to Gary Bang I had the perfect chance to play my plan for the radio.

As soon as he was gone down the alley I got the radio down from the shelf, took the bottom off it and took the string off the rollers. Now you could dial any station you wanted and the pointer pointed at the oldies station no matter what. After I removed the string I tuned the radio to KLOS {a new rock station} and put it back on the shelf.

Hugh insisted he'd figure it out right away. I said it'd take him at least a little while, no matter when the outcome it was gonna be hysterical. A little while later Micah came striding back thru the shop sucking on his cigar, smiling {it's good to be the boss}. We were all working away smiling inside in anticipation of the pranks unraveling. All was right with the world at that moment and I couldn't wait.

About a half hour or so later with a showroom full of customers Micah came back in the shop, looked me right in the eye as I looked up to catch his expression, wheeled toward the radio, reached up to change the channel and his hand stopped halfway. He stood there for a long second looking at the dial with his arm half in the air knowing that what he was hearing was never played on his station {when they only play fifteen songs it's easy to keep track}, but the needle didn't lie or did it? After that moment of indecision he took his arm down and looked at me {who was trying to watch him and look like I was working on the job at hand and ignoring him at the same time}, his head tilted like the RCA dog's and he walked back up front.

When he walked back towards the front Carlos leaned out from his area and as soon as Micah was up front burst out laughing {Chopper was catching on}.

That was the signal; I couldn't hold it any longer and fell out laughing. When I stood back up Hugh was laughing so hard tears were streaming down his checks and Carlos was wiping tears from his checks as well.

Micah came out and stared at the face of that stereo a half dozen times that day before he finally shut it off. When he did he turned and looked at everyone of us like he was gonna say something, I just don't think he knew what.

We could tell by the look on his face he was pissed. He knew something was up, he just didn't know what. The rest of the day we worked in silence; that was better than Elvis every five minutes anyway.

The next morning Chopper was already there {snitching} and Micah was fixing the stereo dial when I walked thru the door. Chopper was a good dude, even though he tattled a lot, he didn't know any better, you just had to keep an eye on him all the time.

If you didn't you might miss something like him coming to work wearing his wife's Gloria Vanderbilt jeans and not believing they were for women. Or wearing his Gucci loafers riding his Shovelhead Dresser to work from Palmdale, he was an absolute crack-up to have around.

He was quite a dashing figure on his maroon and white dresser, with his Gucci loafers, Gloria Vanderbilt highwater jeans, high school varsity leather jacket and the biggest pair of aviator's goggles you've ever seen in your life.

Hugh and I spent all one week convincing Chopper that bikers called their bikes their knobs and when they invited chicks for a ride they asked 'em if they wanted to ride their knobs.

At first he wasn't having any of it, every time we told him that he'd look at us and go "nooo, issnot true?"

"Oh yes it is Carlos," we'd tell him. "Ask Micah."

We coached Micah on the deal as soon as we dreamed it up. When Carlos went to him he agreed completely and helped clinch the deal throughout the week by reaffirming it to Chopper every time he mentioned it.

By Thursday he'd be doing something and when you walked by he'd look up and go "knob?"

"That's right Chopper, knob." I'd toss over my shoulder at him laughing to myself at the same time.

Finally Saturday noon came and it was the end of the week, when we were leaving we reminded Chopper about "knob" leaving that on the stove to simmer over the weekend.

Monday morning came, no Chopper. By seven-thirty we were beginning to wonder, when we heard his dresser turn in the alley. He was an awesome sight to behold he'd gone all out this morning; he had on his wife's Gloria Vanderbilt highwaters, black to showcase his white socks and tan Gucci loafers, a Cordovan jacket, his aviators goggles and a purple hand print on the side of his face.

He parked his bike at the end of the row, scowling in our direction the whole time. Which in itself was kinda' funny to me because it's awfully hard to look tough while you're wobbling backwards into a parking space on tippy toes, just barely in control, teetering on the brink of a spill the whole way.

Once he was parked and off the bike we could tell he was furious. He ripped the goggles off his head and hollered **"KNOB SHIT"** as he stormed past us into the shop. We took a moment to laugh without him seeing before we went in to find out what happened.

Once I'd gotten a grip I headed in to hear the story. Micah already had him inside asking him what happened when I walked thru the door. In Chopper's own words **"I TELL HER MY KNOB, SHE SLAP ME ON FLOOR!"** When we heard this we couldn't contain it any more and fell over laughing.

Chopper was pissed and stormed off; we went to our areas and laughed for another half hour and in spurts the rest of day. By the end of the day we had him convinced that he'd asked the wrong girl.

He'd asked another Mexican gal at a bar in Palmdale, she answered him with a slap so hard it knocked him off his stool onto the floor and left a mark on his face. We started convincing him that Mexican girls didn't know that about bikers and white girls did and if he'd asked a white girl he wouldn't have gotten slapped. His answer to all this coaching and information was "ohhhh, nooo." When he said this you never knew quite what he meant or if he even understood what you said.

A few weeks later we were standing around figuring out who was the senior man in the shop. When it was determined that it was Chopper we began a campaign to educate him on the duties of being the head mechanic. This one took some time to get into Chopper's head, it was hard to overcome his shy nature and get him to go off like he did, but it was worth the time it took to set it up and see it thru.

After weeks of consulting him on every job we did to make him think his word mattered. We finally had him convinced that Micah would pay him more and he wouldn't have to work so hard if he'd step up and take his place as the head mechanic. Micah wasn't supposed to be the one to quote the jobs; he only did it because Carlos wasn't doing it.

As this was worming it's way into his brain he'd stop what he was doing whenever Micah was out in the shop talking to a customer about a job and listen to the conversation, trying to get a grip on it. Chopper had only minimal skills as a wrench and not enough of a grip on English for much of a detailed explanation to get thru if you wanted to teach him something, so I'm sure he didn't get much of any conversation he was listening to.

After weeks of goading Chopper finally snapped one afternoon and jumped into the middle of Micah's conversation. Pushing Micah aside, he started shouting about being sick of Micah taking his money and that he was the head mechanic and he wanted his money now. He marched thru this whole tirade in horribly broken Spanglish that you could only catch every few words of, until he heard us laughing.

When he heard Hugh and I roaring with laughter and saw the "what the fucks your problem" look on Micah's face he knew he'd fucked up and we'd talked him into it again.

If looks could kill we'd've been dead a thousand times, both Carlos and Micah gave us the death stare. Carlos went back to his work like Micah told him to. Micah retrieved the customer who'd headed up front to get outta the line of fire when the action started and finished his business.

When he was done he called me into his office and told me to leave Carlos *and* the radio alone. After he was done with me he told Hugh the same thing. It was gonna be hard to get anything going with Chopper for a while; he wouldn't even look at Hugh and I for a month.

During the month that Chopper wasn't talking to us we got another wrench. A dude {he hated to be called dude} from New York named Snake. I knew Snake briefly from my Venice Beach days. We'd partied together quite a bit before his wife came out from New York, after that I didn't see him until the day he walked into Micah's.

The next day he'd moved into Choppers work area and Chopper never came back until Friday afternoon. When he did come back he walked thru the shop on his way up front quickly, only smiling as he passed, not even slowing when spoken to. A few minutes later he was headed in the other direction, on the way by he waved and said "see you" but didn't even slow down, he did the same thing to Hugh and was gone.

I continued to fuck with the radio every chance I got, always looking for ways to liven up the work day. One morning after Al'd finally taken back his pickup {I'd had plenty of time to get Christine back on the road. I was just far more concerned with feeding my addictions and getting worse all the time and he knew it} Tammy was driving me to work and heading back to Orange County for work herself {we'd hooked up after she left Mex and he'd gone to jail. This was before he and I were sentenced for our drug bust}, so it was early in the morning.

On the way thru Hollywood I jumped off at the Cahuenga exit, shot over to Hugh's apartment and left a note on the seat of his scooter that said "the early worm gets the bird, nyuck, nyuck, nyuck."

The nyuck, nyuck, nyuck came from Curly on The Three Stooges. When I got back in the car Tammy and I laughed about it all the way to Canoga Park. I knew it'd just jack his ass up completely until he figured out it was me.

I got there so early I had to hang around the streets of Canoga Park for about an hour until Micah got there. It was a trip to watch all the street people and junkies that panhandled up and down the sidewalks all day crawling outta whatever hole they slept in that night and starting their day of busy nothingness. I remember thinking like I always do "glad that isn't me." Little did I know how short the time would be before it was.

Micah got there around seven and not long after we heard the roar of Hugh's shovel as he blasted down the alley out back. He came striding into the shop, threw his gloves on his bench and went straight up front with a worried look on his face. A few minutes later he came out and asked me if I'd left the note on his bike. When I broke up laughing Micah said "see", Hugh's face straightened out and he laughed a little, but quickly told me I was a sick fuck.

As soon as Micah heard the nyuck, nyuck, nyuck he knew it was me, being a fellow Three Stooges aficionado he recognized Curly's laugh immediately.

We went back to work and about an hour later Hugh asked me while we were eating breakfast what the note meant.

I told him "itdoanmeansheeit" and went back to eating breakfast. He looked at me like I was nuts {I probably am} and asked me what the fuck that was supposed to mean.

I explained to him that it came from a Zap comic book character from the late `60s, early `70s named Mr. Natural. Somewhere in each story other characters would ask him "what does it all mean Mr. Natural?"

His answer would always be "doanmeansheeit."

Hugh's answer to that was "man you're an old fuck."

Mr. Natural's answer inspired me so much that I actually had a tattoo done of him on the left side of my neck, he's pointing at his head and pointing up at mine, with "doanmeansheeit" as a caption, kinda tells ya where my head was at doanit? Back then I never thought I'd live this long and figured I'd go out with a bang of one sort or another. By then there'd been so many near misses that just by the law of averages and the way I lived I was getting close. I firmly believed in riding hard, dying fast and leaving a good looking corpse.

Despite my constant disruptions Micah and I were friends. He was going thru some bullshit of his own at the time that would put him off his feed once in a while, but on the whole he was quick to laugh at or respond with a joke and though he had some pretty black moods at times he was a good guy. We became friends enough that I was invited to spend Thanksgiving with his family that year.

It must've been nice to have a family like that, I wouldn't know I wasn't close to my family, in fact I don't think I'd ever even been close to myself at that time in my life. I just drifted from one party to the next staying high and doing just what I needed to do to squeak by on the fringe. Watching life from a drug-induced distance, only getting involved enough to stay high and never staying in one place very long.

Sometime around the first week of December of `88 Mex and I went back to court for our drug bust. The dump truck talked us into going to a drug diversion program through the court. If we pled guilty in exchange for drug diversion the charge would be stricken from our records when we successfully completed the program.

He wouldn't hear of taking it to trial even though we had a dozen witnesses that'd testify that they saw the cop take the dope out of his shirt pocket just like we did. He said it didn't matter how many witnesses we had the court would still side with the cop and for putting the court through the trouble of having a trial before they found us guilty we'd pay a much heavier cost than if we'd just plead out and go thru this little obstacle course of court appointed bullshit.

We went thru the formality of the court appearance in the morning and the probation department interview right after lunch. When they were done they informed us we'd be notified by mail sometime in the next ninety days of their determination and given further instructions at that time.

With our day shot we went out and partied the rest of the day. It took us hours to get home because we stopped at every bar we knew between Compton and Buena Park and Mex had at least one bunch of beers at each one. It's amazing how much you can drink when you're wired. Only problem is you better find a place to lie down before you come down. If you're still on your feet when the speed runs out and all that alcohol hits you won't be for long.

Myself I'd quit drinking the day of my wreck so I busied myself with the old standbys speed-n-weed. I felt I was making a wise decision giving up alcohol simply because I never woke up {when I did sleep} feeling like hammered shit anymore and I had already found it much easier to convince a cop that I was sober when I didn't smell like the dumpster behind a brewery.

Months earlier I'd gotten a mailbox in The Valley because I spent more and more time there, that way I wouldn't miss any court papers when they came. If I had to take the long way around the hill to lose this case, I didn't wanna lose the race before it ever got started. I was spending more and more time in The Valley every week and figured I'd probably move out there as soon as things completely fell apart down south, which wasn't gonna be long by the feel of things.

I was coming home to an empty apartment more often than not now. Sometime I'd come home to a place that looked like a tornado hit it. That'd be Mex coming home after a however many day long bender angered to find Tammy wasn't there, having a fit and leaving or passing out in the middle of the floor.

Sometime I'd come home to a cleaned house and no sign of anyone for days. One of those days there was a note on what I called a bed from Tammy telling me she needed to talk to me with a number to reach her at.

Since I was there right then there was no sense putting it off. I knew what she was gonna say before I ever called her. The last few times I'd seen her and Mex together it was a fight. After that the only one I saw at home with any regularity was Tammy. We'd have coffee spiked with a rock for breakfast in the morning before we went to work becoming friends over the common ground of drugs.

When I called her she said her car was running funny and she didn't dare to drive it because of the way it shook and asked if I'd take a look at it for her. When I said I would, she gave me directions to her friend's house where she'd been staying lately. I got off the phone and headed over to the house. All this was before Al took back his pickup.

When I got there I found the U-bolts holding the driveshaft loose and getting looser. A couple minutes with a ½ inch wrench solved that problem and the car was good to go. After the car was fixed she told me that her and Mex had a big fight and he'd left there drunk and proceeded to get drunker until he got busted for DUI and possession. He was in jail then and she'd chosen to take that opportunity to cut the cord with him. The lease on the apartment was up in few days and since she was losing her job she wasn't gonna keep the place.

We spent that night together and started hanging out together full time; she'd moved all of her stuff out earlier so there was just my little bit of shit that I could pack up and have in the car in half an hour and Mex's stuff. As she was looking through their bedroom for anything she'd left behind I found about a half dozen of my T-shirts Mex had helped himself to and a few other things that'd been missing for a while as well.

We just left his shit were it lay after I got my stuff out of it and left. That evening we drove out to The Valley so I could put all the stuff I didn't need every day in my storage unit. I was now officially homeless, I stayed with Tammy at her friend's house, but that was a bad situation made worse by my being there.

Right after I hooked up with Tammy was when Al asked for his truck back, the registration was due to expire and he wasn't gonna renew it. Tammy followed me out to Venice Beach one evening and I brought Al his truck. Now I had no wheels which sucked because it was the first of a new year. Starting out the new year afoot and homeless was a huge tumble down the spiral and a bad omen of things to come.

The first few months of every year is slow in a bike shop just like everywhere else. There were plenty of days when it didn't pay to make the trip to Canoga Park to stand around the shop hoping something would happen. That was why I started dealing to supplement my income. Now it made sense to drive to Canoga Park and hang out at the shop during the morning while all the dealers were still in bed. If no work came in by lunch I'd make my calls, get my dope and take off for the day, go pedal the dope make my money and do it all again the next day.

I looked at it like I was doing my fellow mechanics a favor by not being there competing with 'em for every job that came thru the door. Micah didn't agree with this theory of mine, although I worked on percentage which meant I got paid for the work I did, not the time I was there. Micah had it in his head that he owned me from seven in the morning till five in the afternoon and shouted just that belief during one of our heated arguments on the subject. My answer to that was "you're outta my fucking mind" and out the door I went, telling him to call me when he had something for me do besides argue, which really pissed him off.

I was really diving headlong into the abyss now, and nobody was gonna keep me from fucking my life up to the point of no return, nobody!

This blowout and one or two more caused Micah and I to come to the conclusion that we made much better friends than we did workmates. One rager was created by a busy body, soap opera sucking, shit-stirring fat fuck named Dan that used to hang around the shop all the time.

A friend of mine had an 80 inch FXR that had cracked cases around the barrel base stud bosses that no one could seem to fix for very long. I told him I could fix those cases and build him a screaming 80 inch motor to boot that'd blow the fenders off even some of the mild strokers that were running around The Valley.

At the same time Micah'd worked out a deal with Dan to where he would build two strokers, one for him and one for Dan. Dan would pay for both kits; Micah's kit would be his payment for the work.

When I found out about this I kidded Micah about getting his fenders blown off by a stock bike when he was done. He just glared at me and said "we'll see." Micah and I had different ideas about building fast motors, he subscribed to the popular stroker mentality that longer is faster, it might be but not for very long.

The longer the stroke, the shorter the engine life, the more the vibration and the tougher it is on all the related components. Another thing about the kits of the day was the plug fit tolerances used in assembly to eliminate any breakin time. If you only got thirty-five hundred miles out of a hotrod motor you didn't wanna spend five hundred to a thousand miles of it breaking it in, you wanted to jump on it and do wheelies right away and worry about it on the other end.

I thought a little differently; build all the horsepower above the pistons by increasing the compression ratio and the amount and density of the mixture thru the use of machining processes, basic parts changes and enhancing the flow characteristics of the heads. The rest of the motor is blue printed to reduce the inherent friction in every internal combustion engine and reduce breakin time and vibration. This allows more of the horsepower that the motor makes anyway to go to the rear wheel instead of being spent to turn the motor.

If you do the same thing all the way thru the rest of your drive train to your rear wheel and go belt to belt to lighten all reciprocating weight and rotating mass you'll have a pretty fast rocket that'll last ten times longer than a stroker and probably outrun all but the biggest ones to boot. Not only that but the cost to the customer is considerably cheaper and he's not riding around on something he can't get parts for if he rides far from home and has a breakdown.

Anyway as the motors were being built George and I couldn't wait to see the looks on Micah and Dan's faces when a well massaged stock motor left their strokers in the dust and I couldn't wait to see the look on George's face when he could actually romp on his bike again and not break something.

On this particular morning I was prepping George's motor for the oversized top end studs that I had specially made by ARP for this application. The project manager had called earlier and said they were ready. With those studs I could mock up the motor, clay and cut the pistons for valve clearance and begin finish assembling the lower end.

While I was working Dan walked up and asked what I was doing.

I told him "I'm building a motor that'll eat your strokers for breakfast" and went back to work.

He said "oh" and walked away.

Not two minutes later Micah came screaming out into the shop mad because Dan told him I said Micah didn't know what he was doing and that the motors he was building were shit and wouldn't run.

I fuckin' snapped and jumped in Micah's shit with both feet. When I found out what'd been said by the fat shit I went after his fat ass. Right about the time I punched thru both sides of a wall and knocked the gasket board off the other side Dan took off like a shot out the front door.

Micah got outta the way after the wall surrendered; I had to hit the wall, Micah'd been in an as near death a wreck as you can get in and live to tell about it, shattering his face and a few other things years earlier. One punch in his reconstructed face could've and probably would've killed him, no matter how pissed I was he was my friend and I couldn't hurt him like that for any reason.

The fault wasn't Micah's anyway it rested squarely on Dan's shit-stirring shoulders and now that I knew that, he was gonna pay with a few pounds of flesh and the ass-kicking of his life. I shot out the front door after him and around the corner onto the side street where he'd parked in time to see his Mercedes burning rubber in the opposite direction down the street.

Sully the tattooist was outside on the sidewalk in front of his shop. As I walked up to him he said "I've never seen that fat fuck move that fast in his life, now I know why. What the fucks going on over there? I heard it all the way over here."

"I just lost my job, that's what, see ya later."

When I walked back into the shop eye contact was avoided by everyone. Micah was the only one that had anything to say. He wanted his wall fixed and then he wanted me gone, but for now he just wanted me to leave. We'd worry about the wall later.

When I got back to Tammy's friend's house, Tammy was thrilled to hear the news. She'd gotten rid of one drunken unemployed bum and picked up another unemployed drug addict all in one maneuver. An addict that was headed for the bottom even faster than the drunk she'd gotten rid of.

There was no way this was gonna last very long and it didn't, after a couple weeks she disappeared from her friend's house like she disappeared from the apartment. Now I was really fucked, I had too much stuff with me to hitchhike with and all the rest of my shit was out in The Valley miles away.

Another orphan that was a permanent resident of the house I had to get away from fast had a son that was squatting in an abandoned house a little ways away, it was someplace to go for now. We took a drive up there and he introduced me to his son. The place was nothing more than a shooting gallery with a revolving door.

In the garage was a `56 Chevy pickup truck that someone had incorrectly butchered a smallblock into. Donny told me if I could make it run I could drive it. I guess the kid had been driving it till he fucked it up and was waiting for someone to fix for him so he could fuck it up again.

I hung around there for a little while doing nothing and getting high, Tammy stopped by long enough to get laid a few times and that was about it. One day I was sick of being there and went out and fixed the truck, when it was fixed I loaded all my shit in it and headed for The Valley. I had to take surface streets because I'd only fixed it long enough to get my shit to The Valley with. To do any better a job would've required money for the correct parts and the time it'd take to do the job right.

I wasn't gonna waste the time, I just wanted outta there. I got out to The Valley, stored my stuff and headed back toward Norwalk. I kept noticing cop cars relaying me all the way to the house in Norwalk. I didn't wanna bring it back to the other place cause it was too far to walk back to the freeway so I dropped it off with Donny, he could bring it back over there.

When I got there Donny told me why the cops'd been following me. His spoiled little fuck of a kid thought I was fixing the truck for him or something and reported the truck stolen when he found it gone.

Donny'd told 'em I didn't steal the truck and not to arrest me, but to keep an eye on it to make sure it was coming back. Anyway when I dropped the truck off to him Tammy and the whole crew were there. As I was walking away from the house towards the freeway her and her friends were screaming shit like "glad to see you go, you piece 'a shit loser, yah you fuckin thief get the fuck outta here and don't come back." I listened to that shit till I was outta earshot. It only took one ride and I was in The Valley.

Freefall

That first night I hung out with Snake in his garage till he called it a night. Then I walked around The Valley aimlessly till I couldn't walk anymore. I sat on a bench in a little park on Victory Avenue until the cops came and rousted me.

I was just about to lay down when they noticed me sitting in the dark and couldn't resist giving me a hard time. When I answered their first question with my driver's license, they immediately quizzed me about being so far from home, so late at night, sitting in the darkest part of the park. I told 'em that as of a few hours ago I was homeless and although I lived in Buena Park when the license was issued, that was not the case any longer and at that moment I didn't have a clue what to do. I worked in Canoga Park and that was the only place I could think to go. I was sitting there because that was were my feet'd said whoa.

The cop tossed my license to me and told me to leave the park saying he figured I had enough problems for now without adding an arrest to the list. I agreed, thanked him and walked on my way to wherever.

Down the street from Micah's was an all-night dinner. I wandered in there and sat down to nurse a coffee till it gave birth. I slipped a little rock into my drink to keep me going into the day and tried to figure something out for a place to crash. The only thing I could think of was sleeping in my storage area at night and panhandling or whatever during the day. I didn't know what to do, fuck I'd never been homeless before, at least not without Christine. I felt pretty well fucked!

I sat there watching the condensate trickle down the window while I tried to think of who I could call for some help. The only one I could think of was Clay up in the bay area; everyone else was fading away like I was. I wasn't gonna call Clay. I could handle this, as long as I had a supply of dope I'd be alright. I had good connections; I'd get a little dealing going on and be back in the saddle in no time. I could fix this. Shit, how much worse could it get? This wasn't so bad. Once the sun came up, this'd all blow away like so much smoke. Yah right!

When the sun came up I walked down Sherman Way to Winnetka Avenue and checked my mail. Then I walked up Winnetka to Roscoe Boulevard and headed towards Canoga Avenue and my storage area. While I was walking along Roscoe a brown El Camino pulled to the curb, it was one of my old customers from Micah's that I'd become friends with while building his bike, he was also one of my connections.

He and his ole'lady were on the outs as usual, his place was empty now and he offered me a place to crash and a bike to build. He had the parts to build a bike, but not the skill. I'd build the bike, split the profit when it sold and be back in good shape.

Meantime if I got rid of some dope here and there I'd be even better off when the bike sold. I knew this wouldn't be so bad, in a few days I'd have the bike built and be back on track. In the meantime there's plenty of dope to do and I had a roof over my head, bottoming out didn't seem so bad.

For the next few weeks I sucked up as much dope as Al would lay out and built the bike we talked about. It wasn't anything at all, just a stocker thrown together as cheaply and quickly as possible for fun and profit. Of course once the bike was done another friend of mine and a long time business associate of Al's took the bike as payment for a long outstanding debt, so much for back on my feet in no time. While the battle for the bike was going on Al's wife of sorts came back after yet another spun-out fling with some dude at the beach.

Both Al and his ole'lady'd fried themselves on coke years before and didn't really need drugs to have a life of hell on earth; they were like fire and gasoline, always at each others throats about every little thing. The best thing they could've done was go their separate ways, for the sake of their sanity and everyone else's around them as well. Al was pretty tightly unwound, always dishing out ultimatums. His frenetic personality was always in the forefront ready to freak out at every little thing; his ole'ladies mission in life was to keep him freaking out every waking moment of his life without exception.

While I was at Al's I had my final court date for the shrooms, the probation department had given the go ahead for my diversion. I had one year to complete a drug rehab program of my choice and attend so many NA or AA meetings, my progress was reported to the court monthly by the rehab unit.

I found a rehab right down Desoto Avenue from Al's, within easy walking distance and cheap enough that I could afford it, considering I didn't even have a job.

The very first meeting I attended I was so fucking high I was a constant disruption because I wouldn't keep my mouth shut for more than a few seconds at a time. Every time the counselor asked a question I had a smartass answer for it and a hundred jokes to tell after the answer.

The counselor got so frustrated that she finally gave me a chance to run the class hoping I'd take the hint and shut up. Instead I jumped at the chance to be the consummate bad influence and dismissed the class an hour and a half early. After that she had her hands full trying to get everybody to come back and finish. We finally did and after the class, she in her most professional manner told me that she'd never had to deal with anyone as distracting and unruly before in all her time counseling and she hoped I could be more constructive at the next meeting.

I attended only a few more meetings because I couldn't afford the thirteen dollars it took to attend each meeting and was no more constructive than at the first, I was too poor to pay attention. I didn't have a steady job, what money I did get went to feed one habit or another depending on what I needed at the time. I was still working on Christine one piece at a time as I could afford it and was slowly but surely getting her rebuilt. I attended a very few NA and AA meetings. I thought these people were absolutely pathetic and most of 'em were living proof that "drugs were for people that couldn't handle sobriety."

I attended one meeting in Canoga Park that was mostly cokeheads. This one dude got up to the podium to witness or share, whatever they call it. Before he even spoke he was pasty faced and pouring sweat. His purplish white knuckles had a death grip on the front of the podium like it was gonna fly away and he was shaking like a leaf.

When he started to speak the first thing he said was that he was a friend of Bill W and if it hadn't been for him and his program he'd still be smoking an ounce of coke a day and that thru the help of the friends of Bill W he'd been clean for two months and it was the best time of his life and he was looking forward to a sober life with all the new friends he'd made in the program and thanks to the four meetings he attends every day and all the support he gets from every one of his ten sponsors he'd win his battle with cocaine, alcohol, pot, pills, his wife and kids, his job, the neighbors, the world and waking up in the morning if he could ever fall asleep.

He finished this little tirade a weeping, sobbing, shaking mess. As he was being helped away from the podium in the silent aftermath of his quivering psychotic meltdown, I heard myself saying out loud, "dude if being sober has you this fucked up, you better get ahold of Bill W and have him get you some dope before you blow a gasket!"

I said this as a joke, but every head in the place snapped in my direction simultaneously. If looks could kill I'd've been dead twenty-nine times. The counselor dropped the crybaby and started screaming at me to get out. The crybaby'd been leaning heavily on the counselor and couldn't catch himself before he hit the floor face first, splitting his lip, bloodying his nose, and giving him an instant egg over his eye.

"NOW SEE WHAT YOU'VE DONE," was the cry from the counselor as she waded thru the sea of desks to get at me while everybody else was headed in the other direction to help the crybaby. He was really balling now, blood spraying everywhere from his busted lip and bleeding nose with every gut wrenching sob and wail he emitted. He sounded like a three year old that fell off the swings and wanted his mommy.

The counselor was now in my face like a Marine Corps Drill Instructor, which is a bad place to be over something as stupid and petty as this. She instantly got clothslined back out to arms length and warned to stay back or else. As I headed for the door she fell in behind me screaming for someone to call the police. I walked back over to Al's from there and never went to another one of those stupid meetings.

I say stupid because you won't quit till you want to and all the meetings in the world aren't gonna change that fact. If you don't want a fucked up life don't start using drugs to begin with. Any use will fuck you up, simple as that and you won't ever see it coming till it's too late.

Thru Al I met a whole new circle of cranksters that I drifted into the company of, one of them managed the Kandy Kat, a neighborhood tittie bar in Chatsworth. My time at Al's wasn't but a few weeks, he wanted to start doing bike work out of a little building he had next to his house, which would've been fine except the neighbors immediately had a fit about all the loud traffic. Not a good thing for a drug dealer to have, so that was stopped.

Being a renter Al had rules to live by, the first time the landlord saw me he talked his way out of it. By the next time it happened a friend and huge supplier had been busted with a massive quantity of crank, which temporarily put a hitch in the giddyup of The Valley's drug trade and made some rent payments late.

My illegal presence and Al's ole'ladie's boyfriend stopping by to fire a few rounds thru the front of the house one night put Al on the "soon to be homeless" list if shit didn't quiet down around there. Well you guessed it, I had to go, it was a relief to be outta that war zone, you never knew when the next battle was gonna start or how long it was gonna last, the only thing for sure was it was never gonna stop till one of those two was dead.

For quite some time I drifted from shooting gallery, to crankhouse, to abandoned house, to anyplace I could get outta sight for a while to lay down or snort a line. I took to hanging around the area of Topanga and Devonshire. My dope source was there and some new constructions that weren't quite finished yet provided someplace to get in outta the early morning fog or rain.

I'd become acquainted with some folks that lived just west of that intersection and spent a lot of my time hanging out at the Kandy Kat just east of there. For a while my whole miserable existence revolved around that one square mile of Chatsworth and how much money and dope I could find in it with as little effort as possible.

One of the many characters that I met at the Kandy Kat was a dude named Silly Billy. He'd come into the bar a few nights a week and hang out. The first time I met him he walked up to me, not even knowing my name and with a perfectly straight face said "ya know I've got five kids and I've only fucked my wife one time. How the fuck did that happen?" I burst out laughing so hard the dancer on stage stopped dancing and looked at me like I was nuts. Everybody else in the bar looked at me the same way till they saw who I was talking to. They'd all probably had an equally underwhelming introduction to Billy as well.

Whenever he came into the bar, he always had something equally as crazy to say. Always with a straight face and he always walked away looking bewildered, as if he just couldn't figure something out.

One evening I was standing by the front door when he came in. After breaking us all up, he went over and sat down by the jukebox. After that every time I looked over at him he seemed to be digging at something in his arm. I finally went over and asked him what he was doing. He held his arm up so I could see and said there was a worm in it and he was gonna get it out. I looked at his wrist were he'd pointed to the supposed worm and told him "that's not a worm, that's your vein."

"Oh yah, are you sure?" Was his answer.

"Trust me, you don't wanna fuck with that," I told him and walked away.

A little while later we snorted some dope together out back. When we were done I went in the office and he went back to his seat out front.

Later I walked back out to the front and saw him digging at his arm with a Buck Knife. A few minutes later he walked up blood streaming down his hand from a huge gash in his wrist, held up a three inch section of the vein and said "see I told ya it was a worm." It was only a few minutes before the ambulance got there, good thing the station was close or that spun cookie'd've bled to death.

Sometime I went a couple days without eating; I never stooped to eating out of a dumpster though. As long as I had dope I didn't need to eat that much and if I couldn't find anything else I could always find dope. The manager of The Kat hooked me up with another customer because he had a rare bike and was pretty cool for a supposed lawyer.

He had a Ford pickup with a powerglide transmission that only had first gear. A powerglide only has two speeds, so driving it around the surface streets wasn't bad, it was better than nothing.

Vince also had a Harley that wasn't running quite right, so I made his Harley roar again and he let me drive that pickup. That gave me something to carry my tools with me in. "Have tools will work," was my new name. At least till I got enough to buy some dope and some bike parts, then I'd get high and go park at my storage unit and work on Christine till I ran outta dope or money or parts.

This wasn't the best life, but it was better than the lives of the people I saw in the alley behind the shop in Lynwood. If I was lucky I got a chance to take a real shower once in a while. Otherwise I'd take one outside with a stolen hose at whichever unfinished house I could get into in the early morning hours.

Having the pickup kinda gave me a home on wheels. When the end of the day came after The Kat closed I'd drive up this dirt road that some friends lived on, park and throw my sleeping bag in the back to crash until the sun came up. I didn't think the bottom was so bad, in a few weeks into months I definitely might get Christine done, if the dope held out.

At The Kat I met a classic example of meth bipolarization and Anhedonia. This dude named Doc was flushing his life away with crank while trying to drag himself thru a black hole of depression. If he never got high he'd literally sleep his life away and not think a thing of it. His girlfriend leaving him had caused him to begin wallowing in an Olympic sized pool of despair and self-pity. The way he carried on I thought it'd just happened and sympathized with him at first, but when I found out it'd been over two years my first reaction was what a fuckin' baby, get a grip and move on.

It was hard to catch Doc in anything but a head hung morose funk. Once in a while he'd come to life and talk about the things he wanted to do, but before he was done he'd find any number of ways to shoot himself in the foot and put an end to any ambition he might have. For a few minutes every few weeks he might have half a smile on his face. The rest of the time you'd think he'd just lost his best friend if you saw him at all.

He'd lost his job because he slept thru whole weeks without ever leaving the house. When they shut his power off he solved the problem by climbing the pole near his house and using a set of automotive jumper cables turned it back on. That lasted a long time {about a week}. He was the most depressed person I'd ever met over a girl in my life. It was depressing me to be around the crybaby so I just disappeared and left him to his misery.

Methamphetamine Psychosis At It's Finest

While I was hanging out at The Kat I also got a chance to see the most shining example of full blown methamphetamine psychosis I've ever heard of. I was introduced to a guy named Jim. At one time he'd owned a vending machine service that serviced all the tittie bars in The Valley. Jim'd become immensely attracted to the dancers at these bars and took up using cocaine to have something to lure the girls back to his house with, so he could have his way with 'em. He created quite a little pussy palace for himself with a hot tub outside that had a desert island motif and all kinds of sex toys and porno movies n-shit.

When the girls started becoming more interested in crank than coke he changed his habit and fried to a delicate crunch every brain cell he had in a very short period of time. He became delusional and paranoid to the point of no return, refusing to leave his house because he thought that everybody and I mean *everybody* was an FBI agent spying on him.

He lived on Roscoe Boulevard just west of Topanga Canyon Boulevard. In his front yard, with railroad ties, cut down telephone poles and plywood, facing both directions he erected a billboard that said "help me I am being imprisoned in my own home against my will by the FBI and other government authorities without the benefit of counsel or relief. Under the writ of habeas corpus I cannot be held more than seventy-two hours without being formally charged with a crime. If someone would notify the proper authorities of my situation I would be set free. Someone please help me". That's not word for word but that was the drift of it. He also had this painted on the sides of the van that he drove around in and hundreds of thousands of this same thing printed on little slips of paper stacked several feet deep on a table in one bedroom. Each one was painstakingly hand printed, cut neatly and uniformly stacked.

Before he went crazy with the billboard and shit, he actually got dressed in a suit and carrying a briefcase full of those little handbills went down to the FBI building in L.A. and handed them out to passersby while he made a loud, prolonged, vocal protest in the lobby about being held prisoner in his home. He had an absolute flippin fit at the receptionist when she reminded him that he wasn't in his home, he was downtown. He did that shit every day until they finally got sick of it and had him removed from the property.

After that he got weirder and weirder. He boarded up all the windows in his house from the inside and became obsessed with everything being an antenna that was transmitting everything he said to the FBI.

He cut up his hot tub with a chainsaw in the middle of the night because he said it was an antenna. He threw his dog over the fence into the neighbors yard and refused to let 'em bring it back because he said after he cut up the hot tub antenna, the dog was barking to the FBI in a secret code, telling 'em what was going on. He refused to pay the water bill because the water was full of microphones.

He was so spun, he took the ringer out of his phone and would call you all worked up over something and tell you to call him back in fifteen minutes.

When you told him his ringer didn't work, he'd tell you he could feel the vibrations and slam the phone down.

Sixteen minutes later he'd call you back mad as hell, because you didn't call him back and want you to do it again. He'd get on shit like that for hours and drive you nuts, he was *so* spun that he snorted talcum powder and swore it was the best crank he'd ever done.

He refused to go to the grocery store because there were too many people there and every time he did go he made a huge scene. There was a Ralph's right down the street from his house that was open twenty-four hours. One morning we were in there on the way to his house to check on him and noticed there were hardly any people in there. We thought it might be a good time to get him to get some food in the house.

It took a little while to get him used to the idea, but he came along, finally. As soon as we walked into the store he screamed **"AH HA"** at the top of his lungs, got right in this poor cashier's face and started screaming **"I KNEW IT, YOU CAN'T FOOL ME, THEY'VE TRADED EVERYONE OF YOU FOR FBI AGENTS, YOU'RE ALL AGENTS!"** As soon as he started that shit we grabbed him to haul him outta there, but we didn't get him out fast enough to keep him from scaring the shit outta everybody who heard him.

One night he finally got busted over in Van Nuys driving along in his protest van throwing handfuls of those little flyers everywhere at three o'clock in the morning. In a roundabout way we found out about it and a friend of mine and I went to his house to make sure everything was ok and the place wasn't gonna blow the whole block off the face of the earth because he'd left something on. Who knows what he'd been doing in there, nobody'd heard from him for weeks before we heard about the bust.

The utilities, except the electricity, had been off in the house for a while when we went in; the place was as silent and dark as a tomb. The first thing I noticed was that every hole in everything was covered with tinfoil shiny side to the hole, even the nail holes where pictures used to hang.

The window on the Magic Chef oven was covered with tinfoil. The exhaust fan for the grill had been removed and the hole in the ceiling covered with foil. An acoustic guitar stood in the corner with the strings gone and tinfoil over the resonator hole. Out in the garage the speakers for the stereo were turned upside down so they pointed at the roof and were covered with tinfoil. Everything that had a hole in it was covered with tinfoil.

The house was a typical California ranch. A long hallway ran off the kitchen/living room area to the master bath and bedroom. With three bedrooms and a second bath along the hall. All the way down the hall Jim had strung tripwires. Tin cans with marbles in 'em were tied to 'em as an alarm system. In the bedroom was the ringerless phone.

The whole place gave ya the creeps as you went from room to room seeing firsthand what a complete meltdown looked like close up. I was amazed at the mountain of flyers that were on a table in one of the bedrooms. It looked like he'd made that his printing room. All it had in it was a kitchen table, a chair, pens and paper. It had to've taken him weeks to cut each piece of paper, handprint each one and stack 'em so neatly.

Unless you're charged with a crime you can only be held for 72 hours and littering isn't a jailable offence. Once the cops got an earful of the lunacy that was coming outta Jim's mouth they took him to the VA hospital for observation.

At the hospital they immediately put Jim on Lithium and Haldall which calmed him right down and brought him back from the land of the lost. In a few days he was as right as he was ever gonna be and they released him with a handful of pills and a good luck.

After all that creepy shit, I saw Jim one last time and it creeped me out to be around him so bad I never wanted to see him again. Back then people drifted in-n-outta my life like the wind and I the same in theirs, I used to call it "here taday, gone ta Maui."

Sometime in the midst of all this shit I went to see Micah about a job again; someone had given me the message to call him, so I did. It was a real slap in the face; he hired me to sweep the floor for seven dollars an hour. The job Carlos used to do. I can't believe I took it, I don't know what I was thinking; the first day there Carlos, who was back, was telling *me* what to do. As soon as the floor was swept, he wanted me to work on bikes for seven dollars an hour, while the other mechanics got 50%. I gave him seven dollar an hour work, needless to say it didn't last but a day or two.

4ᵗʰ Of July, Zuma Beach

I'd been stuck in The Valley for months. I had the Ford pickup now and felt like seeing some water. I'd done some bike work that I actually got paid for, so I had some money and some dope. Early on Sunday morning I fired up the Ford and headed down Topanga Canyon Boulevard for PCH. At first I was gonna stop at the first wide spot I saw but the tide was high and there wasn't anyplace to park that was close to any beach. I headed north on PCH thru Malibu, past Pepperdine University and ended up at Zuma Beach when the truck started to run bad.

I pulled into the beach parking lot and parked near the restrooms and showers so I could clean up after I got the truck fixed. It took me until late in the afternoon to find the problem and fix it. As I was packing up to leave for the day the same two sheriffs that I'd spoken to twice and had been watching me most of the day saw an empty beer can roll by the truck, blown by the wind from God knows where.

These two assholes rushed me like I was waving a gun around or something, and me wearing nothing but shorts slammed me to the ground screaming I was under arrest for drinking on the beach.

Once they got me cuffed one picked me up by my hair while the other kicked me in the back and stomach for resisting arrest. They informed me that they were gonna search the truck for drugs, alcohol and weapons. I said "fine", the only thing in there was my dope. The only thing I had was a bluff. I figured they'd give it a quick once over and go back to kicking my ass which seemed like the only thing they wanted to do.

They found the dope and asked me what it was.

I told 'em I didn't know what it was. I'd borrowed the truck from a friend for the day, it'd fucked up on the way out there and I spent the day fixing it and they spent the day watching me do it.

They told me to my face like I was some kind of idiot that the first time they saw me was when they arrested me.

"Okay if I've been drinking, do you smell alcohol on my breath?"

They said they didn't have to, the beer can was all the evidence they needed, then they went back to the bag of dope. I watched 'em take out their little test kit and drop a drop of bleach on some of the dope; it turned into goo at the bottom of the bag and they ran outta steam.

As they dragged me to the car and threw me inside they kept telling me I had one more chance to tell 'em what was in the bag or else. I told 'em their guess was as good as mine and wished 'em good luck.

At the Malibu substation we played twenty questions until the cops gave up. I asked when I was gonna blow in the breathalyzer to prove I hadn't been drinking. They slammed me up against the wall and told me that I wasn't under arrest for drinking, I was under arrest for drugs and put me back in a cell.

The next morning before I ever went to court they woke me up and kicked me out the door, charges dropped. I walked out to PCH and started hitchhiking back toward The Valley. It took me all day to get there and I did a lotta walking. When I finally got there that evening Doc was at the bar, that was good I was gonna need a ride out to the impound yard to get the truck ASAP because the bill was getting bigger every day.

When Vince came into the bar later that evening and heard about his truck, he was afraid the cops would fuck with him over it or something and said he wasn't gonna get it out.

Great now I've gotta get my toolbox and all my shit outta the truck before I lose that too. The next day Doc and I took a drive out to Malibu and got my stuff. The impound yard wasn't gonna let me have it at first, but after a heated discussion on the matter they called the cops and the cops told 'em to release it.

Riding On The Metro

One evening at the Kandy Kat Al showed up wanting to know if I wanted to work. He'd rented a garage out in Simi Valley in the Santa Susanna Knolls. I could crash on the couch there and make some money working on stuff, plus I was closer yet to a good source of dope. Well sure, why not, I wasn't doing anything and it was getting close to the rainy season anyway, time to have a roof over my head.

The next day I moved onto my new home, a grungy old couch in an old gas station in The Knolls. Beggars can't be choosers can they? As bad as I was getting with the dope I could've had it a lot worse. If I could keep it together long enough to get Christine back together again, I'd be all right. I had a shop of sorts now. It wasn't set up for bikes but I could make due long enough to get Christine done. All it'd take is money now to get my frame back from Pete; everything else was ready to go back together.

That morning I met the "crew" I'd be working with, a dude named Monte. The first thing we did as soon as Al was outta the way was duck out to this old bread truck that was on blocks next to the shop and "go bowling."

While we were sitting in there I noticed that the make of the old delivery van was a Metro. "Riding on the Metro" was a popular punk song at that time and it immediately began playing through my head when the thought struck. After that it was a little private joke between Monte and I about riding on the Metro to go bowling and a way of saying lets get stoned in mixed company, namely Al.

Being out there was pretty cool for a while, there was a bar fifty steps in either direction from the door. A bike shop right across the street and a bunch 'a crazy people of all kinds to get to know. Before my time in The Knolls was done I was voted an honorary Knoller by my friends there, which probably doesn't sound like much to you but unless you've been to The Knolls and know some of the folks there you wouldn't understand anyway.

The only thing that sucked about being out there for me was the lack of wheels. Without 'em it felt like you were pretty far out there. It was only a fifteen minute drive to The Valley from there but it was a hell of a long walk, a definite deterrent to a night of partying there. The only entertainment available for the nights when there was no money for the bar was a nineteen inch black and white TV, with rabbit ears covered in tin foil, for slightly better than shitty reception. The only station it got was a WB station from Oxnard.

Out of boredom in the few months that I was there I managed to get myself arrested for carrying a concealed weapon, which would've been a misdemeanor had I not already been a convicted felon. Thru some twist of California law, once a felon always a felon no matter what you do, at least that's how it seemed to be for me. I was held overnight at the West Valley facility and bussed to Van Nuys Court in the morning.

After spending the day there I was released with time served and probation for the gun and the illegal attachment of plates to the car I was driving, which was the reason I got stopped in the first place. I could've been charged with a few other things besides, neither the plates nor the vehicles they came from were mine, shit could've been a lot worse. That right there was probably the stupidest fucking thing I'd ever done in my life, but for the next few months it seemed like I was on a "stuck on stupid" hell ride, doing every idiot thing that came down the pike.

It wasn't long before my welcome at the garage was so worn out it was transparent and so was I because I wasn't seen around there again. That didn't stop me from continuing on down the spiral even further with every step I took.

For a while I had a hundred dollar car. With it, I made a trip down to the shop in Orange County that Pete had moved to. From what I understood he and Vince had a falling out shortly after I'd been fired and Pete'd moved to the Broken Spoke, a bike shop in Fullerton.

My frame had been done for quite some time. When I got down there I was stoked with all the work Pete had done to it, yet managed to keep it looking stock in spite of the stretching and raking.

A `57 straightleg frame was a very rare frame to have and mine was stock right down to the toolbox and sidecar mounts. Harley frames up to `56 were wishbone frames, the front downtubes curved outward before going down to the front motor mount from the steering head. In `57 they straightened those curves and in `58 went to a double drop swingarm frame, making the `57 a one year only frame.

The bill was five hundred and fifty dollars, which of course I didn't have on me at the time, but Pete did the framework for a shop in The Valley called Vic's. I knew Vic well enough and arranged to send the money to Pete and have him ship the frame to Vic, where it'd be much easier for me to pick up in case I didn't have a vehicle. Of course if I had one I'd drive down and pick it up myself. Once our business was done we did another bump to supplement the blast we did when I first got there and caught up with each other before being lost for good.

The old Oldsmobile I'd bought for a hundred dollars was on it's last leg and I didn't wanna break down in the dark on an L.A. freeway this far from home. I lived in the car and it'd suck to leave my house and all my shit in it on the side of the freeway so I got headed back to Simi Valley while it was still light. Now all I had to do was come up with the cash and a few hours of work later I'd be back in the saddle again.

I don't remember exactly how I met Richard and the chronology of things isn't really coming to me. Shortly after I met Richard I parked the Olds in the wrong place at the wrong time and got rousted by the cops. Between my last bust and this one the diversion had defaulted and a warrant was issued. I was taken into custody and shipped to L.A. County the next day. The day after I went before the judge in Metro Court at the jail and sang him a sad song. He reinstated my probation, ordered me to return to rehab in the next thirty days and released me.

It took till the next morning to walk out the door and all day to make it from the central jail in downtown L.A. to Simi Valley. When I got to Simi I walked from the freeway to Richard's. He and I went down to the impound yard and got the Olds outta hawk. If I'm not mistaken Richard loaned me the money to get my mobile home back.

When we got back to his place I parked in front of his house at night to sleep after that.

A few days later Richard and I were talking about ways to make that money fast. Richard was into all kinds of things and knew all kinds of people.

A few days after our conversation he made me a present of a Mossberg 510A pump riot gun. A week or so after that he'd hooked up a way to make money with it. He knew a guy that would pay eight hundred dollars to gun hands that'd go with him to rob mules that snuck in from Mexico to deliver drugs, pot was our target.

We drove over to Tucson and waited in a motel for the dude to show up for the delivery. When he did we took the pot he had and his American money and sent him packing back to Mexico. We drove back to Simi with a trunk full of pot, getting stoned all the way. When we went thru the produce check at the California state line we were amazed that they didn't smell it when we pulled up, we could all smell it like we were sitting in the middle of it. We made it home with no problem and collected our cash the next day.

The first thing I did was get some dope, the second thing I did was get a room at the Motel 6 and sleep one night in a real bed. The shower felt so good I took four of 'em while I was there. I now had the money for my frame, things were looking up finally. I called the Broken Spoke to tell Pete I'd be down first thing the next day to get my frame.

I'd missed a real person by minutes, the shop closed early that day and wouldn't be open till the following Wednesday because they'd all taken off for a bike run up north. Fuck, if I had my frame I could be riding by Wednesday.

The next morning on my way to Richard's house the Olds overheated for the very last time, by the time I got to his house the old thing was hissing and pinging and was so hot it'd barely run.

Well this was fucking great, I've gotta waste almost a week before I can get my frame and now the car was dead, maybe I could fix the car in the meantime. I did a line, dug the tools outta the trunk and went to work. When I got the heads off, the valve pockets in several chambers had huge heat cracks in 'em several were cracked right thru the valve seat. Being a dedicated tweaker always looking for something impossible to fail at, I decided to try to fix the heads.

A friend of mine had a service truck with a welder and a compressor on it. It wasn't too hard to talk him into coming over and welding the cracks for me, then letting me keep The Knolls up with the roaring compressor till the cops came and shut me down.

That's not the first time that'd happened either, on Thanksgiving I'd been porting a set of big block heads. The shop compressor couldn't keep up with the air gun I was using and I was having to stop all the time to let the compressor catch up. Wade and another friend stopped by and before they left for good Wade had gotten the truck, parked it in front of the shop and I was using it to power the gun. The compressor on that truck was a beast and bellowed like one. It put out more air than my gun could use up.

I'd been snorting lines and working on those heads all day and night, I had no idea what time it was or anything when the guy that owned the shop came busting thru the door hollering at me to turn the thing off and leave it off until morning. I didn't realize it was four in the morning; the last time I'd paid any attention was around seven o'clock the night before when Monte'd brought me Thanksgiving dinner. I'd wolfed it down and gone back to work; as long as I had work to do I kept on working. I never even thought of the roaring of that old compressor keeping half of Simi Valley awake.

After I got the welds ground down, I lapped the valves back into the seats by hand, which took a lotta dope and days to do. A new gasket set and I put the thing back together. I made sure it was getting gas and all that shit and turned the key. What a waste 'a time, that thing wasn't ever gonna run again, not with that motor in it anyway.

Sleeping in the car came to an end one night when a cop spotted me getting in the car late at night and not driving away. Just as I got comfortable he knocked on the window and jacked me up, if Richard hadn't come outta the house I'd've ended up taking another ride in a cop car. After that I crashed in a little room above the party house out back of the main house till Richard's mom got sick of seeing my face along with all the other undesirables that dropped in all day every day.

She was sick of the constant party that went on there, it was her house and she was especially sick of me like every other parent had been ever since I could remember. There's been something about me since I was little that scares people, especially parents. They lock car doors at intersections, go outta their way to get outta my way at the mall, avoid eye contact and try to scoot by unnoticed. My buddy Ralph'll tell ya he knew me for years before he ever saw anyone just walk up and start talking to me and it's still that way today.

Anyway we found a friend with a four wheel drive truck, hooked it up to the Olds and towed it thru The Knolls, up Black Canyon Road, past the Dead Head Ranch, almost to the gate of Rocket Dyne. We turned left on Wolsley Canyon Road, followed it almost to the end and turned right onto a wheel rut of a road that lead to an abandoned house and some outbuildings on about sixteen acres of abandoned land and that's where me n-the Olds got dumped.

If I remember right this place was called Hippie Hollow by the folks that I was hanging out with. There were other tenants that lived in this staging area for hell as well, each of us was there awaiting whatever fate the great meth god had in store for us. All of us had more than less ended up there. This wasn't a place that anyone would choose to go; this truly was *a staging area for hell*. The only way to go from here was down.

This place was as close to hell as you could get without getting burned, you could definitely smell the brimstone and feel the heat from there and at the right time of night you could even see the flames.

Now all I had was this end of the world dump and the dope that came through it. **By now that was all that was left, dope**. There was nothing else, but the few things that I could carry in a bag. Everything I cared about was in a storage unit that seemed like it was in another country, outta sight and outta mind. Dope was the only thing here, other than that nothing else at all, nothing but a few abandoned buildings full of tweaked thru remnants of wasted lives, the same thing my life had turned into.

We spent days into weeks doing nothing but drugs; there wasn't anything else to do. The only thing we had in the way of utilities was water from a spigot at the meter up near the end of the driveway. All the wire and plumbing had been scrapped out of all the buildings for dope money. The buildings had stood open for years and were full of trash from all the stuff the cranksters that drifted their way to this end of the world place like me dragged back from dumpster diving, burglaries and all other forms of unsavory activities.

The place came under surveillance shortly after or maybe it was when I got there I don't know. Sheriff's Department helicopters would circle overhead during the day with a dude hanging out the door with a camera, so you kept outta sight as much as possible and tried to not be filmed. When the helicopters weren't circling sometime up to six cars would sit in the turnout on Wolsley Canyon Road and film for hours.

I remember one spun-out afternoon when we dragged a bunch of old furniture, couches, chairs of all kinds and arranged 'em in rows one behind another, kinda' like bus seats and started watching the cops in the turn around right back. They weren't hiding what they were doing, there were six cars, two had parabolic mics sticking out the side windows of their cars and they all had cameras rolling.

To give 'em something to listen to, we started talking about the bus to hell leaving the staging area at sundown and on-n-on, the further on it went the more carried away and outrageous the conversation became. We spent hours spinning all this elaborate bullshit and they spent hours listening.

When we first noticed 'em there was only two or three of us, by the time the sun was going down there were seven or eight of us and we were playing the bus to hell game to best of our spun-out abilities. Once it was completely dark they drove off and the game was over. I got to the staging area shortly after New Years of 1990 and I don't remember leaving there until......

February 23rd 1990, 7:00am

I'd lain down to rest on my pile of rags just before sunup after many hard days of tweaking. When I laid down I got a strong odor of unwashed body and crank. I couldn't remember the last time I'd bathed, but the crank smelled good. I slept the sleep of the damned, not really sleeping just lying still even though my mind was screaming around at warp three inside me.

I'd made a bed from a pile of old mattresses and rags, my sleeping bag and a poncho liner, in what used to be the main bedroom of the dilapidated main house that was my home.

The house looked like a bomb'd hit it and continued to hit it every day. Every inch of the floor was covered in trash from picked over lives; the ceiling had fallen in in many places because the roof leaked like a sieve.

There was broken glass from alcohol bottles and windows, broken needled rusty rigs, ceiling debris and all kinds of filth to wade thru to get to one of the only places where the roof didn't leak. It was there that I awaited my trip to hell. In the middle of the wind whipped rainy nights of that January and February's rainy season I lay there wired staring into the darkness wishing for death or anything to deliver me from this place.

When there wasn't any dope to do, the days without food were sorely felt and the depression that took over was so deep and dark that dying would've been an improvement. Laying on that pile of rags in the dark *or the light*, watching the rain pour in from everywhere soaking everything around my little dry spot, wondering how much further down I could go, how I ever got here and how I'd ever get out was all there was to do.

At 7:00AM on February 23rd that question was answered when every door was kicked the rest of the way off it's hinges and every broken window was broken again as cops from five different departments rushed in, guns drawn, screaming orders. They jacked me up, cuffed me up, stuck some pants on me, stuck my feet in my boots and marched me and the shotgun outside. A few minutes later a cop threw my jacket on top of me and that was how I was taken to the Malibu substation for booking. I was charged with a felon being in possession of a deadly weapon {a sawed off shotgun that the barrel length was a sixteenth of an inch too short on}.

Once in a cell it felt good to take a shower and put on semi clean cloths. When I was booked I weighed one hundred and eleven pounds and although I was still wired all of that day and most of the night it felt good to eat when meals came around. The first thing I did was call Clay to see if he could get Christine before the tweakers at Hippie Hollow invaded my storage unit and scrapped her out. I gave him Richard's number, he was the only one I knew that had a phone and could find Terry.

The only thing I could do was give the key to this gal Terry {one of the other tenants} and hope that she'd hook up with Clay and get at least Christine to a safe place. It had to be done soon because the rent on the unit would be up and it had to be empty before they seized it for the bill.

Clay agreed to come down as soon as he could to take care of it; thank God Terry kept her word and got Christine and as much other stuff taken care of as she could take care of for me too.

The next day I went to court for my arraignment and met my dump truck. I was informed by him that because the case was a felony it'd be moved to Santa Monica Court and I'd be transferred to the central jail that afternoon by the daily court bus. That was not what I wanted to hear, I figured that I could plead out from this court and be back on the streets in a couple 'a weeks after having some detox and recovery time in this country club atmosphere.

Early that evening we were cuffed together two by two and lead to the waiting bus for the trip downtown. On the way out the driveway, I saw in the impound lot across the street the Ford pickup I'd been busted at Zuma Beach in the summer before. It looked like I felt, fucked, rode hard and put away wet.

The next thirty-four hours was spent in a wonderful place called IRC {Inmate Receiving Center}, being stuffed into one overcrowded cell after another in between physical exams, fingerprints, warrant checks, delousing, and getting dressed in. The next place you go is to the nine thousand floor, where a thousand inmates are stuffed into a dormitory with a capacity of three hundred and classified for transfer.

This was a dangerous fuckin' place! At the time of my incarceration the population was roughly twenty-eight thousand inmates in the entire system. The number of blacks was roughly sixty-five percent, the Mexican population was thirty-three percent, the last two percent was white and most of those were suburbanites and kids doing DUI time that had never seen anything like this in their lives. I hadn't either but at least I had the good sense to find my own kind and stay there.

The nine thousand floor was probably the most dangerous part of the jail. The inmates there'd just come in off the street for all kinds of crimes up to and including murder. Gangbangers from every gang in L.A. roamed the dorm in packs, taking whatever they wanted by any means necessary and fighting other gangs for the right to rob somebody of anything.

One of the things that made this place so dangerous, was that everybody that had money on 'em when they came in was allowed to keep forty dollars or whatever they had less than that on their person, because when you got into the population you could go to the inmate store weekly.

This money was given to you in a little manila envelope that you carried in the only pocket you had until you made a money bag of your own. The pocket was on the chest of your shirt so everybody in the place knew you had money as soon as you walked thru the door, making you an instant target.

Another thing was if you had sneakers on, you kept 'em to wear while you were inside. You also kept eye glasses and one religious item, some people had rosaries. If the sneakers couldn't be beaten off your feet or obtained by any other means, the laces would be cut and they'd be slid right off your feet in your sleep. You didn't ever take your sneakers off except when ordered to by a deputy and you used 'em as your pillow when you slept if you wanted to keep 'em.

The second day on the nine thousand floor we peckerwoods {white boys} had gotten ahold of five joints from a friend of mine that was the trustee that handed you your towel roll when you entered the dorm. There were only four white dudes out of a thousand inmates in the whole dorm and we bunked together and never went anywhere alone if we could help it.

Myself and another dude had just come back from inhaling a whole joint in two hits in the men's room and were sitting on the top bunks of the peckerwood area watching the free-for-all going on around us and making the best of a horrible situation.

While we're sitting there a middle-aged white dude wearing gold rimmed eye glasses, new white and black L.A.Gear high-tops, with his envelope sticking out of his pocket wandered by with a dazed look on his face. We'd seen that look on all kinds of faces in the last day or so. When he got close we "hey'd" him over to find out why he was there and to warn him to stick close to this area or else.

He told us that there was some mistake; he was only supposed to do the weekend in jail for DUI at the substation near his home. It was only his second time in jail. The first time'd been his local substation when he was arrested and that'd only been overnight. He was sure the mistake'd be found and he'd be brought back to the right place shortly. We just laughed and explained the odds of that happening before he was released on Monday, if he was released on Monday were pretty slim.

When he heard this he kinda' got this panicky look on his face and said he had to go talk to someone that could fix this. We pointed him toward the window in the control booth and told him good luck and if he knew what was good for him, after he was done getting abused by the deputies that really didn't give a shit where you thought you were supposed to be, he'd better head right back in this direction.

As soon as he was outta sight we forgot about him, there was too much activity to keep track of to keep tabs on just one dude. The next time we saw him he had a black eye that was cut top and bottom where somebody'd punched him in the face hard enough that his glasses {which were gone}had cut him, his shirt pocket and envelope was gone and he was barefoot. He'd never gotten to the window before someone blindsided him, dragged him into a corner and took everything but his blues {jail cloths}.

While he was telling us the story a fight broke out across the room, in an instant deputies with batons were everywhere clubbing every head that wasn't on a bunk or on the floor. After the wave of deputies washed by us we got up topside to see what was going on. In just a few seconds deputies appeared carrying a stretcher, we watched as they loaded a limp black figure on it and covered it from head to ankles, covering the face and leaving the feet exposed. As they were going out the door with the guy the old man caught a glimpse of him and went "those are my shoes!" Nothing he could do now.

Once the body was removed we were all lined up, put out on the roof and strip searched for weapons while they shook down the entire dorm and everybody's stuff in the place. They also had a shitload of blood to clean up because the dude they carried out of the place'd had his throat cut from ear to ear and had bled out pretty fast.

For sixteen hours we sat in the drizzle, the sun, whatever the weather until they were done. When we got back inside the first thing I did was check the mattress that I'd hid the joints in, they were still there. As soon as things quieted down from coming back inside we went to the restroom and smoked another joint in two hits.

When we came back it was real quiet in the dorm. As we walked thru the door stoned-to-the-bone and probably looking it, everybody turned and looked at us that was near enough to notice us.

We went to our area and talked quietly as we sat on the top bunks watching for the next thing to pop off. It wasn't long before there were a few black dudes standing in front of us smiling like we owed 'em money. The littlest one was the closest to us, so he did the talking. He said they were Compton Crips and that if we shared our dope with 'em they'd give us protection, if not they didn't know what was gonna happen.

My answer to them was "what dope?"

"So that's how it is? We'll see **muthafucka!**" They walked away looking at us over their shoulders and whispering and laughing to each other, eventually we lost sight of 'em.

Suddenly we were surrounded by deputies and getting jerked off the bunks, all of our stuff was rounded up with us and brought out onto the roof. We were each stripped by two deputies a piece and searched, including as far up our asses as they could get without transportation. While that was being done everything we had was examined thoroughly by two more deputies. When they were done we were told to give up our dope and the possession would be overlooked. I just looked at 'em like I had The Crips earlier and said "what dope?"

When we walked back in The Crips from earlier were standing by the corner of the control booth waiting to say something when we walked by. As we did they said they had other tricks too and if they couldn't have any dope nobody would. I wheeled around on the punk and hollered right in his face **"I DON'T HAVE ANY DOPE, I DON'T WANT ANY DOPE, SO STOP TRYING TO GET ME TO BUY THOSE PENCIL SHAVINGS YOU'RE TRYING TO PASS OFF AS DOPE AND GO BUG SOMEBODY ELSE!"**

We didn't get three steps beyond the dudes before deputies had us all up against the wall. When they asked me what I was hollering about. I told 'em that that guy'd been trying to get me to buy dope from him for the last two days and wouldn't leave me alone about it. It was him and his buddies turn to get their asses turned into parking garages by those savages. I'd had enough 'a their shit.

The cops still hadn't found the dope, so while our friends were getting reamed out on the roof we smoked each of the rest of 'em in two hits a piece. Operating on the assumption that if it was inside us with nothing but ashes on the outside, they'd never find it. Smoking it all at once was better than losing it to the cops, catching another beef and possibly getting more time. Not to mention possessing dope in any penal facility is as big a felony as dealing is on the street, adding big years to sometimes little cases. Like me, the case I was in there on wasn't really that big, but throw an inside possession on top of it and gladiator school here I come.

When our friends returned from playing "hide the nightstick" with the turnkeys they didn't look like they were in a very good mood. It was a good thing a long list of movement lines had come down and they were starting to be called. Finally my name was called; I'd be going to the modules now, thank God. It took hours of standing in line on the roof before we were finally brought to our assigned areas.

The modules were four to eight man cells tiered up like a penitentiary, the only thing better about it was all the movement lines from there went in the daytime. You didn't have to stay awake for days waiting for your name to be called at all hours of the night or be jacked up every minute for a search or a fight.

I spent a week in the modules before I was moved to a trustee dorm. A trustee dorm is usually your final stop in the big jailhouse shuffle unless you're lucky enough to go to Wayside Honor Ranch or Biscalue Center {probably isn't spelled right, hooked on phonics works for me}, both were minimum security facilities where you actually got to go outside during the day.

The first job I was assigned was officer's salad chef and to do this job you had to be clean shaven. I had a full beard down to the middle of my chest and hair down to the middle of my back and had no intention of cutting it. I did have the intention of finding every way to get over and use my slight freedom to the best of my ability.

As a salad chef all I did was make salads of all different types for the cops. Clean up the area and I was done. There was another dude that worked with me, a black dude from south central named Walker. He was also my Bunkie upstairs. There were only two salad chefs in the whole kitchen and it was considered by frequent insiders to be the best job in the jail. Fuck that! I wasn't shaving.

On my first day at work Walker gave me the grand tour. On that tour while we were visiting one of the elevator crews I was given a donut with frosting and sprinkles on it. Inmates got plain old stale ass, dry as a bone donuts and not too many of those at that.

Deputies got fresh frosted donuts with sprinkles on 'em and filled donuts, éclairs and stuff like that and they all came in right through that elevator. Greasing the right palm with something I could get would ensure my receiving a box of officer's donuts all my own on Saturday morning when they were delivered. These could be sold for money or traded for dope or other items that I couldn't find myself.

It was pretty simple for me to find something to trade with, I had access to everything in the kitchen, even Sherman Block's private freezer full of ice cream and frozen lobster, steaks and gourmet foods from all over the world. While the guys upstairs were eating slop prepared in hundred gallon vats by other inmates who didn't give a shit about anything or anyone; I could make my own steaks and other meals, drink as much milk as I wanted and actually do very little work. They were right this was the best job in the whole jail. I still wasn't shaving.

The next day as soon as I got downstairs I made a bunch of Dagwood sandwiches and brought 'em around to all the different inmates that worked downstairs but didn't have access to the foods that I did. Even though the entire downstairs is wired with cameras I got away with doing this right in front of 'em for days before I finally got caught in the wrong area.

The color suit you wore determined where you could go in the kitchen, inmates that wore all white like me could go everywhere, but visiting the different elevators too frequently and being caught on camera or in person will get someone on your case. For me that was Deputy Alvarez. He was an ex-Marine that thought that the Marine Corps bullshit was good for inmates as well as Marines and tried to force that on his kitchen crew. Not only did he fuck with the crew in the kitchen, but he made our lives upstairs hell as well.

Every evening he was on duty we'd have a Marine Corps style inspection of the dorm, one of his pet peeves was what they called Irish pennants or repelling ropes. Irish pennants are the little strings that hang off the seams of your shirts and pants, repelling ropes are a longer version of the same. In a Marine Corps inspection having any of these will fail you.

Inmates in the county jail made these things called money bags by unraveling socks or underwear elastic waistbands, spinning the threads into another type of thread and weaving a money bag to hide your money in. It was designed to expand as your bank increased, hang around your waist and lay by your balls. Because that was the only place another inmate'd never get caught feeling around and when you get patted down that's the one place they don't feel is your balls, unless the deputy's gay.

The reason you don't want the deputies to find your money is because you're only allowed to have forty dollars, max. If you've got any brains at all as soon as you get assigned somewhere in the jail you start running some kinda' game to make money. Personally I got up to six hundred dollars at one time before I was released. Only problem with that is ya can't take it with ya when you leave, you've gotta spend it before you go. That even poses a problem at the little inmate store, cause you can't walk up and spend a couple hundred dollars every time the store comes around without attracting attention. Sometime rules are just a bitch to live by I'll tell ya.

When guys'd make these bags and everybody makes one, they'd leave some of the strings hangin' from the posts of the bunks that they used to spin the threads on. It'd get this Deputy Alvarez's panties in a wad big time every time. One of the very first nights I was there when he was on duty he came in and had a flippin' conniption fit about a couple 'a strings hangin' off an empty bunk in the back of the room. With the kind of hysterics he threw over those little strings you'd think the world was gonna end.

After inspection was done and he was gone I went in the gear locker and got an old mop head; from the strings on that mop head I hung so much string on the bottom of my bunk it looked like fringe. My Bunkie wasn't a real "rock the boat" kinda' guy, he was more of an under the radar hustler that enjoyed all the comforts that our job gave him and when he saw all that stuff hangin' from the bottom of my bunk he knew there was gonna be hell to pay tomorrow night. All evening long people would walk by and comment on my decorating skills and the probable effect it'd have on my intended victim.

I went thru the whole day doin' everything I could to drive Alvarez nuts while I was downstairs. By that evening he'd already had as much of me as he could handle long before he ever got to our dorm.

The inspection started on the other side of the room. Between the anticipated explosion that was gonna happen when he finally got to me and the looks from everybody near me that was waiting for the same thing, it was all I could do to keep from exploding with laughter before he ever got there.

When he finally turned the corner on our row he was in front of the bunk next to me when he noticed my decorating talent. As he stared at my handiwork a line of purple rose out of his shirt and engulfed his whole head. A nanosecond later every vein in his head was a half inch tall pulsing blue line and he was vibrating. His eyes were on fire and foam was flying from his mouth as he tried to spit out something coherent. After a little spitting and sputtering he finally exploded **"WHAT THE FUCK'S THIS, FOR CHRISS-SAKES?"**

As he was gathering steam I stood there smiling like I knew something I wouldn't tell. When he finally blew I acted as hurt as I could and said in my best effeminate voice "I thought you said you wanted strings" and broke down like my feelings'd just been demolished and I was headed for a double lung sob fest.

When he saw and heard this, the top of his head came off, twirled around in the air a dozen times, slammed back into place and he screamed in incoherent Spanglish for five minutes before he went storming outta the dorm and down the hall. I guessed that was the end of the inspection.

The other deputies had all they could do to keep from laughing in front of us, but when they got in the control booth where they thought we couldn't hear or see 'em they were rolling with laughter and imitating him the rest of the night.

When shift change happened a little after lights out, you could hear 'em telling the story for the new crew and all of 'em laughing their asses off about it again. Walker was amazed I didn't get "rolled up" {sent back to the modules for reassignment} and glad the dorm didn't get tossed over it. I didn't even think about that, but if the dorm'd been tossed and anybody'd gotten busted doing whatever they were doing, I'd've probably had my throat cut in my sleep for being the cause of it.

The next afternoon when we went downstairs he had all this extra work he thought he was gonna pile on me. The first thing I did was make my Dagwood sandwiches and hand 'em out. At my last drop he caught up with me and busted me for handing out unauthorized food to unauthorized inmates and leaving my work area without permission. He brought me back to the control area, gave me blues, made me change right there, give him the whites and rolled me up back to the modules.

I went upstairs got my stuff and reported to the modules. The next morning right after breakfast my name was called for a transfer line and I was back in the kitchen, less than twenty-four hours after the roll up, washing dishes in the officer's scullery.

Talk about panties in a wad, we heard Alvarez in the control room screaming about wanting me gone throughout the entire basement of the jail. When he came outta the control room his face had that pretty reddish purple hue from the night of the inspection. I thought he looked so good in that color that I made it my mission the whole time I was there to keep him colored up like that as much as I could.

The window to the scullery looked right out onto the officers dining floor. You've heard of whistling while you worked. I bellowed Guns-n-Roses songs at the top of my lungs the whole time I worked. Welcome to the Jungle, I Used to Love Her But I Had to Kill Her and Dancing With Mr. Brownstone seemed to be the most disliked songs of my repartua so I bellowed them nonstop the whole time I was washing dishes.

When I wasn't washing dishes I was sneaking food to all my old customers again. You see dish washers wore dirty white suits as opposed to the cleaned and pressed ones I'd worn on my first job, but white was white and it took the deputies a few days to figure out that I wasn't supposed to even be near the reefers now, nyuck, nyuck, nyuck.

When I did get caught again it was by my buddy Alvarez and I was back in the kitchen in even less time after this "roll up". Which pissed him off so much that the purple wave'd wash over him every time he saw me; I always went out of my way to do things that'd make a lifed-out {still living the Marine Corps way in the real world} ex-Marine's blood boil. It was the only form of entertainment in there and what made it so entertaining was the reaction I always got out of him, if he wasn't so anal and didn't react so spastically I'd've quit right after I began. Thanks to my dedication to making his every moment on duty a living hell I was rolled up eleven times by him and brought back in less than twenty-four hours each time, nyuck, nyuck, nyuck!

Since being arrested violated my probation from the Compton Court. Shortly after I was locked up I took a bus ride down to Compton and made my last appearance on that case. The court revoked my probation, gave me time served and my second drug felony went on my record. Now I had two drug felonies, a weapons felony on the way and was working toward another weapons felony and the state of California was talking about instituting a three strike law. Three felonies of the same type and you get life; well I was becoming a two category contestant in that game of roulette and would soon be able to lose on either of two categories or possibly on both at once and get double life. Gimme the dice, it's my throw again!

The next case to be taken care of was the CCW case in Van Nuys. Another bus ride and my probation was revoked there too and I was given time served, that was my first weapons felony. Now that I only had the one case in Santa Monica to have adjudicated I was put on a bus early one morning to go to Wayside. That was fine with me it'd been a few months since I'd been outside except for bus rides, searches or recreation on the roof and I was looking forward to seeing the sun again.

While we were in the transfer cells in IRC waiting to be cuffed I ran into a dude I hadn't seen since I was brought into the jail, we'd gone thru IRC together and got split up on the nine thousand floor.

When we met Armstrong told me he was from south central, what started our conversation was his hair cut. He called it a sprout; it was shaved on the sides and grew straight up on top, making him look like a taller drink of water than he already was. He was six foot six inches with probably six or eight inches of hair on the top of his head which made him look a lot taller. To my five foot eleven inch ass he seemed pretty tall, being as thin as he was exaggerated his height and having to duck thru the doors finished the picture.

Being called for transfer lines always sucked because you spent hours stuffed into cramped little IRC cells waiting for God knows what. You're not told anything about why you were called out. You could either spend it isolated in yourself and probably become somebody's target for something or getting to know more about other people's lives on the streets and how and why they'd did what they did to be where we were. I've always been interested in how we get where we are and what brought us there, that was why The Ghost of PCH interested me so much. I usually spent the waiting time making at least one acquaintance.

When we got off the bus at Wayside, the sun was bright and the air was fresh and clean. That was one thing out of many that sucked about the central jail, the recirculated air. All it took was one guy with a cold to infect the entire jail in just a few days. It's more common to get sick within a few days of incarceration and stay sick until you get out than not. The fresh air and sunshine at Wayside took care of that in just a few days for me.

Once you get your job assignment {everybody works at the ranch} you're pretty much free from seven in the morning till ten at night. All you have to do is show up for work and chow and stand all your counts and formations and you're good to go. They had a library, a game building and movie lounge, a snack bar, a ball field and plenty of room to walk around and enjoy the fresh air and sunshine. It was an easy way to do time compared to the central jail.

Armstrong and I got split up again because we had different jobs. Just like in the military you were housed by the different jobs you did and the hours worked. The job I had the first time I went to Wayside was in the chow hall of course, which sucked because of the hours you worked. Your day started at 2:30AM when you started breakfast. That was finished around 7:30AM. You had about an hour and a half till you started lunch. That was finished around 2:00PM. An hour and a half and dinner got started. That was over between 6:30 and 7:00PM. Once you relaxed a little and got a shower it was nine and lights out was at ten. You did this every day until you got transferred or released. It wasn't very long before life started to really suck.

Life had started to suck for me when I was called for a transfer line one morning for no reason. I wasn't the only one either. Armstrong was standing in the crowd waiting for his bus ride to hell as well. Neither of us could figure out what this was for. We didn't have any court dates or anything like that, none of us did. Whenever this happens without a reason it always makes ya nervous. Mostly because you'd just as soon not go back to the jail until you're due for release and none of us were due for release either.

The reason for the bus ride was some bullshit doctor's visit that turned out to be the drunken jail doctor asking me if I felt ok.

I told him "I did until I got jacked outta bed to ride down here for this bullshit!"

His answer was that he was just doing his job.

The deputy was as nice as the doctor. After he pulled me outta line, shoved me face first into the wall and smacked me across the back of the thighs with his flashlight. He informed me that I should feel lucky to be able to see the doctor. I recognized that mutilated Spanglish accent and told him I'd feel lucky if it was actually a doctor I was seeing.

When he pulled me off the wall and shoved me back toward the line I looked around, it was my old buddy Alvarez. I immediately started in on him. Midsentence Armstrong whispered in my ear "you ain't gonna git back ta Wayside dat way." My mouth clapped shut so hard if my tongue had been in the way I'd've bitten it off. I leaned back and thanked my friend outta the corner of my mouth. You're not supposed to talk in line and I really didn't wanna get popped for that too.

The whole day was a nerve wracker for myself and all the other inmates that got jacked by this bullshit bus ride. After we all saw the doctor which took about twenty minutes we were brought up to the nine thousand floor which was a good sign. If we'd been brought to the modules it would've meant that we were staying in the jail and none of us wanted that. We all sat in the cramped dorm worrying about where we'd go next. When they finally started calling names we listened anxiously for our names in association with the right line.

Some of the guys that came down from Wayside with us got called for other lines. That didn't look real good to us. It was getting pretty late in the day and they still hadn't called the Wayside line, but we hadn't been called for any other lines either. Maybe there wasn't gonna be one today and we'd be stuck here overnight, that'd really suck.

Finally they started calling another line. We all sat there quietly waiting for our names. For each name that was called a little muted cheer went up from that person. ARMSTRONG, he cheered silently. I held my breath, a few more names. FULLER, I guess I was a little too happy. When my name was called Armstrong and I shook hands and cheered quietly. From behind I was hit across the back of the neck, grabbed by the scruff of that same neck, jerked out into the hall, slammed up against the wall face first and pummeled with a flashlight from the base of my neck to my ankles.

When I was finally jerked off the wall and thrown back into line with the admonition "one more sound outta you and the only place you're going is the hole," I knew my buddy Alvarez was right on top of things as usual and had everything under control. As he swaggered past me I thought how much I'd love to see him on the outside and beat him so bad the only thing anyone'd recognize is the smell. He stopped right behind me and looked at something on my back. When he did I noticed that he had his name scratched into the barrel of the Maglight he'd hit me with "Jerry's" it said. He was looking at the white power lightning bolts tattooed on the back of my neck and said for everyone to here, "I bet when the black boys see those lightning bolts, your life won't be worth shit."

Armstrong, who'd put me in front of him when I got shoved toward the line by Alvarez spoke from behind me, "the black boys seen his lightnin' bolts, n-we think he's the powerfulist white boy we know." The other guys in line murmured an agreement and he was about to get really shitty when another deputy jumped in his shit and made him go away.

It was dark when we got back to the ranch, but the fresh breeze felt good and the sprung bed frames {versus the slabs in the jail} were much easier on my bruises.

Because I'd missed work that day my job'd been reassigned {thank God}. I now worked on the outdoor maintenance crew, sweeping, raking and mowing, outdoors all day, what a great job.

Two weeks later I went on another bus ride. This time it was expected, I had an appearance in court on the shotgun deal. It was my Preliminary Hearing. One more court date and I'd know how long I was going to prison for. My dump truck kept saying two years with the priors. With time served and good time I'd be out in seven months if I didn't catch another case inside or fuck up my parole somehow. Needless to say that wasn't what I wanted to hear, but there was no use fighting it. If I lost I'd get my time maxed out just for spite and end up doing years instead of months. Good ole California, come on vacation, leave on probation.

I called Clay that evening and told him what was going on, he'd managed to recover most of my stuff from Terry thru Richard. He had all of Christine except the frame; he said he couldn't find that. I told him it was safe, Pete had it and I'd get it when I got out, but I gave him Pete's number just in case. When I told him about the time he said he'd still have Christine if I was in twenty years, not to worry about her just do the time and get out as soon as I could.

When I came back from court I went to the modules so I knew I wasn't going back to Wayside. The next day I got shipped back to the kitchen. Two days later I got called for a transfer line and thought I was going back to Wayside. Another inmate said I wouldn't go back there because of the time I was gonna get. It was too easy to escape from Wayside if you were determined to. Who in there right mind would try to escape on a seven month sentence and spend the rest of their free time running and hiding till you got caught and got forty years or some crap like that? You'd have to be stupid to even consider it.

The transfer line was for Biscalue Center. **This place sucked!** It was right in the middle of the smoggiest part of the city right near downtown in Montebello. All you could do all day was sit in the dayroom and play cards or walk around the barracks. You *could* read a well worn five year old magazine if you could see thru the graffiti scribbled all over it. We got to go outside for one hour every day and walk up and down the driveway in a line while the deputies watched every move we made and jumped our ass for every little thing, even talking.

Between this place or the central jail I'd choose the central jail at least you could go to work to help kill the time. It beat the shit outta twiddlin' your thumbs and starin' out the window at the smog. Two days of that crap and I was called for another transfer line. This time it was back to the central jail and a run to the Santa Monica court.

My old fuddy duddy of a dump truck'd been replaced by a new female dump truck. She was far more aggressive than the old man. After looking at my case she thought that getting a different judge might help me get a time served and probation outta this and skip the prison bullshit.

I went back to the county jail feeling a little better than I had for a while. This time I was assigned to a mess deck which was like working in the chow hall at Wayside hour wise, it sucked. I worked for this cranked-out deputy, that I know was on crank. He'd drag himself in, in the morning looking like something the cat puked up and half an hour later come bouncing into the mess deck like his feet were on fire and his ass was catchin'. One crankster can always see it in another crankster no matter what uniform they're wearing.

The mess deck I worked on fed the hole, a disciplinary lock up for troublemakers like me. The trustee that worked there was a black dude nicknamed Little Mike because he cut his hair like Mike Tyson. Little Mike was anything but little, he'd been in the county for five years fighting a murder beef was the story I heard. Mike had nothing to do most of the day except work out and it showed, he was built like a rock above the waist, but below he had little toothpick legs because in jail there wasn't any real way to work 'em.

Every day after we were done serving Mike'd come into the mess deck and get as much extra food as he could eat. One day the deputy that ran the deck informed us that we were under no circumstances to give *anyone* any extra food; they'd rather throw it away and waste it than feed hungry people with it, assholes.

The guy that worked next to me on the line was a junkie named Richard, you could tell he was a junkie and had been for a long, long time. Every visible vein on his body was lined with huge blackish purple abscesses from shooting hot Belushies {a mix of cocaine and heroin}. These had to be slammed hot because they'd congeal when they cooled and wouldn't go thru the rig. He was a nice guy to talk to, but man he was hard to look at. Every piece of exposed flesh was covered with huge blackish purple lumps that looked like they hurt a lot {he said they didn't and after the people that ran the kitchen saw 'em when he testified, he didn't work in the kitchen anymore}.

After lunch was served we were cleaning up the mess when Little Mike came in and sat down at one of the tables close to Richard and I. He sat there staring at us for a couple 'a seconds then addressing me said "say man why don't you gimme some 'a that ham?"

"You got nuthin' comin' here dude" I replied.

"I SAID GIMME SUM 'A THAT HAM MUTHAFUCKA, NOW!" He snapped.

"FUCK YOU ASSHOLE!" I shot back.

"I don't think you knows who I is, I's Little Mike! They calls me that cuz I cuts mah hair like Mike Tyson, n-I'll fuck yo cracka ass up muthafucka" he growled.

"I don't give a fuck who you think you are shit-for-brains, you got nuthin' comin' here! Step the fuck off or pay the price asshole!" I growled right back.

He glared at me for a minute then shifted his gaze to Richard who'd gotten a pale green color all of a sudden and was visibly shaking "gimme some 'a that meat!" Richard looked at me; the fear in his eyes was spilling out all over him staining him this greenish white color.

"Tell him he's got nuthin' comin'." I said to Richard.

"You do, n-yo dead" Mike countered.

Richard looked at me, the turmoil in his brain screaming in his eyes.

"Tell him" I nodded in Mike's direction.

"You got nununuthin' cacacomin'" he stammered.

Mike jumped up and charged in our direction. Richard threw the ladle he was holding, turned and ran for the door. When Mike got to me I spun on him and kicked him in the left knee. This stopped him and turned him toward me {he was going after Richard}. When he squared with me I kicked him dead in the crotch so hard it lifted him off the floor about an inch. With a groan he sank to his hands and knees.

I reached under his chin, lifted his head up and drilled him right between the eyes as hard as I could. This split the skin down the bridge of his nose and across both eyebrows. Instantly blood gushed down his entire face. When I let his chin go he fell on his face knocking two teeth out on the red tile floor.

As he hit the floor, four deputies hit me from behind and slammed me to the floor as well, cuffed me, stood me up and hustled me out into the hallway.

While I was standing there they helped Mike out of the mess hall. When they half dragged him outta the door with a deputy on each side he looked at me dazed and slack jawed, blood streaming from his forehead, nose and mouth.

When he looked at me, head wobbling, I growled "**Got it now?**"

Immediately I was slammed face first into the wall and hauled away to the ground floor for Sergeant's Court.

Even though Richard testified in court that Mike'd been the aggressor, I was given eleven days in the hole. When that happened all the attending deputies in the court gave a little yeah and started laughing amongst themselves. They took me straight from the court to the hole, chuckling all the way like kids whose mischief was unfolding just the way they wanted it to.

In the hole Mike was the one that served your food which was a juteball and a cup of water three times a day. A juteball was all the food from the day before meat vegetables and bread ground up, packed into a meatball lookin' thing and deep fried. They tasted like hammered shit if you could even choke one down.

For breakfast the first morning Mike brought me bacon and eggs, toast, milk and an orange. As he handed me the tray he kinda' winked

384 ~ D.C. Fuller

one swollen eye, then walked away. For lunch I got the regular food that was served in the chow hall again.

In the hole you get one hour a day for recreation. When that time drew near Mike came and leaned on the wall of the catwalk in front of my cell and waited for my door to open. I figured for sure that when the door opened he'd rush me and it'd be on. Earlier I'd heard the deputies taking bets on who'd win the fight so I had a good idea that this was orchestrated by the deputies for their entertainment.

When the door opened I sat on my bunk waiting for the rush. Mike just leaned on the wall. All the other inmates exited their cells and started walking up and down the catwalk {that was the extent of our exercise}. When I didn't come out the deputies ordered me out of the cell over the loudspeaker.

As I exited the cell Mike came off the wall toward me with his right hand outstretched. "Name's Leroy n-yo the craziest fuckin' white boy I evah met, whatevah jumps off, I got yo back bro."

"Howdy Leroy, I'm Dave and I got yours too." We turned and walked up the catwalk away from the dumbfounded deputies, who were visibly pissed at an outcome they'd never foreseen.

Leroy and I spent our hour walking back and forth talking. Right after recreation was over, I was ordered to "roll it up" and sent back to the dorm I'd come from. Serving dinner that night Leroy laughed when he saw me on the line. When he got to me he looked me in the eye and said "you was right bro."

"Told ya, come back after chow" I replied. From that day till I left Leroy got all the extra food I could pile on him.

It was while working here that something happened that could've cost me everything and added years onto my sentence. A day or so after I was in the dorm, my buddy Armstrong came thru the door. He'd been released earlier in the week, had only been out for a few hours and had caught another case. He was back and this was his first assignment outta the modules.

Along with him came a few other inmates. One was a young banger from the Eighteenth Street Gang. I worked with a couple of his older brothers and we'd become friends. For some reason he didn't like it that they even talked to me. Well we worked together side by side and they got a kick outta the crazy white boy that fucked with the deputies.

The older guys'd tell their younger brother to leave me alone, which pissed him off even more. He went outta his way to cause trouble for me at every turn. One night while I was taking a shower he came in and told me if I went to sleep that night I'd never wake up. I thought, "fine I've been playing vampire games all my life, fuck with me!"

I stayed down in my part of the dorm all night long, playing cards and what not with friends. About one in the morning somebody pointed out that my buddy'd fallen asleep. I went up and sure enough he was out like a light. He didn't even move when I kicked the leg of his bunk.

I went to the gear locker and got two rolls of toilet paper the first one I wrapped around him kinda' tight from head to toe, the next I wrapped loosely from head to toe. When I was done I lit the toilet paper by his feet on fire and blew the flames towards his head. The loose paper caught and spread real fast and pretty quickly he was burning from head to toe. As soon as he realized what was going on I turned the bunk over on top of him, pinning him to the floor while his skin got seared by the burning paper and he screamed like a little bitch in fear and pain.

A few long seconds after he started screaming deputies rushed in and put the fire out with extinguishers and got him on a stretcher when it came. While he was laying there he said something to one of his brothers who was standing close to him. I didn't hear what he said, but I heard his brother say "no bro, I told you not to fuck around; you got what you asked for esay." The incident report said the fire was started by smoking in bed and the bunk turned over as a result of his thrashing around once he woke up on fire.

We were put out on the roof until the smoke cleared and the dorm was aired out.

After all the smoke cleared and things were winding down Armstrong asked me "say man, wha chu call 'at anyway?"

I thought for a minute and said "a Magic Mountain ride" after the amusement park in Valencia we drove by on our way to Wayside. We both laughed and that became my unofficial nickname the rest of the time I was there.

One night I was walking down the long hall that separated the old jail from the new jail at around three in the morning by myself. The echoes in that football field long hallway didn't let me have a clue where it came from, but when I was in the middle of the hallway someone said **"Magic Mountain."** There was no one in front of me and no one behind me when I turned around and there was no telling who it was. Everybody was calling me that {even deputies} by then, the story about this crazy white boy was one told at least once around that jail system.

A few weeks on the mess deck and it was time for another bus ride. Armstrong and I packed our shit and headed for another vacation at the resort. This time we worked together in the laundry, which was actually the coolest job in the place.

You worked at night and had the least amount of supervision of any job in there. An added plus was the two deputies that ran the place were the biggest shitbirds in the facility. They both rode Harleys and I was pretty sure I recognized the van one of 'em drove.

It took me a few days to get to the office and see the head deputy but as soon as I saw him he recognized me and I him. He'd brought his bike into Micah's to be worked on a few times and I'd always been the guy that did the work. As soon as he recognized me, my work assignment became sitting in the office looking at motorcycle magazines and throwing the lunches to the crew and that was it.

I was getting used to my cushy job in the office when I got called for another transfer line. This was it, my hearing date, by the end of the day I'd know what my time would be. I took the ride to the jail one day, went to the modules for the rest of the day and got bussed to court the next.

It was hot that day and the air in the bus wasn't working, it was a pretty hot ride since the windows only opened a few inches. When we got to the courthouse the holding cells weren't any cooler, the only thing better was you weren't stuck to the guy next to ya anymore.

My dump truck had a deal worked out when I got there. Plead guilty, get six months, no tail, with time served be released in thirteen days. Finally a break, I signed on the dotted line and went to the back of the cell. My day was done now all I had to do was sit in this hot box and wait for the bus to take us back to the jail at the end of the day.

When the time finally came to leave we were all ready to get outta there, it'd gotten well over ninety degrees in that cramped little cell with no AC and only a half pint of warm milk to drink all day and nasty water. The deputies said the AC was out in the whole building. What a bunch of liars, if it was like that all over the building they'd be dying from the heat with their ballistic vests on. Instead they always looked nice and cool and the guys that did go into the courtroom said it was nice and cool in there.

When we got to the jail I got out my calendar, figured my release date and started the countdown. It was hard to go to work or do anything after that. Knowing your release date, especially when you're short is torture. It seems like the closer you get the slower time goes; it takes a week for each day of the last few days to go by.

June 13ᵗʰ 1990

The third morning after court I woke up and ran to the restroom with the screamin' shits, the kind ya get after slammin' some good dope. Early that morning I'd had a dream about snorting this huge line of crank, the dope was so good it made me have to shit instantly, like when we slammed it. As I sat on the toilet waking up I felt like I was getting off on the dope dream, even though it'd been months since I'd even seen any dope other than the joints on the nine thousand floor.

I'd never had a dope dream before; I'd heard people talking about 'em, but they were mostly crackheads. I wandered outta the restroom looking at the clock on the way. I'd have to get up in forty-five minutes for work anyway; I might as well stay up. I sat down at one of the picnic tables and smoked a cigarette. After that I climbed up in my bunk. I must've dozed off because in a dream I heard **"FULLER, ROLL IT UP!"**

I snapped up on my bunk like I'd been electrocuted, but I had ten days left. Had I dreamt this too?

"FULLER, RACK NUMBER 125, ROLL IT UP AND REPORT TO CONTROL AT ONCE!" fuck I was awake that time. I jumped down off my bunk and went to control.

The deputy said "you're not going anywhere like that, go get your stuff and report back here yesterday, move!"

"I've got ten more days."

"If you want out of here at all, you'll do what I tell you, now!"

From somewhere in the dorm somebody said "will you get your shit and get outta here so we can sleep."

I got my shit and headed for the door just as fast as I could. This wasn't exactly the easiest way to do this. Rushing out the door with your pants on backwards and your shirt inside out, tripping over all the stuff spilling outta your arms and trailing around ya. I had to stop outside the dorm door and get some of this stuff straightened up. I got it bundled up a little better and tied my shoes before I got on the elevator. As I stepped out the door of the elevator all the stuff was taken from me by a trustee except my personal things.

It took me twenty-four hours from the time they called me outta my dorm till I hit the last warrant check. I sat there on the bench watching free people walk by outside, my gut in a knot because of this last check. Many a better man than I'd made it to this point and was remoded because of a warrant that'd been overlooked earlier or was issued after your last check.

It was another three hours before I was called to the counter and given my official release papers for the property room. I stepped thru the door, got my envelope of valuables and when the buzzer sounded I stepped outside into a blast of warm downtown L.A. night air that smelled heavenly to me. Actually it smelled like piss, beer and cheap wine.

I walked to the bank of payphones and called Clay. He was as shocked as I'd been about the early release. He'd already made plans with work for nine days from now and couldn't change 'em. I didn't care I was free and nine days'd give me a chance to scrape the money together for Christine's frame and pick it up before Clay got there to pick me up. We'd arranged for him to pick me up and bring me up to his place. I'd get Christine back together there and then the sky was the limit after that.

While I was on the phone with Clay, my old buddy Alvarez pulled up out front in a sheriff's car and got out. While standing behind the open driver's door he took his flashlight outta the holder on his belt, threw it on the front seat and replaced it with a baton, closed the door and walked up the sidewalk to hassle a bunch of obviously intoxicated dudes drinking on the wall down by the corner of the jail. As he walked off I don't think he even paid attention to who was around or anything.

He'd thrown the flashlight on the front seat of the car he was driving, left the windows open, shut off the car and walked down the block a good ways to hassle these guys. When I got off the phone with Clay he was way down the block jackin' up the dudes that were drinking. As I walked by the end of the phone bank the flashlight that he'd thought he was hurting me with was laying on the front seat. I couldn't resist, I grabbed the flashlight and stuck it in the inside pocket in my jacket as I walked past the car.

A few seconds later I walked past Alvarez while he was cuffing one of the drinkers. He looked me right in the eye as I walked past, but in my street cloths I don't think he recognized me.

There's an old jailhouse superstition that says "if you write on the walls, you'll be back," so I never wrote on the walls. I've never heard anything about taking souvenirs though, I considered it as having sentimental value since it and I'd had an intimate relationship. I've still got that flashlight around here somewhere and you'll hear about it again later on.

I'd heard that when you got outta jail your first RTA bus ride was free. I was about to put that to the test, if it wasn't it was gonna be a long walk to Simi Valley from downtown, especially in engineer boots with no socks.

When I got to the bus stop on First Street there were a couple 'a new releases like myself waiting for their buses. They were old hands at the free ride home deal, all you had to do was show the driver your ID bracelet and you were good to go, all the way home. I looked on the schedule and found the bus that ended at Roscoe and Topanga and sat down to wait. I didn't wait long before it arrived; it let me off at Roscoe and Topanga around two-thirty in the morning.

I walked from there to Hippie Hollow which was only a few miles away off Valley Circle Boulevard. Steel toed engineer boots with no socks are not exactly the best thing to walk any distance in. By the time I walked by Jim's old house, noticing the absence of the billboards and thinking he was probably locked up somewhere right now, my feet had huge blisters all over 'em and I was already tired of the pain.

I stopped for a minute and looked at the house. The windows had been opened back up; there were lights on somewhere inside, probably a nightlight. It had a fresh coat of paint and the yard'd been repaired.

The signs of the old billboards were all but grown in with new grass. In a month or two you'd never know anything was there. I wondered if the people sleeping in the house had any idea what'd gone on there just a year ago and what'd happened to Jim. I wondered about a lotta things, like were I was gonna get my first line from; I couldn't wait to gag on the nasty-ass drip of some peanut butter or glass.

When I got to Hippie Hollow it was dark and silent, almost spooky. As I got close to one of the buildings Buster the pitbull started barking at me from inside, the door was padlocked so I knew nobody was home. That meant I'd have to walk thru Box Canyon to The Knolls and go to Richard's house. That was the only other place I could think of to go. I walked into the darkness of The Hollow and headed toward Richard's.

I got lucky right away. I'd walked about a hundred yards up Box Canyon Road when a car pulled up beside me and stopped. I leaned down into the open window and asked the dude if he was going to The Knolls, next thing I knew I was there. As I walked past the train station and the park in the dark it felt good to be free, now I needed to get on with my life, before it got on without me.

I walked into Richard's room and told him to wake up. He sat up and looked right at me with his eyes closed and said "what're you doing here? You're in jail."

"I just got out. Where's your pot?"

"In the top right drawer. Am I dreaming?"

"No, I'll be out in the party room."

"Ok." He fell right back into the position he was in when I *woke* him up. I grabbed the pot and went outside. The bong was where it always was and lighters were everywhere. I loaded the bowl and prepared to go bowling with the big dogs; I inhaled the whole ten hit bowl in one hit, clearing the tube and everything. Not one wisp of smoke went anywhere till I couldn't hold the humungous hit any longer. It seemed like it took me five minutes to exhale the entire hit. When I was done exhaling the entire room was choked with smoke like twenty people'd been partying there for hours.

Once I was empty of smoke my lungs showed me how much they appreciated the weed by giving me a twenty minute coughing fit. Once the coughing was over I showed my lungs I meant business by getting the biggest bowl outta the cigar box of paraphernalia parts and screwing that on. I almost passed out taking that whole bowl in one hit; I was getting close to where I wanted to be.

The next hit was packed a little tighter than the last and it was all I could do to snap the entire bowl, I had to stand up to make as much room as I could to let my lungs expand enough. I got the whole hit in and the standing idea was the one that worked, I got such a rush that I had an outta body experience for God knows how long.

I kinda' came to when I heard from somewhere in the distance "hold on a minute, I gotta check something, I mighta' been dreaming, but **I WASN'T!**" On the I wasn't, I was pulled outta the chair and into a bear hug, Richard'd woken up.

Clay'd talked to Micah for me about doing some porting work for him when I got out to make some quick money. The night before when I talked to him, he told me to get ahold of Micah as soon as I could. Richard was going to The Valley to do a carpentry job that day. I caught a ride over the hill with him and he talked me into eating breakfast at the Bob's Big Boy right down the street from Micah's. After the swill from the county jail, a breakfast of real food threw my body into shock, it was good to be out. The meaning of "the worst day on the street is better than the best day inside" was never clearer than right then.

I walked up to Micah's after breakfast, a few hours later I walked out the door with six hundred dollars for a couple 'a sets of heads. Not bad for a couple hours work, if it was only more consistent it'd be a good money maker. Porting heads was always my specialty; I did 'em from mild to wild, match porting your manifold to the heads and carb body was always included as well as a single angle valve job, with the port radiused to one side of the angle and the chamber radiused away from the other side. One slightly wider angle on the seat provided better heat transfer from the valve and the radiuses kept the mixture flowing fast, only giving it one flat spot to slow it down. This was something I could do in my sleep. Like Micah said "they worked."

From Micah's I walked straight down Sherman Way to Vic's to find out about my frame. The number Pete'd given me almost a year earlier wasn't working, but I knew Vic'd have his new one.

How could I possibly anticipate the news I got? Pete had gotten in a disagreement with his neighbor about his loud music. He'd gone after the neighbor with a baseball bat. The neighbor took the bat away from him and beat him to death with it in front of his two little girls. The shop were he had his frame table closed up shortly after that happened and the owners moved back to Iowa. Now I was out one rare frame and one friend, I didn't know which was worse.

I left Vic's feeling like I'd been shot in the foot; I started walking back toward The Hollow, while I was waiting for the light at Reseda Boulevard a Chevy truck that I recognized pulled to the curb right in front of me. Without looking I jumped in and we took off back into traffic. When that truck dropped me off at Richard's I had an eight-ball of glass in one pocket, a bag of skunk bud in the other and I was only a few feet from the bong, the party was on.

For the next few days I made up for as much lost time as I possibly could in one sitting. I partied till I was talking to myself and didn't quit till I lost the argument.

In I don't know how many days Clay got there, we collected the little shit I had here and there and headed back north within a few hours of his arrival.

Now that I'd hit bottom and was on my way back up it didn't seem like bottom was so bad. It sucked being in jail, but I'd had fun in there at times. It's said that absence makes the heart grow fonder, it sure did for me. The first lines I snorted were the sweetest smelling dope I'd done in a long time and I went back at it with a vengeance. I still wasn't giving dope the credit it was due for putting me there. Even though I didn't get busted for dope directly it was the reason I was there and quitting never even crossed my mind.

The morning of the day I left with Clay I went to Micah's first thing and ported a couple 'a sets of heads real quick, the money'd come in handy while I was at Clay's. I was gonna have to buy a frame now in order to put Christine back together and the six hundred dollars would definitely come in handy for that.

When I finished the heads Micah knew I was leaving and pled poverty, saying he'd send the money within a few days. There wasn't much I could do about it at the moment, but I didn't feel good about that deal. Micah'd never stiffed me before and now wasn't the best time for it to happen, I'd have to wait-n-see.

Twenty-Eight Days Later

One of us had some dope on the way back to the bay area, cause I remember stopping around Castaic for couple 'a minutes to snort a line on a cassette cover and haul ass.

Clay and some of his friends were leaving for Sturgis in a month. I had that long to either get Christine done and be ready to go to Sturgis, or have her done and headed back down south.

Micah wasn't coming thru with the cash as promised and there wasn't anything I could do till I had a frame. Clay being the hustler he's always been went to work. He turned a sow's ear into a silk purse by selling every bit of the few things I had, to come up with the money needed to get Christine together, but get her together I did.

Twenty-eight days later Christine was together but for some reason she wouldn't fire, I was outta money and stuff to sell. Micah still hadn't paid me and I was gonna have to go back to L.A. to get my money and get the old bitch fired up.

We loaded Christine and the rest of my shit, snorted a line of Rosebud Crank a piece and headed south. I was glad, it was too cold and damp in the bay area for me and things hadn't gone quite as planned because of the money thing.

Back To Reality

Clay dropped me at a friend's house in Simi Valley; I dropped in on Moody because he was the only one I knew that wasn't using at the time and I knew I couldn't stay there long. That would force me to get my ass in gear and do something immediately. If I'd gone anywhere else I'd have sucked all my forward progress up my nose before I ever got Christine running and she'd've been left for one drug binge after another and probably ended up being abandoned again for dope.

Once we unloaded my shit into Moody's garage Clay gave me a ride over the hill to Canoga Park. We had breakfast at Bob's Big Boy, then he headed back home. I walked the few blocks to Micah's.

As soon as I walked thru the door at Micah's I had my money. I bought a condenser for my magneto and hitchhiked a ride or two back to Simi Valley. I installed the new condenser and did a little tune-up on my mag; made sure the accelerator pump had a good shot of gas, primed the old bitch and three kicks later scared the shit outta the neighbors when Christine blasted to life.

The next day I was at the DMV when it opened and a half hour later we were legal again, after the DMV I hit every bike shop I knew, looking for a job. There wasn't much luck in The Valley, but I went back to Simi that night with a fresh bag of crank and a fresh set of wheels. After a stop at Richards for some weed I was good to go for the rest of the week.

Undaunted by the lack of success of the day before, I headed in the other direction on my job search. The first place I stopped was The Shop in Ventura. Dave told me that he didn't need anyone at the time, but he knew of a little shop on Channel Drive that was struggling and could use a good wrench. He gave me some directions to the place and I headed for it.

Scooter Stuff was a little mom-n-pop place {literally, that's what most of the people called 'em} on a back street near the center of town. Further down the driveway was a body shop that did trick paint and beyond that was the practice studio for some local band.

At first Larry didn't think he could afford to pay me saying that he didn't have much in the way of service work, he sold a few parts and t-shirts and was just barely squeaking by. I told him the work would take care of itself, I'd see to that, we struck a deal for fifty percent of the labor ticket and I told him I'd see him in the morning. When I left I took a little ride around town to familiarize myself with the place.

When we did the swap meets, we'd attended several of 'em at the Ventura Fairgrounds. I always liked the little seaside town, it was far enough from L.A. to not be affected by the rats winning the race a few miles to the south. The atmosphere there was a lot more laid back; there weren't any traffic jams in the morning and things moved at a much less intense pace.

Within a month I had a constant flow of customers rolling thru the place, as this was happening I was getting to know the town. I'd had to move to some friends of Moody's and now mine as well because Moody's ole'lady's parents didn't want a bad influence and generally all round rotten guy like me in their house. I moved across the valley to Arcane Avenue. Moving for me wasn't much of a big deal, packing and unpacking saddlebags, that's about it. Back then I was back to traveling light, I'd sold off everything but my cloths to get my girlfriend back on the road.

Three months after I went to work at Scooter Stuff we moved from the hole in the wall place to a big storefront on Thompson Boulevard a few blocks west of Seaward Avenue, there was a constant flow of traffic thru the shop and it was increasing daily. I usually had a bike on the lift and two waiting; people that had a less than happy experience with Scooter Stuff in the past were coming back for another try.

Hanging out at the Red Cove in the evenings and on the weekends gave me the opportunity to talk to people, answer questions and get 'em back in thru the doors of the place. Once they were there I dazzled 'em with brilliance {mostly I just told 'em the truth about their problems and how I'd fix 'em}. The hard sells that needed more assurance got baffled with bullshit as well. The one two punch of bullshit and brilliance always seemed to work on even the hard headedest of skeptics, we were doing pretty well.

After we moved up on Thompson I started getting more and more head work to do both from Ventura and shops in The Valley. One day at lunchtime I decided to make it official and got a business license under the name of Ventura Speed in the county of Ventura and a few days later did the same thing in L.A. County.

While Scooter Stuff was thriving I was making the acquaintance of every crankster and partier in Ventura, in fact I was becoming good friends with people that didn't even know me. One evening myself and a friend named Gary were standing outside The Red Cove, a bar were the scooter people hung out. It was a nice night for a "joint session" and watching the traffic go by was the perfect entertainment.

While we were standing there a car pulled into a parking space a little ways down from us with a couple in their early twenties in the car. We weren't quite done with our joint, but not knowing these two we weren't gonna smoke it in front of 'em. We'd just wait till they went in the bar. Instead of getting out they sat in the car occasionally looking at us, but not really staring or being overly nosey.

After a few minutes I figured it'd be fun to go over and fuck with 'em to kinda' get 'em moving along. Gary and I wandered toward the car with a purpose. As we got to it the driver rolled down the window. I said howdy and asked him if he needed anything.

He said he was just waiting for Dave.

I asked him "which Dave?"

When he said the one that rode Christine both Gary and I looked at each other and smiled.

I asked the kid if he knew Dave.

He said he was good friends with 'im and had been for a long time.

I told him that Gary and I were good friends with Dave too and asked him if he had any dope. By this time Gary'd walked around to the other side of the car. He and I were talking across the roof to each other and the guy and his girlfriend who were kinda' surrounded inside their car were probably starting to feel as uncomfortable I was trying to make 'em.

He said he had some dope.

I immediately told him he'd have to give us both a line just for the sake of being a BRO.

He quickly agreed, but said he didn't have anything to do it on or with. He had a cassette tape case and I had a dollar bill and a pocket knife, we were in business and he was about to get schooled. His girlfriend got booted outta the passenger seat, I got in and laid out two massive lines for Gary and I that took most of his bag. I snorted mine, Gary did his. I wiped off the case, put it back where it came from and told him I'd be sure to tell Dave he was good dude. I reached out my hand and said "by the way name's Dave, what's yours?"

The look on his face was priceless. I got outta the car, his girlfriend got back in and as I walked away from the car I asked if they were coming inside. The dude was shaking his head and saying yes while he was backing outta the driveway and hauling ass up Main Street. We walked into the bar laughing our asses off at what'd just happened and so did everybody else when they heard the story.

I'd become very notorious especially to one particular motorcycle cop on the Ventura PD. He made it his mission in life to write me as many tickets as he possibly could in the shortest amount of time possible. He'd write me two or three loud exhaust tickets a day sometime. He familiarized himself with the times that I came and went from the shop and would lay in wait for me. As soon as I pulled outta the driveway his lights and siren were on. All he had to do was see me in traffic no matter what I was doing and I got a ticket for something.

One evening I left the shop and turned toward the freeway on Seaward, just beyond the freeway was a Chevron station on the corner of Harbor Boulevard and Seaward Avenue that I intended to pull into to get gas. To get into the gas station you had to be in the left turn lane. As I'm sitting there waiting for the light to change Officer Dickhead comes flying up behind me lights and siren blaring. He pulls up behind me and orders me over his P.A. to pull across two lanes of traffic to the right curb. I looked behind me and told him I was going into the gas station and he again ordered me to the right curb.

This was the third time that day he'd fucked with me and I was pissed. Without even looking I wound Christine up and dumped the clutch, shooting thru the red light and across the intersection to the right curb. I shut Christine off, flipped down the kickstand and slid off the bike while it was still rolling. Dickhead was still trying to get both his feet on the ground when I grabbed him by his belt and his collar and pitched him headfirst over the embankment next to the road, he tumbled about forty feet into some bushes in the vacant lot at the bottom.

When I turned back toward Christine the people in the cars at the intersection started cheering. I walked back to Christine fired her up and took off to go continue my night elsewhere. I expected to be arrested at any time during the next few days, when it never happened I was kinda' amazed. That'd been the culmination of months of harassment from the little redheaded prick. After that night he got pretty scarce.

A few months before that I'd had three different traffic cases going at the same time, one in Antelope Valley Court, one in Calabasas Court and one in Ventura all on the same day.

My day started with an early morning ride from Simi Valley to Lancaster for the Antelope Valley Court case, court took longer than expected and I didn't get back into The Valley in time for the Calabasas appearance, but I stopped at the court and talked to the clerk to get the amount of the ticket and the warrant so I could pay the ticket when I got paid on Friday and just cancel out the warrant and the ticket all in one. After I got the information I headed for the Ventura Court.

All I did was plead not guilty to get time to get the money together to pay the tickets in Lancaster and Ventura. I was kinda' tryin' to string a couple 'a these tickets along so that one could drop off my driving record before anymore went on.

I'd intended to string 'em all along, but the easiest way to take care of 'em once you miss the court date is to pay 'em and take your lumps at the DMV. This was on a Tuesday. I was putting the finishing touches on a complete ground up rebuild I was doing and hurried to get all this crap done so I could get back to the shop to get Mark's bike closer to completion.

Shortly after lunch Thursday afternoon Mark's bike was ready for a test ride. I rode east on Thompson, took Seaward to the freeway and headed south on the 101. I hit fifth gear at ninety mph, looked in my mirror for cops before I gagged it and saw Officer Dickhead trying to catch me. Since I was on a customer's bike I pulled over immediately, if I'd been on Christine I'd've made him work a lot harder for it.

When he finally caught up with me I was parked, smoking a cigarette. He jumped off his bike with his hands in the air jumping up and down like he'd scored a touchdown screaming, **"I GOT YOU MOTHERFUCKER, YOU'RE GOING TO JAIL, I FINALLY GOT YOU, WAAAAAHOOOOO YOU'RE GONNA GO TO JAIL, WAAAAAHOOOO I GOT YOU!!!!!"**

"YOU CAN'T TAKE ME TO JAIL FOR SPEEDING ASSHOLE!" I yelled over his bullshit victory dance.

"You've got a warrant and you're going to jail, Ha, Ha, Ha motherfucker I got you." While he was saying this a car was pulling in behind his bike. He cuffed me cackling like an old hen to himself, as fast as the car got there he'd been setting this up for a few minutes anyway.

When I got to the jail I called the shop, after a quick call to Biker Bail Bonds I was soon walking down Telegraph headed to the bar to get ahold of someone to come down and let me into the shop so I could get Christine.

When I got to the Red Cove Larry's son and I went to the shop, I got Christine and went back to the bar. Mark had gotten his bike out of impound and rode it to the bar later that night. Since I hadn't gotten a chance to finish tuning it, I told him to bring it back the next day and I'd finish it up real quick.

While all this was going on my crank use was going off the charts, customers brought me bags of crank for tips constantly. I was using so much dope that one afternoon when I pulled up in front of the Red Cove, I was still sitting on Christine fifteen feet from the door, a friend standing inside the door when I pulled up stepped out and said "dude you smell like crank."

I got off the bike and walked inside, as I walked past Brian he started laughing and said he was getting high just off the fumes from me, I was laughing too because I'd just come from paying a traffic ticket at the courthouse, the best place in the world to be walking around smelling like crank.

Sometime in there I moved from Simi Valley to Ventura, I spent all my time in Ventura, only occasionally returning to Simi for whatever. I lived mostly outta my saddlebags and bounced from here to there not really living anywhere. One day a friend whose house I spent a lotta time at and I jumped in her car and went to Simi, loaded up the little bit of stuff I still had there, said "see ya" to the folks I was staying with and headed back to Ventura.

Missy and I'd become good friends, but for some reason our relationship never got much further than that. Part of it was because Missy was very closed up, she spent a lotta time living inside herself and wasn't very open about anything really.

I on the other hand was living at light speed, burning the proverbial candle at both ends and in the middle at the same time.

Missy was the person I was talking about in the beginning of the book when I mentioned someone playing Tetris for three days nonstop. She'd call and say "hey what's up, I'm headed out the door and I'll be there in ten minutes." Three days later you haven't seen her yet, when you walk into her bedroom she's sitting on the bed playing Tetris and has been since she hung up the phone three days earlier.

All the traffic tickets ended up in a thirty day suspension of my driver's license. In order to be able to make it to work each day I stayed with some friends named Jimmy and Deena {sorry if I didn't spell it right} who lived about a hundred yards from the shop on Catalina Avenue.

Jimmy and Deena were two of the first people I met my first day at Scooter Stuff and were two of my best friends in town. I spent a lotta time with 'em, they were both always at the shop and we partied and rode together all the time. They were near me in the pack the day of the Santa Barbara Toy Run when Christine and I drowned out the local news lady as we rode by, while they were reporting on the run.

It was pretty funny in the film clip they ran with the story that night on the news; the reporter was standing on the side of the road looking into the camera with the bikes going by behind her. As she was speaking her commentary she was drowned out by what sounded like a series of small explosions, Eventually you could see her lips moving, but all you heard was Christine burble by at about 125+ decibels. As we faded away her voice came back. Sitting in their living room that night watching the news we all had a good laugh at that clip, mostly because the loudness of Christine was always a source of comment {good and bad}, depending on which newspaper you read.

If you read the Star Free Press, I was the one known as the two o'clock biker and I was actually a topic of conversation {how can we get him outta town or quiet him down} at town council meetings. Myself and Christine were deemed to be a public nuisance by Ventura County and the city of Ventura. It didn't matter much I was losing my license anyway. That'd give 'em time to forget I was around when they didn't hear me roaring thru the streets at all hours of the day and night.

By now law enforcement was figuring out what crank was and how to do roadside tests for it and identify users of it by sight. My relationship with Larry was becoming more and more strained; he was helping too much in the shop. I kept telling him to let me do the jobs from beginning to end; instead he and maybe somebody that happened to be hanging around right then would take jobs apart and lose the parts, put 'em in off the wall places, forget where they put 'em, not label the boxes they were in so we knew what job they came from and shit like that.

This wasn't so bad when you were dealing with stock bikes and parts, but it came back to bite us on the ass when a dude brought in a Sportster Chopper that was in one of those low slung, stretched out, bay area custom type frames that I'd never seen up close before.

I was working on something else when Larry and another dude that hung around regularly took the bike apart, I didn't get to see how anything in that whacked out frame was fastened and Larry couldn't remember his name most of the time. When I asked him for the hardware for the frame he gave me one little coffee can with about half the fasteners I'd need and none of the brackets or hardware necessary to mount anything in the frame.

The reason we had to tear the bike down was a blown transmission case. Not only did the bike have to be torn down. The engine as well had to be torn down so the tranny case could be welded and remachined. They left the engine and tranny for me to tear down. Putting that back together was as easy as it should've been.

When it came time to reassemble the bike, that was another story. I had all the big hard parts, fenders, frame, engine, wheels, front end, gas tank, oil tank, but none of the bracketing to put it all together with and damn few of the fasteners. Larry's answer to that was to replace the stuff and charge the guy for it.

When the bill came in a couple hundred dollars more than quoted and that cost was made up of parts that were on the bike when he brought it to us {the bike was complete when it came thru the door and none of those parts should've had to be replaced} he hit the roof. Later on after the whole mess had been settled on one of my last days there while looking for the parts on a different job, I came across the missing Sportster parts and fasteners in an unmarked cardboard box under a bunch of other boxes shoved on a shelf.

Immediately Larry pointed at me, blaming his incompetence on me, citing me as the one that built the bike, he never told anyone that he took it apart and lost the parts. After that Larry decided that he'd short my pay for the parts. At the same time this was going on we had an increase in our labor rate. At fifty percent my pay should have gone to twenty-one dollars an hour, when it came time to get paid Larry insisted that he hired me at eighteen dollars an hour and handed me the shorted pay like it or not. I took the money and never set foot in the place again.

Dave's Music Box

Larry'd seemed to forget that when I went to work for him he barely had two nickels to rub together and was about to lose those, it'd been my work that put us up on Thompson, nothing he'd done. If it'd been anything he'd done, he'd've been on Thompson when I met him. If my work built him, then he'd be undone after I left right? It wasn't but a few months before there was an empty shop across the street from me with a **FOR RENT** sign in the window.

When I left Scooter Stuff I opened a shop right across the street from him so I could see the look on his face when the people that he thought were *his* customers came and went from Ventura Speed all day long. While this went on he spent his nights at the bar telling everybody how I'd fucked him over and what a scoundrel I turned out to be.

The shop across the street was in the back of the old C-n-E auto parts building, a good friend of mine owned it and a graduate of Drunken-U worked the parts counter and fucked things up in the back when he had a chance. The back was a pretty complete automotive machine shop, albeit archaic and an office that my friends called Dave's Music Box because of the way the stereo got abused in there. It so happened that my friend's name from Drunken-U was Dave too so that worked out quite well.

Dave spent many cranked-up, drunken, week long days staggering around on his lips in there fucking things up and I hep'd. My crank use was off the charts, along with my pot smoking and everything else that I did. Dave wasn't any better; in fact he was probably worse by far because he drank hundred proof vodka all day long like it was water and when he was drunk he never knew what was gonna come outta his mouth or to whom.

One afternoon after he'd been staggering around on his lips since around eleven that morning, the wife of one of the parts accounts parked out front and walked into the shop. The woman was gorgeous and Dave was plowed, not knowing who she was he cheerily informed her that he'd love to suck her clit till her head caved in.

Talk about righteous indignation, she lost her mind. She'd been coming in to pay the monthly bill. That check got torn up and thrown in Dave's face and she stormed outta there so fast it made Drunken-U's head spin.

Of course the result was another lost customer which worked to further the decline of an already dying business. The owner was going thru a personal crisis of his own and paid very little attention to the actual workings of the business any more. He came in every day because we were his friends, we'd get high and bullshit about what was going on. None of it was good and his wife was the leader of the pack that was ruining him, literally.

Although he was convicted in court, I believe the evidence was contrived and he was railroaded by her for financial gain. He was a good friend to me and knowing him as I did I won't believe he's guilty of anything they convicted him of till he tells me otherwise.

Even though I had a place to work, I slept on Christine under some trees in an outta the way spot up near Ojai, which wasn't too bad unless I got caught in an occasional early morning rain. My days were occupied with making the money to get high and staying high until the next day.

I drifted from one spun crankwhore to another. That was why Deena insisted that I move outta their house. I think she was afraid that I'd teach Jimmy my bad habits. Jimmy was in the Navy and couldn't afford to have too many bad habits and he knew it. That didn't keep Deena from being afraid I'd corrupt him with some little spinner that I brought home. Being given the boot had become a way of life for me, I've been a bad influence on everyone I've ever met, hell I was a bad influence on myself and still am.

The evening the axe fell Jimmy and I talked about it, he explained that it was Deena making such a fuss about it that forced him to do it. As far as he was concerned life was a little more exciting with me around. He gave me the best compliment anyone has ever given me in my life, he said I was the only real scooter tramp he'd ever met and he was glad to've known me.

I'm glad he and I got to have that talk, the next day Jimmy was deployed to Italy with his outfit. While his team was eating in a restaurant they all mysteriously contracted an unknown virus, none of 'em survived. Jimmy Earl came home to Kansas City in a box at twenty-five years old; none of us ever saw him again except in the pictures of all the things we'd all done together at his memorial service at the Red Cove.

To this day I believe that Jimmy was killed by his own government. I think the reason they were sent to Italy was to isolate 'em from the American public. They were then exposed by their own government to some type of virus to "see" what'd happen to 'em. I always thought it funny that although they all got sick and died within days none of the other population around 'em even got a sniffle.

Just the other day I was digging through my old stuff looking for something when I came across the memoriam that Deena'd made up for his memorial service. Jimmy wasn't a victim of drugs like so many others I knew, which made it hard for me to accept his death both then and now. He had a good head on his shoulders and was liked by everyone who ever met him. For me his death kinda' severed the tie I had with that group of people forever.

By now I was used to losing touch, I'd lost touch with everyone I'd ever known, that was how it'd been all my life. I was used to being alone and as I got older I got more distant from everyone I associated with. Eventually it just became easier to not have friends, just acquaintances that could be cut loose quickly and painlessly. The only things that were always around were my scooter and my dope. They became my only priorities, everything and everyone else could go fuck themselves for all I cared.

Eventually Drunken-U faded away and it was just me in the old C-n-E building. I can't remember where he drifted off to, I think he'd gotten a girlfriend and a home and was making somebody else's life a wreck for a while as well as his own.

While I was working outta C-n-E another friend and his ole'lady split up and he needed a roommate to help with the bills. I moved in with him for a little while, this brought me into another circle of cranksters. Just moving into the neighborhood and getting to know the neighbors introduced me to even more circles of cranksters.

It seemed that everyone I knew had about the same story. They'd all worked in the oil field when it was booming in Ventura and all began using crank while they were working there because of the long hours and the hard labor. When American oil interests shifted overseas and the wells around Ventura were capped because of politics, the bottom fell out of everything overnight and many people faced with losing everything became crank dealers and cooks. Some survived, some became drunks and junkies, some ended up behind bars and some died in more ways than one, everyone had a story about themselves or a friend, relative or acquaintance that'd met one bad end or another due to their personal economic collapse.

Right then everybody I knew without exception was a crankster, we all lived like vampires, prowling the streets at night on one mission or another, looking for the next buzz, party or dumpster to pick thru. The ever downward spiral I was on was continually getting intertwined with other downward spirals leading me to believe I was doing alright, at least compared to most of my peers who were in the same boat as me and spinning in-n-outta control like I was.

In November of `91 I became the father of an orphaned pitbull puppy who resembled Hemet's dog Kona very closely. I couldn't resist naming my new charge Kona Gold. I used to tell people that if he didn't turn out to be a good dog I'd kill him, skin him, roll him up and smoke him. He must've been paying closer attention than I thought because he turned out to be the best dog a guy could ask for considering the fact that he saved my life on more than one occasion and was ultimately the reason I quit using crank.

Ventura Speed

January first 1992 saw the end of an era for me in more ways than one. California had finally passed a bill to make helmets mandatory for all motorcycle riders and C-n-E was being sold. The owner was locked in the final death throws of his marriage and his life, everything was falling down around him and he had all he could do to keep himself psychologically afloat.

That year the rainy season was the worst in twenty years, The nation watched as KTLA televised the flooding, showing the destruction that occurred when the Ventura river which hadn't had water in it for twenty years swept tourists and homeless alike into the Pacific Ocean with a raging wall of water. Weeks of rain kept everybody on bikes miserable and indoors.

Being California, the rain wasn't gonna last forever, in fact nothing was gonna last more than a few minutes ever. A friend was finally getting his feet back under him after a hell of a bike wreck and getting around to getting another scooter.

Ed was introduced to me by one of Larry's sons' right after we moved up on Thompson. He'd just been released from the hospital after his wreck and wasn't in very good shape. He was just barely getting around, in fact it was probably one of the first times he'd ventured from his house since the wreck.

When I first met Ed I was running wide open with my hair on fire and it wasn't until he was in good enough shape to keep up that we started hanging out. We hit it off right away, especially once he got his Softtail Springer. My favorite thing to do was make Harleys go fast and he didn't wanna keep the bike stock so we made a plan, port the heads,

S&S G series carburetor and it already had a set of slashcut drag pipes to liven up the stocker.

Liven it up it did, that thing'd fly when I got done with it. A month or so after I did Ed's bike I had to move once again, I'm not gonna go into the clusterfuck that was the cause of our having to move, but it was caused by the spinning out forever of the girl that Bill sublet the house from. She'd fried her mind on crank and was being shipped back to her family in Ohio so they could take care of her because she was no longer capable of doing it herself. When we all moved it was purely by coincidence that we all moved out to El Rio.

Ed was becoming quite successful with his chosen profession and was interested in starting a shop as a form of diversification, so while my roommates {Bill and Linda} were moving into a house on Balboa in El Rio. I was moving into a shop on Montgomery Avenue just across Vineyard Avenue from them.

We Turn Dreams Into Nightmares

Was the motto at Ventura Speed, which was located at 534 Montgomery Avenue suite 303 in El Rio, CA. This was the perfect place for making Harleys go fast and testin' 'em to make sure they did before they left the shop. Fifty yards from my front door were two perfect quarter mile long roads that had no traffic on 'em after five o'clock in the evening and were so far out in the country that you'd have to go a long way to find somebody to bother after regular business hours. The fact that after eight o'clock at night you were virtually alone without anyone within two miles of the place was a definite plus that allowed room for a lotta monkey business and extra curricular activities.

For me this was my personal paradise, right down to the creepy voices and conversations that were overheard in the middle of the night in the restroom. The very first night I moved in there I noticed voices when I was in the restroom, but only in the restroom.

Because the complex was new and in the country it was on a septic system. Due to this the restrooms were shared by two adjoining units, two units used one restroom. I simply figured that the guy next to me left a radio on low when he left and that was what we were actually hearing and the weird shit that I thought I heard said was just my mind playing tricks with unqualified sounds.

The next day I was working on something when the neighbor came in and opened his shop. The first thing I noticed when his overhead door went up was there wasn't any radio on. Kona introduced himself to Sterling right away; I on the other hand was a suspect in Sterling's book right away. He'd been a partier at one time earlier in his life and I think he recognized the signs, his motto was now "Drags not Drugs," this was emblazoned on the rear quarter panel of his top alcohol funny car.

I'll never forget overhearing him talking to the landlord a few weeks after I moved in, he was trying to get me booted out because he thought we were a bunch of druggies. Of course I couldn't hear what the landlord said to him but his reply was "I think all he does is sit over there and do drugs, the whole bunch of 'em."

A few days later she came by just to say hi and see what was going on there. She didn't find anything outta the ordinary; in fact myself and a friend were scrubbing the floor to prep it for painting.

The first time somebody used the restroom at night they walked out the door ashen faced and in hushed tones told me that they thought we were gonna get raided. They could hear people whispering on the other side of the door and they were talking about raiding the place. As soon as Jake said that I knew if I was finally losing it after all these years I wasn't gonna be making the trip alone, there'd be at least one person riding that bus with me.

Over the next few months when I didn't have bike work to do I worked on making the shop into my own little world. One of the first things done was a mural on the back wall twelve feet long by four feet tall of a flaming drag bike spelling the words Ventura Speed for the body of the bike in flames {this was also my business card}, with a little bit of track lighting to highlight it and a photoelectric cell controlling 'em so the bike jumped out at ya when you entered the shop it was the first and best of the many decorations in the place.

I eventually had low level lighting throughout with highlighted work stations, electronic door locks, complete exterior surveillance with audio, a forced ventilation system, sealed doors and an air conditioned office. My office was wired so I could watch and control most of the place from my desk. I was always tweaking on something, turning the place into my version of a crankster's paradise.

With the help of my good will ambassador Kona I became just one of the neighbors in a very short time, despite what people thought of me, Kona became friends with everybody in the complex. He had toys in every shop on our side of the building, at eight-thirty every morning he'd go out and make his rounds of the different neighbor's shops. From then until about eleven o'clock I'd see him running by chasing balls and wooden blocks or hear him growling like a wild beast while he was playing tug-o-war with somebody. Around eleven o'clock he'd come in for a drink and pass out in front of his water bowl for an hour or two.

Flying Lessons

When I moved out to El Rio I was kinda' seeing this spun cookie named Frankie, she was good looking as hell, but like so many spun ones she was a few sandwiches short of a picnic. The worst part about her was she wouldn't shut up when she was high, she'd say anything to keep talking. I once spent seventy-two hours telling her to shut up and go away, do you think she'd get the message? It went in one ear and out the other while she just kept right on hyper-babbling away about God knows what.

She was so spun the night I was doing the heads on Ed's bike we had to lock her outta the shop so I could work, she kept hovering around me while I was working, hyper-babbling away about the most stupid shit. I finally hustled her outside pointed her at her car and told her to leave. I walked back inside and locked the door as I closed it; we waited to hear her car start up and drive off, but never did.

A few hours later when no amount of dope could keep my eyes open any longer Ed called a time out for sleep and a shower before I split my head open falling head first onto the bike every time I fell asleep. Ed went to put something in his car, when he came back he told me to look outside. I went to the door and looked, Frankie'd been busy while she was out there, she'd striped the interior out of her car and had it scattered all over the parking lot.

As tempted as I was to leave her right there tweaking until she'd completely dismantled the entire car, I couldn't let her tie up our friend's business's lot like that. In a few hours his trucks were gonna have to be able to back in and load up tools and supplies for their jobs that day. As exhausted as I was I gathered all the stuff up and put it in the trunk, back behind the seats, wherever it was outta the way, we pushed her car outta the lot, closed the gate and rode home with Ed.

The next night while I worked on Ed's bike he and Craig kept an eye on Looney Tunes and made sure she put her car back together. Just as I figured though she didn't remember taking it apart, so after I finished Ed's bike I had to quickly stuff everything where I thought it belonged {I'd never worked on a Porsche 914 in my life, or any other Porsche for that matter} and get it to where she could drive it enough to get it outta there.

She made me so crazy that Kona became allergic to her and started to develop this huge open sore on the side of his neck that no matter what was used on it, it just got bigger and uglier with each passing day. Along with the sore he had the worst case of hives I've ever seen on anything living or dead.

The day I finally got rid of Frankie the sore dried up, the hives went away and almost overnight the sore healed and had fresh hair growing out of it. From there on out every time Frankie so much as called on the phone you could see the hives begin to form on him and if I stayed on the phone long enough he'd be one big fire engine red lump from nose to tail. Fifteen minutes after I hung up he'd be fine again.

One day my neighbors were standing out front talking and drinking coffee. Frankie'd been driving me up the wall over a phone bill that I'd given her the money to pay on her way home weeks earlier. She'd blown the money on dope, but kept insisting she'd paid it and the phone company was lying. I know she hadn't because a week after she was supposed to've paid it I got a shut off notice. When I called her she said she'd paid it and had a receipt to prove it. I told her to bring me the receipt so I could take it to the phone company to prove payment and get a refund. She said she'd be over in half an hour, I didn't hear from her for two weeks.

When I did it was "hi, how ya doin'?" Like nothing'd ever happened, she asked if she could come over. When she got there she hyper-babbled about being clean for two weeks and how clean she was then and on-n-on-n-on.

I told her to get the fuck out, don't even bother shutting up just get out. She continued on until I grabbed her by the seat of the pants and the scruff of her neck and pitched her out the door headfirst into the parking lot. After that I slammed the door and locked it.

I watched her on the surveillance camera while she picked herself up and started hollering crap at the wall in front of her. She continued on till the neighbors started laughing. I think it was the first time she noticed they were there, because she got in her car and left.

I waited a few minutes to make sure she was really gone before I opened the doors again. When I did the neighbors were still outside laughing and talking. Gary said he liked the way I handled my women problems and wanted to know what I called it. I thought for a minute and told him "flying lessons," everybody laughed and we eventually went back to work.

The same neighbors saw Frankie take three more flying lessons before she figured out that I didn't want a thief and liar around me and left me alone. Four months after she finally took a powder, she showed up one day outta the blue, spun right out, hyper-babbling a blue streak. By that time I'd gotten to know my neighbors pretty well, well enough that Sterling knew he could walk in any time he needed something I had and borrow it.

Well he walked in right after she showed up, because he needed to borrow my one inch ball micrometer; she was sitting with her back to him when he walked in. She turned as he came in and said hi. He looked down at her and recognizing her asked with genuine curiosity "how are you, have you gotten your pilots license yet?" And burst out laughing.

I almost fell outta my chair I was laughing so hard, then when I saw the RCA dog look on her face I did fall outta my chair. She had no idea what we were laughing at and was bewildered at first, but started laughing along with us which made us both laugh even harder at her. She was so spun she was a rebel without a clue, but when she left in a trail of laughter it was thankfully the last time I ever saw her in my office.

Though Ventura Speed was a fully licensed and taxpaying establishment that specialized in "warp drive for Harley-Davidsons," the order of the day was monkey business. Every day there was a week long and packed with cranked-up shit to do. Speed-n-weed were the main sources of inspiration, along with the mutterings of the meth monsters that haunted the place. Late at night when the complex was empty was the most fun, you could do anything and there was nobody around to say a word except for the meth monsters.

One of the people that distributed dope for me was a lying, thieving little skunk named Jake; the first time he got dope for this guy he shorted it by half a gram before he gave it to him. Because it was the best dope around he came back for more even though he'd been burnt the first time, but he insisted on using his scale to weight it with. I weighed the dope with Jake watching, he agreed on the weight, I packaged it up even though Jake was fifty dollars short. He assured me he'd deliver the dope and come right back with the money within the hour.

I didn't see him until I left the following message on his mother's answering machine "you got the dope motherfucker, where's my money?"

Half an hour later he was on the phone crying like a girl telling me not to leave messages like that on his mother's machine, she'd hear it and have him busted. I told him I didn't care if he got busted I wanted my money, he countered with the bag was short a gram and the dude wanted his money back. I told him to go get the motherfucker and bring him and his scales to the shop and we'd see who got what when they got there.

A while later he walked in with a dude named Ralph. We sat down to figure out where the shortage was, by simple deduction it was concluded that Jake was the culprit. To solve the problem I cut Jake right outta the loop and told Ralph that if he wanted dope from then on to come straight to me instead of going thru Jake and I told Jake as far as he was concerned I was outta the dope business. It was funny to watch the little weasel break down and cry like the little bitch that he was. That right there began a friendship with Ralph that lasts to this day.

Another one of Jake the Snake's forms of thievery was taking my business cards claiming that he was handing 'em out for me during his travels. He was handing 'em out all right, he'd cross out the phone number for my shop and write in his mother's home phone number {he was a momma's boy}, portraying himself as the owner of Ventura Speed and stealing work from me in that way.

I don't know how long he was doing this and the only way I found out was one afternoon Ralph and I were sitting in my office recovering from the rippers we'd just snorted when the phone rang. When I answered the person on the other end asked for the owner of Ventura Speed, I told him he had 'im. When I said that, he identified himself as a customer from Thousand Oaks and started to complain about the work that'd been done to his Suzuki {I only worked on Harleys and couldn't even spell Suzuki} not being right. I told him I didn't have any customers from Thousand Oaks, didn't work on Suzuki's and asked him what he was talking about.

He then asked if this was Jake.

I said it wasn't, that Jake didn't even work there.

He knew Jake didn't work there, he was the owner was his answer.

I was instantly pissed and explained thru clenched teeth that I owned Ventura Speed and Jake wasn't even so much as welcome in my parking lot let alone in my shop and I only worked on Harleys to begin with. I invited him to come to El Rio to the real Ventura Speed and talk to me.

Later that evening he showed up with the business card that Jake'd given him; I told him that the number that was hand written on my card was Jake's mother's home phone, gave him directions to her house and wished him good luck getting anything but grief from the thieving little prick.

That was the straw that broke the camel's back. I was gonna do my best to smooth everything over with the little scumbag, crankster, fuckhead so I could get him to come to the shop that night. When he got there my intention was to torture a confession out of him then kill him and sink his worthless carcass in the flooded gravel pit next door, ridding the world and me personally of a class A piece of shit.

I must've been projecting this psychically, cause he said there's no way he'd come anywhere near my shop for any reason ever again. He hung up when I called him a pussy and I never heard from or saw him again. Only problem was the damage'd already been done. I can only hope that somebody somewhere got ahold of the scumbag, crankster, asswipe and gave him the beating he deserved. I only wish it could've been me. With any luck at all he got busted and ended up in the joint, that'd fix his wagon.

The Ventura Speed times were an updraught in my downward spiral; the good time of Ventura Speed didn't last for very long at all, but nothing in the world of a crankster ever does, there's too many things against you, the number one thing is what fuels the lifestyle, **CRANK**. Being involved with crank in any way begins the crash. It might take time and you might not notice it at first, but the losing begins with your very first line and depending on your period of use and the depth of your involvement may never end till you're dead.

A few months after moving to El Rio, I ran into a friend I hadn't seen in a while. His relaying of a simple message from his boss to a narc that was setting him up for a drug bust, dragged him into the middle of a drug sting and for his trouble he'd received a conspiracy charge that he was subsequently convicted of and given a year in the county for.

When I ran into him he'd already been sentenced and was trying to get his affairs in order. He'd been ordered by the court to vacate where he'd worked because it was the scene of his crime. Although his girlfriend had a part time job, it wouldn't be enough to keep her afloat until he got out, meaning mostly that she'd lose her new car. There's a long story behind that car that has no real bearing on this story other than this, he was paying for her new car because he totaled her first new car. He couldn't make the payments from jail.

At the same time that this was all happening I was losing my license for either too many tickets once again or driving under suspension, I can't remember which. Very shortly I was gonna need someone to do my driving for a while. For the last month of his freedom I let him use some shop space to make money with. He was an auto mechanic by trade so I let him use my shop and tools to make as much money as he could before he got locked up. I even found him a little work when his ran out.

We worked out a deal, basically I'd take care of Amber while he was away and she'd be my wheels until I could drive again.

A day came when she came to the shop after work. As she sat and cried I knew why, he'd called me earlier that morning and told me he'd left a note and walked out to turn himself in and start his sentence. She was pretty bummed that day and I couldn't help her with it, it was something foreign to me. I was always the one bummed out because I was going to jail, I'd never had anyone I knew besides friends go to jail and that never made me cry.

That first day we hung out and made a place for her to have her stuff, kind of a little office of her own and got high. The atmosphere was a little subdued around there, compared with the usually frenetic activity level in the place. That evening Ralph came over, we mostly sat in the office and watched TV and got high, nothing'd been done so far that day why start now? Around ten o'clock Amber said goodnight. Ralph and I sat up till around three in the morning. We took Kona out and chased possums for a while and that was about the extent of the excitement that night.

After Ralph left I was gonna go to bed for a change, but when I got to it there was already somebody in it. I thought she'd gone home to her moms only a mile or two away. This wasn't something we'd discussed, so I didn't really know what to think when I found her in my bed. I went back in my office, smoked a bowl or two and finally fell asleep in my chair watching TV.

Remember the voices in the restroom? One night Ralph and Amber and I were sitting in the office, probably watching a movie. Amber went back to the restroom, a few minutes later she came back with a weird look on her face and asked if we'd been talking about her while she was in there.

I told her that not only were we not talking about her, we weren't talking at all and we hadn't been, something'd come on the TV that caught both of our attention and we'd shut up to hear it. She said she definitely heard somebody talking about her, at least it sounded that way to her. I told her that I heard voices in there myself and to me they sounded like they were gonna kick the door in and bust the place, but instead they got into an argument about when to do it every time and it never happened, just ignore it.

Another thing about the place was when it was windy it sounded like someone was walking on the roof. One night about an hour after Amber'd gone to bed she scared the crap out of us when she tiptoed into the office and whispered that she'd heard someone walking on the roof and then saw them looking thru the skylight at her.

What cracked me up the most about it was that she didn't have her glasses on and couldn't see a TV ten feet away without 'em. The skylights were twenty-six feet off the floor and opaque. If someone looked thru them during the daylight you couldn't see 'em unless the sun was directly at their back making a shadow on it, let alone in the middle of an overcast rainy night. In that kinda' circumstance they could lay on top of it and you'd never know it, even if you didn't need glasses. I walked her back to bed and tucked her in telling her it was just the creepiness of the place, she'd get used to it.

Over the next few months we became very close, we couldn't help it we were together twenty hours a day. I couldn't legally go anywhere without her taking me, so she got run from one end of town to the other, to The Valley to pick up and drop off work, all the shit that I did as a matter of course during my days of busy nothingness.

It was easy having Amber around, she wasn't a crankwhore, I could trust her, that was the most important thing. Not only was she trustworthy she was easy to look at and quiet, the only time you knew she was around was when she wanted you to. She never followed me around babbling incoherently for a minute let alone for days like some of the other lunatics that'd stuck their noses in my dope bags over the years. That right there was the biggest plus. When we talked about something she actually understood what was said and could follow simple, even complicated instructions without being held by the hand every step of the way. She was also a very good accomplice in my practical jokes, for instance.

The morning of Ed's birthday he called to see if I could bring his car back to him. I'd borrowed it to haul something with earlier and hadn't gotten around to returning it yet, which ordinarily wasn't a big deal. This morning it was, because the night before, leaving a friend's shop he'd forgotten to take the bulletproof American Lock outta his rear pulley and tried to ride away.

He didn't wanna even tell me about it and was kinda' reluctant to tell me why he needed The Truckster at first.

I told him we all make mistakes but this was the funniest one I'd ever heard, because that lock fucked that aluminum pulley up. He was now stuck at home with no wheels on his birthday and bummed out big time.

I made some excuse as to why I couldn't bring the car to him right away while a plan formed in my mind. I told him I'd try to have Amber bring it to him sometime later on that day if I could and hurried off the phone. As soon as I was off the phone with him I was on the phone to the Harley shop, they had one pulley in stock. I dealt with 'em on a regular basis so they knew me over the phone. I told 'em to hold the pulley for me I'd be right there to get it and somebody else would be calling for the same pulley in the next few minutes, when they did, tell 'em you ain't got one and they've been on back order for six months, you don't know when you can get one.

Amber and I went to the Harley shop in Ed's car, got the pulley and went over to our friend's shop where the bike was. When I got there I called Ed to see if he'd had any luck getting a pulley. He was almost crying on the phone he was so bummed. I told him I had no idea where Amber was and couldn't drive the car there myself because of my license situation. He told me that he called the Harley shop and they told him just what I'd told 'em to, that was why he was so bummed, they'd laid it on extra thick to make it sound worse than it could ever be.

When I hung up the phone I went to work; in half an hour I had the pulleys changed and the bike ready to roll. I told Amber to head over to Ed's with The Truckster a little while into changing the pulleys. Since I'd done the headwork to Ed's bike it was almost as loud as Christine. I jumped on it and headed for Saticoy where Ed lived. I have a very distinctive riding style, wide fuckin' open and anybody that knew me, knew when I was headed their way. Christine and I could be heard from miles off long before I was sitting in your driveway.

I jumped on 126 and headed for Ed's house. It was perfect Amber called Ed before she left and said she was on her way, I wanted him to be outside when I pulled up or a little before, so he could hear his bike coming. Even though he had a rocket there he still rode it like somebody's grandmother and I always gave him shit about it.

One night he and I rode to his house early in the morning after a "most of the nighter" at a friend's shop. When we got there he asked me if my front wheel ever touched the ground because every time he looked over at me my front wheel was just skimming the high spots on the road and that was all.

I flew out 126 as fast as that bike would go, passing everything like they were running in reverse. I jumped off at Wells Road making a lotta noise as I downshifted, ripped up Wells Road to Telegraph making as much noise as I could. Left on Telegraph, gag it, right on Nevada and left on Modoc romping on it all the way to his driveway, up the driveway in a small wheelie and my job was done.

Amber was walking from The Truckster parked at the curb up to Ed who was walking outta the garage when I rolled up. They could both hear the screaming bike headed their way and Ed knew it was me tearing 126 apart, but he couldn't figure out what bike it was. He knew it wasn't Christine, but it couldn't be his, it was broken and it might be next fall before he could get it fixed from what the Harley shop told him.

The look on his face when I almost ran him over with his own broken scooter was priceless. I jumped off the bike, wished him happy birthday and we had a good laugh when he said he knew it was me, but as well as he knew that, he knew I wasn't riding Christine. He just couldn't figure out what bike it was and he'd never heard his bike sound like that so he didn't recognize it.

We hung out for a while getting high and then Amber and I headed back to the shop. That was gonna be one of the last happy days any of us had for a while.

Two Blondes

Early one morning Amber and I were returning to my shop from a friend's at around 3:00AM. When we got off the 101 onto Vineyard Avenue we passed a sheriff sitting in the parking lot of a business. He didn't move to follow us, but he did watch us turn down Montgomery Avenue into an industrial area that was empty and desolate after eight o'clock at night and never come out.

That evening before we left for my friend's place I'd taken a shower and hadn't tied my hair back. Both Amber and I had bright blonde hair that hung below our shoulders. I no longer had a beard just a short Fu Man Chu moustache.

About a half hour after we got back to the shop Amber, a friend named Mike and I were about to do some lines when the doorbell rang. Looking at my surveillance monitor I saw it was two sheriffs. I told Mike to lock the door behind me when I went outside. When I got out there the deputies started asking me if Amber was inside. I asked 'em why they wanted to know. Their reply was "sheriff's business, just answer the question."

I don't give a fuck what kind of uniform you're wearing, you come at me with an attitude like that for no reason and all you'll get is ten times more attitude back. So I told 'em "fuck you, this is my turf and until I know exactly what you want her for she's not coming out."

They looked at each other knowing their bluff had been called, one of 'em told me that another deputy had seen her car with two blondes in it turn down here and not come out and knowing this area was uninhabited at this time of night he grew suspicious. They'd found her car parked out front and were making sure she was alright.

Since I had sound as well as picture in my surveillance system I simply said to thin air "unlock the door and send Amber out." The door unlocked and Amber came out and stood close to me facing the cops.

As soon as she did the one that did most of the talking looked at us standing side by side and said "two blondes" and started laughing. He got on his easy-talky and contacted the deputy that we saw on our way to the shop. When asked where he was he said he was in front of Amber's mom's house, he hadn't gotten any answer when he knocked on the door and was waiting to see if someone would eventually show up or open up.

The deputy in front of us told him he'd found the two blondes and they wanted to meet him. As soon as he unkeyed his radio he started laughing again. While he was still laughing the other one asked why we were down here so late.

I told him it was my place of business and we were working.

He asked why we were there at that hour.

I asked him if he'd ever been down there during the day and if he had how he liked working in 102 degree heat and the dust from the rock quarry next door.

In unison they replied "why do think we work nights?"

My answer to that was "great minds think alike, huh?"

They laughed again and asked what I did.

While I was explaining that I made Harleys go fast Mike came out and joined us. When he opened the door I told him to leave it open. from where they were standing the cops could see into the shop all the way to the back, they took in the trick lighting, the David Mann gatefolds covering one wall of my office from floor to ceiling and all the crazy decorations I had everywhere. While we were talking we could hear a car squealing to a stop at the stop sign down the street and then burning rubber thru the intersection.

That intersection had rather deep drainage channels across it and the car jumped wildly as the idiot behind the wheel that thought he might get laid by at least one blonde, did his best to impress the two blondes he thought wanted to meet him. He slide the car sideways into the driveway floored it and came skidding to a stop a few feet from us and started to cowboy his way outta the driver's door. As he did the one cop walked over to the car. The goofy looking redheaded deputy was only halfway outta the car when our deputy pointed at Amber and I and said "there's your two blondes!"

His face turned as red as his hair when he saw Amber tucked under my arm and realized we were the two blondes. He reversed course midexit, slammed the door closed, jammed the car into reverse and burned rubber outta there even faster than he did getting there.

The five of us had a good laugh at the hero. After he was gone the deputies asked if they could check out my shop, always willing to blow my own horn I asked if they wanted the twenty-five or fifty cent tour. When they asked what the fifty cent tour was I told 'em "we go around twice" and we all had another laugh.

I walked 'em all around the shop and showed 'em my machines and my trick lighting, the flaming drag bike on the back wall, they read the poems on the walls and got a kick outta the one that said "having sex with your pregnant wife is like pumping gas into a car that you've already wrecked."

After the tour we walked 'em to their cars and we all wished each other a good night. What they don't know was that the filing cabinet they were standing inches from at one time had two pounds of crank in it and they weren't even outta sight before some was on the glass and we were doing the lines that I'd put in my top desk drawer when they rang the bell.

The Downward Spiral Continues

Only a few weeks later Ed made the worst mistake of his life. He U.P.S.'d an ounce of crank to a friend of a friend in northern California using both his right return address and the dude's right delivery address. He'd declared it as a book when he did it and checked it in with someone who'd snorted a lotta his dope in her time. As soon as he left the U.P.S. terminal she blew the whistle on him and within hours the Ventura cops were looking for him. The dude he was shipping it to got jacked into singing his guts out about Ed and before long the beginning of the end'd started.

As soon as I heard this I told him to go into hiding and have somebody rent him a place in their name and stay outta sight until everything was moved and all ties with his old place were cut. His ole'lady Lori did all the paperwork putting the place and its bills in her name to cover Ed's tracks.

The best thing he could've done was get outta the state altogether, there was a reason why he didn't that I can't remember. Anyway it wasn't long before, thru a wiretap on one of Ed's friends in Florida they found him again. Because his friend in Florida was a big fish in the drug trade there, the cops in Ventura assumed Ed was more than just his friend and began trumping up a case on him that would put him away for quite a while.

I'll never forget the evening we got the call; we'd rented My Cousin Vinnie at Block Buster and were about halfway thru the movie when the phone rang in the office. I jumped up and ran to get it. It was a collect call from "Ed." I could tell by the echo in the background that he was in a holding cell in the Ventura County Jail. When he got on the phone

I asked him what happened. He said there'd been a knock at the door and as soon as he began to open it, it was kicked out of his hands and the place was fulla cops.

They'd found a little bit of dope and some new glassware he'd just bought for his lab that wasn't even dirty yet. They hauled him and Lori off to jail and Lori's brother'd come to take care of her kid. After I got off the phone with Ed I called everyone I knew to get 'em working on the only plan that would have any chance of getting him out. His bail was set at a phenomenal rate because of the wiretapped conversations with his friend in Florida.

The only thing to do instead of wasting his money on bail was get the best lawyer his money could buy and let him get him out thru bail reduction hearings, he wouldn't get out quite as fast but wasting his money on bail and leaving him in the less than good hands of a court appointed dump truck would be signing his death warrant. With one of their dump trucks on his case he'd probably get railroaded into a life sentence.

It was a long night that week as I tried to call in as much of the money owed him as possible and get the best drug lawyer in Ventura in his corner. In the meantime Lori got released after seventy-two hours because she was only there when they busted him, she didn't have anything on her. I can't remember for sure if she was charged with anything or not, I really didn't care. Ed was the one in the most trouble and my concern was getting him the best and most help I could as soon as I could.

Vultures And Rats

You know the old sayings when it rains it pours and if your friends can't fuck ya, who can? If matters weren't bad enough Lori's ex, Craig who wanted nothing to do with her or the kid she'd had by him spent a day or so getting himself as spun as a top. Once he was as delirious as one could get he grabbed a gun and went over to Lori's brother's house to get what he finally decided was his kid. Needless to say he got his dumb ass busted for brandishing a firearm in a threatening manor.

When they got him to jail they pulled the old give us three names routine and he spilled his worthless guts about everything he knew, pounding a few more nails in Ed's coffin and turning states evidence on him even though they couldn't've done much to him for the gun. Brandishing was a misdemeanor and since he didn't have any kind of a record would've been a love tap on the wrist, but the big fuckin' pussy believed the bullshit the cops slung at him and caved before they even put any pressure on him.

He claimed he did it for the good of his child, the one he threw Lori outta his house for having as soon as she gave birth. The whole time she was pregnant the only thing he'd say was it wasn't his, he wanted nothing to do with it or her and as soon as it was born she'd better be gone. To me he showed just what a spun piece 'a shit he was and I was glad he didn't have anything he could roll over on me for.

Don't get me wrong Craig and I'd been good friends at one time, but since the deal with Lori he'd stopped hanging out with anyone and was getting further and further out in left field. He actually went so far as to let himself be evicted to get Lori outta the house. Ed being a friend of both of 'em let Lori move in with him so she didn't have the kid in an abandoned doorway down on The Avenue.

For some reason Craig took this as Ed stealing his girlfriend and got a case of the ass with Ed resulting in some pretty damaging depositions and testimony coming from his mouth in relation to the drug bust.

Myself I always thought that the only good rat is a dead rat and wanted to off the whiney little shit before he ever got to court to corroborate his depositions. Ed wouldn't hear of it, he was afraid that he'd get stuck with the murder too.

"Not if you're locked up when it happens," was always my answer. I wanted to do it during the confusion right after the bust before anything even happened in court.

Once Lori got out she showed her true colors. The first thing she did was sneak over to the shop, steal The Truckster, and give it to Ed's greedy, spun motherfucker partner down in Southgate.

The night I got the call I hid the pound of dope I'd gotten from Ed a few days earlier inside the back bumper of The Truckster just in case thru phone records or wiretaps they'd gotten wind of my association with Ed.

It would be easy enough to explain why he came to the shop and called me on the phone. He came here to get his bike worked on and we were friends. But it would be so much easier for them to tie me into the drugs if they found 'em in the shop. Plus I had Amber to worry about, at the time she was twenty years old. It would've sucked to have her get caught in the middle of this and get hung for something that she just happened to be on the fringe of because of her association with me.

For days after Ed got busted my doors stayed closed and the activity and traffic at my shop was brought to a screeching halt. One afternoon right after it happened Amber and I were just walking out the door to go somewhere when The Truckster went flying out the driveway from the other side of the parking lot Lori behind the wheel and Ed's partner's wife on the passenger side.

Shortly after that Jerry {Ed's partner} called to see if he could come and get the car. I told him he already had and that all my dope was stashed in the car when they took it. When the car got to Southgate the idiot completely stripped it looking for the dope.

What a dope, as if a bag of dope casually stuffed in the bumper is gonna be there after the seventy-five mile drive to Southgate on California freeways.

While Ed was going thru his trial by fire, I had a small battle of my own going on over my driving. It seems the state meant it when they said **NO** driving. I was going to court for my fourth or fifth driving under suspension. The result of that was fourteen days of community service. Instead of dragging it out I chose to do fourteen consecutive days that way I'd only have to cleanup for two weeks and be done with it.

Community Service

On the paperwork for community service it's very clearly stated that you' could be drug tested at any time and if found under the influence immediately incarcerated and charged with another crime.

Figuring that I could handle two weeks of sobriety better than I could more jail time I began the process of drying out. I didn't know I could sleep or eat that much and I had no idea that being clean could be so shitty. Without dope I couldn't get my head off my pillow or outta my ass and you talk about a grumpy mean ass son-of-a-bitch, I fuckin' hated myself.

Convinced I'd never make it without dope, I abandoned the thought of trying to be clean a few days into it and decided to take my chances and go high. There was no way I was gonna make it thru the next two weeks of this shit sober. I didn't make it anyway, the second week into it I came down with the worst flu I'd ever had which lead to bronchitis.

In the middle of the day a deputy had to come from the work release offices and take me back to the shop. When Amber got there she had to make an appointment to see her doctor, what an asshole he was.

I've had chronic bronchitis since I was a kid and know just when it's coming on and what treatments work. When this zit-faced dickhead came into the exam room and asked me what I was there for. I told him what was wrong and what I needed. He told me he was the doctor and he'd decide what I needed. After a hundred dollars of unnecessary tests he prescribed exactly the same thing I told him I needed in the first place.

When they handed me the bill, I paid for the office visit, but refused to pay for the tests. When I told 'em that the tests weren't needed in the first place because he'd prescribed exactly what I told him I needed to begin with, they said they'd see me in court, they never pressed the issue beyond that.

While we were sitting in the waiting room I picked up a Psychology Today magazine because one of the articles was about acid flashbacks. The jist of the article was that if you'd taken LSD fifty times and hallucinated vividly you were clinically insane and needed treatment. I showed the article to Amber and had her read the part about being insane and asked her, "what if you slammed LSD in your Carotid Artery every day for a year and spent most of that time hallucinating."

She looked at me with a wry smile and said "that would explain a lot."

I didn't go back to community service for two weeks. When I finally went back they told me it was a good thing I showed up when I did because if I'd been gone any longer they were simply gonna violate me and send me to jail even though I'd done everything they told me, like calling in every day and bringing a doctor's release with two weeks written in red and circled. According to the deputies no one was ever sick for two weeks.

I only had a few days left when the van our crew for the day was riding in made an unexpected left turn into the back of the admin. building, which only meant one thing, we're gonna get drug tested. The deputy on the passenger side got out and looked into the back; he pointed at the inmates on either side of me and ordered them inside. I almost shit myself when he pointed at 'em. They went inside, a few minutes later the deputy came out alone, got in the van, slammed the door and said "let's go." That day they caught five people under the influence of something. I finally finished my sentence on January 11th 1993, the same day Amber told me she was pregnant and was moving back to her mother's.

Falling Down

Well I was fucked now and pissed as hell. It was the best thing for her and the worst thing for me, it meant that I was basically a prisoner in my shop. To get something as ordinary as a Snapple was a three mile walk to the store and back.

I guess that didn't matter much anyway since Ed's bust I'd kept an ultra low profile. I'd been under surveillance off-n-on for a while. The cops would park an easily identifiable vehicle chock full of surveillance gear in the no parking zone across the street from me in the middle of the night, thinking they were being sneaky and leave it sit there for days. The first time they did it I took Kona for a walk and we checked out the vehicle.

It was loaded to the gills with surveillance equipment that they thought was hidden by the darkly tinted windows. Nothing could hide all the meters and function lights blinking in there all day and night. Not to mention were it was parked and for how long. To countermand their bullshit I put twelve volt computer fans on the windows themselves and left 'em running 24/7 that way when they shot my windows with a parabolic microphone all they heard was the humming of the fans, nothing was ever discussed on the phone, and all calls kept to just a few sentences.

Another thing they tried to get someone inside was this. One afternoon on my surveillance monitor I watched a car with a state license plate pull into the parking lot and park right across from my shop. The driver got out walked up to my door and rang the bell. When I opened the door a detective that I'd seen a dozen or more times at the courthouse asked me if I needed my overhead door serviced.

I told him if I did I was more than capable of doing it myself.

He turned around walked back to the car, got in and drove away. As soon as he was gone Sterling came over and asked me what that was all about.

I told him the guy wanted to service my overhead door. "Bullshit that guy's a sheriff, has been since we graduated high school together," was his answer.

"Maybe he's moonlighting," I said and walked inside.

I knew when the car pulled into the parking lot it was a cop just by the license plate, recognizing the guy from the courthouse only confirmed it. I didn't need anyone to tell what he was; how fuckin' stupid did they think I was anyway?

I let the answering machine do most of the work after Ed's bust, at Christmas time I put a message on it that everybody got a kick out of. "You've reached Ventura Speed where we turn dreams into nightmares. No one can come to the phone right now because we're on strike for lower wages, poorer working conditions, more hours, less breaks, a pink Malibu Barbie Corvette for a getaway car and a GI Joe with the kung fu grip for security, until these demands are met no one answers the phone!" I hope the cops got as big a kick outta that message as everyone else that heard it did.

After Amber left the only company I had besides Kona was Ralph, he was the only one that I hadn't run off because he was the only one that wasn't a known crankster. He'd come over and we'd tweak on shit for a day or so then he'd go home and I'd lock the place up tighter than a drum. The only time anyone knew I was even there was when I walked the dog, that was it.

Around the end of May the bottom'd fallen outta Ralph's life and he left California for good. After that I spent hungry days sitting in an empty shop, the phone'd stopped ringing shortly after Ed's bust because the worst day outside was better than the best day inside and I wasn't going back to jail again. If I did who'd take care of Kona?

I'd finally found something in my life to love besides drugs. Because of him I'd stopped doing the things that'd get me locked up, like going to the bar and driving like an idiot, in fact I gave up almost everything because "what would happen to Kona," was always on my mind.

When they turned my power off because I couldn't pay the bill I went into the power room and switched the wires to an empty unit. When they shut off my phone for the same reason I piggy backed my phone onto the one next door and was careful about using it. From then on to reach me I had to be paged and you'd have to wait for me to call you back, which I sometimes had to wait to do if someone was next door.

Things were no longer spiraling down they were falling straight for the bottom now at an ever quickening pace. Whenever I didn't have any dope, suicide was always on my mind right in front of "what would happen to Kona." I'd plunge into a depression so deep that it'd take me a quarter gram of good dope to get back to near normal. With no money any amount of dope was impossible to get. To get money I started selling off my gold and anything else that I didn't need to live on to get money for as much dope as I could get and a little bit of food.

The unit next door to me was the distribution center for Mission Tortias. Every couple 'a days the manager would bring over a couple bags of chips and once in a while a friend would bring over some of the sandwiches that had gone beyond the sale date from his roach coach. That same friend brought me a case of Hershey's Kisses. I lived on those alone for months.

One day I got sick of being stuck in the shop and rode over to Bill and Linda's for a while. As I rode past a convenience store that was on the way a sheriff that I'd beaten in a court case and had taken it upon himself to make my life hell, chased me to their house and arrested me for driving under suspension, *again*. I was in jail overnight, when I went to court the next day I told the judge that my dog'd been locked in my shop the whole time I'd been locked up and was probably outta food.

He must've been an animal lover, because he said he couldn't allow that and released me on an OR. I walked back to El Rio from the court house. When I was arrested I gave my keys to Linda and asked her to take care of Kona. He wasn't even at the shop he was at Bill and Linda's when I got out.

While I was walking home a line from a Missing Persons song rolled thru my head "only a nobody walks in L.A." It seemed to me that I was fast fading into a nobody, just another junkie on a greased skid headed for Hell and getting burnt to a crisp along the way, again. The only thing that was saving me was Kona, he was the only thing besides Christine that I loved, Christine was a lot easier to take care of than he was, she didn't have to eat and believe me I went hungry many times to make sure Kona had plenty of food.

The last driving under suspension was something like my eleventh and the court was sick of seeing me, to make sure they didn't see me for a while they sentenced me to two months in jail. Now I had a real problem, I'd have to find someone to keep Kona for me; no one I knew could or would keep him for two months.

From back east Ralph found someone. On the day I was to surrender myself Kelly came and got Kona and I, dropped me at the jail and took Kona home with her. No matter what I was gonna go thru in this next stint in the crossbar hotel I knew my baby boy'd be safe and well taken care of.

I'd made a deal with my landlord, who was probably the coolest landlord I'd ever had. She was gonna store my shop for a dollar a month and we'd work out my back rent once I got out. That was until she found my creative wiring in the power room. A few weeks after I was locked up I got a letter from her attorney telling me that they'd found my work to be creative, however illegal and all bets were off as far as our agreement was concerned.

Because I wasn't a real criminal I was quickly shipped to the honor farm up in Ojai to be a gentleman pig farmer for my two months, which was just fine with me. Fresh air and sunshine every day is far better than fluorescent lights and the stinking bodies in the central jail. The Ventura County system was far more obliging than the L.A. County one. The place wasn't as crowded and the attitudes of the inmates were a lot different, the system was more relaxed so in turn the inmates were more relaxed. There wasn't the permeable tension in the air like in L.A. County.

The highlight of my stay there were the brush fires that year. They got so close to us that we could see the flames on top of the next ridge over from us and the sky glowed red at night. It was kinda' scary to lay in my bunk at night with the whole dorm lit in a flickering red glow, smelling the smoke that hung in the air. Rumor had it that people with less than ten days left would be released if the facility had to be evacuated because of the overcrowding it'd cause in the jail if they didn't.

After I heard that I asked the deputy I worked for if it was just jailhouse talk or what. His answer was "until it happens it's all just talk."

I rephrased my question to "has it ever happened in the past" and got a definitive "no." So much for that.

With two days left to go at five o'clock in the morning I heard **"FULLER, DORM FIVE, ROLL IT UP AND BRING YOUR GEAR TO THE DOOR"**. By nine o'clock that morning I was a free man. As I was walking thru the visiting area a friend who'd just been released a few days earlier was walking in. When we were locked up together he always said he'd pick me up when I got out and give me a ride home and true to his word he was there. It never ceases to amaze me how different we all look in civilian cloths. I barely recognized Mike as he was walking up to me until he smiled then I recognized him; we'd done a lotta laughing together while we were locked up.

I hate to let being locked up get to me; it makes time go by too slow, ratcheting the tension level up to unbearable sometimes. It sucks bad enough being locked up, but dwelling on it only makes it worse. Occasionally to the point where you end up in the hole "for your own good," they say. That's the way to make ya feel better, lock you in an even smaller hole.

It was a Thursday when I was released. After I'd gotten Kona, a bag of speed and a bag of weed Mike and I went to my shop. After Mike left I got on the phone and called Ralph to let him know I was out, his sister answered the phone. When I asked for Ralph his sister told me he was on his way out to get me.

Saturday morning Kona and I were sorting thru stuff at the shop. Throwing the trash in the dumpster and getting my equipment together to be sold. I'd talked the landlord into letting me stay at the shop on the condition that I restore it to the condition it was in when I rented it.

Outta the blue Kona got up and headed for the front door, by the reflection on the wall I knew a car'd just pulled in. When I looked out the door a silver Caddy had just pulled into a space across from the front door.

Kona was going nuts before I even knew who was in the car, evidently he knew because he was getting ready to give somebody a hell of a greeting. When Ralph's girlfriend got outta the passenger side

I knew why he was all jacked up. Ralph and Francie were two of Kona's favorite people and they were gonna get it now.

After watching a seventy-five pound pitbull turn himself inside out for fifteen minutes we greeted each other with lines and joints. Then sat down to make a plan to get rid of everything I could, pack the rest and get outta California.

When I'd moved to Ventura in `90 the place was a little slice of heaven. Money, dope and every other form of entertainment flowed like water, prosperity was everywhere. The five military bases in the area bled money like a cut artery. It didn't matter what business you were in directly or indirectly the money you made came from those bases.

In `91 Clinton signed a bill that closed three of the five bases and kicked all the civilian contractors off the remaining two. It was like turning off a spigot, overnight people's lives went in the toilet. People that were living in million dollar homes one day were sleeping in their cars the next. At that time I had a shop full of bike work. One by one my customers came and picked up their bikes, some of 'em in pieces because they couldn't pay their bills, they couldn't even afford to have me put 'em back together. It got so bad I started telling people to bring their own boxes for their parts.

By the end of `93 there was more dope on the street than there was money, a lotta people had pockets fulla dope they couldn't give away, but didn't have two nickels to rub together. This was the economy that I was trying to sell my equipment in. Trying to get enough money to get myself and the few things I was gonna keep outta California.

It was hard to get anything for my equipment, the money I was offered was pennies on the dollar and supplemented with dope for the balance. For the next few weeks I worked day and night getting everything repaired building wise and getting everything gone equipment wise.

After weeks of finagling the best I could do was get enough money together to rent a storage unit and take IOU's for the rest that was owed. One step ahead of the sheriffs Ralph and I moved my stuff to a storage unit down the street. Once that was done we packed up and headed east. I hated leaving Christine for even a minute and it'd been hard for Ralph to convince me to do it. In reality it was the only way I could, the little bit of money I did get, paid for the storage unit and the rest went toward gas for the trip east.

Spun Cookies

On a crappy overcast day in November of `93 the four of us piled into Ralph's sister's Caddy and headed east, leaving behind the place that I thought I'd spend the rest of my life, but not for the last time.

It'd been a long time since I'd been back east. I'd forgotten how green it was back there and how many seasons they had. California has two basic seasons rainy and dry. During the rainy season what doesn't get washed away in mudslides turns green for a little while. Within a few days after the rain stops everything that isn't watered burns brown and stays that way till the next rainy season. I'd been in California so long that I'd forgotten what the rest of the country looked like.

I guess that was one of the things that impressed me once we got east of the Mississippi River. Even in November it was still lush and green a big contrast to the sparsely vegetated, mostly brown desert in southern California and the southwest in general.

The plan was to go back to Ohio. Sell all the dope I could quickly. Come back to California, get my shit and get out for good. I was one strike away in two different categories from being a three strike lifer in the joint. Fuck that, I didn't like California enough to live the rest of my life in one of it's penitentiaries. I didn't lose anything there and if I did they could have it. There wasn't a thing in California that wasn't somewhere else. As much as I liked the Ventura area it wasn't worth the trouble it took to stay there. Not to mention that all I had to do was get one more drug or gun bust and I'd get life under the three strike law.

The economy was in the toilet. The cops'd figured out what crank was and were convinced that everyone in Ventura County was on it. The thing they asked most frequently during a traffic stop was "will you tilt your head back so I can look up your nose?" They had watches with a little rounded triangular shaped appendage on the side that measured your pulse when you laid your finger on it.

The shit was just getting too deep to deal with and I was sick of playing cat and mouse with every cop I saw, or should I say saw me. If you rode a Harley that automatically made you a target of law enforcement and pretty much took the fun outta riding. One afternoon I got stopped riding from Ojai to Oxnard four times. Each time on the premise of a traffic stop, but once they looked up my nose they let me go without even mentioning a traffic violation. This kind of constant harassment wasn't worth sticking around for and after seeing the way they trumped up all the bullshit charges on Ed, lied to get a conviction and railroaded him into some big joint time I was ready to go.

Most of my friends'd fallen one way or another. They were either guests of the state for a while or they'd lost everything and were living in the river bottom. None of these things had any appeal to me. It sure hadn't taken very long for everything to go in the crapper and I wasn't in the mood to go with it. If I did "what would happen to Kona?"

Three days after we left El Rio we were pulling into the apartment complex Ralph's sister lived in, in Union Ohio. The first thing I noticed when I got outta the car was a kinda' moldy cowshit smell and the fact that it was only sixty degrees and I was sweating. I'd forgotten how humid it was back here. When we were driving around I saw cars that were nothing but rust buckets, holey fenders flapping in the breeze when they drove down the street because the mounts or the bolts that held 'em had rusted off years earlier.

You could drive a car around California for ten years with no paint on it at all and it wouldn't rust that bad. One thing I did like though was the **HELP WANTED** signs everywhere. At least there were jobs available here. Just the opposite of California, out there they had signs telling you to go away, there was no work available.

I had mixed feelings about the place, one good thing about it was it was twenty-two hundred miles away from Ventura and all the recent bullshit there. One problem though I still didn't have my driver's license and it'd be months before I could even try to get it back, worse yet I'd have to go back to California to get it before I could get any other and that sucked.

Once we got there we had to find somebody to get rid of the dope for me. It'd been a long time since anyone'd sold any crank in the Dayton area. A lot of people didn't even know what it was. All I got from more than one person was how it'd once been all over the place but they busted a bunch of people who all rolled over on each other and ratted out the cook who happened to be the son of a cop and people'd been killed for being snitches and all that bullshit. I asked 'em how long ago that'd been, the usual answer was fifteen or twenty years ago.

Damn what a bunch of quitters and sissies. It seemed like getting rid of this crank I had wasn't gonna be as easy as first anticipated and it seemed like the only people I knew didn't wanna try very hard to help me get rid of it. All I heard was "if that was coke, I could get rid of it all tomorrow."

Coke was the most underwhelming drug I'd ever tried, the shit sucked, who wants to spend three or four hundred dollars a night on something that only got you high for twenty minutes at a time and was gone before the sun came up? When four hundred dollars worth of crank would keep you high for a month.

The four of us staying at Lana's were my own best customers. We spent days wired for sound with nothing to do but watch TV and shoot the breeze. The ones that did buy the dope spun right out into space and became liabilities to sell to, but I had to get rid of the stuff and get back to California to get Christine. In the next two months I barely made enough money to rent a U-Haul and get my stuff for those reasons.

The U-haul Police

A few days into 1994 Ralph and I rented a U-Haul truck in Trotwood Ohio and headed back to Ventura to get the stuff in storage. We rented the truck for one day local use, kept it for thirty-seven days and drove it from one end of the country to the other, up the west coast, back down and back to Ohio. I'm not really gonna go into that too much because I intend to write another book about that little escapade.

In that trip alone we packed in enough excitement for a whole other book and then some. I'll tell you this on January fourteenth we were sitting in a friend's shop in Port Hueneme when the Northridge Quake hit. We got outta the building in time to see the Ormond Beach Power Plant explode and part of it fly out into the ocean, engulfing the whole area in absolute blackness except for the frequent transformer explosions and the occasional natural gas fire caused by ruptured gas mains. It was creepy driving thru the pitch blackness lit only by the occasional passing vehicle.

We put over seven thousand miles on that truck, had new tires put on it twice and came close to getting busted twice. One time a deputy in Oklahoma City had the container of dope in his hand and couldn't get it open so he thru it back in the truck. The other time two Missouri Highway Patrolmen were using its stash spot for their desk while they searched the truck and their dope dogs were standing right on top of it and never found it.

The reason was it was in the Maglight flashlight {water and airtight} that I'd stolen from Deputy Alvarez. I'd loaned the flashlight to a friend to use while he was working on his pickup truck. He wasn't a very good mechanic and became frustrated with the job he was doing and hurled it against the wall, flattening one side of it from one end to the other, making it nearly impossible to get the end cap off where the batteries went in. When the deputy in Okie City picked it up there were two ounces of good peanut butter crank in it. He couldn't get it open so he threw it back into the truck, if he'd gotten it open this story would've been a lot different and the ending would've been a lot worse.

The U-Haul police was a private joke between Ralph and I because we had so many brushes with the law during our trip. We joked that it would take the U-Haul police to crack the case.

When we got back to Ohio we ran the truck outta gas on the side of I-70 so no one could steal it and left it sitting with the keys in it on the side of the freeway near the airport exit after wiping it down for prints, that would baffle the U-Haul police with bullshit when they found it.

Back in Ohio with another batch of dope even better than the first we looked for more candidates to become roman candles after the first line. We found a few, but they were mostly the ones from the first batch.

While we were gone a phenomenon that I hadn't seen in years and didn't particularly miss occurred, it snowed.

Fuck The Buckeye

When we got back there was a foot of snow on the ground and it was colder than a witch's tit. We pulled up in front of the apartment and started to walk inside. Ralph's sister met us at the door, she let Ralph in then slammed the door before Kona and I could get in. Thru the glass in the storm door she said "you're not welcome here anymore, you can go stay with Vena if you want, she doesn't care" and the inside door was slammed in my face.

Fuck if I'd known that I'd've stayed in California, who the fuck wants to be homeless in a stolen U-Haul truck with two ounces of crank on 'em and no driver's license? That's a sure-fire way to find yourself in jail in a hurry, not to mention once the truck was discovered all my stuff would be seized and "what would happen to Kona" or the near zero temperatures, what a fucking asshole bitch, fuck her.

I drove down to Vena's, when I got there all the lights were on, I stood on the porch for half an hour beating on the door until I was half frozen, no one ever answered the door so I said fuck it. I got back into the truck and headed back to Lana's.

It was near I-70, I'd sleep in the truck with the engine running tonight in front of the apartment that way if anything happened someone there would take care of Kona I hoped. After I got a little sleep I'd head back west and sell dope in the truck stops till I got back to California. Instead of going back to Ventura I'd go up to Clay's and try making a new start.

I parked in front of the apartment and lay down across the seat using Kona for a pillow, as I was dozing off someone tapped on the window, since it sounded like knuckles and not a flashlight I didn't jump up. It was Francie. I cracked the window, she said to come inside, I shut the truck off and Kona and I went in. I listened to the bullshit about it being a government subsidized apartment and how she couldn't have so many people there and Kona especially couldn't be there.

"Why the fuck didn't you tell me that before I left?" At that point I didn't give a fuck what she had to say about that bullshit. I wasn't from there, they were the only people I knew there, if I couldn't stay there she should've said something before I left, then I wouldn't've come back. I wasn't that thrilled with the place or the people either for that matter, I'd only met one dude there that was even halfway cool, everyone else I'd met was an ignorant weak-minded piece 'a shit.

The next few months were like the previous few months, they sucked. It was either snowing, raining or so fucking cold you couldn't stand it. The dope sold slowly because it was so good a little went a long way, all the way to the Montgomery County Jail for animal cruelty.

The cranked-up, drunken lunatic Vena walked over to the local fire station dangling her kid's pet rabbit by it's ears. In front of her kids and a bunch of firemen she whipped out a knife and started stabbing and hacking the rabbit to pieces screaming about it interrupting her while she was talking to Willie Nelson {talk about delusions}.

As she was being taken to jail she was raving to the cops and everyone within earshot about this biker named Dave from California up in Union at the Meadows of Martindale apartments selling the best crystal meth she'd ever done. Fuck, she did everything but shout out the phone number, she probably waited till she got to the jail to do that.

That sure did explain why the Union cops were always driving thru the parking lot. It was a few days before we found out about that shit, but long before we heard about it I became wary. The first few months I was there you never saw a cop in there, suddenly they seemed to be circling like vultures.

My Future Ex-wife

April of `94 the bottom was falling outta everything again like it had been for years. Because of the lunacy with the rabbit everything had to stop once again or we'd all end up in jail. Lana was being evicted because of me, meaning we all had to move. My move was gonna be back to California, fuck this place!

Ralph'd grown up in Dayton and had a lot of friends that he'd reconnected with when he returned to the area. One of 'em had a `70 Dodge van that wasn't much more than one of the rust buckets I described earlier, but it ran and wasn't bad for two hundred dollars. I didn't particularly like Ohio, the weather sucked and once it got warm the mosquitoes ate me alive every time I went outside. If I was gonna be homeless I'd rather do it in California than Ohio.

We were taking our time moving, more playing at it than doing it. Doing anything was difficult for me, it'd been weeks since I'd had any dope and all I wanted to do was sleep. One day while we were walking around in circles trying to get something done a tall, thin auburn haired gal with sparkling green eyes, named Debbie, knocked on the door and asked if we had any papers, we didn't. I told her no; she thanked me and walked away. After that when I'd take Kona over to the park she'd come over and chat while we played ball and whatnot, occasionally she'd bring a joint and we'd get stoned.

She wasn't exactly my type, she was a recently divorced housewife with three kids and though she was nice enough I didn't want any more than minimal involvement because I was leaving to go back to California and I didn't wanna get tangled up with anyone and side step those plans. We were all finally out of Lana's, Ralph and Francie

446

moved two doors down to the apartment of a single mom that Francie babysat for and I slept in my van in the parking lot for a few days till I was ready to leave.

I'd packed everything I could into the old thing and was just hanging out for God only knows what reason. Anyway I got stopped by the cops right in the parking lot of the apartment complex. He wanted to search the van but after I opened the doors and he saw all the shit stuffed in it from floor to ceiling and wall to wall he just asked me if there were any drugs or weapons in it and took my word for it when I said no. his next issue was the no license thing. I gave him a big long story ending with leaving that evening to head back west.

The outcome was that I was to be outta town by the next morning. If I wasn't he'd arrest me and well you should know the drill by now. While I was talking to him Debbie'd driven past, parked, and gone in her apartment. After he left she came out and wanted to know what he wanted. I gave her the rundown, after that we spent the rest of the day together, we went looking for a bag 'a weed and partied until early in the morning.

I finally had to leave to comply with the cops deal from the day before; she told me to write and gave me a hug. I told her I'd be back sometime and left it at that. Kona and I walked over to the apartment that Ralph and Francie were in, the door was locked and everyone asleep so I wrote goodbye on a piece of paper and stuck it under the windshield wiper of the car and left.

Somewhere I Belong

After the recently rodded rotten radiator popped its cork in Williams Arizona we got to Ventura on a wing and a prayer. Four days after we left Union Ohio we were back in the one place that I liked to be, Ventura. I drove to Ed's house, when the door opened, Ed was as amazed to see me as I was glad to see him. I don't know which I was gladder to see, him or the mirror that he broke out and the lines we did. I know both felt good, Ed and I'd become quick friends and good friends to boot, he was getting the shitty end of a big stick and it was far from over.

While I was gone he'd been busted again at the gas station on the corner for simple possession. After the first bust on Modoc he'd been hounded unmercifully everywhere he went. Having cases pending he couldn't even blow town to get away from the constant bullshit. Lori'd been busted for under the influence and ordered into an inhouse rehab where she ran into some real scumbags that got her into slamming dope. Once that needle goes in your arm everything else goes out the window.

Ed'd married her which I thought was a gargantuan mistake, but I kept my mouth shut because at the time she was his soft place to land after the bust on Modoc. Now she was like any other junkie on the street that'd steal anything and everything she could from him. She'd abandoned her kid and her husband for dope and if he left the condo for five minutes she was in there stealing him blind.

She stole The Truckster from him twice while I was there, once she used it to commit a burglary on one of Ed's friends' right down the street from him. The neighbors gave the cops the description of the car and a few days later when Ed was visiting the same friend the neighbors saw the car again and called the cops. When Ed left Jerry's house he was swooped on and jacked up seven ways from Sunday for the burglary.

Jerry was the one that had him released; now they knew who the burglar was for sure. Another time she was caught in the same friend's house by his girlfriend who happened to be home sick the day she broke in.

A few days after I got there Ed and I walked into his house and there she sat with her scandalous new junkie buddy Mario slamming dope in his living room.

Ed was mister mellow, he barely raised his voice when he was furious, the only way you could really tell if he was mad was his color'd change and he'd talk faster. I could tell he was pissed that they were there, but instead of saying anything he went into his bedroom to do a quick inventory.

While he was in there Lori tried to strike up a conversation with me by asking me what I was doing back in Ventura. I told her I was there to put a stop to my friend being ripped off. When I said that her junkie buddy's head snapped up and the color drained from both their faces.

"How you gonna do that" was her next question.

"Kill 'em if I have to."

When I said that it was "we gotta go" and they were gone.

When Ed came outta the bedroom he asked where they were.

I told him they'd suddenly found out how short their lives were gonna be and split.

"The Truckster" was all he said. We went outside and sure as shit it was gone.

Lori called later like nothing'd happened {an oh so typical junkie move}, feigned surprise that someone'd stolen the car. "Oh my God" was her reply, like it wasn't her, as if she'd never done it before and wouldn't do it again if not stopped. Then the tune changed again, suddenly she had it and was gonna bring it back in a little while.

When I got back to town Ed's house was full he had a roommate and shit, so I stayed with another friend up on Vista Del Mar Drive. He was also in the process of losing his life to dope and a myriad of other personal and financial woes. His house was in foreclosure along with the rest of his life, it seemed we were all in freefall with the bottom coming up fast.

I'd blacked out the windows in his garage so the nosey neighbors couldn't snoop around and passersby couldn't see what I was doing. I wasn't particularly doing anything other than working on bikes, but while I was doing that I was getting high as usual.

One afternoon I was headed down to Ed's. I snorted a big fat ripper, put all the shit away in my toolbox and locked it. Walked out the front door and was swooped on by the swat team, DEA, ATF, and a couple dozen local uniform cops.

They had me put Kona in the van and lay down on the ground where they kneed me in the back of the head and neck while they cuffed me and kicked and slapped me around once the cuffs were on {like most chickenshit cops}, holding guns to my head daring me to move or make a sound so they could shoot me.

While they did this the dogs were run through the house, a crowd of neighbors had gathered at the end of the driveway and were screaming "kick him again, he sold drugs to my children. He moved, shoot him!"

Their dope dogs weren't very good because they didn't smell the quarter ounce of dope in the top drawer of my tool box. "There's nothing in here," they announced when they brought the dogs out. Two cops picked me up off the ground and removed the cuffs.

The audience in the street jeered them for that. "You're letting him go, he's a drug dealer" they screamed. "We want him arrested now! Get this filth out of our neighborhood!"

This time I could see who was doing most of the screaming, it was the slut from the house next door. The first time she saw me there she came right over and introduced herself, the problem was she'd done it in front of Steve {whose house it was}. After she'd gone he filled me in on The Whore Next Door, as she was known in the neighborhood.

The next day I was working on a bike in the garage when Steve left for a job he was doing out in Oxnard. Not five minutes after he was gone she came walking down the driveway in a pair of stiletto heels, naked under a skimpy little see thru silk robe that barely covered her crotch. Her freshly manicured pubic hair, all but shaved displayed every fold of her pussy. As she set the two cups of coffee she was carrying on the desk, she let the robe fall open showing me her ample breasts and well toned body. "Not bad for forty-one, huh?" She said as she stripped the robe off and threw it on the desk.

"Not at all" I said as I cupped her breasts in my hands and sucked her nipples one by one. I pulled her close and slid a finger in her soaking wet crotch. As I licked and sucked her nipples and fingered her she collapsed against me "fuck me now, hard," she breathed into the back of my neck. I swept everything off the top of the desk, breaking the coffee cups and splashing coffee everywhere. Keep in mind we're forty feet from the street, with both garage doors open and she's on her back on the desk naked with her legs in the air.

"Let me close the doors."

"No I like it when people see me getting fucked, fuck me hard."

I obliged her, she was hot and those long silky smooth legs felt great wrapped around my neck and head and everywhere else they touched. She came so hard I thought she was gonna drown me. When we were done she hung around the rest of the morning, never putting her robe back on, sticking her big tits in my face to be sucked while I worked. The mailman got an eyeful when he stopped to deliver the mail and the neighbors got an even better eyeful when she walked to the mailbox in nothing but stilettos to get it. I fucked her five more times that morning on the desk, bent over it, you name it.

When Steve got home of course I had to crow about it. He told me to nip it in the bud because her husband was some high muckity-muck in upper-buttcrack and would cause a lotta problems if he got wind of it. For me it was just someone else to do, so it wasn't any problem saying no.

The next time she came over, which was the next day I told her I was too busy to take the time, fooling with her yesterday had put me behind and I had to get the job done today. You'd think I'd spit in her face she got so mad, I told her to come back in the afternoon and we could play slap and tickle to her hearts content.

"My husband'll be home then!" She snapped. Wheeling on her stilettos and stomping off. She looked as good walking away as she did coming toward me. It was a good thing the blood was in the right head this time.

"Hell hath no fury like a woman scorned," kept rolling on a loop thru my head once I realized who it was that was shouting most 'a the shit at the cops. She was mad as hell when they packed up and left.

I let Kona outta the van so he could go potty while I waited for the cops to clear out completely. I didn't wanna be on the street with them around for a number of reasons. My nemesis was the last to leave "I'll get you you bastard, if it's the last thing I do!" She spit at me as she stomped indignantly toward her house.

"Does this mean we're not friends anymore?" I asked her backside as innocently as I could while she was still in earshot.

"We were never friends!" She snapped.

"We sure fucked like we were yesterday morning." I said it loud enough so the ears in the garage would be sure to hear. The clang of a dropped something on the garage floor told me my comment'd hit home. I got in the van and went to Ed's. Steve was there and had a cow when I told him what happened. He apologized for the bullshit.

My answer was "it's the price we pay, for the life we lead" and the conversation moved on to bigger and better things.

It so happened that the reinstatement date for my license and my birthday were one in the same. At two-thirty that morning I was stopped for no real reason by two Ventura cops. The only thing I got was a ticket for driving under suspension and sent on my way with a "fuck you and your license," by the two assholes that stopped me.

At nine the next morning I was at the Oxnard DMV getting my license back, hoping that the judge would be cool and let it slide. If not it would mean another year with no license and I couldn't live like that anymore. I put the case off as long as I could so I could enjoy a little legal driving time. It'd been a long time since I could legally drive and it felt good not to get a knot in my stomach every time I saw a cop.

The next low point in my return to Ventura was the day I had to take Ed to jail to do his time for the possession case from the gas station bust. Not only did I have to take him to jail, I had to keep Lori out of his house long enough to get all his stuff packed into a U-Haul and delivered to his folk's outside of Phoenix so they could store it for him. The first bust hadn't been adjudicated yet, that would happen while he was locked up for the possession charge.

After his things were safely in storage in Arizona I was once again homeless. While I was staying at Steve's Christine'd dropped one of the valve seats that asshole Mel had put in while I was in Colorado rendering her useless. She simply got loaded into the van with everything else and toted around with me everywhere I went. I had a new set of heads for her, but the conversion would cost money and a place to do the work, neither of which was available at the moment.

For months Kona and I drifted around the Ventura area sleeping in the van wherever we happened to end up when I ran outta dope. I did a little bike work here and there the outcome of which was less than stellar, contributing to another ever quickening downward decline.

One evening while I was going to a customer's shop the rearend came apart in the van. We dragged it to his shop and I did the best I could to put it back together with what I had to work with. It kinda' worked, but it made a horrible clunking noise and vibrated like crazy when it got around forty mph. I drove it like an old woman to keep it together as long as I could.

Every Line Is An Adventure

Around the same time the rearend went out Ed was released from jail. A friend told me he'd evicted some people from one of his mother's rental properties and they'd left behind a Dodge van. I enlisted the aid of my best crimey. He and The Truckster and I went over to Buck's. We drug the thing outta the pile of trash it was buried under and towed it over to the customer's shop where the van was with the intension of swapping out the rearends but the new one was a full floating heavy duty rearend and mine was a regular rearend.

Several of the key things like the U-joint yoke and the spring hangers were different and not interchangeable. We'd done all that work for nothing, but we'd had fun doing it and the adrenaline rush from when the cops stopped us was an added plus.

Since I couldn't fix the van, all I could do was baby it around until I could. Bill and Linda'd moved from El Rio to Oak View and I was turning into their driveway the day the rearend finally took a shit and went away for good.

Bill was already in trouble with his landlord for having too much stuff in his yard. It was beginning to look like a tweaker's paradise, which it was. I'd bought a Ford van from another friend for a hundred and twenty-five dollars and brought it to Bill's to work on. One thing'd led to another the way things do in the ever spinning world of a downbound crankster and it ended up being another thing for his landlord to bitch about instead of the replacement for the dying Dodge like it was intended.

We shoved the Dodge over next to the Ford and that became our home for that rainy season. In between rains I worked on the Ford and got it running, despite my best efforts the damn thing would only run on six of the eight cylinders. I couldn't put off my last driving under suspension any longer. The judge didn't give me any leeway at all except with the additional suspension time and I ended up with ten days in jail and only thirty days of additional suspension time.

The thirty day suspension wasn't too bad, ten of it would be spent in jail; the only problem was "what would happen to Kona." Again a call was made to Diane, Ralph's friend that took him before and again they agreed to take him. Her and Kelly came up to Oak View and got Kona and I. Once we got to their house and they found out the whole story they offered me the couch and told me to get my shit outta Bill's and bring it there. Which was very timely since Bill's landlord was up his ass constantly to clean up the property, namely my two vans.

The next day I called Ed and asked him if he was ready for another adventure. "Fuck yah" was his answer. I gave him directions to the place and a little while later we were lining up to go retrieve my two junks full of junk and bring 'em back to El Rio where Diane lived.

I hooked the Dodge to the old Ford and on the six working cylinders that the Ford had we began the slow and strenuous project of dragging the raggedy assed Dodge with the even more raggedy assed Ford all the way from Oak View to El Rio. It was a slow trip. I took it as easy as I could on the old Ford. We didn't have to hurry we just had to get there. We did it in the middle of the night like most cranksters do everything. The reason for that was because if we did it during the day we'd have traffic on Route 33 backed all the way up to Ojai by the time we got to Ventura if we didn't.

When we got off the 101 onto Rice Avenue and started up the incline for the 101 overpass the Ford died, stalling our rolling junk yard in the middle of the road. It was only outta gas and there was an all night station right across the bridge.

I grabbed a can and ran as fast as twenty four years of meth abuse and a pack of Camel straights a day would allow, meaning that I ran about three steps and huffed and puffed while walking the rest of the way there and back.

As I was getting to the top of the bridge, red and blue light was strobing off everything around me. Fuck, the cops were there. When my caravan of crap came into view Ed was sitting in the Dodge, his eyes as big as saucers, gripping the wheel with both hands and staring straight ahead. The cops were still sitting in their car with spotlights trained down each side of the vehicles.

I put the gas can down near the filler for the Ford and walked back to the police car. As I walked up the cop on the driver's side rolled down the window and asked if gas was the only problem.

"Yes."

He said "I don't wanna hear it and I don't wanna see it, get the gas in that thing and get it the hell outta here."

You didn't have to tell me twice. I jumped to it, got the thing fired up and we struggled our way to Diane's and parked the mess at the curb. I borrowed Diane's husband's pickup and took Ed back to Oak View to get The Truckster, mission accomplished. Another adventure under our belts without anyone ending up in jail which was getting to be a popular place for myself and most of my other friends as well.

The second of January '95 I turned myself in for my ten days. I went immediately back to the farm to do my time. I was released the morning of the seventh day due to overcrowding. It was 7:00AM when I walked out thru the release door into the visitors lobby and back to reality. The reality of having three vehicles that didn't run, no money, no home, a raging crank habit and no way to support or fix any of it.

I walked all the way from the county jail to El Rio. As I walked down Nyeland Avenue I could see Kona running in the yard with Diane's dogs. When I got about twenty-five feet away he stopped, his head whipped around and our eyes locked. He was over the fence in one bound and all over me like a cheap suit. I don't know who was happier to see who, I sure was glad to see him though.

When I opened the front door Kona bounded in. When he bounced in the door to Phillip's bedroom, Phillip jumped up figuring he was gonna have to go chase down their escape artist dogs. As he shot out of the bedroom door he almost ran headlong into me surprising the shit out of him. Phillip and Kona'd become big buddies the first time they babysat for me and once again he took it upon himself to be the buddy and head caretaker for Kona.

All I ever heard about Phillip was what a problem he was. The problems he had were common in all kids from broken homes. To me he was one of the coolest sixteen year olds I'd ever met. I don't think anyone gave him credit for being a pretty cool kid, they just hammered on him for the mistakes he made. Hell we all screw up, learn from it and let it go, remember the lesson and not the deed.

When I got out I was in the usual shape, broke and homeless {I don't call camping on somebody's couch having a home, it's more like being a bum}. When I bought the Ford it had some new plumbing fixtures in it like a new low flow toilet and some odds and ends. To get some money I put all this stuff in the Penny Saver for forty dollars. The first night it ran I sold it, that'd give me the money for my reinstatement fee and to get enough insurance to show proof of it to the DMV and of course some dope.

By now without dope I'd sleep for days. With dope I'd be up for days. The only thing that superseded dope was dog food. Kona came first, a first for me in itself. For years dope had come first, last and always.

On New Years of ` 92 I'd walked over to a friend's house a few blocks away to get an eight-ball. When I walked into Bruce's office he had a half ounce lined out on a piece of polished marble, he handed me a tooter and said "Happy New Year, do it all or don't do any." I snorted all of it.

When I was done the top of that marble looked like it'd been wiped clean. I handed Bruce his tooter and exhaled tasting the crank on my breath. He looked at the spic-n-span top of that marble and said "fuck man, I was only kidding, that was supposed to last all night. I didn't think anyone could snort that much dope at once."

As serious as I could, with my straightest face I looked at him and said "I never kid about dope."

"I guess not, I'll never do that again," he replied as he handed me the eight-ball. With our business done I headed back to the house before the cops got thick. Even though I was only walking a few blocks, that didn't mean I couldn't get fucked with especially on New Year's Eve.

That's how deep into dope I was at one time. Without a second thought I'd snorted enough dope to blow out an elephant's heart. The amazing part, I walked back over to Craig's house and fell asleep {the first sign off an overdose, you just shut down until your body burns off the excess dope. You wake up sprung, once that happens you better have something to do} on the couch while watching a movie with Lori and Frankie.

Once I had my driver's license, the next thing was Christine, but first I had to get rid of one of those vans. After doing a compression test on the Ford I decided that it was the one I was gonna get a hundred and twenty-five dollars for at the Pick-a-Part in Santa Paula. Ed and I had one last not so adventurous adventure. He followed me out to Santa Paula in The Truckster, picked me up and we went back to Diane's after picking up an eight-ball with the money from the van. With an eight-ball I could half it giving me a teenth for personal, whack the other teenth back up to an eighth, bag it out and make a hundred and fifty dollars. That was more than enough to pay the rest of my insurance and get Christine back together.

Shortly after this last anti-adventure I had to say good-bye to one of the best friends I'd ever had. Ed'd gotten four years joint time for the Modoc Street bust, which sucked unbelievably. I don't know how he got himself to turn himself in {his parents put up their property}, I couldn't've convinced myself to do it. As close to Mexico as we were I'd 'a hauled ass. For me that'd've been the frosting on the cake of my bad decision making, but back then it's what I'd've done. It sucked losing Ed, he was a good partner in crime, game for anything and could keep his mouth shut, rare qualities in people these days.

While all this was going on Diane's landlord {who lived right across the street} was getting on them about me being there, he didn't like my old van being there and he didn't like me there either. The pressure was mounting daily for me to get moving. I got Christine done, but getting the van fixed was gonna be harder. A rearend was around a hundred and fifty dollars. I didn't have it but the van had to be running so Kona and all my shit could go with me.

After much finagling I found the right rearend behind this guy's shop on Thompson. The only condition was I had to get it out from under the van that weekend because the rest of the vehicle was going to the crusher on Tuesday. Best thing about the deal was it was free as long as I got it out before Tuesday. Hell of a deal at twice the price I thought.

It'd be simple I'd borrow Jay's pickup, they were going outta town for Memorial Day weekend so he wouldn't need it anyway, go pull the rearend on Saturday and by Sunday noon have the van rolling again and be gone when they got home on Monday.

Jay loaned his pickup to a coworker that weekend and the guy never brought it back. Come Tuesday I rode into town early in the morning, the van was already gone. I'd talked a friend down the street into letting me tow the whole thing down there, where I could pull it out, throw the rearend in his pickup and bring it out to the house and take the rest of it to the crusher. Since the van was gone though, that fucked that up and I was stuck at Diane's for a few more days till I could make other arrangements.

What I ended up doing was having a friend tow my van to my friend's shop and living in it there while I did enough work for him on one of his vehicles and regular shop work to pay for everything and put some money in my pocket. He found me another rearend and let me use his tools to change it out one evening outside his shop.

Kona and I were now able to go anywhere we wanted. We lived in that raggedy assed old van parked out front of his shop for two months. When the shop closed we'd hang out till late at night with Drunken-U in a motorhome parked out front or with Johnny, one of the guys that worked and also lived there in one of the back rooms. When we finally crashed in the van, we'd get up around sunrise and drive down to the parking lot for the beach access and sleep until around nine. Wander back to the shop, do some dope and do nothing or something depending on what was available to do.

The highlight of the two months came early one morning {2:00AM early} in Fraser Park on my way up to Bill and Linda's. We stopped there to eat a burrito and enjoy the peace and quiet of the place. While we were there I had the stereo on real low. After I finished my burrito I got the shit out to do a line. Though I was looking down I noticed lights in my periphery and looked up to see what it was. The light wasn't coming from any car and it really didn't look like any light, it was just a greenish glow above me in the trees. I hurried and snorted my lines before anybody got there if anyone was even coming.

I put all the shit away and looked up in time to see a huge mass of little greenish glowing orbs descending all around the van. I quickly rolled up both windows in the van and watched whatever it was descend all the way to the ground like a curtain. I thought I'd finally blown my mind, but when I looked over at Kona he was seein' 'em too.

They descended and kinda' floated all around us filling the clearing I was in as far as I could see. Everything had a weird greenish glow as they swirled slowly around us. Kona's eyes darted from one to another as they drifted in front of his side of the windshield. He'd reach out with his nose and try to sniff 'em and follow 'em from the front around to his side of the van. Then track another one in a different direction so I knew I wasn't hallucinating. Just like they slowly lowered, they slowly rose outta sight.

When they cleared the top of the van the stereo suddenly came back on. I'd never noticed it go off. When the stereo came back on Kona and I looked at each other. "Did you see that bud?" The look on his face was saying the same thing to me. I started the van and drove to Bill's with a severe case of the willies.

When I got there I told 'em about it. They listened to the story and looked at me like I'd lost my friggin' mind. The only witness to this was Kona and he wasn't talking. I guess he didn't want people to think he was nuts too.

A few mornings later I was driving up to the shop from where I parked at the beach access to sleep. When I parked in front of the shop I sat in the van for a moment and looked at the vacuum that my life had become.

At thirty-nine years old, after twenty-five years of meth use I was living in a rusted out van with expired registration that I couldn't get a plate on in California if I wanted to. All it'd take is the right cop and everything I owned {which was mostly junk} would be gone, then I'd have even less nothing. I had no job, no hope, no anything. The only thing that kept me going every day was Kona. Whether I ate or not he had to, no matter what he had to be taken care of. I had a twenty-thousand pound gorilla on my back named **CRANK**, that should've killed me long ago and I'd finally had enough.

I packed up Christine and arranged everything else to ride, collected less than what was owed me and had no clear idea about where I was going. I'd lost track of Clay and my family during one of my stints in jail or the gutter so essentially had nowhere to go for sure. Anyone I knew locally did as much dope as I did so that wouldn't work. I had to get as far away from everyone and everything I knew as I could if this was gonna work. I headed east.

July 24th 1995

I was done. If I didn't do something, I'd really be done for good.
The only place there was anybody I knew was back in Ohio. Four
days later I was in front of Debbie's apartment at the Meadows of
Martindale Apartments in Union Ohio. The same green curtains were
in the windows. No one answered the door though.

I went over to the payphone in front of Our Place and called Ralph.
Francie answered and said Ralph'd just gone to work that week driving
over-the-road. I told her I was at Our Place. At first she didn't believe
me, but she gave me directions to their place down in Dayton and half
an hour or so later my trip was over for now at least.

I'd run outta dope the second day into the trip and just gotten to
Ohio by the skin of my teeth with twenty bucks to spare. One of my
first questions to Francie was if she could get some crank. She just
laughed and said there wasn't any around there, the big thing was coke,
I guess I'd come to the right place to quit.

A Day Without Crank, Is A
Like Day Without Sunshine

I hadn't been back east in the summertime in many years and had forgotten how different the weather was. The change from the hot dry weather out west to the hot oppressively humid weather of Ohio plus the lack of the thing that kept me moving all of my adult life put me in no/slow motion mentally and physically.

If I'd been anywhere that I could've gotten dope my resolve to quit would've lasted only a matter of hours. If I'd had the money to turn around and go back I'd've done that too. That was why I left Crankifornia, to get as far away from it as I possibly could.

In the first hour of the first day in Ohio I'd convinced myself I'd made a huge mistake. The thing that'd motivated me to leave Crankifornia had been concern for the welfare of Kona. The fear that he'd be somehow harmed was the motivation for wanting to quit and it was the only voice of reason amid all the voices of insanity in my head shouting endlessly for a return to the life we'd loved at one time.

The constant jonesing for drugs was a kind of energizer in its own right, it kept me up at night. When I did sleep I had vividly lifelike dreams of doing drugs that woke me up and kept me up, some part of me thinking that I'd actually gotten high in my dream.

A couple'a days after I got to Dayton I was out riding Christine and rode by Debbie's apartment in Union. She was home this time and we spent the afternoon together. I couldn't stay long Kona was home alone and I really didn't have the energy to do much. It seemed like every day

I went without crank the slower I became. The only thing that woke me up was an adrenaline rush like a fistfight or something of that nature.

I'll never forget the day the neighbor's arsonist boyfriend threatened to burn the house and garage to the ground because he thought I was seeing his girlfriend. I think I had a good reason to nip this in the bud since he'd been convicted of arson twice before.

As Ralph was coming in the door from his week in the truck I grabbed him and we hunted the little prick down. After Ralph introduced me to him as The Avon Man, I gently convinced him with a few punches to the face that It'd be in his best interest to never be seen on that block again.

Of course the piece of shit called the cops, when a detective and two uniformed officers asked me about it I denied knowing the guy. I wasn't lying I didn't even know his name, if his girlfriend hadn't pointed him out, I'd've never known him. The detective bottom lined it like this. They knew the guy was a scumbag and probably did something to deserve the convincing little talk we had. If that was the case as far as he was concerned the dude got what he deserved case closed. I told him to talk to the landlord of the place {who'd been his most recent victim} and if they had any questions after that they knew where I was, I never saw him again or heard any more about it.

Other than more frequent outbursts of anger it was getting harder and harder to stay in the moment. It seemed like each day I went without crank my thought processes lost a little ground. At first it was just an irritant because I didn't have a witty comeback or a snappy answer for something. As time went on though not only did I not have a snappy answer, I didn't have any answer. It was the weirdest thing it was like parts of my brain were shutting down. Following a conversation simply got beyond caring about, mostly because it was almost impossible. I'd sit right there looking you right in the eye and in my head be a day behind what you were saying, it was aggravating. As time went on the distance between what I was thinking about and the real world got further and further apart.

As the stifling summer heat gave way to the overcast gloomy fall it didn't compare with the overcast and gloom inside my head. The only thing I was capable of was being a lump. You're pretty damn depressed when you're too depressed to think about suicide. I'd be sitting on

Debbie's couch in the morning when she went to work. She'd find me in the same spot staring at the TV not really even seeing what's on it when she came home.

I don't know how to describe how we came to be together as long as we did or at all for that matter. We were exact polar opposites in virtually all ways. There wasn't any great romance or any great anything for that matter. I think it was just in her nature to feel sorry for and take in strays. I was far from even sociable sometime and the longer I went without dope the less sociable I became and the darker and deeper my depression got.

For some reason she understood without ever knowing exactly how depressed I really was. I'd never experienced anything like this and definitely had no way of articulating it coherently to anyone else. The only thought that got my attention was dope. On the weekends Ralph'd come by and the conversation always turned to doing dope {the good old days} and how much fun we'd had.

Once the excitement from that conversation wore off I was paralyzed from the neck up again. With very little energy and no desire, it was hard to stay focused on anything for more than a few seconds. My thought processes slowed to none. I was literally trapped inside myself and was afraid I'd be that way the rest of my life. I couldn't get outta my own way long enough to even get in the shower for weeks at a time. When I did get in the shower it was all I could do to get out of it.

Into The Void

For almost a year I was lost in place and in my own way every minute of every day. Sitting immobile and smoking weed for self medication for almost a year with the screwed up metabolizism of an ex-crankster packs the pounds on fast. For years after your body stops living on crank your entire system is outta whack. This leads to a rapid excessive weight gain and a depression so deep, the blackness seems as endless as space.

The darkest thoughts crowd into your brain like people into a New York subway car and push and shove their way around in your head fighting to be the one that gets focused on long enough to be acted upon. I'm probably lucky that nothing got that chance. If it took more energy than taking a bong hit or lighting a cigarette {doing both simultaneously required a nap} I wasn't capable of holding the thought long enough.

The simplest thing like sleeping was the most complicated task. For the first few months all I could do was sleep and eat. I could be asleep watching TV sitting up with my eyes open. Nothing would get past my cornea for hours at a time even though my eyes were wide open. Actually going to sleep was impossible most of the time. In more lucid moments I'd become paranoid that I was gonna be this way permanently and then forget the thought altogether in the next second.

While all this and more was going on in my head every second waking or sleeping, it was like the rest of me was completely disconnected from myself. To all who saw me from the outside you'd think I was the laziest, most moronic worthless thing on the planet. I just sat like a lump staring at the TV or empty space sometime if the TV wasn't on.

The next part of the sleep cycle gone awry was the inability to sleep for days at a time. I don't mean like the wired for sound lets go do something can't sleep. I mean this lead weighted, can't get out of my own way, frustrating inability to shut off the freight train of mostly pitch black self-destructive thoughts and countering arguments that were eternally slamming back and forth at each other like tennis balls being shot out of cannons. I actually lost several arguments with myself during that time and still haven't figured out how I managed to do it.

I spent the winter of `95 and the spring of `96 a vegetative lump on Debbie's couch until she'd finally had enough and tossed me out. I can't say as I blame her I was probably the most impossible asshole I've ever met. She always told me that if I loved that life so much I might as well go back to it {kinda' like the shit I said to the dude at the NA meeting}. There wasn't anything more pathetic than a washed up junkie biker. If I hadn't had Kona I would've never left it. I loved crank, there's never been anything that made me feel that good in my life, but here's a little rule of thumb that definitely applies to that feeling good bullshit, "if it feels that good, it has to be bad for ya!" Pertaining to crank no truer words have ever been spoken.

The good that you feel is way too good. When the bad feelings come they're overwhelmingly bad and the longer you felt that good, the longer you'll feel that bad. I spent nine months in the blackest depression you could ever imagine. The day I realized I'd swelled up so much from the lack of crank, the constant scavenging of everything I could get in my mouth and sitting like an unmoving lump, that my cloths didn't even fit me was an even darker day than the rest. Sitting in a depressed blob doesn't pay very well so I couldn't buy any new cloths.

Imagine if you will, being the person taking applications for a job. So far all of your applicants are fairly well dressed, and dressed for the cold weather as well. Then in comes a thing that hadn't seen a barbershop for fifteen years, a hair brush for two years, breath that would knock a buzzard off a shit wagon. Wearing black insulated long johns with purple shorts over top, tucked into knee high, filthy, once white socks, stuffed into ripped out, worn out long ago L.A. Gear sneakers, with a sleeveless shirt under an old work coat that was about two sizes too small. How many call backs do you think I got? Would you call a nasty thing like that back especially if it couldn't remember it's name or what day it was? I think not.

That was how I looked on many of my job interviews in the middle of my depression. One place I went to in that shape actually held the trash can out for me to throw my application in because the girl refused to put it on her desk and wouldn't touch it herself. **I DIDN'T GIVE A FUCK!** At that time in my life I only cared about one thing Kona, as long as he was fed nothing else mattered.

I hated myself and my entire life up to that point, the only thing that mattered was my dog. Debbie used to say that Kona was an angel sent to me in the form of a pitbull to pull me out of the certain death I was headed for. God knew that pitbull dog would be the only thing that I'd care enough about to make me walk away from the life I'd been living.

Despite myself I managed to get what passed for a job thru Manpower working in a factory for a dollar and seventy-six cents an hour plus incentives, the incentives might've brought it up to two dollars and twenty-five cents an hour. The so called incentive plan was the brainchild of the cheap piece of shit that owned Venture Manufacturing. It used to kill me how he'd come in and walk around the shop bragging about the new car or house he'd just bought while the people that worked for him went without food or rest to make just enough money to be considered poor.

He'd walk up and tell you that when you got your break go out and look at the Rolls he'd just had imported from England because he couldn't find one he liked in this country. Always sure to remind you not to get too close to it as he walked away to rub somebody else's face in the shit he'd just made you eat.

I lasted exactly ninety days in that miserable shithole, that was all it took for me to get my CDL back and find a trucking job. While I was doing that Debbie and I patched things up, which was a big mistake. She didn't like the life that I'd led, she didn't even like herself and she never liked me. How we stayed together for almost eleven years is beyond me. To her I was a washed up useless piece of shit that deserved to live destitute in a gutter somewhere and swore on several occasions that if it was the last thing she did in this life, she'd see me there.

Before I could go to work driving I had to try cheating a system I knew nothing about and failed a pre-employment drug test. It'd been so long since I'd applied for a real job I didn't believe a simple drug test couldn't be fudged. Boy was I wrong. The company was what they called proactive though. I was given the opportunity to comply with DOT regulations by going thru an outpatient rehab for five or six weeks. The failure was for pot, something I just couldn't find that much wrong with then or now. After a clean test I went to work on the first of July `96 almost a year after coming to Ohio.

One of the DOT requirements for someone like me was that I be randomly tested every month for the next twelve months after going to work. I made it to whoops. Whoops came in February of `97. By this time Debbie and I'd bought a house together and were hard at work making each other miserable. When I lost my job because of pot again I was the biggest piece of shit on the planet as far as Debbie was concerned. Pissed because she had to carry the load again while I redid rehab and because of life in general. I was at the top of her shit list and maintained that spot till the day she snuck away for another loser that gave her the boot a month later.

For my birthday that year I got a new job with a hillbilly hoodlum that didn't care what you did as long as the freight got there on time. This guy was truly an idiot. He always complained about the money he wasn't making, but wouldn't make a good business decision to save his life. He'd refuse to pay two hundred dollars to fix something in our shop, saying that the trucks had to be running and end up paying two thousand dollars to get the same thing fixed on the road somewhere. The DOT had it in for our trucks because they knew what kind of junk he ran and the stupid way he ran his so-called business.

He made the mistake of trying to get me to steal freight for him by duplicating PO numbers and getting two loads for the price of one. When he was trying to convince me to do it he made the mistake of telling me that a load of stolen scrap paper'd bring him twelve thousand dollars.

I told him I'd do it for six thousand dollars. I figured if I was taking all the risk I should get some of the profit from it. He had a fit, telling me I'd get my usual loaded mileage rate and that'd be it. I just came home empty and really pissed him off. When I got back to the yard and he found out I meant what I said he got in my face, which was the wrong thing to do. His tune changed completely when I knocked him on his ass.

The longer I worked there the harder and longer hours I worked and the less I made, the only thing that kept me there was being able to smoke weed and not worry about being tested. When a new general manager came to town after the owner screwed the best one he'd ever have, shit started to roll downhill fast. The guy was dumber and drunker than the hillbilly hoodlum he worked for, which made for some even worse decision making and poorer work relations than before.

Being my typical rebellious self I was quick to let everybody know what I thought about this drunken idiot. As things deteriorated within the company the drivers were the ones that suffered the most because they were the ones getting cheated outta their pay every week so the owner could keep up his overly extravagant lifestyle. They finally used a fender bender accident caused by the lack of working trailer brakes on the trailer I was pulling as a reason to drug test me illegally and terminate me. On December seventh of `98 I was gratefully fired from a truly dead end job.

Shortly after I left, their whole house of cards came down when the owner's son was caught dealing crack outta the offices after hours. Not only that but they started being kicked outta the places were we loaded because of their junk equipment and their refusal to fix it. It was the best thing that could've happened to the assholes, truly poetic justice.

After that I had my own business until May twenty-seventh 2004. The low point in that period was when Kona died of cancer on September twelfth 2001 the day after the World Trade Center attack. On May twenty-seventh `04 after a succession of equipment failures and other setbacks I was at the end of my rope business wise, waking up on the twenty-ninth unable to move my right arm clinched the deal.

In order to get my right arm back three discs were removed from my neck and a titanium plate was installed to keep my head from falling into my plate at dinner. It took five months of doing as much nothing as possible to recover from the surgery.

In November of `04 I finally went back to work, all of this time the love hate relationship between Debbie and I grew. She just loved to hate me. Somewhere amidst all the other mess we got married for God knows what reason. This did nothing, but make Debbie hate me more. We came from two totally different ways of life and agreed on pretty much nothing. Everything was a fight started by an insult or accusation, just being in the same room was a reason to insult each other. Our relationship was more toxic than any drug-induced relationship I'd ever had.

Debbie snuck out of our home without so much as a word on the thirtieth of March of ' 06. Leaving me for some guy she'd been seeing on the side for about a year. My first and last thought was good riddance to bad rubbish. I'd rather be alone than be in a constant shouting match with a lying, cheating, opinionated, narrow minded, psychotic bitch. A few months after she left, my stepdaughter, the only good thing that came from our relationship told me one too many times that I needed to write a book, so here I am. If it wasn't for her help getting this project started it might've never gotten off the ground.

That pretty much chronicles some of the highlights and most of the lowlights of almost a lifetime of drug use that started nearly forty years ago. Four years of amphetamine use, twenty-one years of methamphetamine use interspersed with every other drug under the sun, lots of LSD, PCP and all forms of hallucinogenics, drowned in alcohol and smoked out with pot, hash, opium and anything else shoved in a pipe, a needle, in your mouth or up your nose.

I'm No Angel

At fifty-one years old I've been clean for twelve years. The first year I underwent the absolute worst depression any person could endure. I'd lived under the influence of crank for so long that without it I was like the walking dead. The only thing that kept me going at all was Kona. He was the only reason I didn't put an end to the blackness I endured every minute for that first year of cleanliness. The only clear thoughts I had were that I needed dope and he needed care and not necessarily in that order.

At times it was all I could do to get moving enough to walk him a few times a day. These few walks a day took everything I had to get off Debbie's couch and out the door. I think the only thing that kept me from going back to Crankifornia besides lack of money was the constant verbal beating I took from Debbie about being a washed up biker junkie. It was a constant reminder of why I'd left Crankifornia to begin with.

The next thing I managed to do was quit smoking cigarettes, though not near as tough as quitting crank, it wasn't easy. By the time I'd gotten around to giving up cigarettes I was a pretty dedicated smoker. I'd spent a year sitting on the couch staring thru the TV chain smoking Camel straights, which'd gotten me up to around two packs a day, more than I'd ever smoked in my life. My theory had always been that if it didn't get me high it wasn't worth smoking. I couldn't afford to smoke that much weed, cigarettes were the substitute. Quitting smoking to Debbie was just another reason for her to start another fight about something. According to her smoking doesn't hurt you and the only reason I did it was to have a reason to put her down or start an argument. Yah right!

It's been so long since I've smoked a cigarette that the only thing I can remember about quitting was that I did it a week before Christmas. Since I left Crankifornia I've managed to whittle my addictions down to what I think is the most innocuous of all "drugs," pot, that being my oldest and least devastating of all addictions. I really can't believe that pot is that destructive, the only problem I've ever had with it is from the law. Pot's never made me wreck a bike or a car. I've never OD'd on pot or heard of anyone else doing it. I have OD'd on Lucky Charms cereal because I had the raging munchies on pot. I OD'd on rhubarb pie a few times too, but never on weed. To lump pot in with any other drug just isn't right in my mind. Even pot isn't used with the frequency it once was though.

More Than One Way To Die

I've watched as my friends and acquaintances killed themselves and others on crank though. One friend fell asleep at the wheel when he ran outta dope and hit another vehicle head-on, killing a young mother and her little girl on impact. He was so relaxed because he was asleep that he got thrown from the vehicle and received only a few cuts and bruises. This happened shortly before I left Crankifornia for good. I'm not positive of the outcome, but the last thing the rumor mill cranked out before I left was forty years for each death.

In Crankifornia if the sentences ran concurrent that would be thirty years before parole eligibility, if run consecutively that would be seventy years. It really doesn't matter. With that kind of time your chances of drawing a free breath again are pretty slim at his age. Another friend got twenty-five years after being busted for crank distribution and sales. At fifty-three years old he'll be seventy-two before he's eligible for parole. **FUCK THAT!** I have no intention of spending my life behind bars, having to fight for my life every day. I'd rather live in a ditch first.

I've had many friends turn into babbling idiots from using crank, more than I care to remember. I think that was because the dope years ago was much better than it is today, the dope today fucks people up because it's garbage, made from garbage, cooked in garbage cans.

I recently watched the HBO special on meth. It showed people slamming dope in their carotid arteries while they were standing up. If you did that with the dope cooked years ago you'd be a black and blue mess from falling down, not to mention how bad you'd smell from shitting your pants. I used to slam my dope sitting on the toilet, because when it hit you there was no way you could control yourself for the first few minutes after blast off. If your blast off was anything less than I just described the dope went back to where it came from because it was bunk.

I had to give up slamming the shit because the high was more of a spinout than snorting the shit was. For me slamming it was just too good a buzz. I couldn't function with a traffic jam for a brain. It took me some time to figure out exactly the kind of buzz I wanted to get from crank. Each method of ingestion has a different buzz to it. Slamming it is the most intense of 'em all. It'll make your hair stand on end even if it's two feet long and fuck you up so that you can't stop twitching for forty-five minutes or so if you've got good dope.

Snorting it was a much slower blast off and a longer less intense buzz, that was much easier to function on. A few minutes after you snort a line you can feel the niacin rush coming up your back and washing over your head, like an internal wave of heat and hebie-gebies that'll smooth out once the rush gets down your face to your chest. The buzz from this is far more conducive to getting a job done than slamming it could ever be.

Smoking it never appealed to me, because I didn't get off at all smoking it. It did very little for me. I had quite a few friends who started smoking it when they finally fried their sinuses and couldn't snort anymore. The few friends that resorted to smoking after years of snorting lost some part of their minds fairly shortly afterward. Not only did they loose their minds, they developed a respiratory ailment where their lungs filled with fluid continually as if they had permanent pneumonia. Their teeth that'd been fine when they started smoking literally rotted off at the gum line in a matter of months and they developed sores in their mouths to the point where they couldn't eat anything for the pain, yet they continued to smoke the shit.

I had kind of a weird thing happen to me for a while. It was like my nose grew a mind of its own. Whenever I even thought of snorting a line my nose would close up like someone had stuck a finger up each nostril, before I could even get the mirror out. By the time the lines were made I couldn't breath thru my nose to save my life. I couldn't even pour water thru it, it would close up so tight. It got so that Ed would have to lay out lines behind my back and I'd have to grab the tooter and snort 'em before my nose knew what was going on. I remember walking into his house, getting the high sign, spinning around, grabbing the tooter and snorting my lines all in one motion just to be able to get 'em up my nose before it closed up. Weird huh?

My alternative to snorting was eating or drinking it in coffee or alcohol. Once or twice I've wrapped a little bit in a small piece of toilet paper or a rolling paper, kinda' like a pill and swallowed it before too. The buzz from this was very mellow and a good work buzz. The only problem with that was it took at least an hour or more to get off on it. Once it kicked in it was the longest high ya'd get from it. I've eaten some on one morning and not needed a booster till the next morning. You have to put it in something that'll mask the taste or prevent ya from tasting it cause it's the nastiest tasting shit you've ever imagined.

It doesn't matter how you do the shit you begin dying from the very first line and for quite a few people the first line is all it takes. I saw a girl do her first ever line, turn from the mirror and keel over dead on the spot. I've also known people that fried the one working brain cell they had and became for all intents and purposes vegetables incapable of anything that we'd call coherent for the rest of their lives. Without family to take care of 'em they became one of the street urchins you see eating outta dumpsters and sleeping in doorways incapable of even panhandling because they're too fucked up to even speak.

I had a girlfriend like that once, when we met she was okay, but as time went by she got further and further out in left field, until one day she just stopped coming around. She stopped showing up for work, lost her home and everything else. One day I was riding down Ventura Avenue north of town kinda' out in no-mans land, there wasn't anything around there except old rusted out oilfield equipment and junk like that when she stepped outta the trees at the side of the road and started waving frantically for me to stop. Recognizing her I did, but regretted it immediately.

She didn't recognize me at all, which was a good thing. By the look of her she hadn't seen soap and water since the last time I'd seen her and it'd been a long time since she'd looked in a mirror. She had huge sores all over her face where she'd picked holes in herself and was completely unintelligible because she was speaking in what I used to call warp-mumble. An unintelligible way of speaking that spun-out cranksters develop as their faculties fade away. The only thing I could do was ride away. I don't even think she knew I was gone because she was still standing in the same spot babbling away at thin air when I looked in the mirror and hadn't even moved the way a normal person would to track the leaving vehicle that was me.

I used to tell new people that came into my circle not to even try to keep up with me when it comes to staying awake or doing dope. For some reason I could run circles around everyone when it came to getting high and staying high. My friend Ralph poo-pooed me when he first started hanging out at my shop with me thinking it was just some kind of macho bullshit I was running on him.

One evening a friend dropped me off a cloths drier because mine had bit the dust. The drier'd sat out on somebody's porch long enough to become full of leaves and cobwebs. When he dropped it off Chuck warned me not to hook it up without cleaning it out first so it wouldn't catch fire the first time we used it. I was working on something else at the time and couldn't take the time right then, so I asked Ralph to tear it apart for me and clean it out. A little way into the project he asked me how far I wanted it torn down. I told him all the way because it had shit all the way up into the top of it.

He got it torn down to the last screw and told me he had to go home and rest, he'd be back the next day to put it back together. Shortly after he left I finished my project. When I walked up front Amber was gonna load some stuff up to take to her mothers to wash and dry. I told her to wait a little bit, in about an hours time I put the drier back together and had it working.

By the time he came back not only was the drier working but the last of many loads was almost dry in it. This kinda' chapped Rooster's hide, so the next time something like that happened he tried to tough it out and ended up passing out right next to me while we were working. Told ya!

I've seen too many people die too many ways using this shit. I guess the most merciful is just dropping dead. Sitting in prison or being a prisoner inside your own head has gotta be the worst. Unable to get thru to the world around you because of concrete and steal is almost as bad as the walls built inside your mind by deluded, incoherent, paranoid thoughts and the psychotic chaos that cooking your mind creates between your ears.

Another friend lost everything to crank and was so far gone that an unreasoning paranoia took over which caused him to run off into the night never to be heard from again', except when he was found in a ravine not far from were he'd taken off from with a broken neck, leg and ribs where a large rock had broken his fall. I doubt he even knew what hit him and I bet after he ran off he didn't live much longer than a half hour, that's about how long it took to get there from where he'd run off from.

In twenty-five years I've seen many a walking dead created by crank. The thing is that these people were like me, they operated on the fringes of society. Most left their families behind when they left home and lived a wild life outside mainstream society as members of bike clubs or the associates thereof. Living life from one line to the next, only caring about the next party, fully aware of the price they'd pay for the life they'd lead and ready to die in a bike wreck or shootout, not frying their brains to a crackly crunch and ending up a warp-mumbling semi-vegetable instead.

Today meth has become the scourge of mainstream society, ruining the lives of fathers and mothers as well as the children they bring into the world. Before they even get a chance to fuck their lives up themselves, their parents have trashed any chance they ever had or some miserable piece of shit capitalizing on the gullibility of children has gotten 'em hooked on the shit in the fifth grade for the lust for money. **THIS SHIT HAS GOTTA STOP, NOW!**

When crank was an unknown thing that fueled outlaw bike clubs it was one thing, but it's now on every street corner in every city and town in this country and in other countries where it isn't regulated as severely it's becoming the fuel the propels national work forces until they drop dead to be replaced by another crankster that will use it to death.

METH has become a worldwide problem that is gaining momentum as the number one killer drug of all time; eclipsing heroin and cocaine at the same speed it drives people off the deep end. You don't have to be in a box in the ground to be dead. You can be just as dead to the world living in a cardboard box in an alley trapped inside your mind. Living in a world of delusion and paranoia surrounded by yourself. Locked in a prison inside your head that no key can open.

Lithium and Haldall can bring you around to some sort of sanity maybe, if you have the resources to get help. Very rarely does anybody come back enough to be anything more than a burden to the family that's trying to help them once they've gone that far. What if you don't have any support system. Do you want to take that chance? do you really want to push yourself into the abyss of Methamphetamine Psychosis? Never to return.

Can you deal with losing yourself in a tiny Ziploc of white powder? How do you explain to your family that you'd rather spend your time in a baggie alone than with them? Why would you put the people you claim to care for thru that kind of misery? **WHAT THE FUCK'S WRONG WITH YOU PEOPLE? ARE YOU OUTTA YOUR FUCKING MINDS?**

Garbage In, Garbage Out

I feel very lucky that I quit using crank when I did. The dope that I did while cooked in various labs all over Southern Crankifornia and Methico was cooked by "professional" cooks that invested time and money into glass labs and manufactured the best crank available at the time.

Every ingredient in crank is toxic and caustic to the point of causing nearly instant death if ingested in even a small amount. Thru the processes of extractions and bondings created with acids, heat and chemical reactions the ingredients are transformed from their original chemical compounds into the drug known as crank or publicly known as **METH.**

The dope that I did was for the most part cooked from nearly the same recipe the Nazis perfected before WWII and was essentially unchanged except for the use of ephedrine as the base chemical versus the original Benzedrine grit from the German recipe. This more pure form of the drug still exacted a heavy toll on the mind and body of the user, but more from fatigue and neglect than anything else.

Once a user took a break, got some sleep and nourishment under their belt they usually returned to "normal"{for a crankster normal is being high, sobriety is an ever deepening pit and the only way out is getting high again, that's why it's so addictive} till they started another run and were a few days into it. That's when the delusions start again.

There were people that flipped in or out and had to be cut off by their suppliers, that wasn't necessarily done to protect them or out of concern for the user, but more for the cook or the dealer. Having a spun-out crankster running loose with your dope in his pocket and brain is the greatest liability that a cook or dealer can have. The way it was prevented in the old days was the word was put out about the junkie and they were simply shunned by everyone until they went away and bothered somebody else.

If the hint wasn't taken and acted upon correctly by the junkie more severe measures like a good ass-kickin' were in order, that usually got the message across. Once the problem cooled their jets for a while and proved that they weren't a problem anymore they were usually allowed back into the circle, but kept an eye on from there on out. Occasionally the offending junkie that just couldn't get the message became coyote bait, but that was pretty rare.

When crank was pretty much confined to the outlaw world we policed our own. You never heard about what went on in the subcultures that crank flowed like water in because it didn't come into your homes on the evening news and your neighbor wasn't the one getting busted for cooking the shit in their garage and shit like that. There was also an "honor among thieves" code that we lived by, that for all intents and purposes was ingrained in the people that traveled in those circles. Dope was very rarely cooked in neighborhoods full of people, if for no other reason than the possibility of detection and the subsequent arrests and prosecution that followed. We also didn't do the stupid shit that people do today to get money for their dope. We didn't fuck with citizens.

Back then there was an acknowledged code of silence that we all lived by also. If you did get busted you took your lumps, did your time and kept your fuckin' mouth shut. As with any outlaw organization of the time the penalty for snitching was death and that was just a given. Not so today though, it almost seems that when people get busted today they can't wait to start singin' about everything they know and even shit they don't.

The only way to cook a good product is in an all glass lab. Eli Lilley Drug Company doesn't make their prescription drugs in trash cans with garbage they buy off the shelves at K-Mart. The crank of today is cooked from shit like lye, carburetor cleaner, Drano, diesel fuel additive, iodine, battery acid, anhydrous ammonia and sudo-ephedrine in galvanized trash cans or tin paint buckets, heated with dime store hot plates and condensed thru wound copper tubing and rubber hoses.

This makes an already dangerous process even more so by the lack of control, and an already dangerous drug even more so by the contaminated shit that's in it. When this stuff is being cooked it needs a controlled environment, get it too hot and the whole mess becomes an accident looking for a place to happen with disastrous results.

All of these modern day ingredients while possessing some of the properties of the originals also contain contaminants that can't be removed and are included in the finished product in one form or another. Cooking the shit in galvanized garbage cans and tin paint or tar buckets, with wound copper tubing for a condenser add further adulterants to the product by leaching them into the mix from the metal during the cooking process.

None of these things can be measured or even recognized by the dumbass cooking the shit in his garage, more than likely it never even crosses his or her mind. Lets face it the guy cooking the shit in his garage with a recipe he got off the internet or that some other crankster gave him, hasn't a got clue about the real chemistry involved in drug manufacturing all he knows is that he's gonna be the next millionaire drug dealer and he certainly has no conscience or concern for those around him or that buy his product.

The meth of today is far more poisonous than the crank of yesterday simply because it contains all the adulterants and contaminants from the back yard garbage can labs and the bullshit ingredients it's made from. The crank of yesterday was bad enough.

After snorting a line the first night I moved into my shop in El Rio, I waited till the drip was done, walked outside and cleared my sinuses by blowing the snot outta my nose onto the asphalt driveway.

A year later in spite of countless rain storms and hosings down of the driveway the residue I snotted onto the driveway had eaten its way thru the asphalt to the sand base beneath and is even now probably getting the potato bugs in that sand high. It's hard to believe we'd even consider putting that shit up our noses. Especially to me, someone who won't drink Coca-Cola because as a kid I used it to take the rust off my bicycle rims. The addictive power of meth is unbelievable and unexplainable but the most overwhelming one I've ever experienced.

That meth was cooked in glass labs; I helped cook some of it with the best ingredients that money could buy. Now all the real ingredients are unobtainable without control numbers and the same goes for the glassware needed to cook the real thing. Cooking in glass is the only way to cook uncontaminated dope no exception. **THE SHIT OF TODAY ISN'T WORTH DOING, STAY AWAY FROM IT!** I know it's hard to quit, but if I can do it so can you. **I GOT HERE, YOU CAN TOO!** Nothing will change till you change it. No one can get you off it but you. You made the choice to use it, now you have to make the choice to stop. You have to believe me when I say, there's no such thing as a retired junkie, dealer or cook and if you're a chronic user, you're a junkie. I don't care what you think or who you think you are, you're a junkie, the lowest form of human on the planet, one step up from garbage, hence "garbage in, garbage out."

"Spare The Rod, Spoil The Child" Proverbs 13:24

Although I ran amuck as a Godless heathen for a long time, I'm not. The belief in God was instilled in me at a very early age. I grew up in a very small rural town in Maine and though I resisted constantly, my family attended church and I attended Sunday school every Sunday. My mother was a Sunday school teacher. I think she was there mostly to blister my wayward ass when I was bad {my antics weren't reserved just for school or the neighborhood}, which was every waking minute. Even though getting me to settle down and pay attention was a job in itself, it doesn't mean that I didn't know what they were talking about.

I remember one Sunday morning in my very own mother's class when we were given a coloring assignment. Now this wasn't the first time I'd seen crayons or anything like that and I wasn't raised by wolves or savages. After the crayons and assignment were handed out my mother stepped out of the room for a minute. I was working along just fine till I realized my mother was gone. Realizing my mom was gone, I marked my face up like a wild Indian on the warpath and started running around the room whooping like a savage and tormenting the other kids.

Not realizing yet that sound traveled, I was shocked when the teacher next door came flying thru the door, snatched me up, found my mom and remanded me to her custody. My mom was beside herself, she brought me back into our classroom and in front of all the other students hauled my corduroy pants down around my ankles and blistered my ass with a yardstick {she started with her hand, but my calloused butt required firmer measures} until I was hopping up and down squealing for mercy, promising to never do it again.

After that I was stood in the corner for the rest of the day, which was a good thing I couldn't've sat down anyway. Church and Sunday school ran concurrently and my father was in the church choir. When we met at the car the first thing he noticed was the war paint on my face and the way I gingerly tippy toed across the parking lot not wanting the heavy corduroy fabric to rub on my blistered hind end. Of course he had to ask what this was all about. By now my parents were well versed in all of my antics and I was the stupidest little hooligan you could ever meet.

Instead of telling the truth, with my mother right there I began to spin this tall tale about two of the other kids and bla, bla, bla… resulting in another blistering before we got in the car and my mouth being washed out with soap when we got home because I started swearing at my dad midblistering.

Can you imagine what kind of a person I'd be today if my parents'd let me get away with acting that way? Even if I learned nothing else I learned that there were consequences for every action you take. People today aren't taught about consequences, this all started during the permissive and promiscuous `60s and has snowballed into the outta control society we have today.

When I went to school we said The Lord's Prayer every morning right before the Pledge of Allegiance and were taught the golden rule "do unto others as you would have them do unto you" in school, church and home, now that's illegal because some atheist fuckhead didn't like it, fuck that piece of shit. Common courtesy and common sense were ingrained into children as a matter of course, parenting was left to the parents not interfered with by neighbors and government, people minded their own fucking business instead of interfering with everyone around them.

Sadists like the hypocrite Dr. Spock hadn't written their drivel yet. What better way to mask your sadistic ways than preaching the opposite while secretly torturing your own children. In my estimation that one hypocritical asshole started the problems we have today with his "never hit your child, reason with 'em bullshit."

How do you reason with a shrieking two year old? Parents now don't even try, they just walk along like nothings happening while everyone around them has to listen to the little heathen, instead of correcting 'em at an early age so they grow up knowing right from wrong. The ball of inconsideration, self-absorption and meism that is now the driving force and one of the major problems with society was started rolling by that one hypocrite's deceitful publication.

What is the problem today? Four generations without consequences or God is a major part of the problem, the me generations or more appropriately the "hurrah for me and the hell with you" generations. People today don't give a shit about anyone but themselves, they think anything they do to anyone they do it to is just fine and how dare you say something to the contrary.

Our society is now governed by the greed and selfishness that the late `60s and early `70s spawned. Special interest groups forcing their own agendas on the majority of the public, removing God and common courtesy along the way. Forcing society to accept increasingly more abhorrent behavior as the norm every day.

Lying, cheating and stealing are now things we take for granted in every aspect of our lives. The nightly news is nothing more than a smoke screen to hide the truly heinous shit our government does to us every day. Our political leaders are the biggest liars and cheats the world has ever seen next to our so-called religious leaders, who're running neck and neck with them. Greed governs our lives and is allowed to flourish under the watchful eyes of a shadow government gone berserk with the lust for power and wealth. All the while claiming "God wills it" much like the Templar Knights of the crusades while they plundered the wealth of the Arab nations in the name of God.

When anyone does get caught in the wrong today, they either have a condition or a disease or it was somebody else's fault or they didn't know they weren't supposed to do that. No one takes responsibility for their own actions anymore. No matter what happens it's always someone else's job or responsibility. Like the fat bastard that tried to sue the fast food companies because he weighed four hundred pounds, on the pretence that no one told him that if he ate forty big macs a day he'd blow up like a balloon. Granted the suit didn't go anywhere, but how fucking stupid can you possibly be?

Couple this mentality with the multi-orgasmic high of the garbage called meth and holy shit look out! You have a pack of spun cookies out-n-about at all hours of the day and night looking for anything that isn't nailed down and can get them their next high. Carjackings, robberies, burglaries anything that they can snatch and grab. Worse yet the one that just fried his last brain cell and dove headlong into the abyss of Methamphetamine Psychosis and is so paranoid he thinks the world is out to get him and tries to get them first.

Or the stay at home mom that's so far into the meth abyss that all she does is sit in a locked bedroom neglecting everyone and everything while she smokes, snorts or slams herself into a full blown delirium, until she considers her own kids or her husband a threat and acts on the paranoid delusion, killing her entire family. When she's caught it was the drugs fault she's a good person and would never do that. Or that same mom that becomes so immersed in meth that she just leaves home one night and never comes back because dope has become more important than anything else.

All of the excuses are bullshit. We all have a choice. We all choose to use or not, if you choose to use {which is the path of least resistance today}, you've chosen to be an addict. Very few people can turn away from meth {it took me twenty five years to wake up} once they've started the downward spiral, not of their own free will anyway. The choice is usually made for them when they get busted or killed either by the drug or the drug dealer and I don't mean the dealer's gonna kill ya with a gun or knife {or maybe he will, I would've if I felt I had to}, I mean with the garbage from his garbage can lab.

Meth is the biggest lie of all. The good feeling is way too good, I was hooked the first time I used it. In my mind it was the answer to all my prayers. When in actuality it was the cause of all my problems and ruined me for life.

Anhedonia is the medical term for not giving a shit about anything and not experiencing pleasure because you've overloaded that part of your brain with crank so much that it's fried to a delicate crunch. After twelve years of being clean I still can't get too excited about anything. Oh I have my little moments when I feel good about something, but generally I haven't been truly happy in years.

I'd venture to say the happiest moment of the last twelve years was when I came home and found my ex-wife gone. Just the thought of never having to fight with her about everything I did or said was exhilarating for a moment, then reality set in. Fifty years old, alone again, a house that I can't pay for, that I don't even own or want because I hate where I live, not one but two bull dogs to take care of {that'll be a problem when I try to rent a place}, living two thousand miles from where I want to be, and no actual means to make the change. I was working a dead end job for a bottom feeding trucking company that would never go any further than I'd already gotten. The day I started at this place I'd already gone as far or as high as I could go for that company.

The answer to everything for them was never go home, run yourself to death, never get a vacation. Christ how dare you think of wanting to get away from the junk equipment they ran and the constant stress of trying to navigate thru a sea of increasingly ignorant drivers. Every time I came in from sometime up to three weeks away from home they'd be pissed when I wanted to go home for awhile to get away from the bullshit, yet they deserved time off from the office jobs according to them and took it whenever they damn well pleased.

Because I couldn't leave the dogs at home alone for weeks at a time they now had to come with me which meant I had to go from a worn out piece of junk that at least ran to a piece of real junk that belonged in a junkyard and was a hazard to itself and everyone around it on the road.

The stress of trying to keep the rolling wreck outta the ditch and away from the other vehicles on the road was exhausting. The truck I drove before though old and worn out at least would go down the road without taking off for the ditch or the vehicle next to it and would actually get out of its own way. This piece of junk I got stuck in was an accident looking for a place to happen in slow motion. This translated into having to drive fifteen or sixteen hours every day to do the equivalent miles the other truck did in the legal eleven. The only problem with that was after eight hours of keeping this thing between the ditches, let alone in one lane I was so exhausted I couldn't go any further.

The owner of the truck did all he could to fix the problems that were causing the ill-handling. The problem was the thing was just worn out from front to back and fixing one problem just shined a light on more problems and did little to improve the handling overall. As the cost of doing business increased and the truck spent all it's idle moments in one shop or another addressing the myriad problems it was plagued with, the final outcome was that the truck cost more to run than it was making and I was laid off.

The upside of this was I had time to focus on the narrative that you're almost done reading now. My daughter and I started this project in July `06 by Christmas time of that same year I'd only completed fifty one pages of the manuscript and was becoming more and more frustrated with the lack of progress.

That was when I put this project in God's hands and let him drive this bus for a while. Since then he's provided me with everything I've needed to tell this story. Sounds crazy doesn't it? Try it yourself, even if you've never prayed in your life, even if you don't believe yet. It's really very easy and can be done anywhere, anytime, one thing I'll tell you he likes to be called **GOD** or **LORD**, both will get his attention equally well.

Another tip, you have to open your heart and mind to him, he's already got your soul, he's the one that gave it to you, in case you didn't know. Once you've done that in your own words ask him to please help you with any and all problems and issues that you have and don't forget to thank him for getting you this far in one piece. Especially if you're life's a wreck of addiction, ignorance, and poverty of all forms and you feel abjectly hopeless, put it in his hands and you'll be amazed how quickly it'll turn around. He's always listening and he wants to hear from each and every one of you. Whatever you do don't forget to thank him for listening and for all the things he's done for you. Just say a little thanks to him for even the smallest forms of relief and pretty soon you'll see the changes beginning to occur and gain momentum as you talk to him and he in turn talks to you.

By talking to you I don't mean a voice echoing out of the sky, I mean subtle things at first, like something going your way for once. When it does thank him immediately. A simple "thank you Lord" will suffice. Pretty soon you'll notice more and more things starting to go in the right direction and the darkness in you and around you lifting.

You're probably thinking that I'm some bible thumping holy roller that's on a soapbox trying to convert you. I'm not, I don't attend church and haven't since I was a boy. I don't believe in the organized religions of today. I do believe that every so-called religious leader of today is a liar and a charlatan, out to take you and everyone else they can get their hooks into for all they can get. God wants you to be prosperous, but not at the expense of others like the fakes that call themselves men of God.

You don't have to believe in them, in fact doing so is against God's word, they are all false prophets and should be shunned. God asks you to believe in him and him alone and his teachings. If you don't know what they are get a bible and start reading, you'll know soon enough. Ask him every day to put "the white light of Jesus" over you and everything you do and you'll see a change immediately, don't forget to thank him and you'll be as amazed as I am every day at the things that come your way.

This book that you've nearly finished reading was written by him thru me. For years I've known that he had a purpose for me simply because I should've been dead a long time ago. There are things that happened in my life that should've taken it a long time ago that I purposefully left out because I didn't want anyone to try them at home. I lived on the wrong side of the tracks, the law, society and everything people call good and right until 1995 {but I never forgot God's laws, there's a big difference, the laws of man today are made to protect the elitist government from the people they're oppressing more and more openly every day, the things we see on the news are spun to make us believe it's for our own good}. Just the amount of drugs I did and the way I did 'em should've killed me before I was twenty-one. They only made me stronger while other people fell by the wayside from overdoses or fried every last brain cell till they're nothing more than walking dead.

While they were dropping like flies around me, I drifted on from one circle to the next doing twice as much, twice as long and am here today to tell you about it, with my mind, body and soul intact. In 1995 I tried to sit down and tell a story on paper. The resulting crap I wrote sounded like a preschooler and looked like it was written in crayon. After seeing the first page in type I chucked that idea, not wanting to embarrass myself to myself any further. The next time I tried it with my wife who immediately thought it should be done her way before we even got through the first page. After her fifteen minute rant about how stupid I was and how the book had to be done her way or else it was wrong, I just said fuck it.

Her daughter, actually my stepdaughter whom I now call my daughter had some friends that she'd wanted me to meet for some time, but not with her mother around. Once her mother left we all got together for dinner one night. After dinner we all went into their game room and sat around mostly listening to me tell stories. The next day Gina told her that if she wanted me out of the trucks {Jessie hated to have me out trucking, it worried her constantly}, I should write a book. With Jess's help and God's typing ability here it is. I hope something in here will spark your desire for a better life and show you the road to it.

The first thing you have to do is get yourself off drugs, no matter what they are. For me like so many people today my drug of choice was crank, meth whatever you want to call it. I loved crank the very first time I did it, eventually to exclude everything else in my life during the last few years of my addiction. Then along came Kona, Debbie said he was an angel sent to me from God in the form of a pitbull {thank God for dogs} because he knew that was the only thing that'd get my attention. Kona brought me to her because she was a caregiver and she took me in at a time in her life when she couldn't handle one more burden, but did so anyway.

She took me in and supported me thru the worst part of my life change, when everyone had for all intents and purposes written me off. Her and Ralph {mostly her} held me up and gave me the time and place I needed to get thru the most ungodly depression and withdrawl anyone could ever endure. She also spent a lot of time hunting down and hooking me up with the people in my life that meant a lot, whom I'd lost. I'd left everything, everyone and a place I really loved to be to get away from crank, that was the only way it was gonna happen and God knew it. That was how I ended up where I am today.

Towards the end Debbie and I were like fire and gasoline. I deeply resented her "my way or the highway" attitude and not being allowed to ever have my things around me like she did or have a space of my own with my things around me in what I thought was *our* home. Every time I slowly created a space I would eventually come home from work and find she'd rearranged my space to suit herself once again and my things got strung all over the house, shoved into drawers and closets {I'm still finding things I thought had been thrown away years ago} or thrown out in the barn, never to be seen again. She'd proudly display her latest attempt at my emasculation and get mad as hell when I wasn't ecstatic about it. Her idea on that was it was her house and if I didn't like I could get the fuck out.

We never really got along that well. She thought she was so much better than me because of the life I'd led and took every opportunity to tell me in so many words what a piece of shit she thought I was and how I'd ruined her life. Personally I thought dropping out of school, having a kid and marrying a heroin addicted cokehead at sixteen was the start of that ruin, but I could be wrong. In spite of all this, there'll always be a place in the back of my mind that is grateful to her for all she did for me, not the least of which was leaving. Like Kona she'd served God's purpose in my life, then went away.

Like many things in my life I tried to hang on long after the bottom'd fallen out {if there ever was a bottom to our relationship}, hoping that things could be made right with a little bit of give and take. What was happening was she was taking what she thought she deserved and I was giving myself away to try to at least keep the yelling and name calling down to a roar. All the while resentment was building in me to intolerable levels. I was always on the verge of another explosion as she verbally hammered nails in the coffin containing our marriage. It's said that actions speak louder than words, that's only true to a point. Debbie would do some very wonderful things for me, then throw them up in my face so continually that it'd come to a point where I wished she'd stop doing anything for me and leave me alone.

She was actually one of the most shining examples of the me generation I was talking about earlier, though we were the same age she'd been brought up to respect nothing or no one unless they had something she wanted or could do something for her. When that ran out so did her fake respect or loyalty and I became shit under her feet to be discarded. She lives on the premise that "because I'm here, I deserve whatever I want and it should be handed to me because I want it," whereas I was taught that you worked for what you want, that's the only way you'll ever get anything.

One day she did leave me alone, I came home to an empty house, once Jessie brought the dogs back to me I only contacted her one or two more times and then severed all contact with her. Each time we spoke she'd go off on a screaming fit about what a piece of shit I was and how one day I'd get what I deserved if she had anything to say about it. It didn't take long for me to decide it wasn't worth wasting the cell phone minutes for the cussing I'd get so I changed my number and never spoke to her again.

Repressed Depression

That's the only thing I can think to call what I went thru for years after I quit using crank. The initial shock to my system when I stopped was unreal to say the least. The longer I went without it the worse the shock got and the deeper my depression got. I was so depressed that I couldn't sleep. When I did go to sleep I simply keeled over on Debbie's couch for a while. I wasn't interested in sex or anything else for that matter. I might go as long as three weeks without a shower and not move off the couch except to use the bathroom or get something else to eat.

None of this was very good for a new relationship. Debbie was full of insecurities anyway that I made worse by my lack of interest in her. The beginning of a relationship is supposed to be when you can't get enough of each other. I'd already had enough of me, let alone her. The only thing that I responded to was when Jessie's older sister picked on her, that sent me over the edge instantly.

Debbie would ask me if I was seeing another woman or if I thought she was sexy, all kinds of things to try to find out what the matter was. The problem was I didn't know for sure what was wrong with me. I'd never experienced this before in my life so I didn't know what to say and trying to think of an answer in my lead weighted brain was only more aggravating. I'd get mad at myself because I didn't know what to say and snap at her or say the first stupid thing that came into my clouded, ultra slow moving mind and sound like an idiot.

I hated myself more each day as my brain slowed down to a crawl. Trying to just watch TV was almost impossible. I couldn't keep up with the dialogue, my brain moved so slow. The only emotion that was still working at all was anger. I got pissed at the drop of a hat over

493

the stupidest things and the things I should've gotten mad about I completely ignored. It's like I'd been rewired backwards or something while I wasn't looking.

Crank'd made me normal, when I was high I was very laid back and easygoing, always cracking jokes and playing pranks, making fun out of even the most mundane things and generally having a good time. That was all gone and I didn't know where or how to get it back. I was so frustrated with myself that I couldn't stand it.

One night I was staring thru the TV, chain smoking Camels. Sometime in the early morning hours I said fuck it and decided to leave Kona with Debbie and head back to Crankifornia alone. In fact I wasn't even gonna get Christine outta Ralph's garage, fuck that piece of shit, who needed it? I was gonna just get up and head down to I-70 a few miles away and head west in my old van until I ran outta gas, then I'd hitchhike the rest of the way.

As soon as I stirred, Kona opened his eyes. While I put my sneakers on he got off the couch and stretched. I gathered up the few things I had at Debbie's and put 'em in my bag. As I walked to the door I told Kona to stay here, the only time we'd ever been separated since I'd gotten him was when I was in jail. I liked his company so much that after I got him one by one I gave up all my old haunts to be with him all the time. When I told him he was staying there he looked at me as if to say "yah right!" Kona had the most expressive face anyone has ever seen on a dog. He couldn't speak but what he was thinking was clearly displayed on his face and there was never any question about what he was thinking. Those of you that knew him know this to be very true.

As I walked to the door telling him he was Debbie's dog now to be good for her, his "yah right" expression turned to "fuck you, you're not going anywhere without me!" Being the bundle of emotional frayed knots that I was, I fell down on the floor next to him crying, hugged him to me and cried for hours. That was the second time since I'd run outta dope that I was willing to just abandon him because I couldn't get a grip on being clean. The first time had been in a truck stop in Kansas because he wanted to sniff around a little bit before he pooped. It was my first full day without dope and it was hot as hell, I got so bent outta shape that I went storming off, jumped in the van and started to drive away.

Realizing what the fuck I was doing I stopped and punched myself in the head a few times. I looked in the mirror and he was trotting after me with this "what the fuck did I do" look on his face. I opened the door and let him in apologizing all over myself to him and hugged him crying. He hated it when anyone cried and he'd never seen the mess that I was becoming come from me before. I was the one that was always ready to play and was always laughing. He didn't know what to think of the new me and neither did I. I do know that neither of us liked me very much.

Debbie had a lot more faith in me than I did in myself back in those days {maybe because she just didn't know}. It was months before the fog began to lift enough that I could fool everyone but me into thinking I was better. Debbie used to accuse me of wanting to go back to my old girlfriends in Crankifornia. She was right about one thing and it wasn't the girls, it was crank. I craved it morning, noon and night. Shortly after I came to Ohio I parked Christine for good because she was just a huge trigger that brought on an overwhelming desire to get high.

As time passed the fog never got much better, I just got better at faking it kinda' like a "I went insane a long time ago, I just act sane now" thing. She helped me get all my driver's license shit cleared up, I was gonna have to do something pretty soon I couldn't spend the rest of my life in the dumps whether I was or not. I had to buy all new cloths because I was swelling up like a new balloon since I didn't have crank to regulate my metabolizism anymore. The months I'd spent sitting on the couch eating almost everything in sight were taking their toll on my waistline and everywhere else.

At the height of my weight gain I blew up from one hundred and fifty pounds to two hundred and sixty pounds. That right there is enough to depress a normal person, let alone one that's already so depressed he goes in the bathroom to sit on the toilet and cry for hours at a time over God only knew what. I used to do that with great regularity while Debbie was at work and the kids were in school and to this day I still don't know why. Funny thing though {actually not so funny} when something happened that required any emotion other than anger there just wasn't anything there, it was like the well was dry. I was truly the Anhedonia poster child if ever there was one.

Not being independently wealthy I had to go back to work and the only alternative to building bikes was driving trucks, which sucked big time. I hated being gone six days a week and never having any time for myself for only four or five hundred dollars a week. Anytime I complained about it though Debbie accused me of not wanting to work and bottom line as much as it sucked, I had to work.

For almost eleven years I dragged thru life living in a repressed state of depression every minute of every day. My energy never came back to an even near normal level and the only real emotions I felt were a morose kind of sadness and anger at even the most trivial things. I drove all over this country hating my job, myself, my everything, disgusted with myself and almost everything around me. That made life inside my head a living hell all the time. I had no one to even talk to about how I felt, if I said anything to Debbie, she either went off about how she was more depressed and had been longer than me or how I was trying to use it as an excuse to not have to work.

In order to avoid the constant insults and accusations I had to stop talking to her about anything other than useless shit like the weather or what happened out on the road. Even those topics usually resulted in some kind of disagreement or other. It became easier to just not speak at all. Every time I opened my mouth she jumped down my throat with her shit. She was always more tired, or sicker or whatever. When they removed three discs from my neck and screwed a titanium plate into three of my vertebrae her neck hurt more than mine and I was a faker, feigning pain for sympathy and using it as just another way to get outta working.

After I recovered from the surgery I went immediately back to work. A little over a year later was when I came home to an empty house at least that was some relief from the constant upbraiding I got from her about everything I did or said and it made me feel a little better and a little worse at the same time.

On the next trip out I stopped at the North Little Rock Petro Truck Stop for fuel and a restroom. When I came outta the restroom there was a person working in a kiosk across the way that sold "Trucker's Choice" vitamins. I'd seen their vending machines in truck stops all over the country and was curious about their products because for ten plus years I'd been looking for a natural supplement that would at least give me a little energy boost and had tried all kinds of stuff that hadn't worked. This was the first time I'd seen anyone at the kiosks that I could ask some questions of.

I talked with the dude at the counter. While I was doing that he poured me a one ounce sample of a liquid vitamin mixture called Turbo Power. I drank it down and continued talking to the guy. In only a few minutes the fog that'd been between my ears for over a decade lifted and for the first time I actually felt like doing something. My ass wasn't dragging anymore and I felt better than I ever had since I'd quit crank. I walked away with a thirty-two ounce bottle and have never regretted it. In fact when I got laid off one of my biggest concerns was how I'd be able to keep getting my Turbo Power. None of the truck stops near me carried it, after a call to the company I was on their auto ship program getting it almost $10.00 cheaper than in the truck stops and it comes right to my door.

I'm not gonna make any claims here. I am gonna say that after ten years of searching I finally found something that made me feel a lot better and every day I took it I felt better and better. The proof came in the pudding when I ran out and went without for almost a week. The fog came back and I couldn't even get outta my own way again, it was the same feeling as running outta crank. When I finally got some again I swore that'd never happen again if I could help it. It happened one more time just a week or so ago when the Memorial Day holiday interrupted the shipping schedule and I was out for two days before it was delivered, it was all I could do to get outta bed.

I don't make any guarantees and neither do the manufacturers, all I can say is that it worked for me. It's totally legal and one hundred percent natural and if I was kicking crank I'd give it a try, it'll go a long way to getting your energy level back up and keeping the "deadly killer fog" outta your brain. The contact information is as follows, the product you want is called Turbo Power, the company is BioRite Nutritionals, E-Mail address is info@findctn.com, the phone number is 1-877-484-2300. Tell 'em Dave Fuller sent ya, not that that matters at all. All I can say is try it, it beats the hell outta the alternative. I hope it works for you like it worked for me and good luck.

Triggers

Triggers are what the experts on addiction call the things that make you want to go back to using {relapse} after you've been clean. I thought leaving Crankifornia would be enough to make quitting a breeze, **HA!** After using meth for 25 years there wasn't anything that wasn't a trigger for me, even sleeping was a trigger because when I slept while I was using I'd wake up just to do a line and go back to sleep.

I was conditioned like Pavlov's dogs everything I did I either did a line before I did it, while I was doing it, or when I was done doing it, sometimes all three. I used to love to ride. Sometime I'd take off on Christine and ride all day with no real place in mind, just riding for the sake of it no matter what the weather or anything. When I got to Ohio for good, that ended pretty quickly for several reasons. **1.** There wasn't anywhere to go but to a bar and I didn't drink. **2.** The weather fuckin' sucked, it was so humid that by the time I sat thru two traffic lights my balls were stuck to my leg and I looked like someone'd turned a hose on me. **3.** The roads sucked as bad if not worse than the weather. **4.** The drivers sucked as bad as the roads and the weather combined. **5.** The whole time I was on Christine, the few times I did go riding, all I could think about was getting high.

By the time I got back to Ralph and Francie's, I was jonesing so hard that all I could do was sit there and sweat like a fiend and think about dope. As I thought about it I could smell it and taste it and sometime I actually felt like I was high for a minute or two. When I slept I had dreams about snorting dope that were so vivid I'd wake up and run to the bathroom because I'd have to shit like when I used to slam it.

Every day without dope, I sank deeper into the depressing reality that my twenty-five year speed run was done. It was probably by the Lord's design that I couldn't find a job. I had formulated a plan to go back to Crankifornia in the very first days I was in Ohio. Whatever job I got would give me enough money within a week or two to get me back. I knew it'd take two hundred and thirty dollars in gas to get back. If I worked three weeks or a month depending on how much I got paid I'd have enough for gas and an eight-ball or two when I got there. I'd whack one into two, keep the pure one for myself and sell the whacked one in The Valley where people had money and never think about the bullshit of quitting again.

I'd leave Kona with Ralph, he loved Ralph and Francie almost as much as he did me and he'd get used to being Ralph's dog in due time. I thought I was ready to quit, but the jonesing was getting worse each day and I was gaining weight like there was no tomorrow. I even took to snorting the ephedrine tablets that Francie's son would bring home and think I was getting off; actually the only thing they really did was stuff up my sinuses and give me a headache. **What a fuckin' weakling idiot, huh?**

Sitting like a vegetable on Debbie's couch was the only real safe place I had. It was the only place that didn't remind me about dope at least not until I went outside. Ralph's sister's old apartment, the first place I came to in Ohio was right across the way and we'd done a bunch 'a dope there. It's a good thing I hadn't done any with Debbie or she'd've been a trigger too.

A couple times I walked over to the back of Lana's old apartment and looked around the place where I hid the dope outside when Vena killed her kid's rabbit and ratted me out in front of the fire station. After she did that I hid the dope out the back door for a while so it wasn't in the house if the cops did kick the door in. Of course there wasn't anything out there. I knew it before I ever walked over there the first time.

Staying at Ralph and Francie's drove me almost off the deep end, because I'd done so much dope with 'em that that was all I thought about when I was around 'em, especially Ralph. He'd get in on the weekends and start drinking before he ever got home, by the time he got there he'd have a good buzz going and inevitably our conversation would turn to the "good old days" when I had the best dope around and lots of it. Then after he got a few more beers under his belt he'd say "let's go get some crank."

I never disagreed that firmly. While outwardly I said no, inside my brain was screaming YEEES, but it never happened. Ralph'd done his time cruising the couch like a vegetable while I was still runnin-n-gunnin out in Crankifornia. He hadn't had any crank in years as far as I knew, for me it'd only been a few weeks, the smell and taste of it was still fresh in my mind. After he passed out I'd be up till the wee hours of the morning jonesing.

By the time the cold weather came I'd outgrown all my cloths, adding to the depression and the inability to look for work, not that it mattered much I'd already been turned down at all the bike shops in the area and didn't have my CDL yet. I just sat on Debbie's couch, a washed up junkie biker, depressed and alone in my head with the fog between my ears and my cigarettes.

The trigger thing is still going on today, twelve years later. Every time I hear a Harley it makes me think about the "good old days." When we first moved into the house where I'm writing this Christine got stuck out in the barn and buried under a bunch of my old shit so I knew she was there, but I really couldn't see her. Just looking at her took me back to a place I didn't need to go. After Debbie left I brought her in the house with the intention of rebuilding her and riding again, but shelved the idea when I did finally do some riding.

Remember when Debbie left, I had to change owners and trucks. My new boss had become the not so proud owner of an S&S powered Ultra chopper that wouldn't run to save its life. He got it home and that's as far as it got. He hadn't been able to get it to run since he got it there. I told him I'd hook him up and took two weeks off to get my shit switched from one truck to another and work on his bike.

As rusty as I was, it still felt good to get my hands dirty on a scooter again. Once I got the wrenches in my hands it all came back to me and I got it going and stopping pretty quickly.

One Sunday when I finished everything I took it out for a ride for a few hours. Even after eleven years clean it brought back the jonesing before I was a mile from his house. If I'd had any idea where to get some crank I'd've done it. Riding sober felt good, but riding high would've been paradise to me. At least now I know that it'll still be a trigger if and when I get another bike. Maybe if I get a Honda it won't have the same affect.

It was around that same time that Ralph bought some coke. When he told me about it I went up one side of him and down the other. After I lit into him about it he got rid of the rest of it.

I even rode down there and tried to talk him into getting me some of that and I don't even like coke and would've hated myself for doing it, but I tried. I rode Paul's bike a few more times after that not as far or as long, but each time I did the thought of doing a line crossed my mind a time or two which isn't exactly what I'd call jonesing.

I also have another more pleasant type of trigger. In a lockbox that I open every few years or so, I have all my old paraphernalia that I used to do my drugs with. In that stuff is the waterproof bottle that I used to carry my dope in for several years. Every so often I'll open that bottle and take a whiff. It still smells like the killer crank that it last contained almost twelve years ago. You'd think that'd make me jones for the dope, but it doesn't. Oddly enough it starts a "movie" in my mind's eye of the "good old days." In this "movie" while I'm sitting on the bed in my present day home I see all my old friends and the things we used to do. I wonder where some of them are. Unfortunately I know where some of them were buried, which hospital others ended up in and which prison system still others are a part of.

I thank my lucky stars that unlike so many of my friends I escaped all that and am still a "free" man. Unfortunately that freedom has come with a price that sometimes feels like more than I owe and other times doesn't feel like enough.

Broken

Broken is the only way to describe how I feel about myself most of the time. At fifty-one years old when I should have my house paid for and be a little comfortable in my life the exact opposite is true. The house my ex-wife bought eleven years ago that was abandoned by her fourteen months ago so that she wouldn't have to work, is in foreclosure {mostly because I don't want to be here} and soon I'll be back to square one again, a hard place to be at fifty-one.

Some of the physical and mental effects of meth are still with me. Even after twelve years I still see crystal creatures occasionally, they don't bother me, I know exactly what they are, they're the residue of years of meth abuse. The other thing that happens to me is a feeling like somebody's putting a cigarette out on my foot or hand or arm, a spot on my skin suddenly feels like it's on fire. To get it to stop all I have to do is push on it like you would a cut to make it stop bleeding.

These things are minor but I know they're related to my excessive meth use because they're both generated by the parts of the brain that meth most directly effects. If these things are all I have to endure for the rest of my life they're a small price to pay for the life I led and my near sanity. I can hang with that, I'm not gonna live that much longer anyway.

Everything that I once enjoyed doing is now out of reach either by design or the lack of the financial means to obtain them which at one time was a good thing. Even though I sometimes think of the life I led and the drugs I did, I could never go back to that simply because I know the damage that life will lead to, much sooner than later. That's why I'm writing this to show you that meth is not only a road to nowhere, it's a road to minus nowhere.

The time you spend using meth doesn't count in the game of life. It's as if you're not even on the planet and when and if you get that monkey off your back, it's like you dropped outta the sky. You're here, you're clean, now whatta ya do? The only way to avoid this dilemma is never begin using in the first place, that's the only way. If you're using, the sooner you stop, the less time lost and the easier the recovery. Every minute you spend under the influence of meth is an hour wasted that you'll never get back. Waste enough of those hours and they turn into....

A Life Wasted

Sometime I honestly feel that I'd've been better off to've died with my friends in the drug deals that turned into gun battles or ODing like so many did. I feel like the time that I spent runnin-n-gunnin was all a waste and somehow the world and life in general got by me and I'm so far behind I'll never catch up. When I was using I was as blind as any crankster believing that the next pound sold would be the turning point and that I'd be able to finance a real life with drug money and make that work.

It doesn't work that way, the words "easy come, easy go" are some of the truest words spoken and include everything even your life. If it sounds too good to be true, you can bet it is. The only direction you'll go while you're using is backwards/downwards. If you start cooking and dealing you'll only go further backward/downward faster.

Let's look at it from society's point of view. When you're just a user you have a disease. A disease can be treated and given enough time and the right environment overcome and the user can become a sober productive part of society, maybe.

When you're a cook or dealer you are the disease and the only way to cure a disease is to obliterate it one way or the other. The way to obliterate a dealer or cook is to remove him from society by any means necessary. In most cases this means incarceration. In some of the most extreme cases this means gunning you down in your front yard or living room, wherever you choose to make your stand. Unless you're like all the other criminals of today and give up as soon as the door gets kicked in.

The paranoia and psychosis that go along with meth use is compounded by a thousand when you're cooking or dealing. Every crankster is an adrenaline junkie. The crank simply fuels the excitement, picking up where adrenaline leaves off. Propelling you into a psychotic world of midnight mayhem. Add to that some paranoia and sprinkle a few handguns around and you've got a deadly combination that can blow up in God knows whose face at the drop of a hat.

I can't tell you how many friends I've talked down off the ledge of insanity over something that they didn't even remember after they'd slept and come back to the real world. It's too easy to convince yourself to do the thing that'll hurt you or others the most when you're under the ten feet tall-n-bulletproof influence of meth. No crime is too heinous, nothing is sacred, nothing else exists except you and what you want.

Meth is the most addictive and selfish drug there is. The only people that aren't hooked on meth the first time they do it is heroin addicts whose soul has already been swallowed by something else. Meth'll get you off coke {unless you're smoking crack, it takes it a little longer} in a New York minute. It'll make you believe it's your savior, all the while sucking the life outta you ten times faster than anything you've ever done before.

Meth fueled the Nazis and the Japanese during The Second World War. It wrote their battle plans and fueled their invasions. Driving the Axis Powers to commit the most insidious crimes ever perpetrated by man against man. In the end the hollowness of meth's unreality caused the implosion and almost complete annihilation of both those societies, along with the victimization of the other countries and ethnicities that the cranked-up lunatics deliriously considered their enemies and the wasting of millions upon millions of lives. See how well it worked for them, what makes you think you'll fare any better when you let the meth monkey on your back?

The Terrible Lie

I know why meth is so attractive, why you do it, why I did it and why so many people are sucked into the vacuum of it today. **LIFE SUCKS!** If you're from anything but a privileged background life is a struggle, struggle to get good grades so you can go to a good college or sometimes just a struggle to get something to eat. If you've overcome that struggle and managed to do it without meth. Then comes the struggle of maintaining good grades to get a good job or the struggle to eat again tomorrow.

Anytime during that process if you're introduced to meth it'll become your lord and savior. Giving you the energy to study endlessly or party endlessly which is more often the case or end your desire to eat. Lets face it studying is boring, the adrenaline junkie that a crankster becomes {if you think you're not one when you first start, you're wrong, you're a junkie after the first hit} is fooled into believing that crank'll make it OK. By the time you're halfway thru school {if you make it that far} you're so sprung you've got a new set of friends and together you become cook and distribution system all rolled up into one. When you flunk out you don't care, you've got a new profession that'll bring you more money faster than working ever could and it will, until.

Maybe you're not lucky enough to be able to go to college and are relegated to working all your life. Crank'll make a long day fly by and you'll go home with energy to spare. Maybe you'll use it to spend time with your kids. Maybe you'll use it to make more kids to spend time with. Who knows?

Maybe you're the stay at home mom whose husband you make more kids with and the extra energy and time you have are just what you think the doctor ordered. At first it's great, you feel great every day. Nothing is too difficult, no day too long, with mother's little helper up your nose, in your arm or in the pipe you can handle anything. Eventually you end up sitting behind locked doors, smoking, snorting or slamming your soul away while your kids are thoroughly neglected and your life turns to shit.

Your husband's now so spun and so hooked that he spends his evenings out in the garage with a crankster buddy of his cooking up another batch of dope in a garbage can lab, because by now he's lost his job and he's convinced himself that he'll make ten times the money cooking dope anyway and he will, until.

Maybe you were born with a silver or gold spoon in your mouth and have more money than brains. You only see your parents when you want something, the rest of the time you spend with people like yourself, young, dumb, n-fulla cum. One night at the club or some party someone turns you on to something "better than coke" and you're as hooked as you'll ever be from that day forth, until.

Meth fits into any scenario, it's a chameleon that'll convince anyone of anything, a black hole that'll suck everything in your life into it including you and spit you out debilitated and broken in more ways than one.

Until

The front door gets kicked in and you're gang rushed by fellow cranksters that want what you've got and don't care what or who they've got to do to get it. Not your buddies {they're probably the ones that kicked the door in}, nor your kids nor anything else mean a thing to these pieces of shit. All they want is everything they can take including your life if need be to get it.

How about that same front door getting splintered by body armored cops that probably won't kill you unless you're stupid, but who have a fate worse than death waiting for you after you've been drug thru the court system backwards like it was one big knot hole. After you're stripped of everything you ever had by the Zero Tolerance Act and are now completely at the mercy of a judicial system gone berserk, this is only the beginning.

After months sometime years in jail you end up in one of this country's many overcrowded gladiator schools where you really have to fight for your life every day, because you just can't do your time anymore. You have to belong to a gang just to survive and to belong you have to be ready to fight and die for the gang or the little bit of concrete and steel that you'll never own, but has become the only thing you can possess until your release date which may never come if you catch another case or two along the way.

While you're going thru your hell, your kids are going thru a hell they didn't ask for and will never get out of. The hell of being wards of the state and then foster children in less than ideal conditions. Not knowing what happened to you or to them, being treated like a number in an already overworked, overcrowded system buckling under the weight of irresponsible addicted parents and "rebels without a clue." Children having more children because they thought it would make them grown up or they just didn't think at all, just like their parents and everyone else around them.

Maybe you never get busted at all. You simply squirt your life out the point of a needle on the end of a syringe till you're found dead in a shooting gallery or on a pile of trash in an alley or in your own bedroom with the needle that killed you still in your arm, like some of my friends. You could suck on a glass dick till you suck the life outta yourself. Losing your teeth, your self-respect and your soul along the way, long before you lose your life, crying about the wreck your life is all the while.

Sounds wonderful and glamorous doesn't it? This too could be you! The graveyards, prisons, alleys and locked bedrooms are full of people that thought it couldn't happen to them, they'd only use a little bit and then quit. Or they believed some idiot that told them that meth wasn't addictive and they could quit at any time. Well I'm here to tell ya it's all a lie, a meth myth, bullshit whatever you wanna call it. Meth is the most addictive drug on the planet and the most destructive bar none, you'll never win in a battle with meth.

The only way to not get hooked is to never try it. If you do there's a 99.999% chance that like me you'll be hooked from the very first time and a 100% chance that you'll fuck your life and yourself up irreversibly before you get busted or get any kind of help at all.

The More Terrible Truth

Meth begins to change you from the very first time you use it. I'm the only person I know that that didn't happen to except for having to learn how to live with the depression once I quit. I never became the twitching, stammering incoherent mess that most people become eventually, some with the very first line or hit. I've seen people spin right out into space from their very first line and not come back for a long time and when they did it was only partially.

The people that don't lose it are a vast minority compared to the ones that do and you have no way of knowing which side of the mirror you're gonna fall on, till you snort the line. Much like playing Russian Roulette, you just don't know. You could slam your first rig full and rip your heart wide open from the mixed signals your brain sends it. You won't know till you pull the trigger and then it's too late.

Do you really wanna find out how bad life can suck? If you think life sucks now, how bad do you think it'll suck when you end up in the joint at eighteen or nineteen years old? How bad will things suck doing life on the installment plan, in-n-out of the joint all your life till you hit the three strike law and end up doing life without. How bad will life suck when you're in restraints, locked away in a dingy little room a danger to yourself and others, pumped fulla shit to keep you quiet?

If life sucks now will it be any better ten years from now when {if you live that long} all you have is your addiction and a cardboard box {or worse} to call home? How do you think your family will feel when you rob them of everything they've ever worked for to support your habit or you give up everything you ever had for the same thing? What will your kids think as they watch you get cuffed and stuffed, while they get dragged off to children's protective services?

All these things and more have a very good chance of happening from the very first time you use. Something as simple as a traffic stop can turn into a two or three year trip to prison. Why would you want to risk that and for what? An artificial feeling that will fade and leave you feeling ten times worse than you felt to start with. Remember **"what goes up, must come down"** and the crash isn't worth the high.

Not everybody's life has to be as exciting as James Bond's, nor can it be. Life doesn't have to be a thrill a minute, in fact it just isn't. When you're high you're the only thing that's changed, the life that you're so bored with is still all you've got. Just because you've slammed a rig fulla crank doesn't mean that anything other than your perception has changed. You're still in the same old town with the same old people and when the shit wears off that's still were you'll be. That's probably the worst part about the terrible lie of any drug, nothing changes {at least not for the better}. Fact of the matter is, it only gets worse {look at the world today} and if you think otherwise you're just lying to yourself or listening to the lies from the dope, the meth monsters.

The only one that can change your life is you! For better or for worse and the only one that has to live with your decisions is you, yah right! If you choose to become a social cripple by frying your brain with drugs you're not only hurting yourself, you're becoming a burden to the already overburdened society around you. A moment's pleasure can cost a lifetime of misery. **You can fly up real high, but you'll fall down real far!** That roller coaster to hell isn't any fun and once you're there you might not come back.

As each member of our society loses control of themselves and removes their voices from the masses it becomes easier for the greedy to take advantage {for our own good}. By becoming an addict and giving up your intellect to the mind numbing effects of drugs you empower someone that doesn't give a shit about you, except what they can get from you or run your life with their agenda which makes life suck even more. Get outta the bag, take back your life, add your voice to the masses and stand up for the radical changes required to make all our lives better!!!

The Ravings Of A Madman

"The easiest way to control the masses is to keep the women pregnant and everyone else addicted to drugs." Illuminati doctrine on controlling the will of the people.

"As a nation of all time, we will live for all time or die by suicide." Abraham Lincoln.

Both of these quotes apply to society now more than ever. By becoming addicted to drugs you're surrendering to the Illuminati {known today as the Freemasons and the Skull and Bones} without a fight. The Illuminati is the ultra-power behind the power, a secret society of ultra-wealthy Satan worshippers that are working behind the scenes to create the **"New World Order"** an oppressive, elitist, fascist government controlled by a handful of ultra-wealthy families like the Rothschild's, the Bundy's and the Rockefellers who are connected by marriage and a common goal. Their whole goal is to enslave mankind while attaining ultimate control of the entire world. That means everyone except the members of their secret society. No one will be spared the cruelty and injustice of this Satanic cult.

Addiction is a disease that we choose to have, it's the easy way out. By choosing to be an addict you're playing right into the hands of the people that want to rule the world. Think about it. As an addict what consumes your every waking moment? Getting high and staying that way! As long as you're thinking about that you're oblivious to what's going on in the world around you. This effectively eliminates millions upon millions of the opposition by dumbing them down to what's really going on around them. Dumbed down by the effects of mind numbing, thought altering drugs taking your attention away from life and focusing it on your own chemical suicide.

If you're one of the truly unlucky addicts the world over to be busted for your use, you're also playing into their hands because felons can't vote. Eliminating millions and millions more of the opposition. **Only you can make the choice to make sure your voice is heard.** If you're on drugs of any kind get off 'em before it's too late. It's the only way we can regain our freedom. We give away our freedoms every day by caring more about our own petty bullshit junkie lives, when we need to be clearheaded and aware of what's really going on in the world and resisting the so-called authority.

The fascists that want to enslave you, have brought you the drugs that are the chains by which they'll own you. If society continues down this path of chemical suicide they'll win without ever a shot being fired. All the wars and manmade disasters since the civil war have been brought to you by the same group of terrorists that claim to be fighting terrorism, including the alleged World Trade Center attack. That was done by our own government to push the Patriot Act on the American public {for our own good}.

George W. Bush is only the latest terrorist to be forced on the American people. He wasn't even elected to the Presidency, he was strong-armed in by the people who pull the strings. His father was the one that first spoke the words **"New World Order"** to the American people. Both of their administrations are nothing more than smoke screens to hide the real truth and the huge advances the Illuminati are making toward their goals. They're both puppets of the higher power, demigods, tools of the elitist fascists that are really calling the shots. When their usefulness is over they'll be cast aside like so much trash, which is really what they are.

If you think I'm crazy type in Illuminati for the keyword in your Google search engine. Then watch the videos of Dr. Stanley Monteith, read the history of the Illuminati and the bios of the thirteen families that are the kingpins behind the overthrow of the world as we know it. Don't have a computer, go to the library and log on to one of theirs. What you find will scare you straight, if it doesn't then you're living proof of everything I've said. You're one of the dumbed down minions that the Illuminati are creating by systematically dismantling our education system, controlling the media and addicting us to drugs.

When I was an addict I didn't care if the world fell down around me as long as I could get high. Life sucked for me just like it does for everyone that gives up their dreams and future for a bag of dope and a place to do it. My dreams weren't quite the same as everyone else's though. The only real dream I had was to have a Harley and ride all over the country, beyond that I never dreamed.

Once I became an addict it was easy for me to live out my dream, it was easy to be a bum on a Harley riding from one buzz to the next oblivious of the world around me. Fight, Fuck or Party was my motto and that was all I lived for. While I was living my "dream" the world moved on without me. It took years for it to happen, but imperceptibly I became the dinosaur that I am now, mostly because of drugs and the lack of caring they bring about.

The thing I'm mad about the most, is that everyone else isn't as mad about this as I am. WAKE THE FUCK UP!!!!!!!!!!!! Get off the dope, not just crank, all of it, take back the power of the people before it's too late. The clock is ticking and the enemy is winning without any resistance from the people whatsoever. Muslims aren't your enemies, they're leaders have been duped into this holy war created by the elitists just like we were by our so-called leaders. The real enemy is your own government, Republican or Democrat it doesn't matter they're only playing us against each other in a mock battle to hide the real agenda of the ones that control them.

If something isn't done by everyone and soon, it'll be too late! I know you think I'm nuts, maybe not! Maybe for the first time in my life I'm on track. Maybe it's you that's nuts for not doing something sooner. If you think I'm crazy let's all try a little experiment. In the upcoming 2008 elections write my name in for president. I guarantee you that if not one vote was cast for any other candidate on voting day meaning I got one hundred percent of the votes. I'd either be assassinated or the government of itself, by itself and for itself would simply refuse to acknowledge the election and continue on plowing our rights under like so many weeds.

Self-made Outcast!!!!!!

I don't fit in your world and won't go back to the one I came from. I know too much and everyone else knows too little or refuses to acknowledge what they know for the sake of the status quo. **FUCK THE STATUS QUO!** If the boat doesn't start getting rocked now it'll be too late. Once we're all slaves the global revolution will be that much harder to realize and make happen. **GET OFF DOPE! TAKE BACK THE POWER OF THE PEOPLE! RISE UP AND CLAIM THE PROSPERITY AN INFORMED AND EDUCATED POPULATION CAN CREATE. IT DOESN'T HAVE TO BE THIS WAY! LIFE DOESN'T HAVE TO SUCK!!!!BUT ONLY AS AN INFORMED, VIABLE, GOD KNOWING SOCIETY CAN WE EFFECT THE NECESSARY CHANGES. HELP ME, HELP YOU, HELP YOUR NEIGHBOR TO HELP ALL OF US!!!!!!!!**

In my next offering from the bottom I'm gonna take you all by the hand and we're gonna play connect the dots, with the dots being very close together.

I'm gonna show you exactly how thirteen ultra-wealthy, elitist, separatist, Satan-worshiping families control the finances of the world and have orchestrated every crisis the world has known since 1774 to bring about the **"one world government"** envisioned by them. How thru credit, the media, your government and addiction to every drug known to man {especially prescription anti-depressants} they are getting closer to reaching their goal of ultimate control every day. How we can get control and change this whole world into the happy, peaceful, prosperous place it should be and how this relates to the addiction problems of today.

In the meantime get off all the dope. Clear your minds of the fog that addiction brings, open those same minds and your eyes as well. Open your hearts, buy a bible and start reading it. Begin praying and changing your lives and things will start getting better.

If you don't subscribe to any religion, so what! Simply read and believe and talk to God yourself. He's the only one that can help you get to the place you'll need to be to be happy. Only he can help us all with the **radical changes** that need to happen to make our world a place where no one needs drugs to be happy and everyone is as prosperous as they want to be.

In **GREED, the coveting of our lives**, we're gonna identify the true enemy of the people and the ways they use to enslave us and best of all how to stop it. Till then, **GO WITH GOD.**

"THE WORST DAY CLEAN IS BETTER THAN THE BEST DAY WIRED! YOU WON'T FIND HAPPINESS IN A TINY ZIPLOC!"

7/7/07

My Own Living Hell

At sixteen years old I had my first tweak.
What I thought would last all night, lasted two days short of a week.
It made me feel like I wanted to feel like this all the time.
The king of the mountain, but the mountain was only mine.
Now twenty-five years later, I write this down
to tell you what I was to find.
I can't think, I can't sleep, I can't drink, I can't eat.
Al my possessions are gone, I'm on the fuckin street.
I've lied, I've cheated, I've conned and I've stole.
It was Satan in disguise, aiming for my soul.
I want to turn and run, I want to live to tell.
How METH and I created my own living HELL.
I know only two kinds of people now, the ones
that I use and the ones that use me.
You'll be no different if you're as foolish as me.
Just go ahead and use and you'll see!
Orin Hughes Jr.
Orin is a friend still battling his meth
monster, pray for him. Dave Fuller.

9484071R0